MAN IN BIOSPHERE
A CASE STUDY OF KHANGCHENDZONGA BIOSPHERE RESERVE

MAN IN BIOSPHERE

A Case Study of Khangchendzonga Biosphere Reserve

Editors
Dr. Ramesh Chandra
Dr. D.B. Mondal
Dr. Arun Kumar Singh

Anthropological Survey of India
Kolkata - 700016

GYAN

Man in Biosphere : A Case Study of Khangchendzonga Biosphere Reserve

ISBN : 978-81-212-1162-8

Published in 2013 in India by
Gyan Publishing House
23, Main Ansari Road, Daryaganj,
New Delhi - 110002
Phones : 23282060, 23261060
Fax : (011) 23285914
E-mail: books@gyanbooks.com
website: gyanbooks.com

Laser Type Setting : Rajender Vashist, Delhi
Printed at : Chawla Offset Printers, Delhi

CONTENTS

Foreword 7

Preface 9

List of Contributors 13

1. Introducing Khangchendzonga Biosphere Reserve: 15
   Umesh Kumar and *Arun Kumar Singh*
2. A Study in Ecology and Conservation in Khangchendzonga Biosphere Reserve of Sikkim Himalayas 31
   Umesh Kumar
3. Cultural Landscape of Fringe Villages: A Study in Khangchendzonga Biosphere Reserve of Sikkim Himalayas 65
   Sudhansu Gangopadhyay
4. Economic Life in Fringe Village: A Study in Khangchendzonga Biosphere Reserve of Sikkim Himalayas 111
   Subrata Ray

5 Traditional Art, Craft and Performing Art: A Study in Khangchendzonga Biosphere Reserve of Sikkim Himalayas. 141
   Krishna Basu

6. Impact of Tourism: A Case Study of Khangchendzonga Biosphere Reserve of Sikkim Himalayas 195
   Amitava Dinda
7. Growth of Urbanisation in Yuksam: A Study in Khangchendzonga Biosphere Reserve of Sikkim Himalayas 265
   Gautam Kumar Bera

8. The Lepchas of West Sikkim: A Study in Khangchendzonga Biosphere Reserve of Sikkim Himalayas 293
Krishna Mandal

9. Man, Nature and Spirit: A Study on the Lepchas and the Bhutias of North Sikkim in Khangchendzonga Biosphere Reserve 335
K. M. Sinha Roy

10. Health, Illness and Role of Ethno-Medicine among the Lepchas Living in Khangchendzonga Biosphere Reserve of Sikkim Himalayas: A Study on Traditional Knowledge 373
Sumitabha Chakraborty

References 433

Appendix 441

Glossary 445

Index 447

प्रो. कमल कांत मिश्रा
निर्देशक
PROF. K. K. MISRA
Director
TEL 91-33-2286 1781/33/1697
Fax 91-33-2286 1799/1685
Email : director@ansi.gov.in / hohq@ansi.gov.in
ansihead@gmail.com
Website : www.ansi.gov.in

भारतीय मानवविज्ञान सर्वेक्षण
संस्कृति मंत्रालय
भारत सरकार
भारतीय संग्रहालय परिसर
27, जवाहरलाल नेहरू रोड कोलकाता - 700 016
ANTHROPOLOGICAL SURVEY OF INDIA
MINISTRY OF CULTURE
GOVERNMENT OF INDIA
INDIAN MUSEUM COMPLEX
27, JAWAHARLAL NEHRU ROAD, KOLKATA - 700 016

Foreword

The present volume is an outcome of the research project undertaken by the Anthropological Survey of India under its Eleventh Five Year Plan Project – Man and Environment. Out of 14 Biosphere Reserves of India, the study of six Biosphere Reserves have already been completed, which are Nilgiri, Sundarban, Pachmarhi, Khangchendzonga, Similipal and Nandadevi. Of the six studied Biosphere Reserves, the reports of Nilgiri, Sundarban and Pachmarhi have already been published. The present volume on Khangchendzonga Biosphere Reserve (KBR) is fourth in the series.

KBR was conferred the status of Biosphere Reserve on 7th February, 2000 by the Government of India. The KBR is repository of various types of flora and fauna, many of which are endemic to the region. It is also the abode of many communities like the Lepchas, Bhutias, Gurung, Rai, Chhetri etc. The present study is interdisciplinary in nature and aims at elucidating and analysing the process of development and conservation along with cultural diversity of the area in the broader framework of ecology, economy and society. Altogether nine scientific personnel were involved in this study.

The present study was conducted in three areas of KBR, which are Yuksum, Lachen and Dzongu of North and West districts of Sikkim. Ecologically and culturally these three regions vary considerably. The issues which have been covered in the present volume are ecology, change and conservation; cultural landscape and economic life in fringe villages; traditional art, crafts and performing dance; impact of tourism; growth of urbanisation in Yuksam; ethnography of the Lepchas; man-nature-spirit relationship among the Lepchas and the Bhutias, and indigenous health practices among the Lepchas.

It may be worthwhile to mention here that there are many studies available on biodiversity aspects of the Biosphere Reserves (BRs) of India, but there is hardly any study which throws light on the cultural diversity alongside biodiversity. It also assumes significance in the light of fact that traditional communities inhabiting the BRs of India have devised over centuries such practices which have helped conserving the biodiversity of the BRs.

I am indeed delighted that the scholars of the Anthropological Survey of India drawn from different academic disciplines have contributed to this volume, making it multi-disciplinary and worth reading. I congratulate all of them individually and collectively for this noble venture.

I am sure this volume is going to be very useful to the academic world as well as to the administrators, planners and the managers of forests.

Prof. Kamal K. Misra

Preface

The growing conflict between man and his environment has forced the intelligentsia of the present generation to think deeply on the issue of environment, its degradation and conservation. This problem has also become acute due to the various developmental programmes undertaken by different societies located in different geo-ecological and cultural zones of the world in general and India in particular. The conflict between man and environment reached to the alarming stage in the early part of 1960s when the developmental process had accelerated to a great extent. Environment started degrading and a situation had arisen where the existence of human society appeared to be at stake. With this background United Nations Organisation started pondering deeply and directed its sister organisation UNESCO (United Nations Educational Scientific and Cultural Organisation) in the year 1970 to come out with detailed research programme on the concept of man and biosphere. Accordingly, Man and Biosphere Committee was constituted in the year 1972 to demarcate the Biosphere Reserves in different biographic zones of the world where the ecosystem was critical from survival point of view. Indian 'Man and Biosphere Committee' demarcated 12 sites at the first instance and later added two more sites. Thus, presently India is having 14 Biosphere Reserves which are spread all over the country right from the Himalayas to the sea of Andaman and Gulf of Mannar. The present volume deals with the biological and cultural diversity aspects of Khangchendzonga Biosphere Reserve, which is located in the three districts of Sikkim viz., North, South and West. The KBR is a new Biosphere Reserve with an unique ecological condition, which primarily varies from tropical climatic condition to the high altitude alpine climatic condition. Due to its varying altitude flora and fauna also vary along with other life support systems like soil, water etc. The volume also tries to understand the process of development in the form of tourism and its impact on the conservation of the fragile ecosystem of KBR. The Anthropological

Survey of India decided to undertake theme based research studies in three areas of KBR, which are Yuksum, Lachen Dzongu and their adjoining areas. Ecologically and culturally also these three regions vary. There are only two traditional communities living in these areas namely the Bhutias and the Lepchas along with migrant Nepalese population.

Dr Umesh Kumar, while studying the ecological change in KBR has focused on anthropogenic pressures and tried to under its impact on the ecology of KBR. Dependence of the population on forest is well visible because fuel and fodder resources are accessed from the forest. The report comes out with an interesting finding that people are willing to help in conservation efforts of the government provided their socio-economic concern are taken care of. In addition, the local NGOs are helping in the conservation efforts by creating public awareness.

The second report by Dr S. Gangopadhyay deals with the cultural landscape of the fringe villages of KBR. The basic objective of this study is to understand the changing cultural landscape in terms of economic resource management by the village population. Yuksum of West Sikkim and Lachen of North Sikkim were selected as two villages for comparative study. It has been felt that both the areas have different pattern of cultural landscape. It has also been noted that transhumance as a system of livelihood is losing its importance and settled agriculture is becoming important economic occupation for the people of both the areas.

Shri S. Roy has studied the economic life in fringe villages of KBR conducting two case studies – one of Yuksum and another of Lachen. It deals with the primary and secondary occupations in these two villages. It also tries to deal with economic potentiality of the tourism industry in the context of declaration of KBR.

Smt Krishna Basu while studying the traditional form of art, craft, music and dance tries to understand the impact of tourism on material culture of the communities living in KBR. It may be mentioned here that tourism has created a demand for artifacts and the local community has responded in a big way because they see it as an area where there are enough economic opportunities.

Shri A. Dinda's report deals with the impact of tourism on KBR of North and West districts of Sikkim. Due to its unique natural setting, KBR is attracting substantial number of international and Indian tourists throughout the year. The local community has responded in a positive way and it has become a major source of income. No doubt there has been some negative impact of tourism. However, due to awareness programme undertaken by different NGOs, environmental degradation has been arrested to a great extent.

Dr Gautam Bera's report on the growth of urbanisation in Yuksum tries to understand the process by which the village of Yuksum is getting transformed into an urban area. Yuksum, which is historically an important centre in the political history of Sikkim, is slowly emerging as a nodal centre to support tourism and related activities in West Sikkim.

The report on nature, man and spirit by Shri K.M. Sinha Roy deals with the interface between the symbols of human understanding taking into consideration the Lepchas and the Bhutias of North Sikkim. Living in close proximity with nature, the Lepchas and the Bhutias have developed a good understanding about the natural objects which is both benevolent and malevolent. Accordingly, they try to appease both forms of nature for better sustenance in the rugged terrain of Sikkim Himalayas.

Dr S. Chakrabarty has studied indigenous health practices of the Lepcha community of KBR. The study shows as how people have developed their own indigenous method of health practices with the help of ethno-medicine, especially the Lepchas of KBR. The Lepcha community lives in close quarter with the nature which has helped them develop unique system of ethno-medicine based on medicinal plants, which is practiced by the medicine man of the community.

Smt. Krishna Mondal has dealt with the community and their life cycle which revolves around various economic activities in KBR. All the research reports, which have been included in this volume, reflect on changing pattern of biodiversity and cultural diversity in KBR and analyse how different communities living in different locales have responded to the changes which they are witnessing.

Ramesh Chandra
D.B. Mandal
Arun Kumar Singh

List of Contributors

Amitava Dinda, Research Associate (C), Anthropological Survey of India, Eastern Regional Centre, EN-79, Sector-5, Salt Lake City, Kolkata-700091. e-mail: amitavadinda68@yahoo.com

Gautam Kumar Bera, Research Associate (C), Anthropological Survey of India, Eastern Regional Centre, EN-79, Sector-5, Salt Lake City, Kolkata-700091.

Krishna Basu, Research Associate (C), Anthropological Survey of India, Eastern Regional Centre, EN-79, Sector-5, Salt Lake City, Kolkata-700091.

Krishna Mandal, Anthropologist, (C), Anthropological Survey of India, Eastern Regional Centre, EN-79, Sector-5, Salt Lake City, Kolkata-700091.

K.M. Sinha Roy, Anthropologist (C), Anthropological Survey of India, Jagdalpur Sub-Regional Centre, Chhattisgarh.

Subrata Ray, Research Associate, Anthropological Survey of India, 27, Jawaharlal Nehru Road Kolkata -700 016.

Sudhansu Gangopadhyay, Cartographer, Anthropological Survey of India, Jagadalpur Sub-Regional Centre, Chhattisgarh.

Sumitabha Chakraborty, Research Associate (C), Anthropological Survey of India, Eastern Regional Centre, EN-79, Sector-5, Salt Lake City, Kolkata-700091.

Umesh Kumar, Human Ecologist, Anthropological Survey of India, 27, Jawaharlal Nehru Road Kolkata-700016. e-mail: umeshkumarpb @gmail.com

1

Introducing Khangchendzonga Biosphere Reserve

Umesh Kumar and *Arun Kumar Singh*

INTRODUCTION

Biodiversity is the totality of genes, species, ecosystems and habitats in a region. Biodiversity constitutes resources upon which humanity depends and it is fundamental to the fulfillment of human needs. Increasing human interventions on the ecosystems have accelerated the process of biodiversity loss. An environment, which is rich in biological diversity, offers the broadest array of options for sustainable human welfare and for adaptation to change. Loss of biodiversity has serious economic and social costs for any country. The experiences of the past few decades have shown that as industrialisation and economic development take place in the society, the patterns of production, consumption and needs change, strain and even alter ecosystems. If one traces the linkages of biodiversity, it is observed that human population and its interventions have been the major factors for enhancement in the extinction process. Conservation and sustainable use of biodiversity, hence, are fundamental to sustainable development. The mapping of mega-diversity zones indicates that most of the mega-biodiversity zones are found in South America, Central Africa and India/ South China. An assessment of biological diversity at world level (Hannah and Lohse, 1993, Mittermeier, 1988) reveals that Asia is the most threatened continent. Perhaps, the best approach to understand biodiversity is to look at it in a hierarchical manner in which biological organisms are organized. The smallest unit starts from the diversity contained in the genetic material of individual organisms and then goes on to encompass the biological communities in which species are organized and on to the ecosystems in which they exist. Biodiversity is recognized at three levels *viz.*, genetic, species and ecosystem levels (Fig. 1). At all three levels of biodiversity, the components are dynamic in space and time. The genetic composition of species changes over time in response to natural and human induced selection process. The ecosystems strongly respond to external dynamics and internal stresses.

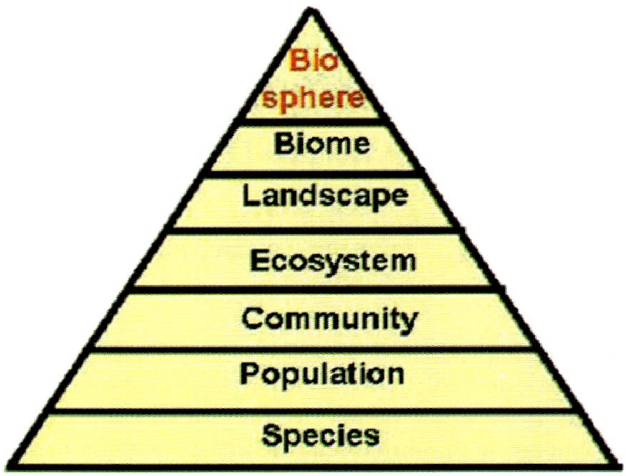

Fig. 1. Hierarchy of Biological Organisation.

Based on IIRS Report on Biodiversity Characterisation at Landscape Level, 2001

Ecological systems do not exist as discrete units but represent different parts of a natural continuum in the form of landscape. Landscape can also be considered as a higher level of biological complexity, immensely useful for understanding various complex processes. While biodiversity is usually considered at the species level, maintenance of biodiversity requires management at higher levels of organization, particularly at the landscape scale, which includes human beings also.

To preserve species diversity most effectively, management plans must preserve the habitats and landscape structures needed by the target species, rather than simply preserving the species in isolation from the larger, potentially changing environment. Management practices aimed directly at a particular species run the risk of losing ecosystem functions which might actually be crucial for the target species, but remained unknown when the management plan was created. Furthermore, maximizing benefits for one species may threaten others. The ideal is to preserve overall ecosystem health, including species diversity. It can be best accomplished by integrating it into the fabric of social, environmental and economic canvas.

This has led to the process of sustainable development where man and environment are integrated together for a better future for all the living being. These considerations led to the origin of the concept of Biosphere Reserve. The initiation of Biosphere Reserves goes back to the "Biosphere Conference" organized by UNESCO in 1968. This was the first inter-governmental conference examining as how to reconcile the conservation and use of natural resources, thereby foreshadowing the present-day notion of sustainable development. This Conference resulted in the launching of the "Man and the Biosphere" (MAB) Programme of UNESCO in 1970. It aimed to facilitate resolution of increasing conflict between the people and Protected Areas

BIOSPHERE RESERVE AS A CONCEPT

The UNESCO's framework stipulates that Biosphere Reserves (BRs) should be representative of a bio-geographic province and should have appropriate zoning system with legally constituted and minimally disturbed core zone. In addition, the site should contain unique and pristine biodiversity, ecosystems and landscape suitable to explore and demonstrate approaches to sustainable development and should be of appropriate size to serve three functions, viz., conservation, development and extension of logistic support. It is aimed to bring at least one representative site in the country within each bio-geographic province under the network of Biosphere Reserves.

BRs are designated to deal with important questions of reconciling the conservation of biodiversity, the quest for economic and social development and maintenance of associated cultural values. Some important aspects of Biosphere Reserves delineates conservation of landscapes, ecosystems, species and genetic variations; economic development, which is culturally, socially and ecologically sustainable and extension of logistic support for research, monitoring, education and exchange of information related to local, national and global issues.

Launched in 1970, Man and Biosphere (MAB) programme covers different ecosystem types from mountain to the sea, from rural to urban systems as well as social aspects. MAB has proposed an interdisciplinary research and capacity building aiming to improve the relationship of the people with environment. In order to achieve the stated objectives it targets biodiversity from the ecological, social and economic dimensions.

In nutshell, the Biosphere Reserve (BR) is expected to fulfill three basic functions, which are complementary and mutually reinforcing:

(A) Conservation function - to contribute to the conservation of landscapes, ecosystems, species and genetic variation;

(B) Development function - to foster economic and human development which is socio-culturally and ecologically sustainable;

(C) Logistic function - to provide support for research, monitoring, education and information exchange related to local, national and global issues of conservation and development.

The Ministry of Environment and Forest has launched the Biosphere Reserve (BR) Programme since 1986. The specific objectives of this Programme are:

(A) to conserve the diversity and integrity of plants and animals within the natural eco-system

(B) to safeguard the genetic diversity of species on which their continuing evolution depends,

(C) to provide areas for multi-faceted research and monitoring,

(D) to provide facilities for research and training, and

(E) to ensure the sustainable use of natural resources through most appropriate technology for improvement of economy and living standard of local people.

ISSUES LINKED WITH BIOSPHERE RESERVE DEVELOPMENT IN INDIA

In the context of India, human population living within the Biosphere Reserves has always been a matter of conflicting interests and debate. These considerations prompted UNESCO (1996) to move away from the earlier held view of concentric rings of core, buffer and transition zones, to a more flexible way of looking upon the local needs and situations. The flexibility and creativity in the Biosphere concept need to be seen from the point of view of both biodiversity as well as the cultural diversity. The benefits of cultural diversity at societal level are comparable to those accruing from the biodiversity. It is important to allude that, while the issues of biodiversity have been addressed at length and caught attention widely, the cultural diversity has not been touched upon and left to the point of oblivion.

The BRs of India are also the abode of many traditional societies who have always been an integral part of the ecosystem functioning there, living close to the Nature. Living in the areas rich in natural resource, traditional societies fulfill many of their livelihood requirements from the rich biodiversity around them. The ecosystems such as forest not only meets a variety of livelihood needs of the forest dwelling societies, through products such as timber and non-timber forest products, but also sustain traditional shifting cultivation and agricultural practices contributing to the food security of the people within the BRs.

So far the management efforts has largely been centered around protection of natural resources within BRs from the outside impacts, but at the same time restricting the use of these resources by the local communities residing in the BR. The concept of sustainable use of resources yet has not taken due to lack of location specific understanding on how the resources should be managed. Of late emphasis is laid on the aspect that the eco-development should also combat problems of community participation in forest eco-system management/rehabilitation directly. What more is required for the management of natural resources is linkage with reinforcement of traditional system of land-based activities based on the traditional value system of local communities.

The BR management, therefore, necessitates not only understanding of ecological issues but also the socio-economic and cultural issues linked with the former. Understanding societal perceptions of natural resources as a cultural resource – often seen through the conceptual framework of sacred species, sacred groves, sacred water bodies, sacred landscape or even sacred mountain system- and its relationship with conservation need to be integrated in the management strategy. In order to achieve this, conservation-linked development strategy has to be based on a value system that people can understand, appreciate and accept. It, in turn, requires appropriate institutional arrangements for peoples' participation, through a 'bottom-up approach', ensuring that each household takes part in the decision making process at the lowest level in the hierarchy keeping into consideration the gender sensitivities.

Before going into the details of Khangchendzonga Biosphere Reserve (KBR), it will be proper to deal in brief the ecological details Sikkim because the KBR is spread over the major areas of Sikkim specially the districts of North, West and South Sikkim

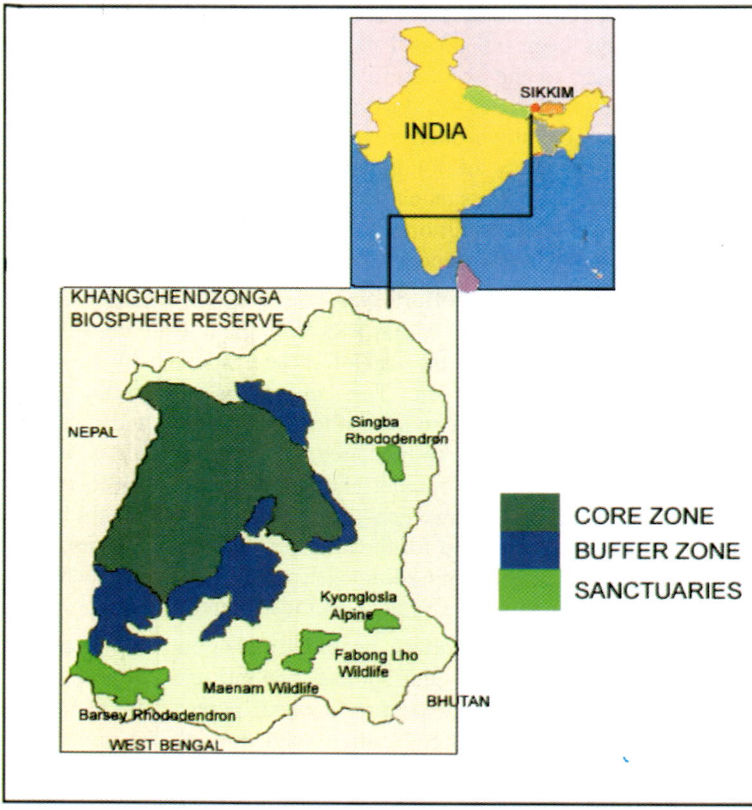

Fig.2 Khangchendzonga Biosphere Reserve.

PHYSICAL FEATURE

Sikkim is situated in the eastern Himalayas between 27°5′ and 28°10′ north latitude and between 88 °4′ and 88°58′ east longitude. It comprises an area of 7299 sq km. The state is bounded on the north and north east by the Tibetan region of China south east by Bhutan, south by the Darjeeling district of West Bengal and west by Nepal. The mountainous terrain of Sikkim possesses a series of interlacing ridges raising range above range from south toward the snow-clad northern hills. In the south the State opens into the plains of West Bengal with a steep fall in altitude over 5000 metres down within a distance of about 100 km. The State is almost rectangular, 113 km long and 64 km wide. It is entirely hilly with altitudes ranging from 300 metres to about 8500 metres above sea level.

The present territory of Sikkim forms parts of the inner Himalayan range of mountains which project southwards. The Singalila and Chola mountain ranges running southward from the main chain of the Himalayas separate Sikkim from Nepal on the west and from Tibet on the east. The main pass on the Singalila range is the Chiabhangjang La. The Chola range separates itself from the main chain at Denkhya at about 4500 to 5100 metres above sea level. A number of passes like Tangkar La, Nathu La, Jalep La open through it into the Chumbi valley. From the eastern flank of Singalila range rises the mighty snow peaks of the Mount. Khangchendzonga (8445 metres), one of the highest mountains in the world. Between the Singalila and the Chola ranges, there are several deep valleys. The largest among these valleys is the Tista valley through which runs the Tista river, from north towards south. Two principal valleys situated in the northern part of Sikkim, the Lachen on the west and the Lachung on the east form the origin and the basins of the two rivers, the Lachen and Lachung respectively which converge at Chungthang to form the principal Tista river. The river Rangit which is the largest tributaries of Tista also flow from north towards south, almost parallel to the Tista river, in the western region. At the southern border of the State, the Rangit turns towards east until it joins the river Tista near Tista town. Among the four districts of Sikkim, the north, east, south and west, the northern Sikkim region constitutes the north district which is predominantly a high altitude region interspersed with deep valleys. The southern part of Sikkim is divided into the three districts, east, south and west by the two major rivers, Tista and Rangit as they flow parallel to each other in the north-south direction. The region east to Tista forms the eastern district, the region between Tista and Rangit forms the southern district and the region falling west to the river Rangit forms the west district. High altitude regions abound in the eastern district along the Tibetan and Bhutan borders and in the western district along the western high ranges bordering Nepal.

Lying immediately opposite Bay of Bengal, Sikkim receives the full impacts of monsoon storms from the south thus acquiring the leading feature of its climate, i.e., dampness and heavy rains. The altitude ranges from 300 metres to 5000 metres and above. The lands in Sikkim can be broadly classified into the following categories according to altitude.

1. Lower Hills	Tropical	300-500 m
	Subtropical	500-1500 m
2. Mid Hills	Temperate	1500-2000 m
3. Higher Hills	Temperate	2000-2700 m
	Subalpaine	2700-4000 m
	Alpine	4000-5000 m

A brief analysis of rainfall data available from stations in Sikkim indicate that the mean annual rainfall is minimum at Thangu (821.1 mm) at 3812 m altitude and maximum at Gangtok (3494.5 mm) at 1818 m altitude. The two high rainfall areas been identified, the one in south east including Mangan, Singhik, Dikchu, Gangtok, Karponong, Rongli, Gnathang etc. and other in south west corner including hilly areas. Between these two regions lies a low rainfall region around Namchi. The rainfall in this area is about half of that former regions. In general in Sikkim, rainfall is heavy and well distributed during the months from May to September, of which July is the wettest month in most places. Rainfall is moderate in the April and October. It is low from November to February. The intensity of rainfall during south west monsoon (July to October) decreases from south to north while the distribution of winter rainfall is in opposite order. While monsoon contributes to the major part of the rains in Sikkim, yet the convective rains greatly account for the substantial rainfall during pre-monsoon and post-monsoon periods.

FLORA

The forest types are sub-tropical broad leaved hill forest, Himalayan wet temperate forest, and temperate broad leaved forest, mixed coniferous forest, sub-alpine a forests and dry alpine forest (Fig. 3). Dominant species of the temperate forests are Phalat, Shrub live oak, Ghoge champ, and Cinnamon. The mixed coniferous forests occur in higher altitude with fir, East Himalayan fir, Maple, Spruce, Juniper and Rhododendron. In the Alpine scrub and grasses, the common shrubs and herbs found are Primrose, Rhododendron, bottled gentian and stagger weed. There are many medicinal herbs in the Reserve like Aconite., Kutki root, Spikenard, Rhubarb and Ginseng. The endemic flora of KBR are Anemone, Uvaria, Sikkim Rhododendron, Sikkim Mahonia.

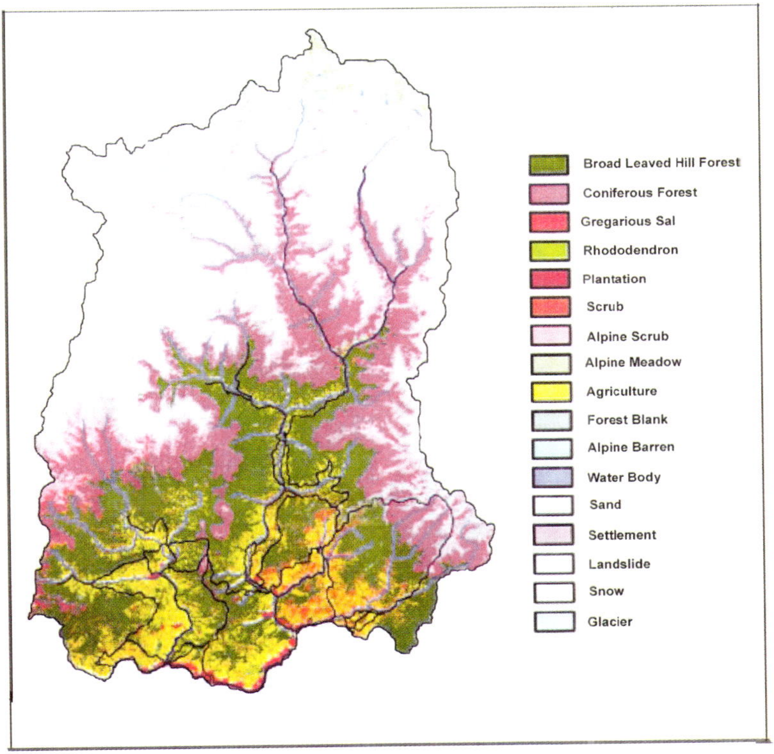

Fig. 3 Vegetation Type in Sikkim.

Tropical moist deciduous sal forest ranges from the altitudes of 300 m to 900 m. This is the climax type of vegetation in the foothills of Sikkim. As altitudes changes from 900 m to 1800 m, the forests also gradually changes from tropical to sub-tropical forests. The vegetation gradually changes from sub-tropical to sub-temperate in the altitudes ranging from 1800 m to 2400 m and afterwards the vegetation becomes distinct temperate forests. This type of forest is found between the altitudes of 2700 m to 3700 m. The vegetation type above 3700 m comprises of typical moist alpine, dry alpine and alpine meadow. A typical situation is found after an altitude of 4400 m. where the tress growth is completely arrested.

FAUNA

The high altitude regions of Sikkim harbour the rare and endangered species of animals. The snow leopard of alpine land holds the position at the apex of the biological pyramid. Himalayan red panda, musk deer, nayan or the Tibetan sheep, bharal or blud sheep, Himalayan tahr, marco polo sheep, marmots and monkeys are a few animals are found here. This reserve also harbours many species of birds. The pheasants include monal, trogopan and blood pheasant. The other species are Tibetan snow cock, Himalayan snow cock, snow partridge, Lammergier, forest eagle owl, Tibetan horned eagle, owl, eagles, falcons, hawks, snow and rock pigeon. Tibetan sheep, Musk deer, Monal pheasant, Snow patridge, Red Panda are endemic fauna of the KBR.

PEOPLE

Sikkim was originally referred to as '*Denzong*' by the Tibetans meaning 'the land of rice'. The present name Sikkim has been derived from Limbu words meaning 'new place' which referred to the new kingdom founded by Penchoo Namgyal in 1642. The Lepcha called this place as '*Nyemae-el*' or 'heaven'. Presently the population of Sikkim consists of three major ethnic groups, namely the Nepalese, the Lepcha and the Bhutia. In addition, there are some smaller groups also belonging to different other communities. The Lepcha were the only inhabitants of Sikkim untill the 16th century. They are believed to be the aboriginals of Sikkim. They are referred to as 'Rang-pa' or 'the people living in the ravines' by the Tibetans. They are short, well built and different from other groups, though definitely of mongoloid descent. A resemblance between the Lepcha language and the Khasi language of the Khasi tribes in the eastern hills had been established. Before the advent of Butias, they were worshippers of nature and they paid obeisance to mountains, rivers and forests. They are firm believers of spirits. Khangchendzonga mountain range is considered to be the abode of theor good and evil spirits. The Lepcha name of this mountain range is '*king-tzum-song-bu*' which means 'highest over our heads.' The majority of Lepcha are Buddhist but a few of them are Christens also. Presently the Lepcha are protected by tribal welfare measures and they happily share their fortune and destiny in common with other ethnic groups in the state.

The Bhutia of Sikkim are the descendents of the migrants mostly from Tibet and to some extent from Bhutan. They are called *'Kham-pa'* or the immigrants from the Tibetan province of Khams. By religion, they are Buddhist and their language is derived from Tibetan. Before the advent of the Bhutias, there was no organized central political structure in Sikkim. They played a significant role in the establishment of the Sikkim kingdom in 1642 in collaboration with the local Lepcha chiefs. The Lamaism or Tibetan Buddhism is recognized as the state religion. The Nepalese came into Sikkim during the 18th and the 19th centuries. Presently, they outnumber the other major ethnic groups. Settled agricultural practices were introduced in large scale in Sikkim only with the advent of the Nepalese population. Among other communities noteworthy are the Gurung and the Limbus.

LAND USE SYSTEMS

The general topography of the State, soil type, rainfall and distribution, natural streams, landslides and status of land erosion and traditional land use preferences are among the many factors which determine the land use pattern. However, in Sikkim certain established, major land use patterns can be recognized which are as follows:

1. Agriculture system is adopted by most of the households, in which livestock, vegetables, fruit crops, trees, fodders etc. constitute minor and subsidiary components.
2. Agro-forestry system with large cardamom as the principal commercial crop, interspersed with utis (*Alnes nepalensis*) plantations which provide the necessary shade, humidity and nutrients by way of litter fall to the principal crop.
3. Fruit crops based horticultural system as existing in Lachen and Lachung valleys for apple cultivation and in and around Singtham for mandarin orange cultivation.
4. Plantation crops based land use system such as tea plantation in Temi-Tarku
5. Specialized horticultural system such as vegetable production and seed potato production in higher altitudes.
6. Forestry covering one-third of the geographical area of Sikkim in which some land is apportioned for social forestry and silvi-pastoral systems.
7. Alpine and sub-alpine natural grass lands which are grazed by sheep, yak and to some extent upland cattle.

Agriculture

Land use for agricultural operation is an established practice among the settled households in Sikkim unlike most of the other north eastern hill regions. The importance of it lies in the fact that nearly 84% of the population in Sikkim inhabits the rural areas and majority of them have agriculture as the main occupation. The number of operational landholding in Sikkim is about 14% of the total available land. Agriculture forms the major component of the mixed farming system adopted by the majority of the settled households. Livestock and other components play a subsidiary role in this mixed farming set-up. A characteristic feature of cultivable landscape of a Sikkim agricultural household is the existence of beautifully laid out terraces, most of which are crescent shape narrow benches built across the mountain slopes. They possess a lengthwise gradient of 2 to 3 % and small shoulder bunds along the outer margins. Terraced lands and valley lands are chiefly utilized for paddy cultivation. Within a agricultural household, a portion above the terraced land is left un-terraced to grow maize, millet and vegetables. Some fruits trees, a few bamboo bushes and fodder trees invariably find their place in each farm household especially on irrigation and drainage channel embankments. Most commonly, field crop production is taken at a slope of 30 to 40%, though in higher altitude above 1500m, agricultural operations do take place at 60 to 70 5 slope. Cropping intensity at lower altitudes lends itself to multiple cropping while at mid altitudes, double cropping is quite feasible and at higher altitudes only mono-cropping is adopted. Climatic topography and soil constraints impose great limitations on crop production, especially the production of cereal grains which on unit area basis is not as much remunerative as in the plains.

Horticulture

The climatic and ecological conditions vary greatly within a short span of distance in Sikkim and as such the adaptability of crops suffers a limitation beyond certain narrow ranges. However, such variations favour growing of varieties of fruits, vegetables and other commercials crop like ginger both during seasons and during off-seasons at different altitudes. Important fruit crops of Sikkim include mandarin orange, guava, lime, lemon and temperate fruits like apple, pears and plum. The main orange belt is around Singtham in the East Sikkim, the orange cultivation is noticed in the north and west districts as well. Some orange orchards problems are facing the problem of decline, which could be averted by using systematic planting method, fertilizer application, plant protection measures and overall management. Apple cultivation, which is mostly confined to the Lachen and the Lachung valleys in the north, also faces problems because of very old plantation and affliction to apple scab disease. Large cardamom is a traditional commercial crop as well as the most important cash crops. However, recently it has become diseased and because of this the production has suffered. The disease is yet to be identified. However, the experts suggest that if replaced by better germplasm, the disease can be overcome.

Ginger is the second most important cash crop after cardamom. It has potential to even push the paddy cultivation to the back ground in the years to come. Commercial production of vegetables on large scale is highly promising around the major developing town of Sikkim as well as in higher altitudes especially in the north where the potential for the production of off-season vegetables is highly feasible. Lachen and Lachung valleys hold out to be the centres of vegetable production in future. While potato cultivation in the mid and higher hills is highly popular among the farmers of Sikkim, potato seed production in high altitudes is yet another instance of horticultural land use of commercial production. Tea is a major plantation crop recently introduced in Sikkim.

Alpine and Sub-Alpine Grazing Land

These lands constitute about 14% of the land area in Sikkim. About 8000 sheep and over 3000 yaks utilize these lands for grazing. Though the quality of these grasslands is not good, considering the number of animals they sustain, the grazing intensity is not so high as to cause any appreciable deterioration of the condition of these lands. In contrast the *gocharan* land which is part of the forest areas constituting about 10,400ha is highly degraded and the *khasmahal* land making up about 28500 ha of the forestlands is severely stripped off its tree cover.

Barren and Uncultivable Lands

These lands constitute about 28.64% of the total area of Sikkim, mainly consisting of glaciers and snow-clad ranges and thus unproductive in so far as agricultural and allied operations are concerned.

The Problem of Soil Degradation

Unstable geological nature of the soils and the steep hilly terrain makes the soils of Sikkim highly prone to erosion and related problems. Among the major factors leading to soil disturbances are intensive agricultural practices, denudation of forest cover, heavy rain and construction of roads. Overgrazing in the *gocharan* lands and excessive tree felling in *khasmahal* lands led to extreme soil degradation in these areas.

KHANGCHENDZONGA BIOSPHERE RESERVE (KBR)

KBR is one of the newest Biosphere Reserve established in Feb. 2002 (Fig. 2). It has an expansion of nearly 70% of the land area of the

Sikkim State covering the districts of North, South and West Sikkim. Its boundaries lie between Latitude 27°15′ North Latitudes and 88°02′40″ East longitudes. The core zone is extended on an area of 1784 sq. km. and is surrounded by four buffer zones of nearly 835.92 sq. km (Table 1). In the KBR the altitude varies from 1220 metres from the mean sea level to 1880metres.

Table 1. Geographical Area under core and Buffer Zones

Sl. No.	*KBR components*	*Area (sq.km)*	*Geographical position*
1	Core Zone (CZ)	1784	Existing Khangchendzonga National Park
2	Bufffer Zone 1 (BZ1)	154.48	Portions of Lhonak valley
3	Bufffer Zone 2 (BZ2)	55.29	Areas of west of Chungthang valley
4	Bufffer Zone 3 (BZ3)	29.37	Portions of Tholung valley
5	Bufffer Zone 4 (BZ4)	596.78	Along Indo-Nepal boarder, CZ and some reserved forests
	KBR Total	2619.92	Falls in the North, West and South districts covering 36.92% of the state.

The Reserve covers mainly the two districts of State i.e., North and West district. In the North district Chung Thang is the subdivision office and in the West district Gylalsingh and Yuksam are the nearest places.

Main Features of KBR

The main features of the Kangchendzonga Biosphere Reserve are as follows:

- It has the country highest peak.
- More than 70% of the Reserve is covered by dense forest.
- It has a wide variety of biomes from broad leaved forest of oak-castanopsis, temperate coniferous, rhododendron forest to dry alpine resembling cold desert of Asia.
- KBR consists of Trans-Himalayan zone and the extension of Tibet plateau.

- It is home to various endemic and endangered flora and fauna, and the endangered red panda and Himalayan bear.
- There are more than 5000 species of angiosperm, 4000 species flowering plants and 450-500 species of orchids and 300 species of ferns and allies.

It also has over 400 species of butterflies and moths, 140 species of mammals and about 600 species of birds.

- It forms catchment areas to the tributaries of the two main rivers Tista and Rangeet.
- There are altogether 24 villages in the fringe area of the KBR of which 14 villages are in West district and 10 are in North District. There is one forest village – Tshoka - which is in the core of the KBR.
- It is also becoming important from tourist view point; both Indian as well as foreign tourist visit the Reserve regularly.

2

A Study in Ecology and Conservation in Khangchendzonga Biosphere Reserve of Sikkim Himalayas

Umesh Kumar

INTRODUCTION

The Biosphere Reserves (BRs) of India are the abode of many communities who have always been an integral part of the ecosystem functioning there, living close to the Nature. Living in the areas rich in natural resource, traditional societies fulfill many of their livelihood requirements from the rich biodiversity around them. The ecosystems such as forest not only meets a variety of livelihood needs of the forest dwelling societies, through products such as timber and non-timber forest products, but also sustain traditional shifting cultivation and agricultural practices contributing to the food security of the people within the BRs. But the human population living within the Biosphere Reserves (BRs) has always been a matter of conflicting interests and debate. These considerations prompted UNESCO (1996) to move away from the earlier held view of concentric rings of core, buffer and transition zones, to a more flexible way of looking upon the local needs and situations. The flexibility and creativity in the Biosphere concept need to be seen from the point of view of both biodiversity as well as the cultural diversity. The benefits of cultural diversity at societal level are comparable to those accruing from the biodiversity.

The BR management, therefore, necessitates not only understanding of ecological issues but also the socio-economic and cultural issues linked with the former. It is, therefore, necessary to understand the societal perceptions of natural resources, as a cultural resource – often seen through the conceptual framework of sacred species, sacred groves, sacred water bodies, sacred landscape or even sacred mountain system. In order to achieve this, conservation-linked development strategy has to be based on a value system that people can understand, appreciate and accept. It, in turn, requires appropriate institutional arrangements for peoples' participation, through a 'bottom-up approach'.

The present study on Khangchendzonga Biosphere Reserve (KBR) in the Sikkim offers an opportunity to investigate the following objectives:

OBJECTIVES

(A) To map and analyse the change in land use and land cover in the selected villages.

(B) To elucidate and analyse the availability and use of forest resources by the people.

(C) To analyse the impact of grazing on the ecosystem.

(D) To find out the people's attitude towards conservation against the backdrop of enforcement of Biosphere restriction on use of natural resources.

(E) Role of the non-government organisation in conservation.

STUDY AREA

The present study refers to the area specially the KBR in the Sikkim (Fig. 2). While attempting to study the area the study is limited in terms of both space and time. Out of 14 revenue villages lying in the periphery of KBR in West District, the two villages -Yuksam and Dubdi - were selected. From North District, Lachen, Gnon-Samdong and Lyngzah villahges were selected for the field investigation. There is preponderance of Bhutia community in Yuksam while the Nepalese are a major community in Dubdi revenue village. The Lachen village is inhabited primarily by the Bhutia who call themselves Lachenpa. The other two villages namely Gnon-Samdong and Lyngzah fall within the Dzongu reserve area and is uni-ethnic. They are inhabited by the Lepcha community.

The principal occupation of the people living in these villages is agriculture supported by animal husbandry. The agricultural system is on subsistence level. With flourishing of tourism in Yuksam and Lachen some people have found engagements in this industry also as they work in hotels and transport sectors. Only a few villagers are in service.

METHOD

Both primary and secondary data have been used to fulfill the objective of the study. In order to gather the primary data field investigation were carried out in two phases- November and December, 2006 and April and May 2007. Remote Sensing (RS) and Geographic Information System (GIS) tools were used to find out the land use and land cover of the area. The data pertaining to fuel wood consumption was culled by adopting a weight survey method based on fuel consumption over a period of 24 hours. For this investigation was carried out in 55 households. During the survey the each sample stakeholder was visited and the head of family was requested to monitor the amount of fuel wood that would be burnt during that particular day. The wood was weighed by spring balance before its use. On the next day, the remaining wood was weighed and deducted from the original bundle to calculate the actual consumption per day. Time spent for fuel wood collection was noted when the members of the households went to the forests.

Participatory Rural Appraisal (PRA) technique was also used to collect the information of preferred species for fuel wood consumption, timber and fodder. Paired resource ranking method was adopted to find out the availability of natural resources and preference in the use of resources.

Based on observation on human needs and biosphere interference, a conservation attitude survey (CONVT) was conducted in some of the important fringe area settlements falling in the North and West Sikkim. Contingent valuation method (CVM) within the ambit of ecological economics with emphasis on willingness-to accept (WTA) and willingness-to-pay (WTP) approach was adopted for these settlements located crucially with respect to KBR. This was done to understand the ways the concerned population or the stakeholders express the environmental conservation concerns. The basic premise of the this valuation is that the environmental conservation costs of enforcing BR principles of restrictions of the use of natural resources shall also be borne by the local population or the stakeholders within their socio-cultural and economic framework of subsistence. To interpret the possible underlying issues, the entire responses to the questionnaire were further categorized into: conservation driven concern, socio-economic driven concerns, willingness-to-accept (WTA) and willingness-to-pay (WTP) concerns and participatory concerns in the BR concepts.

Besides, the qualitative information were gathered on role of NGO in conservation efforts through observation and discussion.

LAND USE AND LAND COVER

Satellite imagery (1:50000) IRS-1A, LISS-II, FCC of bands 2, 3 and 4 were interpreted for forest cover and other land-use employing a photo interpretation techniques for the year 1999, in conjunction with the Survey of India topographical maps by Chhetri et al.(2002). The interpretation of the imagery shows that 30.55 percent of the area is under snow cover. It is followed by Fir-Rhododendron forest, dense mixed forest and alpine pasture which occupies 20 percent, 16 percent and 12.49 percent of the area respectively (Table 1).

Table 1 Areas under broad land use/cover of KBR

Sl. No	*Land use/cover*	*%*	*Area km²*	*NDVI values*
1	Dense mixed/conifer forest	16	419.19	more than
2	Open mixed/conifer forest/ silver fir-Rhododendron forest	20	523.98	0.2-0.27
3	Degraded mixed/conifer forest	7.14	187.06	0.12-0.19
4	Scrub land/forest blank	2.63	68.9	0.05-0.11
5	Alpine scrub/pasture land	12.49	327.24	
6	Alpine barren land/barren land	9.92	259.9	0.01-0.04
7	Snow cover/glaciers	30.55	800.38	
8	Rivers/streams/lakes/exposed soil	1.27	33.27	less than 0.01
	Total	100	2619.92	

Based on Report of Maharana, I., Rai, S.C., Chettri, N., and Sharma, E. 2000.

Areas under different land-use/cover show that agriculture is the predominant non-forest land-use, occupying 14% area. A total of 77% of the area has forest which include degraded forest (having sparse vegetation), open forest and degraded forest (Table 2). The majority of the forest land is degraded category (crown <20%), 19% open forest (crown <21-40) and 19% dense (crown >40%).

Table 2. Area under different land-use/cover categories in Yuksam-Goechhala trekking corridor

S. No.		*Land-use /cover*	*Area*	
			(ha)	*(%)*
A		Built -up Land	65	2
B		Cropped Area	533	14
C		Conifer-Rhododendron		
	1	Dense	466	13
	2	Open	377	10
	3	Degraded	231	6
	4	Total	1074	29
D		Mixed-Broad Leaved		
	1	Dense	223	6
	2	Open	343	9
	3	Degraded	1058	28
	4	Total	1624	43
E		Rhododendron	30	1
F		Alpine Scrub	40	1
G		Forest blank	100	3
H		Waste Land		
	1	Rock outcrop	45	1
	2	Land slide area and sand cover	58	2
I		Surface water bodies	140	4
		Total	3709	100

Based on data used by Chettri. S., Krishna, A.P. and Singh, K.K. 2002.

In the Tsong area the plantation is the dominant land-use followed by sparse vegetation and agriculture. Plantation has occupied 45% of the area while area under sparse vegetation and agriculture including settlement are 40% and 15% respectively (Fig. 1). Large cardamom is the major plantation crop followed by some fruit trees like pear, guava and banana. Ginger does not grow in that area for the altitudinal height of the area is more than 6000 feet.

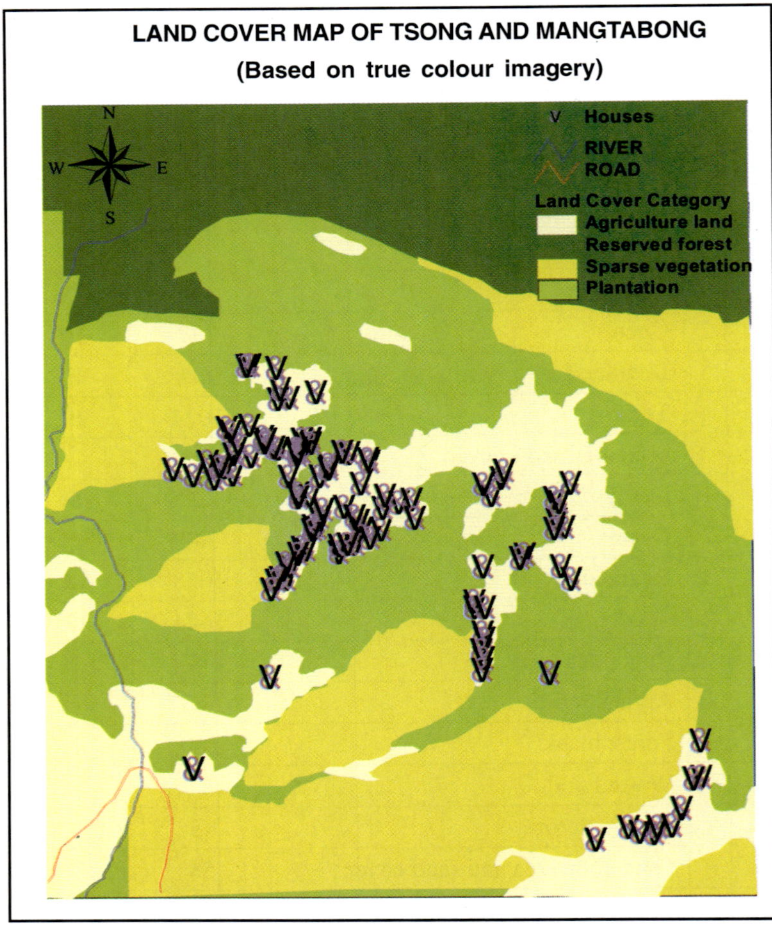

Fig. 1. Area under different land use in Dubdi are

During the ground truth testing in the course of field survey it was established that the vegetation adjacent to the settlement has very few woody trees. Consequently in order to meet the need for fire, fuel and timber woods the villagers depend on the reserved forest.

AVAILABILITY AND SPECIES PREFERENCE

Population living close to BR is highly dependent on forests in the buffer zones, be it for non-timber forest products (NTFPs), including extraction of medicinal herbs, litter, wild edible fruits, and other minor forest products (MFPs). Although the timber cutting is strictly prohibited, it seems difficult to stop the collection of fodder and fuel wood such as rhododendrons- a keystone species acting as biodiversity indicator of the region. Keeping in mind the aforementioned need of the villagers a study on the availability and preference of resources for fuel, timber and fodder was carried out in the month of November- December in Yuksam and Dubdi villages while in Lachen, Linzah and Gnon-Samdong it was carried out in the month of May and June. Revelations of studies are mentioned are below.

Fuel Wood

Fuel wood provides the major proportion of household's energy consumption in the domestic sector, while commercial alternative energy sources contribute very little. The consumption of fuel wood varied amongst stakeholders with respect to different physical and economic factors. Pair-wise ranking of species used as fuel wood at Yuksam and Dubdi Blocks have been presented in the Table 3. There are altogether 13 species used as fuel woods. The availability of status of this 13 species suggest that Uttis is most widely available fuel wood followed

Table 3. Pair-wise ranking of species used as fuel wood in Yuksam and Dubdi Villages

Sl. No.	*Local Name*	*Scientific Name*	*Availability*	*Preference*
1	Bajrant	Quercus lamellosa	11	13
2	Jat Katus	Castanopsis hystrix	01	12
3	Phalanth	Quercus lineata	05	11
4	Jhinguni	Eurya acuminata	07	10
5	Asare	Viburnum codrifolia	09	09
6	Bans	Dendrocalamus sp.	12	08
7	Mahua	Engelhardtia spicata	10	07
8	Uttis	Alnus nepalensis	13	06
9	Pansi	Sorbus sp.	02	05
10	Kharane	Symplocos ramisissima	04	04
11	Argali	Edgeworthia gardeneri	08	03
12	Tusare		03	02
13	Panyun	Prunus cerosoides	06	01

by Bans, Bajrant, Mahua, Uttis and Assare. The other species are available less widely. But the preference wise, Bajrant is the most preferred fuel wood species followed by Jat Katus, Phalanth, Jhinguni and Asare. The least preferred species is Panyun. A co-relation between the availability and preference shows that except Bajrant, Assare and Jhinguni, the other species, which are in high in preference list, are not abundantly available. Moreover, Jat Katus is the second most preferred fuel wood species but is least available in the open forest. The above analysis reveals that except Bajrant, the other preferred species are less in number. It means in order to procure these species they have to depend on the reserve forest. Secondly, the excessive exploitation of this species will further reduce their availability in the open forest.

In Gnong- Samdong and Linzah villages of Dzongu area there are altogether eleven species identified by villages as fuel wood (Table 4). Interestingly Chilloni, Uttis, Lapsi and Mahua are among the most preferred species. Among the least available species are Tooni, Kaulo, Saur and Malato. Other species are moderately available. The preference

Table 4. Pair-wise ranking of species used as fuel wood in Dzongu

Sl. No.	*Local Names*	*Scientific names*	*Avail- ability*	*Pre- ference*
1.	Chilloni	Schima wallichii Chis.	11	11
2.	Phalant	Quercus lineate	6	10
3.	Katus	Castanopsis hystrix	7	9
4.	Saur	Betula cylindrostachys Wall	3	8
5.	Panisas	Tectona myriocarpa Heurue & Muell	5	7
6.	Utis	Alnus nepalensis	10	6
7.	Mahua	Engel hardtia Spicata Bl.	8	5
8.	Lapsi	Spondias axillaries	9	4
9.	Malato	Macaranga pustulata	4	3
10.	Tooni	Cedrela Toona roxb.	1	2
11.	Kaulo	Machilus edulis	2	1

wise the Chilloni ranks the first followed by Phalant, Katus, Saur, Panisas, Uttis and Mahua. A co-relation between availability and preference shows that Chilloni is most widely available as well as most preferred fuel wood species. But other species, which though rank high in the preference list, are either moderately available or least available.

Fuel Wood Consumption Pattern

In order to find out the consumption pattern of fuel wood, 45 households were taken as sample, the details of which are given in the Table 5 In the Yuksam Block only those settlement have been considered which are dependent on Khanchendzoga Biosphere Reserve for fuel wood consumption. These settlements are Tshoka, Geychen, Norbugang, Khongtay and Yuksam. The settlements which are not dependent on Khanchendzoga Biosphere Reserve are Kopchey, Mantabong, Topsing, Gofa Danra, Dostang and Mangsabong.

Table 5 Fuel wood consumption pattern in different villages

Settlement	*Number of households*	*Total Population*	*Sample Size*	*Fuel wood consumption pattern*	
				Kg/captia /day	*Mg/yr*
Yuksam	364	1951	15	4.73	3368.303
Dubdi	69	402	10	3.5	513.555
Lachen	1609+12	2955	5	5.0	5334.475
Linzah	80	397	5	3.8	550.639
Gnon-Samdong	66	401	10	3.6	526.914

The consumption pattern of fuel wood is estimated to be 3368.303 Mg yr-1 in the village of Yuksam dependent on KNP corridor. In case of Dubdi it is 513.555 Mg yr-1. The consumption pattern of fuel wood in Lachen, Linzah and Gnon-Samdong is 5334.475, 550.639 and 526.914 Mg yr-1. The average consumption of fuel wood in Yuksam and Dubdi Blocks together is 3881.858 Mg yr-1 while in two villages of Zongu the average consumption of fuel wood is 538.776 Mg yr-1.

Species Under Pressure

The inventory of resources used for fuel wood at low and high altitudes shows that the trees surrounding the village vicinity, irrespective of species, have the maximum pressure of fuel wood extraction. Nevertheless, certain species are preferred over others for the fuel use because of their better burning quality. Bajrant (*Quercus lamellose*), Chilloni (*Schema wallachi*), Jat Katus (*Castanopsis hystrix*), Phalant (*Quercus lineate*), Jhinguni (*Eurya acuminate*), Katus (*Castanopsis hystrix*) and Aassare (*Viburnum codrifolia*) are the most preferred species at low altitude. At high altitude *Rhododendran spp*., *Quercus lineta*, *Quercus lamellose*, *Betula alnoids* and *Magnolia spp*. are the preferred species used as fire woods. But the availability of these preferred species in the forest is facing tremendous pressure. The settlements at high altitude viz, Tshoka, Lachen and Thangu are the major consumer of fuel wood. Many species from natural forests especially *Rhododendron arboretum*, *R. barbatum*, *Magnolia spp*. are cut for use as fuel.

The above discussion shows that the people in the surrounding of the forest area tend to collect fuel wood repeatedly from the same patch of the forestland. The forest cover in close proximity to the settlement and camping sites experiences maximum pressure. After the supply from the closer points decline, people penetrate further and further into the forest widening the area of impacted zone. In addition, the other factor that has put pressure is the selective use of species of choice for fuel. In recent years the quality fire wood trees have become sparse. Now the quality of the available fuel wood is poor and the shortage of good quality fire wood has led to widespread switching over to inferior quality fuel wood. The distance covered and time devoted in collection of fuel wood from surrounding forest is an indicator of fuel wood availability and scarcity. High pressure was observed in Monastery forest at Dubdi and trekking corridor of Yuksam-Gochala. It is apparent that if the harvested quantity exceeds the production capacity, one would not lose the growing stock but also biodiversity. The wood for fuel is derived from live, dead and damaged trees and woody shrubs.

The large scale felling of trees and shrubs along the trek route and camping sites is accelerating the degradation process. Forest is becoming thinner, leading to erosion of top soil and disturbing the ecology of the area. The present practice of fuel wood extraction if continued may have drastic effect on ecosystem structure and function. Extraction of fuel wood were slightly reduced after the intervention by Sikkim Biodiversity and Ecotourism Project, But the impact of extraction would still be substantial because much of the extraction is concentrated in the forest surrounding settlement and trekking corridor. Impact of fuel wood extraction on biodiversity can be minimized by promoting use of alternative fuel resources.

Sikkim biodiversity and Ecotourism project promotes alternative use of firewood through various awareness programmes and capacity building training. Lodge operators in Yuksam are now using alternative energy like kerosene and LPG for tourist purposes. Porters are now able to hire blankets while on treks to minimize use of firewood for heating. A code of conduct has been developed by a Yuksam based NGO named Khangchendzonga Conservation Committee (KCC) for visitors. The travel agents association of Sikkim has adopted a code of conduct where alternative energy on treks has become mandatory.

Timber

The PRA conducted in Yuksam and Dubdi Blocks with respect to the timber used by the villages reveals that there are eight species of timber woods which are preferred by the villagers. Of these Uttis, Siris, Katus, Okhre are abundantly available while Kaulo, Tooni, Tarsingh and Chanp are least available respectively (Table 6). Though the Chanp wood species is least available but the most preferred one. It is followed by Katus, Okhre, Kaulo, Uttis, Tooni, Siris and Tarsingh. Thus one finds that except Katus, Okhra and Uttis, other species are not available in abundant. As such in order to procure these species they have to depend on the buffer forest of Khangchendzonga Biosphere Reserve.

Table 6. Pair-wise ranking of species used as timber wood in Yuksam and Dubdi Villages

Sl.No.	*Local Name*	*Scientific Name*	*Availability*	*Preference*
1.	Chanp	Magnolia sp.	1	8
2	Katus	Castanopsis hystrix	6	7
3	Okhre	Litsae citrate, Juglans regia	5	6
4	Kaulo	Machilus edulis	4	5
5	Uttis	Alnus nepalensis	8	4
6	Tooni	Toona ciliate	3	3
7	Siris	Albizzia lebbeck Benth	7	2
8	Tarsingh	Beilschmiedia sikkimensis	2	1

Fire wood stacked at the base of the house.

Tiber collected from the forest being sawn.

Table 7. Pair-wise ranking of species used as timber wood in Dzongu

Sl.No.	*Local Names*	*Scientific names*	*Availability*	*Preference*
1.	Chanp	Magnolia sp.	2	8
2.	Malagiri	Cinnamomum Cecidodaphne Meeissn	1	7
3.	Kimbu	Morus indica L.	4	6
4.	Okhare	Litsae citrate, Juglans regia	3	5
5.	Katus	Castanopsis trixhys	5	4
6.	Kaulo	Machilus edulis	7	3
7.	Utis	Alnus nepalensis	8	2
8.	Tooni	Toona ciliate	6	1

In case of the two villages of Dzongu namely Gnong-Samdong and Linzah, there are eight timber species preferred by the villages. These are Chanp, Malagiri, Kimbu, Okhare, Katus, Kaulo, Utis and Tooni (Table 7). Among these species the Uttis is most widely available followed by Kaulo, Tooni, Katus. The least available species are Malagiri and Chanp. Interestingly the least available of species like Chanp, Malagiri, Kimbu and Okhare are the most preferred ones. The co-relation between availability and preference suggest that in the want of preferred species in the open forest, the people depend on the buffer forest of Khangchendzonga Biosphere Reserve.

Fodder

In all the studies area the people rear cattle which include sheep, goat, cow, ox and dzo. In order to feed them they require fodder which includes the leaves of trees and grasses.

In Yuksam and Dubdi area, there are 13 species of grasses which are used as fodder (Table 8). Among them the most widely available grasses are Gaglatu, Banmara, Rattnoli and Elame. The least available grasses are Duari, Kurkuro, Mirre, Bans, Chiple and Kamle. But preference wise the most preferred species is Amliso followed by Bans, Kurkuro, Chiple, Kamle and Galatu. The least prefer are Elame, Banmara, Mirre and Rattnoli.

Table 8. Pair-wise ranking of grass species used as fodder in Yuksam and Dubdi Villages

Sl. No.	*Local Name*	*Scientific Name*	*Availability*	*Preference*
1	Amliso	Thysanolaena setosum	08	13
2	Bans	Dendrocalamus sp.	04	12
3	Kurkuro		02	11
4	Chiple		05	10
5	Kamle		06	09
6	Gaglatu		13	08
7	Phultarul	Diascorea sp.	07	07
8	Kurro		09	06
9	Duari		01	05
10	Rattnoli	Polygonum molle	11	04
11	Mirre		03	03
12	Banmara	Eupatorium adenophorum	12	02
13	Elame		10	01

Table 9. Pair-wise ranking of grass species used as fodder in Dzongu

Sl. No.	*Local Names*	*Scientific names*	*Avail-ability*	*Pre-ference*
1.	Chiple (Kuhlonpe)	Bucklandia populnea Br.	1	22
2.	Thotne (kundyyum)	Polygonum molly Wright	5	10
3.	Unieu (tongtok)		11	9
4.	Piray Unieu (Lukship tongtok)		7	8
5.	Banso (Bamboo)	Dendrocalamus Helmintonii Ness, Arn and Sikkimensis Gamble	10	7
6.	Ratnaulo	Polygonum molle	9	6
7.	Amliso	Thysanolaena maxima	8	5
8.	Okhare	Juglian regia L.	6	4
9.	Banmara	Eupatorium Adenophorum Spreng.	2	3
10.	Tetepati	Artimesia indica	3	2
11.	Dhokrephal (Domari reep, only for goat)		4	1

In the studies villages of Dzongu of 11 species of grasses are used to feed cattle (Table 9). Among them the most available species are Unieu, Banso, Ratnaulo, Amliso, Piray Unieu. The least available species are Chiple, Banmara, Tetepati, Dhoakrephal and Thotne. But the preference for the species suggest that Chiple is the most prefer species but it is least available. It is followed by Thotne, Unieu, Piray Unieu and Banso while the least preferred species are Dhoakrephal followed by Titepati and Banmara.

In Yuksam and Dubdi blocks, there are 18 species of trees, leaves of which are used as fodder (Table 10). Among them the most easily available species are Billoni, Nibara, Gugun, Dudilo and Asare. The least available species are Titepati, Dudilora, Chindde, Khosmiri and Pipale. The preference wise the most preferred species is Dudilora followed by Bad, Dudilo, Nibara, Gugun, Phuto and Tooni. The least preferred species are Billoni, Titepati, Asare, Bajrant and Jhinguni.

Table 10. Pair-wise ranking of species used as fodder (except grasses) in Yuksam and Dubdi Villages

Sl. No.	*Local Name*	*Scientific Name*	*Availability*	*Preference*
1	Billoni	Mae chisia Don.	18	01
2	Nibara	Ficus hookeri Mig	17	14
3	Gugun	Saurauria nepaulensis	16	13
4	Dudilo	Ficus nemorates Wall	15	15
5	Asare		14	02
6	Bad	Banyan	13	16
7	Bajrant	Quercus lamellose	12	03
8	Payale		11	11
9	Tooni	Toona ciliate	10	08
10	Phuto		09	12
11	Kaulo	Machilus edulis	08	09
12	Khanyu	Ficus cunia Ham.	07	10
13	Jhinguni	Eurya acuminate	06	04
14	Pipale	Piper longum	05	07
15	Khosmiri		04	06
16	Chinde	Pentapanax leschennaulti	03	05
17	Dudilora		02	17
18	Titepati	Artemesia vulgaris	01	(Used by goats)

Table 11. Pair-wise ranking of species used as fodder (except grasses) in Dzongu

Sl. No.	*Local Names*	*Scientific names*	*Availability*	*Preference*
1.	Nibara	Ficus hookeri Mig	15	15
2.	Dudilo	Ficus nemorates Wall	14	14
3.	Baral		13	13
4.	Lali	Amoora wallichi	12	12
5.	Bar (banyan)	Terminalia bellirica	2	11
6.	Gagun	Saurauria nepaulensis	1	10
7.	Khanyue	Ficus cunia Ham.	10	9
8.	Kabra	Ficus infectoria	11	8
9.	Labar	Ficus elastica Roxb	8	7
10.	Chulitaro	Brassiopsis mitis	5	6
11.	Phalant	Quercus lineate	6	5
12.	Katus	Castanopsis trixhys	7	4
13.	Kutemero	Litsea polyantha	9	3
14.	Jhinguni	Eurya acuminate	3	2
15.	Titepati (Bush)	Artemesia vulgaris	4	1

In the Gnon-Samdong and Lyngzah villages of Dzongu, there are 15 species of trees, the leaves of which are used as fodder (Table 11). Among most easily available species are Nibara, Dudilo, Baral, Lali, Bar and Gagun. The least available species are Titepati, Jhinguni, Kutemero and Katus. Interestingly, Dzongu area presents a case where the most abundantly available species are the most preferred species.

In the last ten years the population of Sikkim has increased by approximately 33% (Census of India, 2001) thus putting even more pressure on resources. In the fringe areas, traditional agriculture and pastoralism exist. Agriculture is at subsistence level, with high dependency on natural resources in the surrounding forest. The practice of livestock rearing to supplement agriculture and generate direct income is quite prevalent. Open Grazing (e.g., yak grazing on alpine pastures) is practiced for the most part of the year, with limited stall feeding. In order to meet the fuel timber and fodder needs, the villagers are largely dependent on the Buffer zone forest of KBR. It is likely to have long-term impact on habitat in KBR. Increased habitat degradation may lead to some adverse effect on rare or endangered species.

LIVESTOCK RESOURCES AND THEIR ECOLOGICAL SUSTAINABILITY

Livestock wealth of Sikkim is constituted by about 0.4 million livestock and 0.3 million poultry which play a significant role in the economy of the region (Balraman and Golay, 2001). The domestic livestock of Sikkim include cattle, goats, pigs, yaks, horses, ponies, mule and poultry. The cattle population of the Sikkim is largely non-descript. However, they carry some exotic blood owing to the influx of animals from the nearby cross breeding centres of Darjeeling and Kalimpong. The local 'siri' cattle are predominant in numbers but poor in milk production. Since 1980s Department of Animal Husbandry has introduced foreign cross breed cattle like Jersey, Brown Swiss and Holstien. The stock of sheep in Sikkim include three main variety which are the Tibetan breed sheep, reared in the northern high altitudes areas for producing fine wool, 'Gharpala' and 'Banpala'. The 'Gharpala', is smaller breed and 'Banpala' a larger variety. The main distinguishing feature lies in the mode of rearing and subsequent adaptation, i.e., the Garpala sheep are homegrown and Banpala are migratory and graze at different altitudes during the course of the year. Marino, Corridate and Rambouillette have been used for upgrading the local sheep for better wool production. Goats are the popular livestock reared by most of the households. They are mostly non-descript and used for meat purpose. Pashmina goats called as 'changra' locally are found in Lhonak and Cholamu grazing grounds in the North Sikkim. Pig rearing is a commercial enterprise among the people of Sikkim. The small black pig, which is the original breed of Sikkim, has been experimented with cross breeding for upgrading of local pigs. Yorkshire breed is also used in the pig-breeding programme. There is preference for black colour pigs among the people here and in recent years, the Hampshire has become very popular. Ponies and mules are used in north, south and west Sikkim for transport. Especially in the northern high altitudes where road transport by other means is rather difficult, use of ponies and mules is imminent. Horses are used by the military personnel for transport of goods considerably. Some herds of buffaloes are maintained in the south, east and west

Sikkim and they are mostly maintained by grazing. In the west, buffaloes are grazed at even as high as over 2000 meters altitudes. The yaks are reared in the north, east and west high ranges. *Bho* yaks are bigger in size and more wild in nature are reared in the western ranges. *Aho* yaks are smaller and are noticed in the north and the north-eastern high altitudes. The poultry in Sikkim are mostly local and non-descript. Black Austrolop, Rhode Island, Red and White, Leghorn have been used for distribution among people and for upgrading the local stock of chickens. Commercial hybrid broiler and layer strains are also available for rearing. Among the ducks, local varieties predominate.

Feeding and Management Practices

Livestock feeding and practices prevalent in Sikkim can be discussed under two major categories, namely, stall feeding adopted by the settled farm households and migratory livestock rearing in high altitudes.

Most of the settled agricultural households are situated within an altitudes of 1800 m and they almost form the bulk of the farm community of the Sikkim. In the mixed farming setup such as noticed among these households, livestock rearing is an important component of aspect of their total economy to supplement and complement other components of farming. Hence, the livestock are not kept as a specialised enterprise, but an efficient means of utilizing farm by products and waste as well as to be utilised for work, manure and products such as milk, meat and eggs. But there specific communities who rear livestock in migratory condition. Gurung community rear sheep in western hill range and while the Bhutia community of Lachen and Lachung rear yaks, sheep and uplands cattle in the north under migratory conditions.

In the order of number of households maintaining different kinds of livestock, cattle rank foremost followed by chicken, goats and pigs. The number of the households maintaining sheep and ducks are quite negligible. In earlier times, when forest and common grazing lands were within easy access of people, grazing alone was the mode of maintaining livestock. Presently among the settled households of Yuksam and Dubdi blocks, stall-feeding is practice as rule and grazing is either within farming hold or in the nearby forestland. Judging from the extent of households utilizing the cut jungle grass, it is clear that forest lands continue to be an important source contributing towards the fodder needs of cattle in these areas. An important limitation here is the expenditure on labour for grazing animals or bringing cut grass from jungles, though the charges for forest grazing or cost of cut grass itself is very nominal.

Tree leaves form the main forage are utilised nearly by all the households. Various agricultural by-products and crops residue are utilised by most agriculturalist households. While the use of cultivable fodder is absent, some households use locally available wild plants and shrubs such as 'amliso'(*Thysanolaena agrostis*) 'dhutesaro' (*Setaria palmifolia*) etc. Forage is offered mostly at specified times generally twice a day. The animals take this feed in feeder made of bamboos within stall or on the open grounds. A scarcity in the availability of fodder particularly grasses during winter (December to March). It is during this period when tree fodders are used in large quantity.

The high altitude ranges beyond 1800 m are of particular mention because of the extreme agro-climatic situation prevailing there. In the Lachen valleys, potatoes, vegetables, and rearing of sheep, cattle and yaks under migratory conditions constitute the major activities of the people. Besides Lachen and Lachung valleys, Nathula range in the east and the high mountains of the west are the areas where above-mentioned practices prevail.

Goats

Goat ranks next only to the cattle. Goat is a popular domestic livestock with the households of Yuksam and Dubdi. Stall-feeding of goats is quite common in KBR. However, in some cases, goats are let loose for limited grazing along with cattle and sheep. Generally goats are fed on forage which are given to cattle, namely, tree leaves and cut jungle grasses. 'Thithepathi' (*Artimisia vulgaris*), wild plant, is collected and given to goats as feed. This plant is otherwise used as green manure in paddy fields. It has some aromatic alkaloids and is not relished by other livestock. During scarcity conditions, even weeds such as 'Banmara' (*Eupatorium sp.*) have been observed to be nibbled by goats freely in many households. Goats are mostly reared in bamboo enclosures raised from the ground often with a small open run. The cut fodder is given to goats in feeding racks made of bamboo so that both sides of the rack could be used for feeding without spoiling or wasting the fodder.

In the high altitude areas of north Sikkim, particularly in the grazing areas of Lhonak and Cholamu the Pashmina goats are reared. They are locally known as 'Changra' and are reared in limited numbers.

Sheep

Sheep are reared mostly by the traditional shepherd tribe in Sikkim, namely Gurung community in western Sikkim, some Tibetan and Bhutias in Lachen and Lachung valleys. Western Sikkim seems to offer a conducive climate and better grazing conditions for sheep rearing. Here few individual households together hire a herdsman to look after sheep flock commonly owned by them, who moves with sheep in high altitude areas for grazing them for considerable period. Similar practice is followed in Lachen and Lachung valleys also.

The Tibetan breed of sheep requires special mention as they are confined to the high altitudes in the northern Sikkim and produce fine wool. They have good carcass weight also. The two locally recognised breeds of sheep are the *Banpala* (forest grazing sheep) and the *Gharpala* (home reared sheep). Sheep are entirely grazed in forest. There are two shearing seasons in a year namely October and April. The 'Banpala' sheep give on an average one kg of wool per annum.

Pigs

Rearing of pigs is an important enterprise among the people. One remarkable feature of piggery is that they are reared in stalled conditions and not allowed to scavenge. Moreover, the terrain of the hills is not conducive for pigs to graze around freely as they become unmanageable if allowed free movement. The pigs are fed on concentrate mixture consisting of maize, maize cobs, barns and little salts. In most instances, shoots and tubers of plants are added to the concentrate. Squash is a most commonly grown vegetable in almost every farm hold in Sikkim where pigs are grown and this forms an important feed ingredient. Pear frits, the trees of which are abundant in the study areas are also one of the commonly fed items. Another feed ingredient is the 'chang' waste. Chang is liquor brewed from the millet ragi an consumed in almost all households. The leftover waste is available to be fed to pig and poultry.

Poultry

The estimated number of chickens per 100 operating households in study area has been calculated to be 426. 75 percent of the households. Most of these birds are non-descript and local. They are all purpose birds not specifically meant for production and marketing, but to satisfy own needs and the requirement nearby. The chickens are allowed to take care of themselves during the day. Use of cooked rice as feed is quite common. 'Chang' waste is also often fed to these birds. Besides, broken rice grain and other waste grains are also given as feed. The chickens roam freely in the open during the day time and returned to their wooden or bamboo enclosure during at dusk.

Yak

Yak is considered as native of Tibet. This animal has the ability to withstand extreme cold conditions. Because of its sure-footed nature, it is useful beast for transport in difficult mountain tracts. The yak is quite hardy and thrive well on the coarse fodder available in the alpine range. During the winter season, the yaks are taken to lower reaches. They are herded only when they are to be taken to lower grazing lands. Milk of the yak is has high fat content. Milk is mostly used for domestic needs and its by products, viz., curd, butter and 'churpi' (dried cheese) are sold in the market. The 'churpi' remains consumable for months together in the dry form at room temperature.

Blankets and carpets made of yak hairs are quite valuable and fetch good price in the market. Usually, male stock is slaughter for meat and females is retained for breeding. There are no special sheds for yaks but some wooden or stone enclosures are used to keep the pregnant yak cows and the newborn calves during the night. Such shelters are provided sometimes right in the grazing ranges.

Dzo

The dzo is the hybrid of cattle and yak. The first dzo was brought from Holong in Nepal in 1971. They are quite hardy and most useful for transport. In fact this animal has the ability to survive in both high as well as low altitudes. Because of this unique ability, it is a very useful beast of burden in West Sikkim particularly in Yuksam-Gochala trek route. This trek route begins from Yuksam, the climate of which can not support yak and goes up to Gochala which is situated in high altitude areas. During the monsoon season, these Dzo's graze freely in the semi alpine pastures in a semi-wild state, without caretakers. Only when the tourists season begins from September onwards, are they are brought back from these heights. They are used to carry the camping gear and rations of the trekking groups. Each Dzo can carry up to 60 kg load on very steep slopes. Currently, there are 200 families owning 375 Dzos from the villages of Yuksam, Tsong, Tshoka, Chongri, Sindrabung and Uttrey in West Sikkim.

Mules and Ponies

In addition to yaks and dzos, mules and ponies are also reared in the northern high altitudes for being utilised for transport. In Yuksam areas also in order to meet the transporting requirement of the trekker, mules and ponies are extensively used.

Grazing Routes of Migratory Livestock in North Sikkim

Tibetan plateau is contiguous with the undulating alpine plains of North Sikkim and earlier to the closure of Tibetan borders, the Lachen and Lachung people (Bhutia) as well as those near the Nathula range had the benefit of free movement into the Tibetan lands for grazing their animals. Presently about 70 households in Lachen have yaks and sheep. Each household has a few heads of yaks and 50 to100 sheep. For grazing there is a norm followed by the people that for grazing their animals they must move together to any area so that good grass in that area will not be eaten away by the early grazers but would be equally available to all animals when grazed simultaneously. The following grazing route is normally followed by the Lachen people:

Month	*Gzazing Area*
March, April, May	Lachen
June, July	Thangu
August, September, October	Lachen
November, December, January, February	Dolep, Salep

In high altitudes of north Sikkim, a place known as Cholamu serves as a good grazing ground during winter. Here, snow fall is much less because heavy winds carry away the snow and the summer grass which is left on the surface as dry grass is grazed by yaks in the winter. In addition to cattle, sheep and yaks, ponies and mules are reared in Lachen region.

Tibetan settlers at Thangu, which is at an altitude of about 4500 metres, also possess sheep and yaks. The animals are not brought down below the level of a place called Donkun. There is common belief among them that the moving of sheep towards the southern side i.e., the lower altitude below Donkun may kill the sheep.

Lachung valley is also inhabited mostly the Bhutia and few Tibetans. The Bhutia of Lachung of have most of the livestock in this region. The settlers who hold small lands just sufficient for their dwellings also possess a few sheep and yaks. The following migratory schedule is adopted by these people.

Months	*Grazing Areas*
October to March	Chungthang
March, April	Lima (Lachung)
May to August	Yangthang
September	Lima (Lachung)

ECOLOGICAL SUSTAINABILITY OF PASTORAL SYSTEM

The fodder availability for the livestock is abundant during the summer months in the alpine pastures. However, it is the long harsh winter when heavy snow covers the winter pastures that really test the resilience of man and beast alike. Unlike the Trans-Himalayan region, which is characterised by much lesser precipitation, the moist meadows of KBR receive heavy snowfall making it difficult for the livestock to access forage during winter. This the time when the herders have to shell out money to provide supplementary feed especially to the milking animals. This essentially means that the livestock numbers are regulated by the availability of forage and feed supplemented with cash input in ensuring uninterrupted supply to the livestock round the year. Ecological sustainability of livestock rearing in KBR is further understood when seen at specific animal level.

Sheep herding (*Banapala* sheep)

The semi nomadic shepherds mostly Gurung have been following this traditional source of livelihood since ages. Sheep is raised mainly for wool and meat. The wool from the indigenous breed of sheep is used for making *Bhurkan* (mattress), *Raadi* (blanket) and *Lakuni* (Jacket) using the traditional handlooms and Majito (*Rubia cordifolia*) as the natural dye. The sheep are slaughtered for meat in religious ceremonies and social function.

In late spring, the sheepherders migrate to the high altitude pastures and return to their villages by late autumn. The sheep herders have tremendous knowledge of the alpine flora and fauna. During summer, these herds reach out to the alpine pastures and the caretaker stay in makeshift sheds made of polythene and bamboo poles. The sheep are grazed in the adjoining meadows. Heracleum (Ganer), Allium prattii (Dandu), Selenium tenuifolium (Cheeru), Kobresia capillifolia (Sun buki), Deschamapsia cespitosa (Chamrey), Kobresia duthiei (Bhalu buki) etc.

are some preferred fodder plants. Major impacts accrue on account of movement of men with their livestock in alpine eco-regions. As inbuilt mechanism for ecological sustainability, the people who practiced mono cropping of paddy in summer, used to invite these herders to manure their fields which were left fallow in winter. A unique symbiosis existed between nomadic sheep herders and sedentary paddy cultivators. Sheep herders received shelter and ration for them and fodder for their flock for staying in the field. In return, the paddy cultivators got manure for his paddy fields. In fact the fallow paddy fields used to serve as winter pasture for the sheepherders. In recent years, most of the winter pastures have been lost due to adoption of multi cropping practices by the cultivators and the fields are not left fallow at any time. Consequently, with this reduced access to winter pastures, sheep herders were forced to reduce their herd size. Hence, these herds are nowadays forced to spend the winter in the large cardamom and fallow fields adjoining the villages. Large cardamom cropping and trekking tourism serves as an alternate source of income to these ex-sheep herders. Presently there are 17 herder families owing about 1000 sheep from the villages of Dhoopi, Narkhola, Karjee, Yangtam, Rungdung, Tsong, Melli and Sardung in West Sikkim which graze in the alpine pastures. Out of 17 families, three families of herders belong to Tsong.

The sheep herds descend down to the people's fields during winter. So the impacts associated with the yak herding in the temperate and sub-alpine winter are not there. The perception of the villagers is that since the impact of sheep herding is limited, if the sheep herders can be made aware to stop poaching and reduce firewood use then at the current stocking levels, this would be a sustainable practice. The herders with their immense knowledge of alpine meadows and regular visits to the alpine meadows can in fact serve as an excellent group for possible partnership with the Forest Department to patrol and conserve these meadows. They can be trained to become a part of the '*Himal Rakshak Force*'. The sheep herders can monitor the temperate and alpine forests during the monsoons.

Sheep grazing at higher reaches near Thangu.

Yak grazing at higher reaches near Thangu.

Yak Herding

Yaks are exotic to the alpine meadows of west Sikkim. Prior to 1975, only the royal herd of the king (Chogyal) of Sikkim was there. It was only in the middle of the twentieth century that the yak herding livelihood was imported from Eastern Nepal to the pastures of Khangchendzonga region. These yak herders practised subsistence level pastoralism and also carried out trans-border trade with remotest villages of Nepal bartering rice, salt and other rations with butter.

Impact of grazing in the alpine eco-region include use of Rhododendron and Juniper firewood in large quantities, poaching of wildlife, smuggling of endangered medicinal plants like kurki, jatamanshi, bikh etc for trade, trampling by yaks, presence of ferocious dog disturbing ground nesting birds and smaller mammals.

They use alpine pasture for six months and temperate pastures for the remaining six months. By late autumn, the yak herders start migrating down and cross the high altitude passes to reach the safety of the sub-alpine and temperate pastures. When these passes get snowed, it is difficult to cross over and ensure the well being of the herds. During this time the yaks herds take over the temperate pastures at lower altitude which are vacated by the cattle and dzo during their own migration. The winter pastures for the yak are mostly the Sub- Alpine Fir and Temperate Oak forests. These exist in the Singalila range at Kalijhaar, Gosha, Chewa Bhanjyang, Phalut, Singalila etc and the Oak forests at Nayapatal, Deoningaley Dhaap and Chtrey. However, there is hardly any natural ground fodder available in these habitats, forcing the herders to chop down large forested areas to promote grass growth and do extensive lopping of trees. The heavy precipitation, coupled with steep slopes and trampling by yaks result in heavy soil erosion and within a few years turns into stone and rock desert.

With the merger of Sikkim into India, development activities have accelerated and it has opened new opportunities for contractors and builders in infrastructure development projects. They hire some of these yak herders in relation to their work. Now some of the yak herders have left their traditional herding activities and entered in cash earning avenues.

Pack Animals (dzo and horse)

Pack animals are a major source of livelihood for the villagers and are engaged in trekking tourism. The herders of pack animals can also be made a part of 'Himal Rakshak Force'. Recently the numbers of pack animals, especially horses have shown a rapid increase, the villagers felt that that some kind of regulation is needed to restrict their numbers. In addition, the villagers are of the opinion that compared to the dzo, the horse has higher impacts. However, this view of the villagers do not appear to be correct as most of the horse herders are Tibetans while the most of the native of surrounding villages are either the Bhutia or the Nepalese. So it is more of a community specific view rather than based on facts.

CONSERVATION

People's participation in conservation efforts related to Biosphere Reserve is very important. Equally important is the people's attitude towards conservation. In the following paragraphs the people attitude towards conservation and nature, people's participation and role of NGOs have been discussed.

Conservation Attitude Survey

Imposition of Biosphere principals in terms of conservation entails certain restriction on the use of Biosphere resources and it translates in to some costs, which people have to bear. In order to know the people response towards such restriction a conservation attitude survey (CONAT) of approximately 20 % of the households was carried out in the selected fringe areas settlements of West Sikkim to determine how local communities and stakeholders express their concerns about environmental conservation.

Contingent valuation method (CVM) within the ambit of ecological economics with emphasis on willingness-to accept (WTA) and willingness-to-pay (WTP) approach was adopted for these settlements located crucially with respect to KBR. This was done to understand the ways the concerned population or the stakeholders express the environmental conservation concerns. The issues which are important both for the policy makers and stakeholders were considered for CONAT. The basic premise of the this valuation is that the environmental conservation costs of enforcing BR principles of restrictions of the use of natural resources shall also be borne by the local populations or the stakeholders within their socio-cultural and economic framework of subsistence. To interpret the possible underlying issues, the entire responses to the query were further categorized into: conservation driven concern, socio-economic driven concerns, willingness-to-accept (WTA) and willingness-to-pay (WTP) concerns and participatory concerns in the BR concepts.

Table 12A. Conservation Attitude Survey

Village name	*Sample size*	*Conser-vation Concern %*	*Socio-economic fuelled concern' %*	*WTA driven concern %*	*Partici-patory concern %*
Yuksam	10	90	80	100	100
Norbugang	06	67	30	85	90
Khongtay	07	85	57	100	100
Tsong	37	76	62	95	100
Mangtabong	30	73	56	90	100
Khecheopalri	07	85	71	100	100
Rambyathang	05	60	20	84	90

Table 12B. Statistical Derivation

Response Category	*Mean*	*Variance*	*Std. Deviation*
Conservation concern	76.57	116.94	10.81
Socio-economic Concern	53.71	396.27	19.91
WTA Concern	93.43	047.95	06.92
Participatory Concern	96.43	033.67	05.80

Table 12C. Correlation of Responses of Different Categories

A.	WTA and Participatory Concern	0.9090
B.	WTA and Socio-Economic Concern	0.9341
C.	WTA and Conservation Concern	0.9751
D.	Conservation and Socio-Economic Concern	0.9313
E.	Conservation and participation Concern	0.8465
F.	Socio-Economic and Participatory Concern	0.9180

The socio-economic and ecological indicators of the settlements covered in this study were established during the survey (Table 12A). The six settlements selected for the study lie in the close vicinity of buffer zone of KBR. CONAT interviews were carried out with random sampling framework in these settlements. For covering a total of approximately 433 households belonging to these settlements, 102 households were actually surveyed. Settlement wise overall positive conservation responses in the categories A, B, C and D were derived (Table 12B). The average positive ratings obtained ranged from 40 to 100 percent. The general positive responses were observed to be high except within the category B (Table) with high standard deviation (19.91) and variance value (396.27). This points out that the "socio-economic driven concern" expressed by the respondent are weaker compared to responses under other categories. It is partly because growth of tourism, particularly adventure tourism, has provided opportunities to the people of the area to economically engage themselves with this sector. The correlations of responses of different CONAT categories were established. The best correlation was observed between WTA/WTP and conservation concern (Table 12C). The results show that the people are willing to accept as well as pay for the sake of the conservation because they are worried about the adverse impact of the degradation of forest cover on the overall biodiversity. Moreover, the economy of the village to some extent now revolves round the tourism. It was closely followed by WTA/WPA and socio-economic concern and conservation and participation concern. Socio-economic driven concern has shown good correlation with WTA/WTP, conservation and participatory concerns. Therefore, despite best of conservation attitude initially, socio-economic condition of the people play a crucial role in maintaining or toning down the conservation attitudes of the community living close to BR area.

The study also throws light on the fact that conflicts are likely to crop up only when the real pressure of conservation restrictions begins to affect socioeconomic conditions of people living in fringe area settlements, in the absence of viable alternative to their traditional dependence on BR resources.

The key to resolution of potential man-biosphere conflicts over resource use lies in the social, economic and environmental concepts that are pillars of sustainable development. Policies for BR should give careful attention to the participation ofstakeholders as well as their perceptions, in the light of recently implemented joint forest management strategy. Such an approach ensures that stakeholders do not become antagonists, provoking conflict in BR areas.

People's Participation

A participatory approach involving stakeholders is essential for effective management of natural resources and ecosystem conservation in BR. Such an approach must imply traditional knowledge and traditional conflict prevention strategies in the management of BR resources. For example, in certain parts of North Sikkim, close to the BR, local communities have a system known as *zumsha* concerned with the social, developmental and environmental issues of local significance. The local governance system of Lachen valley is unique. This system is called the *Dzumsa* system. The literal meaning of this is 'gathering of people'. It is the traditional institution entrusted with task of administering and organising activities within a given territory. The general council of the *Dzumsa* is compose of household heads. The head of the Zumsa is known as *Pipon*. This system of self-governance was initially established during the first half of the 19th century in order to provide structure and cohesion to the societies and the activities of the people and was operative in Lachen and Lachung blocks of the Sikkim. In the year 1970s, when the Indian Government initiated the reorganisation of the Sikkim's administration and introduced the *Panchyatiraj* system, the *Dzumsa* was officially recognised as system of self-governance in place of *Panchyatiraj*. This system continues to function even today in Lachen and Lachung. The *zumsha* system prescribes and regulates activities such as grazing, tree felling and of medicinal plants and herbs, taking of full account of traditional ecological knowledge and imposing penalties for violations. Grazing is permitted only when complete care is taken to retain the regeneration capacity of rangeland. This includes allotment of a particular piece of land for grazing, determination of the number of the cattle allowed to graze, guidelines about the correct season, and suggestions concerning the times when cattle should be left in and brought out of the forests. Granting by the *zumsha* the right to fell the trees and collect medicinal plants and herbs, with the recommendation of Pipon, is also based on traditional ecological knowledge with the little danger of over exploitation. Such factors as socioeconomic status of household and systematic allotment of area for collection, considering the capacity for ecological regeneration, are also taken into account in the granting of rights concerning quantity, species, etc. Other forms of local traditional knowledge can also be integrated with the BR management to make it more efficient.

Sacred Landscape and Conservation

Sikkim is known as '*Demazong*' which means "hidden valley full of treasure, fruits and flowers". It is land of hydraulic culture where almost every water body, be it small or big, is treated as sacred. In fact the sacredness begins at species level and reaches up to the landscape level with the Mountain Khangchendzonga acting as guardian deity (Fig. 2).

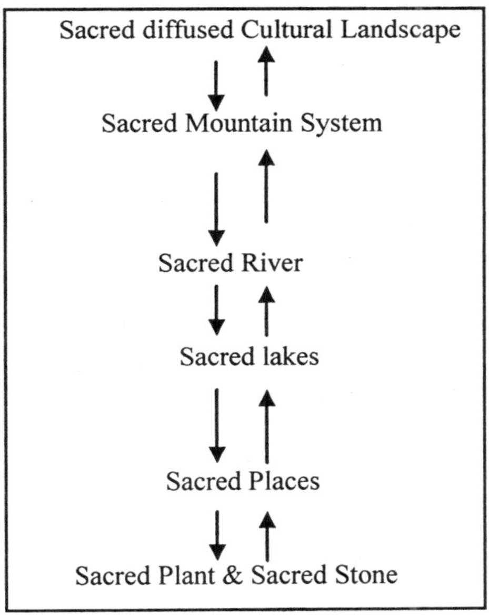

Fig. 2. Organic Relation Between Man and Nature.

People residing in and around KBR venerate and propitiate their deities of local pantheon, regional level and above all the Buddha. The deities are related with nature and its components. There are some festivals and rituals to be observed during the year. In the month of August, 'Panglhabsol' festival is celebrated and Buddhist lamas perform rituals and offer prayers in the name of the Mount Khangchendzonga. The monk and devotees go up to Dzongri 'Dhaplha gang' to offer prayers and rituals to Mount Khangchendzonga for good harvest and to make the whole region free from diseases and any king of natural disaster. There are altogether 109 known existing large and small lakes in Sikkim regarded as sacred by the people. Besides all rivers a and springs are also regarded as sacred. People dare not pollute these water bodies. In fact, the people of Sikkim even apprise the outsiders also about the sanctity of these water bodies and the kind of the nature's wrath they might face if they pollute the water bodies. Of 109 lakes, seven lakes are considered holy and believed to be having power to fulfil the wish of the people. Therefore, they are also called as wishing lakes. These seven holy lakes are Khecheoparli, Kathok Tso, Bar Cho Marpu, Phu Cho Karpu, Ka Bur La Tso and Dafuk Yum Tso. These lakes are considered as seven offering bowls to the Mount Khangchendzonga. Besides, there are four holy caves in the four directions of Sikkim, viz, Lhari Nying Phu in the North, Dechen Phu in the west, Khandu Sang Phu in the south and Bas Phu in the east directions. These caves are religiously protected and people do not disturb the flora and fauna of these areas.

Even at meso and micro level, every landscape be – it high land or low land–every streams and big trees and caves are believed to be the abode of a guardian deity which (*Yulha, Zibda*) are worshipped with great devotion by the local monastery in the morning rituals. Every human habitation and places which have the footprints of human being are decorated with wheel of life, eight lucky signs, prayer flags, chorten etc. The prayer flags can be seen almost every where in Sikkim- on hills, along the water bodies, beneath a big trees and on building tops. It seems that the sanctity to sacredness flow from the religious rituals.

The whole region seems to reverberate with the hymns of Buddhism which has permeated the life of the people. The religion is not an external element to the people but has brought together both the man and nature to interact on day-to-day basis. Consequently it has led to emergence and operationalisation of organic relationship between man and the nature (Fig. 2). This relation is world apart from the Newtonian reductionist approach which put emphasis on the importance of parts. It is, on the contrary, a holistic relation where man interacts with nature with respect and treats it as a living entity.

Role of NGOs: Ecological Sustainability

There are two non-government organisations (NGOs) namely Khangchendzonga Conservation Committee and Mutanchi Lhom Aal Shenzum (MILAS) operating in the West and North Sikkim. While the former is operative in Yuksam area, the latter is functional in Dzongu area. Both of them have done wonderful activities regarding conservation of natural resources in their respective areas by through mass awareness programme. Various exchange programmes with outside people are arranged for building conception of conservation among the local people. At Yuksam, the main entry point to the KBR, the government office does not contain any information pertaining to reserve thus leaving the KCC with the sole responsibility of providing all park visitors with reserve information. In addition, the KCC has created awareness among the local people regarding use of polythene. Now the people collect the polythene bags at one garbage centre instead of throwing here and there. In an effort to stop the use of wood for water heating and coking by the tourist going to Gochala, the use of kerosene stove is being promoted. In addition, KCC is also promoting the home-stay tourism in the area to benefit the local people. Recently they are involving in programmes related to capacity building.

CONCLUSION

Nested in Himalaya the KBR requires management of both natural ecology and cultural landscapes. Agriculture is at subsistence level. The practice of livestock rearing to supplement agriculture and generate direct income is prevalent in the region Human population living close to BR is highly dependent on forests in the buffer zones, for timber and non-timber forest products. An effective conservation policy requires a strategy based on provision of alternative livelihood options and additional resources, to defray the pressure and dependence in the BR resources is also important for the efficient management and conflict prevention. This can be achieved by capacity building in local communities to enhance the productivity, thereby reducing dependence on biosphere resources that are likely to be subject to restrictions. Local communities must derive direct and indirect benefits in the implementation of overall BR concepts, with due concern for effective implementation mechanisms.

Provision of alternative livelihood options and additional resources, to defray the pressure and dependence in the BR resources is also important for the efficient management and conflict prevention. This can be achieved by capacity building in local communities to enhance the productivity, thereby reducing dependence on biosphere resources that are likely to be subject to restrictions. In summary, the most important initiative to be implemented concurrently for effective conflict prevention necessitates that ecosystem protection has to be based on participatory approach wherein community is given responsibility for effective monitoring and exercise of traditional rights and forms of resource use.

ACKNOWLEDGEMENTS

The author is grateful to Dr. V. R. Rao, Director-in-Charge, Anthropological Survey of India for giving me the opportunity to do field work in Sikkim. The author is also indebted to Dr. Ramesh Chandra, Deputy Director (C), North – West Regional Centre, Dehradun, and Dr. A. K. Singh, former Senior Human Ecologist for their untiring effort in finalizing the report. The author is grateful to Department of Forest, Tourism and Police and other government departments of the Government of Sikkim for extending all possible and co-operation. The author will ever remain indebted to the Khangchendzonga Conservation Committee and the people of Yuksam and Lachen for their unconditional help and co-operation. Last but not least, the author also acknowledges all team members of the project for their cooperation without which the work could not have been done successfully.

3

Cultural Landscape of Fringe Villages: A Study in Khangchendzonga Biosphere Reserve of Sikkim Himalayas

Sudhansu Gangopadhyay

INTRODUCTION

The Khangchendzonga Biosphere Reserve (KBR) is named after god Khangchendzonga and third highest peak of the world (8598 m). It is also highest in altitude among the 14 biosphere reserves in India. It covers an area of 2619.92 sq. km including core and buffer zones. Incidentally, it is second in respect of core area of all the biosphere reserves in India. Its boundary follows peak line of Singalila range in the west and in the east it follows line of the stream. In the south, it touches to the line of the forest differentiating buffer zone from fringe villages. The Reserve does not have any human settlement except Tsoka inside area in west Sikkim either in core or buffer area though surrounding fringe villages are found in southwest, middle and northeast. The people of fringe villages are basically Bhutia and Lepcha though few Nepali people are seen to inhabit specially in the southwestern part. By virtue of being place for enjoying eco-tourism through trekking in deep forest and in hilly terrain of Khangchendzonga and place of cultural and historical heritage, some fringe villages like Yuksom, Tsozo, Khechedpalri got exposures since 1995. Again the merger of Sikkim with India in 1975 and subsequent acceptance to democratic set up of multi party system from Buddhist monarchy leads to development and tourism activities which starts to reflect in post 95 era of contemporary situation.

The contemporary situation had brought changes in cultural landscape in fringe villages in the form of economy, resource management and cultural life. The pattern of cultural landscape is an important subject matter specially in the area such as Yuksam of West Sikkim or Lachen of north Sikkim where exposures have imminent either due to tourism or increasing network.

STRUCTURE, EXTENT AND AREA OF THE RESERVE

The KBR consists of two zones namely core and buffer area basically, though fringe villages are engulfed with the buffer area mainly in the southern and western part of biosphere. The KBR has wide variation in altitude lying between 27°15′ north 27°57′ north and 88°02′ east - 88°40′ east. The core and four buffer zones cover an area of 1784 sq. km and 835.92 sq. km respectively. The reserve spreads in three districts of west, south and north district. The KBR as a whole is bounded by Singalila range in the west while its eastern and southern part follows more or less the upper limit of village forest. The northern limit of the reserve runs following the course of stream Gomachu and Pokechu approximately. But the line demarcating KNP and buffer zone is not uniform while buffer zone ends with touching village forest line at its southern part. The core area is known as Khangchendzonga National Park which is entirely protected from any kind of exploitation. The buffer zone which guards forest species, wildlife and glaciers, lie between core and fringe villages. The buffer zone has four segments which have known as zone I, II, III, and IV. West Sikkim lies at zone four while Dzongu area lies at the end of zone three and the zone one and two touches the northern most Sikkim and north of Dzongu respectively. The area of buffer zone I, II, III, and IV are 154.48, 55.29, 29.37 and 596.78 sq.km respectively. The zone four is large and spreads in west and south district. The zone of third is least in area lying in Dzongu area of north district. Again the buffer gap widens upto 154.48 sq. km. near upper part of Lachen valley while this gap is less in the southern part i.e. 55.29 sq. km. The buffer zone consists of reserve forest of coniferous, temperate and subtropical nature of species.

The next part of the reserve is fringe setup which has 23 revenue villages and one forest village (as enlisted by forested department) as juxtaposed to the buffer zone of the reserve. As per enlistment of forest department, Government of Sikkim, fringe setup covers 14 revenue villages in west Sikkim and 9 revenue villages with one forest village in north Sikkim. In this way it has about 1479 households having population of 8250 persons in west Sikkim and while North Sikkim has about 2563 households with total population 7763 persons (Census : 2001).

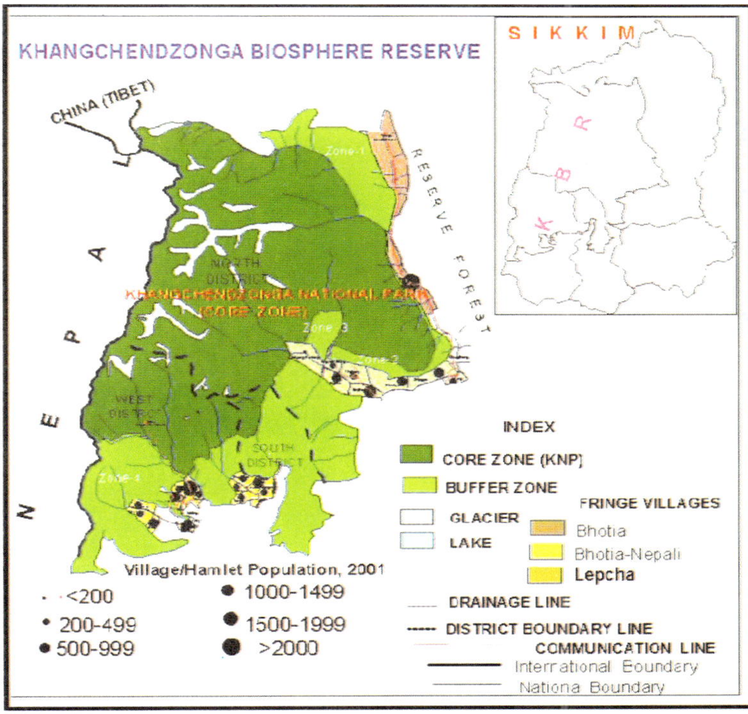

Map 1. Khangchendzonga Biosphere Reserve.

The total geographical area of fringe setup villages is 221.72 sq.km. Bhutia and Lepcha are in majority in north Sikkim. Bhutia locally known as Lachenpa are concentrated mostly in Lachen. The Lepcha is found mostly in Shipgyer, Tung, Salimpakel, Lingthem, Lingthen and Sakyong – Pengong of Dzongu area. Unlike the concentration of Bhutia and Lepcha by majority in north Sikkim, west Sikkim has the concentration of Bhutia, Lepcha and Nepali in different proportions though Bhutia and Lepcha are found in great proportion in some villages.

The fringe villages hold significance since they are the entry points to enter into the reserve for trekking into the base of Khangchendzonga or enjoying the nature. In this way, some of the fringe villages have become the place of a great deal of human activities related to tourism. Yuksam and Lachen of West and North Sikkim Districts respectively may be cited as an ideal example to prove the case. However, the villages of Dzongu area are yet to attract the tourist at a larger scale for entering the Dzongu area requires permission from the government owing to its being a restricted Lepcha territory. Therefore, fringe villages have been studied by the social scientist not only for noting down the changes of economy, resource management and cultural setup of this people but also to observe and understand the underlying factors seemingly responsible for inducing changes.

The names of fringe villages are as follows:

Table 1. Fringe villages

Sl. No.	*Fringe villages*	*Location*
1.	Topung, Singrangpung, Nambu; Yuksam, Dubdi, Tsozo, Khaehedpalri; Meli, Melliaching; Dhupidara, Labdang, Narkhola, Kongri Mangnam	West Sikkim (Rathang Valley)
2.	Sakyong-Pengtong, Linzah-Toloung; Tingbong, Lingdem, Lingthem, Salimpakel, Shipgyer, Tung	North Sikkim (Tolung Valley, Dzongu area) North Sikkim (Middle Tista Valley)
3.	Lachen, Lachen forest village	North Sikkim (Lachen Valley)

Source: Forest Department Government of Sikkim, 2007.

IMPORTANCE OF KBR

The KBR is named after third highest mountain peak Khangchendzonga (8598 mts). The entire land is seemed to be lying under mighty god Khangchendzonga holding banner of victory and seated on a snow lion and therefore the entire landscape is sacred to the Sikkimese people. The major festival is *Phang Lhabsol* to be held in connection with the worship to mountain god. Similarly, the Lepcha has also a great attachment to this mountain since the base of the mountain is seemed to be *mayel* land (ancestors' place) from where *mayel* people (ancestors of the Lepcha) have come. The present land of Sakyong-Pentong, Linzah-Toloung, Tingbong, LIngdem, Lingthem and erstwhile Shipgyer has very close similarity with mythological land *mayel* as believed by the Lepchas and expressed by Geoffrey Gorer

(1938) in terms of rough terrain and inaccessibility. Thus the reserve is cared and guarded by the local people due to its cultural attachments.

Apart from this, ecologically it has great significance since it is a store house of water resources locked in form of number of glaciers and lakes which provide supply of water to the major river system of Rangit and Teesta (Table-2). It is also global hot spot for biodiversity. Its diverse forest species with many pristine patches and tropical, temperate, coniferous, rhododendron and alpine meadows type of species; turbulent streams, wide variety of birds, flower plants and above all panoramic view of mountain terrain has given invaluable gravity to the biosphere reserve area.

The floral and natural diversity of KBR as follows:

Table 2. Floral and natural diversity of KBR

Floral	*Nos.*	*Natural*	*Nos.*
Species of flowering plants	4500	Mountain peaks	28
Types of orchids	448	Glaciers	21
Types of rhododendrons	36	Lakes and wet land	227
Types of bamboo	20	Rivers and streams	104
Types of butterflies	700	-	-
Types of birds	550	-	-

KCC report, 2007.

METHOD

Methods used in the present study with regard to selection of villages, collection of data and duration of field work have been elucidated below.

Village Selection

Yuksam, a fringe village of KBR, has mainly been selected mainly due to economic and ethnic diversity and presence of as many as 16 hamlets. Secondly the degree of accessibility are different among settlement units of Yuksam.

The second village selected for the study is Lachen. Lachen

consists of two hamlets located at entirely two different geographical locations i.e. one at lower elevation while other at higher elevation. Hamlet situated at higher altitude is vacated in winter and people move down to hamlet at lower altitude. The locational factors are guiding forces for economic activities in two seasons - winter and summer. The above mentioned reasons have necessitated selecting this village for study. The selection has also been made in order to know how the village of having background of pastoralism, agricultural and trade activity with Tibet under transhumance system has responded in switching over to diversified occupation: hotel, transport business and subsequent change in level of education and lifestyle with attachment to traditional value.

Data Collection

The data collection was done at both secondary and primary levels. At secondary level land related information was gathered from Survey and Settlement Office while map of KBR was accessed from Forest Department. The other information on forest, people, economy and infrastructure were collected from the concerned offices including Census Office. The village level information was collected through interview. A total of fifteen percent of households were covered. The households were selected through random sampling method.

Field Work

A preliminary investigation was undertaken at Yuksam village in August 2006 and later on a detailed village level survey was conducted during November and December 2006. On the other hand detail village level of survey was done at Lachen in similar fashion during May, June 2007.

OBJECTIVE

The study was undertaken with the following objectives.

The basic aim of the study of the KBR is to describe the pattern of cultural landscape in terms of economy, resource management and some aspects of cultural life of the people of both the villages i.e. Yuksam of West Sikkim and Lachen of North Sikkim. The similar and dissimilar situations in the cultural landscapes of the two villages are also attempted to study in order to understand underlying principles which may be due to different exposures to transport network, tourism and other development activities in contemporary situation.

STUDY OF FRINGE VILLAGES

Yuksam

Yuksam is one of the 23 fringe villages as enlisted by Forest Department of Sikkim. It lies in the far western corner of Sikkim. The western part of the villages is bounded by Rathungchu while its eastern part is delimited by Yuksam reserve forest. The northern limit is marked by hills stream known as Paha-khola. The southern boundary is delimited by Dubdi and Labbing revenue villages, while Tsozo and Khchepaldri are seen on the western edge of this village.

Literary meaning of Yuksam is meeting place of three superiors. It is also a place where Buddhist monarchy was initiated by Bhutia lamas by way of consecrating Phuntsog Namgyal with the title Chogyal meaning king of righteousness. Yuksam being the first capital of Sikkim since 1642 has its significance as a place of *Lhakhang* i.e. altar for offering prayer to the *Khangchendzonga* deity and center of gateway to have entry to Khangchendzonga Mountain leading ultimately pouring of trekkers and nature and tour loving people. Incidentally, it is the last settlement unit beyond which lies KBR. Apart from its historical event, Yuksam had been considered the *Lhakhang* i.e. altar for making offer to the *Khangchendzonga* deities. The lakes, peaks, streams, rivers, caves, big trees and even landscape are believed to be guarded by *Khangchendzonga* deities. Therefore Yuksam being place of installation of Buddhist monarchy and belief of being place of deities of the area have become place of pilgrim to the Sikkimese people in general and Bhutias and followers of Buddhism in particular. Thus, it houses few monasteries out of which Dubdi is the oldest monastery founded by Lhatsum Chemo in 1701.

The average altitude of the village is 1780 mts. The terrain is by and large rugged and rough though northern part i.e. Gechen and eastern part of Khyongte has gentle slope due to foot hill position and the central part in the Yuksam Bazar shows plain land. Similarly, Ramgeythang has developed plain land inspite of location in hill slope. The southern part is marked by rugged terrain. Rathangchu is the main drainage line though few hill streams pass through the village. Yuksam is considered as highest rainfall area which is encircled by snow capped mountain peaks including Khangchendzonga as third highest peak, river valley, falls and laxurian growth of forest species of coniferous, temperate, rhododendron and orchid etc. Yuksam is the most busy locale through which tourism takes place to visit the snow capped peaks of the reserve through trekking inside the jungle upto the base of Khangchendzonga. Tsoka a hamlet of Yuksam lying inside the KNP is also an added attraction to tourism.

Lachen

The village Lachen lies in the valley of Lachenchu. It is the last settlement unit of North Western part of KBR. The village is divided into two parts -. lower or southern part and upper or northern part. The lower part has Lachen (3000 m.) as permanent settlement and is village's headquarter. The upper part is known as Thangu (3658 m.) and is summer settlement where agriculture starts in summer season with the melting of snow. It is also the place where high altitude cattle meet in summer. Both parts of the village are separated by narrow forest cover.

Literary, the term Lachen means great (*chen*) pass (*la*) which covers a geographical area of 36 sq. km. Unlike Yuksam it is basically homogeneous village with Bhutia as major ethnic group locally known as Lachenpa.

Lachen being the last settlement unit of north western part of KBR has its significance as habitational place at the altitude of 2926 m and practices agro-pastoral economy. It had great historical and cultural attachment with Tibet before 1962. The striking point is that the village spreads in two parts of which Lachen (2926 m) is main part and known as winter settlement while Thangu (3658 m) is the upper segment and known as summer settlement. It is also important that village Lachen is very near to snow line. As a result of it, the area is struck by severity of the winter in the major part of the year. It is also lying very near to the core area of the KBR. In addition, the people of this village practice pastoralism and agriculture under transhumant system.

Like Yuksam, the Lachenpa of Lachen consider mountains, streams, trees, stones and hill slope as sacred. The Lamaism and monastic life influenced by Buddhism has a great bearing on economic activities pursued by the people.

Environmental Background of Fringe Villages

The lower part has very rugged terrain with deep gorge due to structural weakness and enormous cutting by the Lachenchu. There are number of sites lying between Lachen and Rabom (southern limit of Lachen village) where thin agricultural field surrounded by thick forest cover exists. The field sites are Raboam, Latendanga, Tselep, Chaten and Lachen.

Unlike the lower part, the upper part becomes wide and has gentle slope where agricultural operation continues to a great extent. Potato is the major cash crop here. The agricultural fields stretches in south-north direction and include places like Zeema (I, II, III, IV), Yunga, Thombuk, Samdong, Yathang, Kalep, Thangu, Toga (opposite to Thangu), Chopta, Byamzee. All fields have good fertile land. It is also striking to note that the northern segment of the village is having flat terrain with thick soil cover.

The village is drained by many small tributaries including Lachenchu. The small streams lying north to south in the upper part are Lhasa chu, Kalep chu, Gyamthang chu, Gay chu, Taram chu while Raboam chu drains the lower part. The upper part has thick soil cover and less stones. The village Lachen due to its position in the great wide valley receives more rain (1485 mm annually) compared to Thangu (531 mm annually). Chopta chu is marked as a northern limit of the village, while Raboam chu is the southern limit. Narrow river plain along with surrounding rough terrain characterizes the lower part while its northern counter part is marked by wide plain of gentle slope. The scenic beauty of Chopta valley, Byamjee, Lahasa valley, Moguthang and Donkung-Cholamu has added special attraction to the tourist and trekkers. The trekking route moves along the stream line of Pokechu and it is very enjoyable to the foreign tourist.

Yuksam

Yuksam is a multi-ethnic village. The communities inhabiting the village are the Bhutia, Limbu/Subba, Lepcha, Chetri, Sherpa, Mangar, Gurung, Newar, Tamang, Rai and Damai. Among them, the Bhutia and the Limbu/Subba are the dominant groups. The Bhutia and the Lepcha are basically Buddhist by religion while other belongs to Hinduism. However, there are few families who are Christian. The total population of Yuksam is 1968 which consist of 366 households (Table 3). The sex ratio is low, as there are 1010 males as against 958 females. The table shows the population strength including male and female ratio against the respective hamlets of the village.

The present day Sikkim originates from Yuksam which had it reputation as being the first capital of Sikkim established in 1642 with the consecration of the first king Chogyal Phuntsong Namgyal by the three lamas. Therefore, Yuksam means meeting place of three monks. A stone throne shaded by a three hundred year old fir still stands as witness to such historical incident in Nobugung of Yuksam village. The

Table 3. Population and Households Yuksam 2006

Sl. No	*Hamlet name*	*Community name*	*House-hold nos.*	*Male*	*Female*	*Total*
1.	Tsoka	Bhutia	10	14	13	27
2.	Thunga	Subba	5	13	16	29
3.	Gechen	Bhutia	22	65	71	136
		Subba	9	28	25	53
		Sherpa	7	14	12	26
		Mangar	3	5	4	9
		Chetre	3	8	7	15
		Rai	1	1	3	4
		Total	**45**	121	122	**243**
4.	Khoyongtey	Limbu	32	97	96	193
		Bhutia	4	13	8	21
		Lepcha	8	20	25	45
		Chetri	2	6	6	12
		Sherpa	1	-	4	4
		Rai	1	2	3	5
		Dorjee	1	3	2	5
		Total	**49**	141	144	**285**
5.	Norbugang (Nupgaon)	Bhutia	23	57	64	121
		Lepcha	7	15	28	43
		Sherpa	3	7	7	14
		Rai	1	2	2	4
		Behari	1	3	1	4
		Total	**35**	84	102	**186**
6.	Khamtong	Bhutia	2	4	6	10
		Lepcha	1	2	3	5
		Gurung	1	2	2	4
		Total	**4**	**8**	**11**	**19**

(contd...)

Sl. No	*Hamlet name*	*Community name*	*House-hold nos.*	*Male*	*Female*	*Total*
7.	Yuksam *bazaar*	Bhutia	26	63	71	134
		Chetri	3	7	4	11
		Newar(Pradhan)	2	4	7	11
		Gurung	2	5	6	11
		Sherpa	2	5	5	10
		Lepcha	1	2	3	5
		Tamang	1	1	2	3
		Rai	1	2	1	3
		Behari	1	4	3	7
		Total	**39**	93	102	**195**
8.	Kopche	Gurung	5	12	19	31
		Chetri	5	12	10	22
		Bhutia	2	8	6	14
		Newar (Pradhan)	1	2	4	6
		Damai	1	1	1	2
		Total	**14**	35	40	**75**
9.	Gufedanra	Subba	3	6	11	17
		Gurung	1	3	6	9
		Lepcha	1	4	1	5
		Total	**5**	13	18	**31**
10.	Sapse	Limbu	5	17	17	34
		Bhutia	1	5	2	7
		Total	**6**	22	19	**41**
11.	Ingtang	Bhutia	4	15	8	23
12.	Topsing	Gurung	16	45	37	82
		Subba	8	18	15	33
		Mangal	1	4	5	9
		Chetri	1	3	3	6
		Total	**26**	70	60	**130**
13.	Mangshaboong	Limbu	46	139	102	241
		Chetri	1	03	03	6
		Total	**47**	142	105	247

Sl. No	*Hamlet name*	*Community name*	*House-hold nos.*	*Male*	*Female*	*Total*
14.	Tinting	Limbu	24	70	60	130
		Chetri	9	33	29	62
		Gurung	2	16	7	23
		Total	**35**	119	96	**215**
15.	Dosthang	Kami	10	30	20	50
		Subba	6	13	12	25
		Lepcha	5	17	13	30
		Gurung	5	14	7	21
		Sherpa	1	2	4	6
		Rai	1	2	1	3
		Total	**28**	78	57	**135**
16.	Ramgeythang	Lepcha	14	42	45	87
		Grand total	**366**	**1010**	**958**	**1968**

Source: Data was collected during field work by the author.

village Yuksam being the birth place of Buddhist monarchy has a number of monasteries in an around the village with Dubdi monastery as oldest monastery established in 1701. Similarly the whole region lying below Khangchendzonga is considered as hidden treasures and sacred regions. Yuksam is, thus, considered the Lhakhang or alter for paying offerings to the Khangchendzonga deities. Similarly it is believed that all the physical objects including mountain, peaks, rivers, lakes are guarded by Khangchendzonga deities and hence any human induced perturbation will ultimately lead to serious calamity. Thus Yuksam and surrounding areas are thought as holy land which, in turn, ultimately helps protect the reserve.

Yuksam (1780 mtr.) being the last settlement unit has the advantages of being the take off point to higher reaches of Khangchendzonga mountain since British period. It has emerged as one of the preferred tourist places since 1995 after the emergence of Pelling as a significant tourist spot.

By virtue of being place of such historical and cultural significance and gateway to Khangchendzonga, Yuksam is visited by people from different states, foreigners and nature lovers since 1995. The change from Buddhist monarchy to democratic system of governance after the merger of Sikkim with India in 1975 and subsequent development of tourism in post 95 period has brought changes in all spheres of life for the people of Yuksam which hitherto were basically dependent on agricultural with maize as dominant cereal and cardamom as an important cash crop. Although few of them had sheep or yak which they used to graze at the higher reaches. Gradual coming-up of hotels, shops, restaurants and showrooms of handicraft items in response to cater to the demand of the tourists have helped transform the economy of the village from traditional to modern ones. The establishments of institutions in recent times such as Khangchendzonga Conservation Committee (KCC), Community Information Centre, Khangchendzonga National Park (KNP) office etc. coupled with provision of telephone and home stay facilities (above Kopche settlement) have provided momentum to tourism which, in turn has, generated diverse economic opportunities to the people of the Yuksam.

Lachen

The village of Lachen is basically uni-ethnic in character though there are few Tibetan families also. There are altogether 224 households inhabiting at Lachen and Chaten (Table – 4). In the present scenario, the sites lying north of Lachen specially Thangu, Zeema and Yathang are preferred by people for inhabitation for a longer period of the year. It is also striking to note that few people have set up camps at Mangan or Gangtok in order to run their business. There are about 23 Tibetan households out of which 18 are permanent settlers at Chaten while five of them live at Thangu. It is also to be mentioned that people of Lachen Valley locally known as Lachenpa having faith in Buddhism are identified in two ways i.e. general people know them as Ma-pong and Tha-Chang (Lama). In this way they are also known as Kya-sher i.e. people with hair or without hair.

In the Lachen valley, Lachen is the only settlement unit which is permanent while Thangu is the extension of it and serves as summer settlement. Beyond Thangu, one comes across the Dokpas community who move along with their cattle at higher altitude. In this connection it is to be mentioned that the Lachenpa is a territorial identity which is normally used by the Bhutias who came early in the seventeen century. After that, the Tibetan came in 1959 and they also identify them as the Lachenpa which means the inhabitants of Lachen valley. But it is seemed that the Bhutia Lachenpa treat Tibetan as refugees as they have no land or voting right in the traditional caste council known as *Dzumsa*. The Lepcha and the Nepali are later migrants to the Lachen valley but they also call themselves as Lachenpa. But in true sense it is used by

Table 4. Population and Households Lachen, 2007

A: Lachenpa - Bhutia

Sl.No.	*Hamlet unit*	*Households*	*Population*		*Total*
			Male	*Female*	
1.	Lachen (non-Lama, public)	145	377	325	702
2.	Lachen (Lama)	15	35	23	58
3.	Chaten	11	25	23	48
4.	Thangu	4	12	8	20
5.	Zeema	2	7	5	12
6.	Yathang	1	4	2	6
7.	Rabom	4	10	7	17
8.	Dokpa (Lachenpa)	7	22	18	40
9.	Mangam	2	3	3	6
10.	Gangtok	10	16	15	31
Grand total		**201**	**511**	**429**	**940**

B: Lachenpa - Tibetan

Sl.No.	*Hamlet unit*	*Households*	*Population*		*Total*
			Male	*Female*	
1.	Thangu	5	12	9	21
2.	Chaten	18	64	56	120
Grand total		**23**	**76**	**65**	**141**
Lachen total		**224**	**587**	**494**	**1081**

Source: Details as per data collected during field work of the author

the Bhutias who are the earliest settlers and have the voting right in their traditional caste council. In recent times the young generation address the other communities like the Tibetans or the Nepalese as the inhabitants of Lachen i.e., the Lachenpa for honour. Thus, this kind of address is also a change among the young generation in treating other communities as the inhabitants of the valley.

The habitation sites are determined on the basis of their suitability for longer stay. It is also to be noted that all other hamlets except Lachen mainly practice agriculture. Again, the sites lying north of Lachen raise potato and other vegetables while the sites lying below Lachen raise mainly maize.

CONTEMPORARY SITUATION

Yuksam

Yuksam has now emerged as one of the preferred destinations for tourists, trekkers and pilgrims alike. According to an estimate by TECS, numbers of tourists in Pelling has touched to 63600 (sixty-three thousand six hundred) in 2001 of which the village Yuksam has got a sizeable share. As per KNP office statistics at Yuksam, the number of trekkers passing through Yuksam between October 2005 and September 2006 has touched the figure of 3488 of which 1986 are foreign tourists.

The establishment of Khangchendzonga Conservation Committee (KCC) in the beginning of 1996 with basic aim of conserving natural and cultural resources in the event of tourism, inception of KNP office has helped made the people aware about the danger of ecological degradation and importance of conservation. Similarly, Community Information Center, opened in 2001, is also imparting computer training to the people of area. The opening of Siddhi Associate Private Limited, a financial institution, in 2001at Kopche of Yuksam village has helped people by lending them loan on easy terms.

The history of the first school in Yuksam dates back to 1942 when first primary school was opened. Later, it was elevated up to class X. Now there are number primary schools in different hamlets of the village such as Tingting (1981), Ramgeythang (1982), Mangsabung (1981). Lately two English medium schools have been opened one each in Kheyongtey (1998) and God Shepherd (2003) at Yuksam Bazar. These institutions also provide employment to the people of the area.

Lachen

Unlike Yuksam, Lachen underwent a major change after the sealing of Indian border with Tibet in 1962. It practiced basically pastoralism, agriculture and trade with Tibet under trance human system. The post 1962 situation affected the trans-border trade and a shift was observed with more emphasis on internal trade. But the post 2000 period also witnessed the beginning of a new industry in the form of tourism in the area. The hitherto restricted areas have now been opened for tourists.

It, in turn, has provided immense economic opportunity to the people of the region particularly Lachen. Now one finds a number of hotels, shops, vegetables stalls, telephone booths and different type of transports catering to the needs of the tourists. The package tour of Lachen and Lachung, Gurudongmar and Chopta valley along with trekking tour to Green Lake in Lachen valley have helped promote tourism prospect and market economy to a great extent.

The oldest government schools dates back to 1913. Now it has been upgraded up to class X in 1996. In addition, some new schools have also been opened at Thangu and Moguthang in the year 1985 and 1986 respectively. These developments have brought about a change in the economy of area wherein the traditional economy of agriculture and pastoralism is giving way to market economy with tourism being the most promising industry in the region.

PATTERN AND DEVELOPMENT OF CULTURAL LANDSCAPE

Yuksam

Tourism has brought about a sea change in economy of the village and surrounding area exemplified by the opening of a number of hotels, restaurants, shops, showrooms and handicraft selling centres. It is striking to note that Yuksam Bazar has ten hotels out of sixteen hotels in this village. Of the remaining six hotels, about three hotels are located at Kopche and one at Gechen. There is one or two lodges at Tsoka, the last settlement unit inside the area.

There are four grocery shops and three stationary stores at Yuksam *Bazar.* These shops not only meet the needs of the people of the village but also of the surrounding villages. Similarly, opening of telephone booth in 2006 and extension of internet service by community information centre heralds the beginning of a new era for region. The opening of showroom of handicraft items made of locally available raw materials like bamboo, wood or wool in November 2006 at Yuksam Bazar has also helped popularize the local handicraft among tourists. As mentioned earlier many hotels have also come-up at Yuksam, the details of which are given in Table 5.

Use of Pack Animals

The keeping of Dzo and Horse as pack animals is an important activity. They are used to carry luggage in hilly terrain specially where no other alternative exist except trekking. These animals are used to carry luggage during trekking, expedition, project work etc. Normally the

Table 5. Ethnic-Beneficiary Group Hotel Business : Yuksam 2006

Sl. No.	*Hamlet name*	*Ethnic-beneficiary group*	*Numbers*
1.	Yuksam Bazar	Bhutia	9
		Sherpa	1
		Total	**10**
2.	Kopche	Gurung	2
		Sherpa	1
		Total	**3**
3.	Gechen	Subba	1
4.	Tsoka	Tibetan	2
		Grand total	**16**

hiring rate of a Dzo or a horse is Rs. 250/- per day The pack animals are specially required by foreign tourists. It is observed that about a total of 1986 foreign tourists came between October 2005 and September 2006. It is seen from the register of KNP that about 586 and 458 pack animal were put into service as against 612 and 439 foreign tourists respectively during October 2005 and April 2006. Therefore, these animals are a source of income for the people. These animals are kept by the people of Yuksam, Gechen, Yuksam, Khyongtey, Norbugung and Tsoka (hamlets of Yuksam). Hamlets or villages lying at lower altitudes below Yuksam do not keep them.

At Gechen, pack animals are found in large number compared to other settlement units. It may be due to the fact that the many of the keepers of pack animals come from Nepal or Darjeeling along with their animals and live in rented house of their relative in order to accompany the trekking teams. This situation is not prevalent in other hamlets like Yuksam and Khyongtey. This finding is corroborated by the fact that Gechen has a large number of room available on rent.

Home Stay and Room on Rent Facility

The introduction of home stay facility at Yuksam and some of its hamlets since 2000 have opened up a new economic opportunity for the people of Yuksam since 2002.

It is observed that home stay is mainly preferred by the foreign tourists during March, April, May or October, November when the existing hotel capacity gets saturated. The tourists prefer to stay at home specially at Yuksam Bazar, Khyongte, Norbugung or Gechen because it gives them opportunity to understand and enjoy the local cultural, in addition to local foods. Out of a total 11 cases of home stay facility, Yuksam Bazar alone has five while Khyongte has four and Norbugang and Gechen have one each. In this home stay arrangement, the Bhutia is the major beneficiary group having seven such facilities while the Limbu have four (Table 6).

In case of providing room on rent, Gechen comes first among all 16 hamlets. Gechen being the last hamlet unit before going inside the reserve and having plain land at the foot hill has the advantage of giving shelter to the keepers of pack animals (Dzo and horse) required for carrying luggage of trekking teams. The keepers of pack animals are people from Nepal or Darjeeling area. Apart from this, room on rent is also provided to accommodate official or teachers. The details of the numbers of rooms available on rent during 2006 are shown in Table 6.

Table 6. Details of room available on rent Yuksam : 2006

Sl No.	*Hamlet Name*	*Rooms*	*Ethnic-beneficiary group*
1.	Gechen	21	Bhutia – 10 Sherpa – 6 Manger – 3 Chetri – 1 Rai - 1
2.	Yuksam bazaar	8	Bhutia – 8
3.	Kopche	7	Chetri – 2 Bhutia – 2 Gurung – 2 Damai – 1
4.	Mangsaboong	2	Limbu – 2
5.	Tintin	1	Chetri -1
6.	Ingtang	1	Bhutia – 1
7.	Dosthang	1	Kami – 1
8.	Ramgeythang	1	Lepcha – 1

The most beneficiary groups in this regard is the Bhutia followed by the Sherpa. The other beneficiary groups are the Limbu, Chetri, Mongar, Lepcha and the Gurung.

Transport System

The replacement of SNT service being in vogue upto 1997 in the route of Gezing – Yuksam or Jorthang – Yuksam with vehicles like Mahindra Swari, Max Mahindra, Tata Sumo, Commandar, Maxsha etc. have brought about a positive change in terms of speed, availability and catering to the needs of tourists. The present private transport system operates between Yuksam – Gezing, Yuksam – Jorthang and Yuksam – Gangtok. It has added to the comfort of the tourists. At present, there are 19 vehicles plying in the same routes (Table-7). In respect of numbers of vehicles, Yuksam Bazar comes first as there are about nine vehicles there. With regards to community ownership, the Bhutia posses eight vehicles out of a total of 19 vehicles. Kopche is the next after Yuksam and it owns four vehicles. The names of Ingtang, Tinting, Dosthang and Gechen hamlets also need to be mentioned though there are only three vehicles, one each in each village.

Table 7. List of vehicles for Yuksam : 2006

Sl. No.	*Hamlets where vehicles owner resides*	*No. of vehicles*	*Community owned*	*Year of opening*
1.	Yuksam bazaar	9	Bhutia – 6 Gurung – 1 Newar – 1 Behari – 1	3 – 2004 2 – 2003 1 – 1998 1 – 2000 1 - 2005 1 - 2006
2.	Kopche	5	Limbu – 2 Chetri – 1 Newar – 1 Tamang – 1	2 – 2005 1 – 2002 1 – 2003 1 – 2006
3.	Tinting	2	Bhutia – 1 Chetri – 1	1 – 2004 1 – 2005
4.	Ingtang, Dosthan, Gechen	3	Kami – 1 Bhutia – 1 Subba – 1	1 – 1999 1 – 2005 1 - 2004

Livelihood Pattern

The tourism coupled with opening of schools and offices of government and non-government institutions and organizations have opened-up new vista of economic opportuny for the people of the area.

As regards the activities directly related to tourism like working as porters, cook and guide it is observed that Yuksam, Gechen, Khyongte, Tingtin, Topshing and Mangsaboong are taking lead in this respect, though there are variation among them specially with regard to the availability of porter, cook and guide (Table-8). Among all the hamlets, Yuksam, Gechen and Khyongte are the centres of tourism activities by virtue of their location near the market centre and being close to the KBR, but the distant settlement units like Tingting, Mangsaboong or Topshing are also striving to reap the fruits of tourism. On the other hand, small hamlets like Ingtang, Ramgeythang and few other settlements are lagging behind in this respect. The hamlet-wise list of porter, cook, and guide given below provides a clearer picture (Table 8).

Table 8. List of Porter, Cook, Guide Yuksam 2006, Hamlet wise

Sl. No.	*Name of hamlet*	*Porter*	*Cook*	*Guide*
1.	Gechen	22	7	1
2.	Thunga	3	-	-
3.	Khyongtey	18	16	-
4.	Yuksam Bazar	20	1	6
5.	Norbugung	7	-	-
6.	Kopche	-	-	1
7.	Gufedanra	4	-	-
8.	Topsing	19	3	2
9.	Sapse	4	-	-
10.	Mangasaboong	12	1	-
11.	Tingting	13	-	1
12.	Dosthang	3	-	1
13.	Ramgethang	2	-	-
14.	Khamtong	1	-	-

Number of cook and guide is reported at Tsoka, Ingtang.

Lachen

The cultural landscape of Lachen has greatly been modified in the post 2000 period. The traditional economy has been replaced to some extent by market related economy. Of all factors, tourism is the most important one. The different aspects of new economy has been successfully incorporated by the Bhutia Lachenpas compared to other communities. Nevertheless, benefit of modern economy percolates to the other groups as well particularly to Tibetan. Another significant development is the continuing of economic activities through out the year at places other than Lachen which was earlier restricted to summer season only and that too remain confined to agriculture. In that way, new dimension in cultural landscape has also reached to other sites such as Thangu, Kalep, Yathang, Chopta which basically did not have any function except in agricultural season before pre-tourism phase i.e., year 2000. However, the new form of economy is changing the landscape as it is now dotted with hotels, shops, restaurant etc. and new mode of transport system. Accordingly role of traditional caste council (Dzumsa) in new economy has also undergone changes though the basic tenets of council have remained unchanged. The function of community information system by way of imparting computer training, role of school and level of education, initiative of social welfare department and handicraft centre, inception of angora rabbit farm, health centre and Rabom hydroelectric station have also played significant roles in developing new mind setup and acts as an agent for change in economy and way of life.

Emergence of Hotels, Shops

The people of Lachen have reputation in trade activities with Tibet 1962. The absence of trade with Tibet under transhumant system after 1962 has led Lachenpas to orient themselves to new pattern of business activities related to internal trade with Gangtok and Kalingpong instead of Tibet solely. The sale of agricultural commodities which were normally used by labourers engaged in GREF mainly and government employees and defence personnel to some extent was being done through the retail shops few years back. Again, luggage was carried to the places at higher altitude with the help of horse or yak in connection with expedition, trekking and defense work. But the post 2000 scenario with the advent of tourism opens a great market for hotel business and it also resulted in the opening of a number of shops. The grocery or stationary items are largely used by hotel owners, tourists, GREF workers and defense personnel. In this way, in Lachen a large number of hotels and shops have come into picture.. The providing of room on rent as source of livelihood is not so much in practice as only two such cases could be found. Similarly home stay facility is not so common here as seen in Yuksam.

The opening of hotels and shops are post 2000 events when large number of have begun to come, in addition to expedition teams, officials and research personnel. According to an estimate (Tourism master plan of Sikkim 1997 – 2011, Vol. V, Tata Economic Consultancy Services, New Delhi, 1998) north district receives tourists to the extent of 5300 and 10600 (projected figure of 2001 and 2006 respectively). also the number of lodges which were four in 2001 have increased to 22 lodges in current spell (Table 9). The numbers of lodges are concentrated maximum at Lachen, while Thangu has four lodges.

Table 9. List of Lodges in Lachen: 2007

Sl. No..	*Hamlet units*	*Numbers of lodges*	*Ethnic group*	*Year of opening*
1.	Lachen	16	Bhutia Lachenpa	2001-4 lodges, 2005-5 lodges, 2006-3 lodges, 2007-4 lodges, total = 16
2.	Thangu	4	Bhutia Lachenpa	2001-1 lodges, 2004-1 lodges, 2005-2 lodges, total = 4
3.	Chaten	2	Bhutia Lachenpa	2005-1 lodges, 2007-1 lodges, total = 2
Grand total		22		

In respect of ethnic group in hotel business, the Bhutia Lachenpa are ahead of other groups. Tibetan does not have any lodge. Again maximum numbers of lodges come into scene since 2004. However, one tourist lodge is opened at Chopta valley near Thangu under supervision of tourism department government of Sikkim. In the event of increasing tourism it is also observed that the main settlement unit of Lachen has become congested due to more numbers of lodges. It has also been observed that many households have diverted their homestead land for construction of lodges. Consequently, now less land is available for homestead for growing vegetables.

The rising number of shops has become new phenomena with the coming of large numbers of tourists. The shops keep grocery and stationary items which not only fulfill demands of the tourist, but also meet demand of labourers engaged in GREF or defense personnel in addition to local need of the village. By virtue of rising number of shops, the village Lachen has a developed good trade link with Gangtok. At present there are about 41 shops of various types (Table 10) which are distributed over different places of Lachen village. These shops are mainly owned by the Bhutia Lachenpas while only four shops at Chaten and two at Thangu belong to the Tibetan community.

Table 10. List of shops in Lachen : 2007

Sl. No.	*Hamlet unit*	*Ethnic beneficiary group*	*Numbers*	*Type of shops*
1.	Lachen	Lachenpa	21	Grocery & Stationery
2.	Chaten	Lachenpa Tibetan	1 4	Do
3.	Yathang	Lachenpa	3	Do
4.	Thangchung	Lachenpa	2	Do
5.	Thangu	Lachenpa Tibetan	8 2	Do
Grand total			41	

In addition to this, there are some military canteens which are used by the local people to purchase some items of daily use at reasonable rate. Chaten, Thangu and Zeema, are places where such kind of shops are found.

Transport System

The SNT service was in vogue even before 1995 though operating twice in a week up to Lachen and once daily upto Chungthang. But in the post 1995 period, it has been replaced by introduction of private vehicles which are mainly owned by the Bhutia Lachenpas. These vehicles are maily commander, marshal, tempo tracks, max mahindra etc. There are now 22 vehicles with 2 or 3 trucks owned by the Lachenpas compared to 5/6 vehicles (jeep) in 2001. There are only two vehicles owned by the Tibetans. The vehicles normally pick-up tourists from Gangtok under package tour of Lachen – Thangu – Gurudongmar and Lachung – Yumthang. In addition to package tour, at least one vehicle plies daily between Lachen – Mangan. In that way village Lachen has become more accessible compared to period before 1990 when the only means for movement was by SNT or by defence / government vehicle in case of dire necessity.

Livelihood Pattern

The village Lachen passed through three phases in economic development right from the days of Tibet connection. In the pre 1962 phase, agriculture, pastoralism and trade with Tibet were three main economic activites. In the post 1962 situation after the closure of border with Tibet, the Lachenpas laid more emphasis on agriculture or on commercial activities such as raising of apple and oriented themselves to new pattern business activity such as opening of retail shops, selling of agriculture commodities like vegetables, potato or supplying of chicken birds, goat or sheep to a limited extent to GREF/defence personal or taking contract of road repairing or construction work etc. This phase continued upto the year 2000. The post 2000 period marks the beginning of third phase which has witnessed the growth of tourism coupled with its increasing importance as strategic location. These all have contributed to the development of the area in terms of economic opportunities and connectivity.

RESOURCE MANAGEMENT

Yuksam

Yuksam, having an area of eight square kilometer, is basically dependent on agriculture. As per an estimate by survey and settlement department, the village has 67% land under the cultivation while 22% land is under village forest (Table 11). The village has 11% land under cardamom. The cardamonm is not grown below Kopche due to warm climate (Table 11).

Based on altitude agricultural operations can be put under two categories i.e. upper/northern part and lower/southern part.

The upper or northern part of Yuksom has relatively low temperature for a major part of the year. Therefore, this area is good for cardamom.

Table 11. Land use in Yuksam : 2006

Sl. No.	*Land type*	*Percentage of land in relation to total geographical area of the village.*	*Area in Hectors.*
1.	Wet land	2%	14.17
2.	Dry land including Bazo i.e. fellow land	65%	531.67
3.	Cardamom	11%	86.95
4.	Village forest including Kashmahal and Gaucharan	22%	179.67
	Grand Total	**100%**	**812.46**

Source: Survey and Settlement Department, Government of Sikkim.

Those units are Gechen, Kheyongte, Yuksam Bazar, Norbugang, Kopche. Wheat is also grown to some extent along with maize which does not grow so well due to lower temperature.

On the other hand the southern zone specially below Kopche i.e. Sapse, Ingtang, Ramgeythang, Dosthang, Mangsabung, Topsing has warm temperature but land is rugged at some places of Mangsabung, Ingtang, Sapse or Ramgeythang. Again Mangsabung, Tinting, Dosthang, Ramgeythang have difficulties in irrigating crops due to want of small streams. Therefore potato, cabbage and leafy vegetable do not grow so well. But the area is good for growing ginger and it is grown abundantly. Besides, Mangsabung, Dosthang and Tinting grow turmeric now a days. Presently there are two cash crops grown in these villages which are turmeric and ginger. In addition maize is also a common product here.

Lachen

In spite of having developed market economy, the Lachen by and large still practices agriculture and pastoralism under transhumant system. The regulation of cattle movement in the lower or higher reaches of the mountain and agricultural operation keeping in view the suitability of land and season is the basic approach to continue the economic activities in such extreme environment. It is striking to note that the continuation of the three economic function pastoralism, agriculture and horticulture run in a cyclic order.

Pastoralism

Pastoralism remains the main source of livelihood to the Bhutia Lachenpas since small or vast patches of glacial terrace or hill slope provides different type of grasses like hierocholoa, stipa-agrostics, calamagrastics, festuca to the cattle. There are two types of cattle; one type is suitable for low altitude while other for high altitude. The high altitude cattle are known as Himal type which include chongri, byangloo and fera in case of yak, sheep and goat respectively by the high altitude grazers or the local people. Similarly, the low altitude grazing cattle are known as *Lhonoh* type. They are known as *gera and bheru* in case of goat and sheep to the people of this valley. The high altitude cattle consist of yak, sheep and goat mainly while low altitude cattle consist of cow, ox, Dzo, horse, yak, sheep and goat mainly. The people who rear and moves with the cattle in the higher reaches i.e. above Thangu are known as Dokpa. The Dokpas may be the Bhutia, Tibetan or the Nepali. The Dokpa use to live in the hut made by stone cemented with locally available mud and roof covered with tin / wooden. This kind of habitat is called Dok and the inhabitants are known as Dokpas. It is reported during survey that There are seven Dokpas of the Bhutia community, while there is only one of Tibetan community. Similarly goatwallas rear and move with cattles in the lower reaches stretching from Rabom and adjoining area to Thangu and adjacent area. The goatwallas may be the Bhutias, Tibetans or the Nepalies. Now-a-days they also face many difficulties in free movement due to setting up of camps by defense personnel in higher reaches. The overall strength of cattle has fallen and it is reflected in cattle census of 1977 and 2001 (Table 12).

Table 12. Livestock North district

Sl. No.	*Major Cattle*	*Year*	*No.*
		1977	2001
1.	Yak	2340	1549
2.	Sheep	3977	2325
3.	Goat	8864	8375

Source: Live stock census 1977 and A statistical profile Sikkim, 2002, Government of Sikkim.

At present, very few people are interested to continue the grazing in higher altitude due to hardship as well as availability of other alternatives.

Lower Altitude Grazing

One or two members from every household take the animals for grazing. Those member are called goatwalla. In the winter specially from last week of November to February, cattle stay and move at Laten – Rabong sub area and adjoining places. The cattle move down upto Munshithang with the fall of snow in the winter.

In the 1st week of March, yaks begin their upward movement and reach at Thangu by the last week of May or in the first week of June. Twenty days after the journey of yak or in the 1st week of April, cows and horses start to move up. On their way to sub-areas of Chaten – Lachen – Zematen and Somdong – Yathang – Kalep area–Thangu, cattle pass through with consuming grasses grown in the places. It is to be noted that the cattle in the course of journey to Thangu, do not stay at Lachen or Chaten settlements. Instead they stay at the hills lying above the adjoining areas. This practice is followed possibly to the keep the area clean. In addition, these days few households prefer to give their cattle to the goatwallas, instead of sending one of their family members along with cattle. For handling the responsibility of grazing the cattle, the goatwallas are given money along with ration of rice by the cattle owners. This has happened because nowadays many households are now engaged in more remunerative activities like running of hotel, shops, transport etc.

High Altitude Grazing

High altitude grazing is mainly confined to the area lying between Thangu and Moguthang, Thangu and Cholamu, Thangu and Laser. These areas lie between 3500 m and 4500 m. These areas experience prolonged winter season with snowfall occurring between November and February. The areas are Cholamu area lying along the bank of Phalungchu, Moguthang area along the bank of Lhonokchu and Thangu – Talim area along the bank of Laserchu. These areas have grasses and scrubs with meadows in the glaciated valley which are very good fodder for yak, goat and sheep of *Himal* type. Due to availability of open space in meadow type terrain in those areas, the cattle have enough scope to move here and there in groups in search of forage. All the more, grasses are available in the winter due to sufficient space available at Moguthang or at Laser valley and snow also does not accumulate on the hilly slope. This is also a good reason for continuation of grazing in these regions.

There is one opinion that the cattle moving in the areas of higher altitude in search of grass cause harm the environment by way of consuming grasses and leaves of scrubs which subsequently result in the degradation land and leads to soil erosion. The local people, on the other hand, opine that grasses are renewable resources and grow quickly in the soil enriched with dung of cattle. Further, grazing help curb the excessive growth of weeds. Apart from this, the cattle dung is also collected by the farmers which they use in their agriculture field to make it fertile. Thus, in their opinion cattle grazing do not harm the ecosystem of the area.

Agriculture

Agriculture is the main stay of the economy in the valley till now in spite of development of tourism and other activities. Potato is the major crop of this region though there is limited cultivation of maize also which is grown only at lower part of the valley i.e. Rabom and adjoining area. About 70% of people are dependent mainly on cultivation and merely 50% (68 households) of total household of the Lachenpa Bhutia are the grower of potato. Again about 78% of total agricultural land is used for potato cultivation, while 18% of arable land is devoted for maize cultivation which is restricted to Rabom area only (Table 13).

Table 13. Lachen: Major land Use Area (in hectares)

Cultivated land	*Village forest*		*Total Geographical area of the village*
	Gaucharan forest land i.e. meant for grazing purpose	*Khasmahal forest land*	
442.83	1887.43	1305.49	3635.75

Source: Census of India, 1991.

It is seen that of total available land, a little over 10% land is under cultivation while nearly 90% land falls under village forest i.e. Gaucharan and Khasmahal forest land (Table-13). Out of this a little over 50% land comes under the category of grazing land and remaining land fall under forest and hill slopes.

Apart from potato and maize, wheat, radish, cabbage, spinach, cauliflower, pea are also grown in the valley. Potato, cabbage, cauliflower, spinach and beans are cultivated in the homestead lands at Lachen. In addition, these vegetable are also grown at other places like Zeema, Yathang, Kalep, Thangu, Yunga, Chopta and Beamzee lying north of Lachen.

Agricultural Sites

The agricultural sites may be grouped into three zones according to altitudes (Table 14).

Table 14. Altitudinal tiers, Agriculture sites and Showing and Harvesting time

Sl. No.	*Altitudinal tier*	*Agricultural sites*	*Showing time*	*Harvesting time*
1.	Low altitude	Laten, Denga, Rabom, Selep	December last week	June last week
2.	Middle altitude	Chaten, Lachen and Zeema	Middle of March	August
3.	Higher altitude	Yunga, Thombuk, Samdong, Yathang, Kalep, Thangu, Toga, Chopta, Beamzee	April 3rd week	October last week

It is to be mentioned that the Bhutia people of Lachen posses land which are distributed right from Rabom at lower altitude to Beamzee at higher altitude. The Tibetan also have some land (mainly) at Chaten and Thangu. The Bhutia people of Lachen has fair idea about timing of snowfall and degree of coldness. Their knowledge about vagaries of season and weather has made them prudent cultivators. Following the rhythm of nature they decide sowing and harvesting time of their major crop i.e., potato. Here it is to be noted that the showing and harvesting time is fixed up by the pipon (head of Dzumsa, traditional caste council) with the consultation of lama members of this council.

Potato

Potato is the major crops of Lachen valley. It is grown mainly at higher altitudes which cover mainly Thangu, Toga, Byamjee, Kalep, Yathang, Samdong, Chopta and Yunga though it is also grown at Zeema, Lachen, Chaten and Rabom. In Lachen, potato is grown in land adjacent to permanent settlement. In recent time, due to growing number of tourists, these lands are being gradually diverted for making of new lodges to cater to the needs of tourism. This has resulted in the loss of homestead land. Still about 78% of total arable land is under potato cultivation.

Potato cultivation at Lachen settlement.

The potato land is locally known as Kiyushing. Byamjee, Thangu and Toga are considered best places for potato cultivation for having gentle slope, less stone and getting sunlight. In this respect, *Domepasa* having no stone and *Sakumbi* having no moisture in the soil are considered best land for potato cultivation. Generally black soil, locally known as *sana,* is good for agriculture. But it is also to be noted that potato grows more at higher reaches due to availability of the sun for longer hours of the day. Thangu and Bayamjee may be considered as ideal areas where sun shine is available from March to May which is the potato growing season. Potato has also become a cash crop now-a-days. It is either directly collected by the potato dealers from their door step or people sell it to businessman at Mangon or even at Gangtok at Rs. 200/- per 40 kg.

The people have been growing local variety of potato such as *Kiu Myabu* (red type) and *Kiyu Kabu* (white type) since long time. However, recently high yielding variety of potato like *Kika-kiyu* has also been introduced. Its cultivation requires use of chemical fertilizers as well. Due to high cost involved in its cultivation and adverse impact on soil fertility owing to use of chemical fertilizers, its cultivation is restricted. The potato is preserved using traditional method wherein potato is put in a pit and top of the pit is, thereafter, covered with leaf and soil.

In Lachen no agricultural activities are carried out in winter due to coldness. In order to avoid coldness and rain, the people of Lachen and Chaten nowadays have begun setting-up *Khoo* (green house) through which some vegetables such as ginger, garlic, chilly, onion, tomato, pear are grown even in Lachen and Chaten in the months from February till May. This practice was started about eight or nine years back. There are now about three to four green houses in Lachen and Chaten. One of the green houses has been set-up under the supervision of defence personal at Chaten. Similarly to overcome the shortage of space, vegetables like beans, cabbage, onion are sometime grown along the edge of agricultural plots. Cattle dung specially sheep dung are preferred by them as organic manure.

Horticulture

Earlier apple was a good fruit crop in Lachen and used grow well. However, in recent years, its cultivation has suffered due to damages to plants. As opined by villagers it may be due to use of chemical fertilizer at potato fields which are very close to apple trees. It may also be due to wet condition of soil at Lachen settlement area. The wet condition of soil is caused by interruption in the smooth draining out of water which is attributed to coming-up of new buildings in the wake of tourism. The apple trees can be seen close to the homestead land in main Lachen settlement area.

CULTURAL LIFE

Yuksam

In the village Yuksam, the Bhutia are the dominant community followed by the Subba/Limbu. The presence of other communities like Gurung, Lepcha, Chetri, Mongar, Rai, Tamang and Newar has given rise of heterogeneous culture since beginning. The plurality in maintaining cultural characteristics is seen in the habitat pattern of the respective community. The maintenance of *Ippung* (memorial structure in the name of ancestors) in case of Limbu and *Choten* in case of Bhutia are evidences of maintaining their ethnic identity in the broader matrix of a plural culture.

Religion

Both the Bhutia and the Lepcha follow Buddhism. The Hinduism is by and large followed by the Nepalese community except few who follow Buddhism. This is seen normally among Tamang, Sherpa etc. Life centres around monastery and lamaism in case of the Bhutia and the

Lepcha. There are few people who have converted to Christianity and there is one church also at Kopche.

Both the Bhutia and the Lepcha of the area consider themselves fortunate for belonging to Yuksam. This sense of pride flows from the fact that Yuksam is considered as the *Lhakhang* or alter for offering to the Khangchendzonga deities. The Kartuk lake of Yuksam is thought as sacred lake and people make wishes at this place. Similarly the *Choten* of Narbugang is also considered very precious as it contains soil and water from time when three lamas met to initiate Buddhist monarchy. Dubdi monastery is another important religious place and it has the distinction of being the oldest monastery established in 1701.

Family type

The joint family is, by and large, a norm in Yuksam. A joint family comprises of husband, wife, mother, father, unmarried sister or brother and unmarried or married son. However nuclear family has become common nowadays.

The average size of a household is 5.37 persons. However, the Lepcha has the largest family size (5.94) while the Bhutia has the smallest family size (5.22). In case of the Limbu/Subbha, it is 5.59 persons per family.

Language Pattern

The Nepali is the link language in Yuksam and it is spoken by all ethnic groups. However, the respective ethnic groups speak their own language /dialect among themselves. It is also to be mentioned that present generation also speak Hindi in addition to their own language and Nepali. Again those who are engaged in business / porter / cook / guide / driving speak well in Hindi. Some of them also speak English. In general the Bhutia are ahead of other ethnic groups in terms of speaking multi language.

Deities Worshiped and Festival Performed

The people of Yuksam specially the Bhutia and the Lepcha follow Buddhism while the Nepalese profess Hinduism. Natural objects like stone, mountain peak, hill stream, lakes are considered as different forms of deities. There are many sacred objects around Yuksam. For example, a stone in side the jungle of Sapse settlement area is considered sacred as it is thought to have the impression of foot of Lord Buddha. Similarly there is a stone on the way to Ramgethang and it is worshipped by the Lepchas in anticipation of well being of the hamlet. The water of

Rathangchu river is considered by the people of Yuksam and they carry its water to pour it in the vessel lying at Tashiding monastery. This festival is known as *Bhumchu. Bhum mean* pot or vess and *chu* means water. There are many places and objects around Yuksam which are considered either as sacred or the living place of a deity.

Phanglhabsol is a major festival which is held in end of August to mark the treaty of blood brother hood between the Lepcha and the Bhutia. *Losoong* is another festival marking the end of harvest season. *Dasain* Durga is also a major festival to the Nepali Hindu.

MATERIAL CULTURE

House Type and Building Material

Use of building material like tin, iron, cement and brick are very much common among all communities. Now people are also opting for modern type of house plan. In general, houses are constructed on elevated platform. Wood and bamboo is common material. Corrugated tin/*siru* (a kind of local available grass) is used in roof. The Nepalese usually separate the sheds of domestic animals from their living quarters. The well-to-do people often keep their kitchen gardens and store houses separate from their residential section. A Bhutia house called *khin* is usually of rectangular shape. The Lepcha, Bhutia and the Limbu mostly keep their household materials at ground floor.

Dress

In case of the Bhutia, the traditional dress of the main member is known as the Bakhu. The traditional dress own by the ladies is known as the *honju* which is a full sleeve blouse. A loose sheet of multi coloured woolen cloth made of special design called *pangdin* is used by married. The male Lepcha wears a dress called a pagi. The Lepcha women wear two piece dress. The traditional Nepalese male dress consists of long double breast garment flowing below the waist. A trouser is known as *Daura suruwal.* The female dress is smade of a double breasted garment. It is shorter than the Daura. It is known as *chow bandi choai*. The Nepalese male keeps *khurki*, a very sharp edged weapon.

Buddhism and Local Culture

The impacts of Buddhism and local culture are visible on locally made art and craft items. Thanka painting may be cited as one of the examples in this respect. There are some popular craft items prepared locally like dragons made of champ wood (Ingtang)), dot stand made of bamboo, *dhungru*, made of bamboo, *cho* a kind of broom made of bamboo (Dosthang), *rari* made of wool (Dosthang), dalainchi made of thread taken from Kalimpong (Yuksam), pelung made of cane (Ingtang), *madal* made of champ wood (Dosthang) etc.

Development in Infrastructural Facilities

Rathangchu is the main stream of Yuksam village. Chutachu and Pahakhola are other streams which provide water. Therefore there is no scarcity of water. The supply of drinking water through pipe has started about 24 years back. Electricity reached this place about 20 years ago while toilet facility started in 1995. The supply of cooking gas is in vogue since 2000. The construction of model houses with two rooms, one verandah and one bathroom for all the villagers at Mangsaboom hamlet may be considered as turning point for healthy living since 2001. Road construction upto Yuksam started after 1970. The first primary health centre was setup in 1986.

Lachen

Despite major changes in almost all spheres of life in the post 2000 period due to tourism and other developmental initiatives, the people continue with their age old tradition of maintaining organic relationship with nature which finds expression in the form of worship of nature, be it mountain, rivers or any other natural objects. In addition, they still maintain their traditional village council. Thus the people of Lachen have successfully blended tradition with modernity. Changes are, however, more visible in case of house types, dresses and family type. The village Lachen maintains by and large Tibetan culture. The Bhutia is the major community in the village with only few Tibetan families.

Common Cultural Features

The prayer wheel (*mani*) run by stream / manually to spread the name of Lord Buddha, n*amgosago*(a symbolic frame) set on the tree or put on wall of house to drive away evil forces, *safu*(a kind of structure where *dhupi leaf* – leaf of incense tree) burnt in front of house in the evening or prayer flag set in bamboo pole along the road or in front of house in anticipation of peace for the deceased soul are common features of Lachen village.

Family Type

Earlier polyandry was the base for their social organization. However, now monogamy has become usual. It is also to be added that one polyandry family has been observed among the studied households.

Negotiated marriage is usual though love-marriages are also taking place. Both nuclear and joint families are found to exist in the village. The family size in totality is 4.82 but in case of the Tibetan, it is 6.13 while in case of the Bhutia Lachenpa, it is 4.84.

Language Pattern

Being an uni-ethnic village, the people mainly speak in Tibetan language. However, due to trade link with Gangtok, Darjeeling and other such places since long past and acquaintances through interaction with defence and GREF personnel, tourists and researchers in recent past, they have learnt to speak Hindi as well. Some educated people also speak English. However when they communicate with the members of other communities, they speak in the Nepali.

Religion

The people of Lachen follow Buddhism and hence the blending of Lamaism is reflected in performing worship, festivals and life cycle rituals. It is lying under niyangma-pa sect.

Deities Worshipped and Festival Performed

There are many god and goddess lying in and around the village. They are seen in form of stone, mountain peak, stream or tree. Some of them have been mentioned here like *checharo* (stone god) on the way to Zemu glacier, *deokhang* (stone god) found on way to Laser valley, *chomyu khang or chomummu* (a mountain goddess), *Dongkung* (a mountain god) seen in Thombuk and *phanglabsol god* (Khangchendzonga god). They are worshiped in anticipation of preventing evil forces and for the peace in the village. It is also to be mentioned that the worship is performed individually with the help of lama priest or sometimes they are also worshipped by making idol of flour in the monastery of Lachen by the lama priests. It is also striking to know that on certain occasions deities worship or performing of festivals or rituals are done in collaboration with Dzumsa, village members and lamas of Lachen monastery. It also strengthens the bondage among the people of the village. The feelings of reverence towards nature, which find expressions in the form of worshipping of natural objects as deities, has indirectly helped in the conservation of nature. In this connection, it is to be mentioned that owing to these reasons, Dzumsa and village members under the leadership of pipon (village headman) express their disliking for setting up of a hydropower station in the upper reaches of Lachenchu.

The Bhutia Lachenpa also perform worship of *mamuthugo/ manithoko* at the interval of 3/4 years. It is done for the good of the village because through this worship the presiding deities of soil, sky, cloud, forest/tree, crop and sunlight/fire are propitiated. It is believed that this worship helps maintain balance among different elements of nature and there would be no shortage of crops. It is normally held in the month of May. There are five deities representing five colours. These five colours signify five areas of nature. As for example sky is represented by blue, fire or sunlight is indicated by red. Similarly cloud indicates white colour and forest/tree/crop is marked by green colour while soil is indicated by yellow colour. All this elements are significant parts of nature and they are required for growth of crop and forest. This worship is done by making idol of flour of the respective colour and this worship is performed in the monastery of Lachen. The Dzumsa and village members actively participate in this worship. This kind of worship has arisen a sense of conservation also.

In addition to this, *khabju(* worship to ward off evil spirit), yak race in Laser valley and some other festivals such as *phanglabsol*, *losar* are worth mentioning.

Education and Hygiene

Literacy rate of the village in general is above 50% according to 2000 Census. There are now 20 graduates, out of which 12 are males and 8 females with two graduate engineers and four polytechnic engineers while one female is studying MBBS. This has become possible due to existence of government primary school since 1930 and its subsequent elevation to high school in 1996. The present connection with Gangtok and Mangon has also helped them to go for higher education.

The hygienic sense of the people has improved. Now people have begun using toilets for the last five to six years. Recently the supply of drinking water through pipe has also begun. In the event of increasing tourism, Dzumsa (caste council) has passed order to keep the roads and settlement areas around Lachen / Chaten clean and in this respect people has also been asked to keep the cattle either above or down the hills.

House Type and Building Materials

Being located at high altitude (above 2941m) and faced with severity of winter, houses of Lachen village are made of wood and it stands on an elevated platform to prevent the effect of coldness. A house generally consists of two rooms and one veranda. One of the rooms is used for kitchen. It is also used as living room. The other room is used for worshipping the Lord Buddha. A part of it is also used as bedroom. However, some people have separate bedroom. The underground area of platform is used for keeping fuel woods and other store items.

Some changes in house types have been observed, though the basic structure remains the same. Now more of pucca buildings are seen. These pucca building are made of hollow cement bricks and have concrete roof and cemented floors. Use of glass fitting in window and corrugated tin for roof cover are also very common. To meet the requirements, one or two hardware shops or shop having miscellaneous items have also come-up. Similarly one also come across few foreign liquor shops.

Dress

The *fo-kho,* a traditional dress stretching up to knee and worn by man with a belt round the waist, is not a common sight nowadays. Similarly traditional shoe made of skin-hide of yak/sheep is also not in vogue. Now the people are wearing modern kinds of dresses and shoes. But the *baku*, a traditional dress worn by women, is still in vogue, though *pangden*, another traditional dress worn by married women, is not so much in vogue specially among the younger generation.

Utensils

The utensil of steel, aluminium, ceramic or glass are very much common in houses specially who run hotels or provide tea/food to the tourists or outsiders.

Development in Infrastructure Facilities

Lachen valley is endowed with Lachenchu as main stream and a number of tributaries like Laserchu, Tarangchu, Rabaomchu, Mainchu etc. Water is available for major parts of the year except winter when there is almost no or very less water available in these streams. Supply of water through pipe is recent happening. Thangu has been getting water supply through pipe for the last five years. In order to meet the huge demand of water, a big reservoir has been built last year behind the Lachen settlement.

The cemented footpath inside village Lachen/Chaten is a recent development. The supply of LPG gas was started in the year 2000. It has lessened the dependency on fuel wood. Fuel wood is now stored for winter season to combat intense cold.

Villagers have access to electricity for the last five to six years old.

The supply of electricity has accelerated with the commissioning of Rabom Hydroelectric Station.

ROLE OF INSTITUTIONS

Yuksam

The establishments of some institutions and their role in different spheres such as economy and awareness in conservation of nature, cultural heritage and advanced technology have brought a new dimension in way of life. The community information centre, established in 2002 near Yuksam Bazar, is not only providing training in computer operation but also spreading awareness about health and education programmes through computer, C.Ds etc. Tourists also have access to internet facilities at this centre. The hamlets of the village and other neighbouring villages also get benefit of this facility. It also provides employment to three persons. The acquaintance with advanced technology spreads through this centre to remote part of the village and surrounding areas.

Similarly the Khangchendzonga Conservation Committee (KCC), a community based organization established in 1996 at Yuksam *Bazar* continues to spread awareness about the importance of conservation among people, community stakeholders, students and even visitors through training and awareness and cultural programmes. This also strengthens traditional knowledge of the people related with conservation of nature.

The opening of the office of Khangchendzonga National Park (KNP) in 2005 at Gechen has helped in the protection of forest species. It has also provided employment to the local people. Besides there are other offices and centers also like office of VLW (1981), animal husbandry (1975), sub post office (1973) and health centre (1991). There are primary schools at Ramgeythang, Tingting and Mansaboong village while Yuksam has high school up to class X which was opened in 1980. Two English medium schools have also been opened near Yuksam market (1999 and 2003).

Sidhi Associate Private Limited

A private financial institute named Sidhi Associate Private Limited was opened in 2000 at Kopche. It not only provides loans to the people but also has schemes of money deposit. The people of the surrounding areas are the members of it.

Showroom of Traditional Art and Craft Items

Starting of showroom of traditional art and craft items in November 2006 at Yuksam Bazar may be considered as an important event as it has accelerated the sale of traditional art and craft items made of wooden or woolen goods. It is observed from the register that the showroom sold items worth of Rs. 805/- during the period of 8th November 2006 – 9th December 2006. The products are made of bamboo and woods. The wooden items are procured from Tingting, Dosthang, Ramgeythang, Topsing, Sapse, Yuksam. Even the products of nearby villages are also brought to the showroom for sale. The people from the Lepcha, Kami, Bhutia and the Limbu are engaged in making these handicraft items.

Lachen

The situational compulsion like loss of high altitude livestock and cessation of trade with Tibet due to closure of border in 1962 has forced people of Lachen to switch over to different kind of economy which is marked by more emphasis on internal trade with Gangtok, more emphasis on growing of commercial crops and finding jobs in different sectors.

Post 2000 period witnessed a new change. Tourism has emerged as most promising sector and people of the village have engaged themselves in different capacity with activities related to tourism. Economic activities related to tourism are transport, hotel business, coming-up of different types of shops etc.

It is queer to note that new economic way of life specially after 2000 era is blended with continuing with the practice of worship of deities of natural objects such as mountain, forest, rivers and treating them as sacred objects and places. It is done with active participation of village people, members of Dzumsa and lama priest of main monastery.

Role of Educational Institutions

Lachen is the northern most high altitude settlement of KBR characterized by inaccessible terrain and extreme climate having pastoral and agricultural background under transhumant system. The first school in Lachen was opened in 1930 which was subsequently elevated to class X in 1996. The opening of primary schools at Thangu and Moguthang in 1985 and 1980 respectively was a major leap forward. Presently the literacy rate of the village in general is above 50% according to 2000 Census. Now there are now 20 graduates out of which 12 are males and 8 are females with two graduate engineers and four polytechnic engineers and one female studying MBBS.

Opening up of Different Institutions

The establishment of different kinds of institutions such as community information centre (2001), ICDS (2006), welfare institution, handicraft training centre, Angora rabit farm (2001), health centre, Rabom hydroelectric station (2003) have helped to develop the area. The opening of community information centre has enabled them to use internet facility. In addition, few people have also got jobs at this center. This centre also imparts training in computer's operation. Similarly handicraft training centre provides training to females particularly in respect of weaving and netting of wool collected from sheep or yak. It also imparts training in making of carpets and different types of woolen products though there is not much of sale of these items among tourist. The angora rabit farm at Rabom imparts training related to rearing of angora rabbits and collection and processing wool in order to have finished products. Three or four persons of the Lachenpa Bhutia are engaged with this institution. However extraction of wool from angora variety of rabbit is not very popular. The installation of hydroelectric station at Rabom has resulted in the electrification of entire village. Besides, two/ three Lachen people are also employed in it. A welfare institute is operational in the village. It provides training in tailoring and gives loan to people for self employment. The introduction of ICDS centre in 2006 and opening of a health centre has brought made the people aware about their health, child care and family planning.

Role of *Dzumsa* and Monastery in the Development of Spirit of Solidarity

Lachen has a traditional council locally known as Dzumsa which is an elected body. The members of Dzumsa consist of villagers and Lama of Lachen village. The Dzumsa plays significant roles in solving matters relating to village and family dispute. It also plays a decisive role in fixing date of live stock movement, solving land dispute, discharging social responsibility, initiating developmental activities, regulating agricultural function and even helping in worship of deities and organization of festivals by way of raising contribution and distributing responsibilities among the respective villagers. It takes part in affairs related to implementing of a government project or distribution of seeds or handing over contracts to the suitable persons. Thus it acts as an instrument in developing solidarity among the Bhutia community and bears collective responsibility in performing activities in different spheres.

CONCLUSION

It becomes evident from discussion on cultural landscape in the fringe villages of KBR that the pattern and process of development in studied villages can be attributed to the inter-play of multiple factors. The contrasting locations of two villages namely Yuksam of West Sikkim and Lachen of North Sikkim in terms of altitudes, terrain characteristics, accessibility, precipitation etc., have great bearing on resource management, economy and culture of these villages.

Both the total population and the density of population are higher in Yuksam (total population – 1968; population density – 246 persons/sq.km as per 2006 field work) compared to Lachen (total population – 1081; population density – 30 persons/sq. km as per 2006 field work).

Unlike Yuksam, Lachen had trade link with Tibet and had to suffer economically due to closing of border with Tibet in 1962. The aftermath of 1962 also saw the implementation of restricted area norms by the Government which continued till 1995. Yuksam, however, did not face such situations. As a result, Yuksam had exposure to mass tourism even before 1995 which was not the case with respect to Lachen. Nevertheless, in post 2000 period the number of tourists visiting Lachen is more than Yuksam. Now there are more numbers of hotels and lodges in Lachen compared to Yuksam.

Increasing strategic importance and role of Dzumsa in case of Lachen have played decisive roles in bringing about the development specially with regards to creation of infrastructure and communication network. On the other hand, KCC has factored significantly in the efforts related to making the people of Yuksam aware about the importance of conservation of nature.

The tables 15 provide in brief the comparative situations of both the villages in respect of their changing landscape.

The table 15C depicts general features of cultural life and changes in respect of both the villages.

Increasing importance of tourism in both Yuksam and Lachen has contributed in the creation of a number of economic opportunities for the people of not only these two villages but also for adjoining villages. Nepali has emerged as link language, though of late Hindi is also being spoken by the people of all most community. Tourism coupled with

Table 15. A. Characteristic of Changing Landscape

Sl. No.	*Village name*	*Economic landscape*					
		Hotels	*Shops*	*No.of vehicles*	*Home stay & availability of room on rent facilities*	*Use of pack animals*	*Livelihood pattern*
		Nos.					
1.	Lachen	22	41	22	Not significant in Lachen.	Role of pack animals is not prominent at present in Lachen due to develop-ment of roads.	Employments in schools and different govt. departments, working as contract labourers in P.W.D., GREF and defence establishments, having own business.
2.	Yuksom	16	12	19	More prominent at Yuksam.	Role of pack animals is signify-cant in Yuksam due to absence of metal or wide road inside the reserve.	Employments in schools and different govt. and non-govt. organizations like health centre, midday meal scheme, I.C.D.S, V.LW centres, animal husbandary, post office etc., working as contract labourers in P.W.D., GREF etc., having own business. .

Table 15B. Resource Management

Sl. No.	*Village name*	*Resource management*	
		Resource utilization	*General land use pattern*
1.	Lachen	Agriculture and pastoralism under transhumant system; potato is major cash crop and maize a major cereal but its cultivation is restricted. Khoo (green house) is introduced recently to grow root and vegetable crops under constraint environment.	Cultivated land constitute 10% of total geographical area while village forest including Kashmahal and Gocharan constitute 90%.
2.	Yuksom	Agriculture is a major economy. Maize, paddy, wheat are cereal crops while ginger, turmeric, cardamom are major cash crops.	Cultivated land constitutes 78% of the total area, village forest including Kashmahal and Gocharan constitutes 22%.

Table 15C. Cultural Life

Sl. No	*Village name*	*Cultural life*	
		General failure	*Change*
1.	Lachen	Traditional caste council (Dzumsa) By and large, uniethnic village except few Tibetans.Phanglhabsol is the major festival, though local deities found in and around mountain, lakes, forest. Mostly followed Buddhism.	Material culture such as dress, utensils, housetype. Building materials; awareness in hygienic sense, Communicative language-Nepalee, Hindi adapted, English spoken by few.
2.	Yuksom	Panchyat system, multiethnic composition, ethnic identity by respective cultural uniqueness. Phanglhabsol, Bhumchu and Dasain Durga – major festival. Buddhism and Hinduism followed. Few people follow Christanity.	Changing material culture such as dress, utensils, house type, building materials; awareness in hygienic sense. Communicative language-Nepalee, Hindi adapted among Bhutia and some Nepalese. English spoken by few.

concomitant economic opportunities has also brought with it the elements of modernity. Strikingly, while the villagers have incorporated aspects of modernity in their life, they continue to adhere to the good practices of their age-old traditions.

ACKNOWLEDGEMENT

The author is thankful to Director-in-Charge Dr. V.R. Rao, Anthropological Survey of India, Kolkata for his interest in the study. The author also acknowledges guidance and suggestion made by Dr. D.B. Mandal former Deputy Director, Eastern Regional Centre, Kolkata. At the same time, the author equally admits and remember constant encouragement and wise advice the provided by Dr. A.K. Singh former senior Ecologist, Anthropological Survey of India, Kolkata.

Author is also obliged to extend his thanks to Dr. Ramesh Chandra, Deputy Director, North Western Regional Centre, Derhadun for helping finalizing the report.

The author is also thankful to Dr (Mrs.) Kakali Chakrabarty, S.A (C) and Head of Office, Eastern Regional Centre, Kolkata for her constant support. The author acknowledges efforts of our staff members, Eastern Regional Centre including Mrs. Dipa Pal for patient, intelligent, untired effort and constant touch in typing and altering the manuscripts as and when required.

During field work, the author got help from various officers, researchers and key persons at various places including Gangtok, Yuksam and Lachen of Sikkim state. Gut Lepcha, Official of Forest Department, Government of Sikkim is one of them. Professor Rahim Mandal, Head of the Department of Social Anthropology, North Bengal University is also one of the key persons who made contribution to finish the work. The executive members of Khangchendzonga Conservation Committee (KCC), Yuksam and people of the studied villages deserve special thanks Cho Rabzor, Pipon of Lachen village and Ring Zing Lachenpa of the same village may be mentioned for contributing by way of giving guidance counseling and relevant information. Thanks are due to all of them.

4

Economic Life in Fringe Village: A Study in Khangchendzonga Biosphere Reserve of Sikkim Himalayas

Subrata Ray

INTRODUCTION

Economy is considered as the base of every society. People perform economic activities to fulfill their desired goals for subsistence. Economy involves production, consumption and distribution of the products. 'Production is dependent on the character of the resource available and capacity of the people to utilize such resource through their technologies. Production is distributed and consumed either by individual or within family' (Banerjee, 1990). In case of hunter-gatherer society reciprocative distribution operates. 'Collection or gathering, hunting, fishing and animal husbandry are considered as successive sequences of primitive economy' (Danda, 1991). One of the earlier classifications is of Forde who made five classifications, viz. – food gathering, hunting and fishing, animal herding, farming and industrial economy (Forde, 1934). 'Earlier, the economic resources were rich and the people were dependent on them but nowadays, the economic interdependency is decreasing. Under the development programmes, people also get modern educational facilities which enhance their overall knowledge and provide them into different white collar jobs' (Raha and Chakravarty, 1996).

'Biosphere reserve is the declared protected area of particular geographical environment for conservation of biological diversity through sustainable livelihood, which maintains the ecological balance' (Mandal and Ray, 2007). Being forest inhabitant, people utilize the forest resources and take resort to protect it through traditional form of forest management. Thus, there is a symbiotic relationship between the forest eco-system and the local people. This kind of relationships start to change when forest is utilized as a source of wealth, which may be due to industrial revolutions.

The present study has been conducted in fringe/transition villages of Khangchendzonga Biosphere Reserve (KBR). Keeping this background in mind the two villages namely Dubdi and Lachen have been selected from two contrasting parts of KBR of Sikkim State, which give rise to diverse pictures in respect of environmental, cultural and historical background. The State of Sikkim has four districts, namely east; west; north and south district. Major part of north and west districts with little portions of south district covers the KBR area. About 33 per cent of the total geographical area of the state is under KBR. Due to altitudinal variation, climate of the state varies from place to place. 'Sikkim is situated between 27°05′ to 28° 10′N latitude and 88°04′ to 88°58′ E longitude. Total area of the state is 7096 sq. km.' (Choudhury, 2006). The total population of Sikkim is 540851 (as per Census of Sikkim, 2001). Sikkim is a multi-ethnic, multi-lingual and multi-cultural state. There are three main ethnic groups in Sikkim, like, Lepcha, Bhutia and Nepali.

OBJECTIVE

The objectives of the proposed study are as follows –

- To understand pattern of economic activities of two villages located in the fringe zone of KBR in contemporary situation especially in the context of its gaining special status as Biosphere Reserve.
- To study occupational patterns of the studied villages.
- To observe inter and intra community interactions.
- To highlight the relation between economic potentiality and increasing tourism in the event of declaration of Biosphere Reserve.

METHODS

The anthropological methods and techniques, like- canvassing household census schedule, observation, interview, case study, genealogical method, etc. were taken into consideration to collect relevant data. To know economic life of two villages of fringe villages. Dubdi of

West Sikkim and Lachen of North Sikkim districts have been selected in view of their contrasting features. The village details are given below to understand the existing economic life of the villagers of these two selected villages.

VILLAGE STUDY

Dubdi (West Sikkim)

The first study has been conducted in Dubdi village, under Yuksam – Dubdi Gram Panchayat in West Sikkim district. This village falls under fringe zone of Khangchendzonga Biosphere Reserve. The Dubdi lies juxtaposed to Yuksam village separated by *Chuta Khola* (river) but its physical distance is more because of ragged terrain, high altitude (about 1828 m. to 1981 m.), dense forest and steep slopes. The basic difference between Dubdi and Yuksam village is that Dubdi is away from motorable road, and can be approached with difficulty due to its rugged terrain. The Yuksam village is an important tourist centre, as well as it is an en-route village to get into the Biosphere Reserve area for trekking. In this context, Dubdi also holds importance in tourism related economic activities and having oldest Dubdi monastery which acts as instrument of attracting tourists.

The Dubdi village comprises of two hamlets i.e. Mangtabong and Tsong / Chong. Settlement pattern of the village is of dispersed type. The plinth of the house is made of stone with mud. Walls of houses are made of bamboo splits with mud or made of wooden planks and roof is thatched with straw or tin, based on bamboo or wooden frame. There is no motorable road in this village. Somewhere, the road is made of stone. Drinking water is available from stream and also supplied through pipe. About 89 per cent families get drinking water through pipe. The facility of electricity is also available now. 85 per cent families of the village have electricity. In this village, 18 per cent families have toilet facilities, 26 per cent families have temporary toilets and 56 per cent families have no toilets. There are two primary schools in the village. As per data collected it is observed that in this village, 80 per cent families live below poverty line (B.P.L.) cards who get ration at a minimum rate, 10 per cent families have above poverty line (A.P.L.) cards and 10 per cent families have no card. 92 per cent families depend on fuel wood and only 8 per cent families use L.P.G. along with fuel wood. However, due to lack of supply of L.P.G. on regular basis the dependence of fuel wood is most common situation in general.

Lachen (North Sikkim)

The village Lachen which lies in the northern most fringe zone of KBR has been selected as the second village for the study. The village is under Lachen traditional Gram Panchayat in North Sikkim district. The settlement units of Lachen village stretches from lower reaches of Rabum, Latung and Denga (altitude of about 1676 m.) to higher reaches which goes up to Thangu and Chopta valley (altitude of about 4267 m.). The main settlement unit of Lachen is situated at the altitude of about 2865 m. Generally, the climatic condition of the village is cold. Snow fall is a common phenomenon in winter but intensity varies according to altitudinal variation. The more the altitude the more prolong and severe is winter in Lachen valley. But reversely, at some of high altitudes places, gentle terrains are also seen in the valley. With increasing altitude, the vegetation density also gradually decreases. In the higher most altitude, vegetation becomes almost nil except meadows, grasses and scrubs. Such conditions are visible at some of the places at local level. The Lachen river flows through the village and later it merges with Teesta river at Chungthang. The motorable road passes through the village. Lachen has the usual attraction to attract tourists for its scenic beauty and altitudinal variation. It is a gateway to go to higher reaches of Sikkim Himalayas through trekking. Again it is also a stop-gap place for tourist to visit Gurudongmar Lake and other approachable valleys like – Thangu, Chopta and Laser valley. Settlement pattern of the studied village appears to be clustered type in main settlement unit of Lachen whereas it is of dispersed type at other parts of Lachen valley. Plinth of the houses is made of stone with mud. Walls are made of bamboo splits coated with mud or wooden planks with mud. Roof is made of tin with wooden frame. They build single or double storey house. In case of double storey house, ground floor is used as store room for crops and fuel wood etc. The first floor is used for living purpose which usually consists of bed room, kitchen and room for religious purpose. Drinking water is brought from streams through pipe. The facility of electricity is available to the villagers at nominal rates. In the village, 91 per cent families have electricity, 50 per cent have permanent toilet facilities, 9 per cent families have temporary toilets while 41 per cent families have no toilet facilities. At present the village Lachen has a high school. Among the studied families, 79.62 per cent families have B.P.L. cards and get ration at a nominal rate, 3.71 per cent families have A.P.L cards and 16.67 per cent families have no said cards. They mostly depend on fuel wood however it is worth mentioning that nearly 78 per cent families now have L.P.G. connection to use in their kitchen.

Nonetheless due to lack of regular supply of L.P.G and cold climatic conditions, dependence on fuel wood is still there.

THE PEOPLE

Dubdi

There are 72 families at Dubdi village. Total population of the village is 425 of which males constitute 55 per cent and females 45 per cent. The Nepalese are the main community inhabiting the Dubdi village. It is reported that Nepalese have migrated from Nepal to Sikkim since 19th century (Singh: 1993). Different communities of Nepalese like – Brahman, Chhetri, Limbu (Subba), Rai, Gurung, Pradhan and Kami live in Dubdi village. Generally, these communities follow Hindu religion, except one Gurung family who has adopted Buddhism. The Brahman, Chhetri and Pradhan belong to Other Backward Class. The Rai and Gurung belong to Most Backward Class. The Limbu (Subba) is only Scheduled Tribe and the Kami is only Scheduled Caste inhabiting in the village. Table 1(a) shows community wise distribution of Nepali families in Dubdi village..

Table 1(a) shows that 54.16 per cent families are from the Limbu (Subba) community. Next, 33.33 per cent families belong to Chhetri community. Between 3 to 5 per cent families belong to Rai, Brahman and Gurung communities. The Pradhan (1.39 % families) and Kami (1.39% families) have lowest presence in the Dubdi.

Lachen

'Lachenpa' are the people settled in Lachen. It is observed that *'Lachenpa'* is a territorial identity. However, this identity again is identified by community identity, such as – Bhutia, Tibetan. Later stage some other communities of Sikkimese, though very few in numbers came in due course to live in or by way of gaining marital relation are settled there and start to identity themselves as *'Lachenpa'* as inhabitants of the valley. It is reported that the Bhutias are migrated from Tibet to Sikkim in 17th century (Singh: 1993). Some Bhutias are settled at Lachen and used to call themselves as *'Lachenpa'*. Some Tibetans came in Sikkim from Tibet before 1959. In this village Tibetans are settled in the land of Bhutias in lieu of money. They also identify themselves as *'Lachenpa'*. This sense of identity gradually percolates too few other communities like – Nepali, Lepcha, etc. The Nepalese are said to have

Table 1(a). Community Wise Family Distribution at Dubdi

Community	*Limbu (Subba)*	*Chhetri*	*Rai*	*Brahman*	*Gurung*	*Pradhan*	*Kami*
No. of family (Total 72)	39	24	3	2	2	1	1
% (Total 100)	54.16	33.33	4.17	2.78	2.78	1.39	1.39

migrated from Nepal to Sikkim in 19th century (Singh: 1993). Lepchas are the indigenous and earlier inhabitant of Sikkim. Few Lepcha came at Lachen for working purpose and settled at Lachen. In respect of constitutional status, the Bhutia, dominant community of Lachen belong to Scheduled Tribe. The Tibetan and Lepcha are also given status of Scheduled Tribe. Bhutia, Tibetan and Lepcha believe in Buddhism. 54 families of *'Lachenpa'* i.e. 24.10 per cent of total families have taken for study through sampling. The total population of 54 families is 285 of which male is 53.33 per cent and female is 46.67 per cent. Community wise distribution of studied families are shown in the following table –

Table 1 (b) Community Wise Family Distribution at Lachen

Community	*Bhutia*	*Tibetan*	*Nepali*	*Lepcha*
No. of family (Total studied families 54)	49	3	1	1
% (Total 100)	90.75	5.55	1.85	1.85

The above table reveals that among the studied families, the highest 90.75 per cent families are found in Bhutia community. Next, 5.55 per cent families belong to Tibetan community. The lowest percentage found in Nepali (1.85 %) and Lepcha (1.85 %) community.

ECONOMIC LIFE

Dubdi

The age old occupation of the Nepali people is agriculture. Generally, they practise terrace cultivation. To cultivate their agricultural land they use plough, spade, fork, etc. The agriculture is solely rainfed. Somewhere, stream water is also used through pipe for irrigation. Cattle dung is used as manure. As per data collected 85 per cent families have agricultural land. In this village, agriculture is of mixed type but production is meager. The villagers mainly cultivate maize, millet, large cardamom. Potato, beans, squash, variety of pulses, ginger, buckwheat, cauliflower, leafy vegetables, etc. The cash crop is large cardamom, potato and vegetables. They also produce fruits like- orange, guava, pears, etc., consumable roots and tubers. Their staple diet is rice but due to high altitude and cold climate paddy is not produced.

The people have domestic animal as subsidiary economy. It was observed that 94 per cent families have livestock. They rear cow, goat for milk. Milk and milk products are used for their own consumption and also for sale. He-goats are kept for mutton consumption. Some people rear bullocks for ploughing. Due to restrictions of grazing facilities in Biosphere Reserve area sheep is reared by few households for wool and meat. They also rear poultry for subsistence. To facilitate trekking tourism, some people rear *'dzo'*, i.e., a hybrid animal of yak and cow. When the *'dzo'* is inactive, they sell it and earn some money. Limbu (Subba) people rear pig.

Beside agriculture and animal rearing, the people also depend on other economic activities as their primary and secondary occupation. The economic activities which are their primary occupations are showing in the table 2(a).

Table 2(a) Dubdi: Distribution of Primary Occupation

Economic Activity	*Total*		*Male*		*Female*	
	No.	*%*	*No.*	*%*	*No.*	*%*
Agriculture	119	58.60	108	53.10	11	5.50
Animal rearing	66	32.40	-	-	66	32.40
Govt. service	11	5.50	9	4.50	2	1
Jeep driving	2	1	2	1	-	-
Tourist guide	1	.50	1	.50	-	-
Wood cutting	1	.50	1	.50	-	-
Blacksmithy	1	.50	1	.50	-	-
'Phedangma / Jhakri' (Priest cum Medicine Man)	1	.50	1	.50	-	-
Religious performer (Lamahhood)	1	.50	1	.50	-	-
Total	**203**	**100**	**124**	**61.10**	**79**	**38.90**

Table 2(a) shows that 203 people of both genders are engaged in different types of primary occupations of which 61.10 per cent are male and 38.90 per cent are female. The highest 58.60 per cent people (male 53.10%, female 5.50%) are engaged in agriculture. Animal rearing has been taken as primary occupation by 32.40per cent female. 5.50 per cent people (male 4.50%, female 1%) are engaged in Govt. service. Jeep driving has been taken by 1 per cent male. Below 1 per cent people i.e. male members are engaged in following economic activities like - tourist guide, wood cutting, blacksmithy, *'phedangma / jhakri'* (priest cum medicine man) and religious performer (lamahood). In this table, some economic activities are directly or indirectly related with tourism like – tourist guide, Jeep driving.

The economic activities which are related with secondary occupations are shown in table 3(a).

Table 3(a) Dubdi: Distribution of Secondary Occupation

Economic Activity	*Total*		*Male*		*Female*	
	No.	*%*	*No.*	*%*	*No.*	*%*
Agriculture	55	27	7	3.38	48	23.62
Agricultural labour	41	20.12	27	13.22	14	6.90
Animal rearing	39	19.14	15	7.34	24	11.80
Porter (related with trekking)	26	12.80	26	12.80	-	-
Daily labour	11	5.50	11	5.50	-	-
Handicraft works	9	4.50	6	3	3	1.50
'Dzo' keeper / yakman (related with trekking)	8	3.94	8	3.94	-	-
Milk business	3	1.50	2	1	1	.50
Wood cutting	3	1.50	3	1.50	-	-
Carpentry / masonry	2	1	2	1	-	-
Petty shop	2	1	1	.50	1	.50

Economic Activity	*Total*		*Male*		*Female*	
	No.	*%*	*No.*	*%*	*No.*	*%*
Tourist guide	2	1	2	1	-	-
Cook (related with trekking)	1	.50	1	.50	-	-
'Phedangma / jhakri' (priest cum medicine man)	1	.50	1	.50	-	-
Total	**203**	**100**	**112**	**55.18**	**91**	**44.82**

Table 3(a) shows that 203 persons of both genders are engaged in different types of secondary occupations of which 55.18 per cent are male and 44.82 per cent are female. The highest 27 per cent people (male 3.38%, female 23.62%) are engaged in agriculture. 20.12 per cent people (male 13.22%, female 6.90 %) are engaged in agricultural labour. Animal rearing has been taken by 19.14 per cent people (male 7.34 %, female 11.80 %). Some male members i.e. 12.80 per cent are engaged as porter i.e. related with trekking tourism. Between 1 to 6 per cent people are engaged in different economic activities, like - daily labour (male), handicraft works (both genders), *'dzo'* keeper locally called as yakman (male), milk business (both genders), wood cutting (male), carpentry/ masionry (male), petty shop (both genders), tourist guide (male). Below 1 per cent people are engaged in following economic activities, like – cook (male), *'phedangma / jhakri'* i.e. priest cum medicine man (male). In this table, some economic activities are directly or indirectly related with tourism like – porter, tourist guide, and cook, *'dzo'* keeper locally called as *yak-man*, handicraft works, and petty shop.

Tourism Related Economic Activities

It has already been stated that at Dubdi offers attraction to the tourists. The village is very close to Yuksam village which is an important tourist spot, as well as an entry point for trekking in higher reaches of

Sikkim Himalayas. As such the people of Dubdi village have some scope to engage in tourism related economic activities. As the trekking route comes under buffer and core area of Biosphere Reserve, the tourists as well as tourist guide, porter, cook, *'dzo'* keeper / yakman with *'dzo'* pay entry fee and seek permit from the Forest department to enter the trekking path. The economic activities which are directly and indirectly related with tourism are shown in table 4(a)

Table 4(a) Dubdi: Tourism related economic activities

Economic activity	*Total (M+F)*		*Male*		*Female*	
	No.	*%*	*No.*	*%*	*No.*	*%*
Porter	26	51	26	51	-	-
Handicraft works	9	17.64	6	11.76	3	5.88
'Dzo' keeper / yakman	8	15.67	8	15.67	-	-
Tourist guide	3	5.89	3	5.89	-	-
Jeep driving	2	3.92	2	3.92	-	-
Petty shop	2	3.92	1	1.96	1	1.96
Cook	1	1.96	1	1.96	-	-
Total	**51**	**100**	**47**	**92.16**	**4**	**7.84**

Table 4(a) shows that 51 persons of both genders are engaged in some economic activities which are directly and indirectly related with tourism. About 51 per cent people (male) are engaged as porter in connection with trekking tourism. About 17.64 per cent people are engaged in handicraft works of which 11.76 per cent are males and 5.88 per cent females. Due to trekking tourism, 15.67 per cent males are engaged as '*dzo*' keeper locally called as yak-man. *'Dzo'* is a hybrid male animal (from a cross between male yak and female cow) used for carrying goods and rations of tourists. As a tourist guide 5.89 per cent males are involved. Jeep driving has been taken by 3.92 per cent males. In petty shop 3.92 per cent people (male 1.96 %, female 1.96 %) are engaged. The lowest 1.96 per cent male engage as cook related with trekking tourism.

Lachen

The people of Lachen have combination of economic pursuits viz.

agriculture, animal rearing and herding. They cultivate their land in different altitudes and produce various kinds of crops and vegetables. Simultaneously, they graze their cattles in different altitudes according to the climatic situation and availability of fodder. They practise agriculture as well as animal rearing and herding through transmigrating process during upward and downward movements. The landed property of individual families transmitted from father to son and these lands are situated in different altitudes demarcated by stones, wooden pillars and iron net also.

The traditional and primary occupation upheld by maximum people is agriculture. They practise valley or hill slope cultivation and kitchen garden. It was observed among the studied families that 94 per cent families have agricultural land and 6 per cent families have no agricultural land, in fact except a small amount of homestead land where some vegetable are grown to little extent. The agricultural activities are generally confined in high mountain valley (altitude of about 4267 m.) which centers round Thangu and its adjoining areas. In these areas they mainly produce potato. Beside this, they also grow radish, spinach, cabbage, cauliflower, beans, leafy vegetable ('raishak') for their own consumption as well as to sell the surplus produce in local village market.

The main settlement unit of Lachen (altitude of about 2865 m.) uses to grow potato and some other kitchen vegetables like – radish, spinach, beans, cabbage, 'raishak' (leafy vegetable), etc. which again face difficulties for growth due to scarcity of land in the event of spreading of large numbers of buildings, hotels / lodges. Apple is also grown to some extent in this area. The agricultural operation is also done to a little extent at Temchhi and its adjoining temporary settlement unit (altitude of about 2743 m.). This area is near to Lachen, the main settlement of the valley. Here, they grow potato, radish, apple, wheat, etc. to some extent.

The agricultural operation continues to some extent in the low mountain valley (altitude of about 1676 m.) of Rabum, Latung and Denga area. In these areas they mainly grow maize with little amount of potato, garlic, squash, beans, etc. However, their staple food is rice but paddy is not produced due to cold climate and high altitude. In case of valley of hill slope cultivation they use plough, spade, fork, etc. but in kitchen garden, they only use spade, fork etc. During the month of April, they plant crops and vegetables within low mountain valley (altitude about 1676 m.) to main settlement unit (altitude about 2865 m.)

and adjoining areas. But at high mountain valley (altitude about 4267 m.) they plant crops and vegetables in the month of May. Generally, they preserve potato seeds under ground of high mountain valley where most of them have temporary settlement unit. The timing of cultivation in this valley is determined by their traditional Gram Panchayat (locally called as *'dzumsa'*)

Potato field near Thangu

They depend on animal rearing and herding. It has been observed among the studied family that 70 per cent families have livestock (cow, goat, sheep, yak, dzo, bullock, horse, pig, poultry bird like hen, etc.). The persons who have many cattle migrate with them for grazing. The migratory animal rearing and herding is of two types based on altitudinal variation and varieties of animals. The variety is identified by the communities in their own perception accordingly. The permanent settlement of cattle rearer and herder is situated at main settlement unit of Lachen (altitude about 2865 m.). Usually, those families who have many livestocks keep one or two members in order to look after their cattle. Some other family members provide ration and food for them. The persons who have few cattle or the owners are busy in other economic activities; normally give their cattle to the herders in lieu of ration, food or some money. This system is prevalent at low and high altitude animal rearing and herding. In some cases the persons who have few cattle of low altitudinal variety rear in their cattle shed also.

The first type of animal rearing and herding is extended within low mountain valley (altitude about 1676 m.) of Rabum, Latung and Denga area to high mountain valley (altitude about 4267 m.) of Thangu and its adjoining areas for grazing. In these areas, they rear cow, goat for milk and milk product. He-goats and sheep are kept for meat and wool. Some people rear bullock, horse, 'dzo' for carrying luggage. Bullocks are mainly used for ploughing. Pig rearing is not so common among themselves. But now-a-days pig is kept by few households for flesh of their own consumption and sell. They also rear poultry birds like hen for egg and meat. The rearer and herder of these animals move within low to high mountain valley, called as *'gothwala'*. Generally, during end of November to beginning of March their cattles graze in the meadows of low mountain valley (altitude about 1676 m.) of Rabum, Latung and Denga settlement units. Usually, the animal rearer and herder do not cultivate in these areas because when they leave these settlement units the monkeys destroy their crops. It is reported that during middle of March the herder migrate upward with their cattles to the meadows of temporary settlement unit of Temchhi and its adjoining areas (altitude about 2743 m.). Those who have some agricultural land in these areas also take part in agricultural activities at this time. Generally, during the month of June, they shift upward with their cattles for grazing near Thangu and its surrounding settlement units (altitude about 4267 m.). The persons who have some agricultural land in these areas also engage in agricultural activities at this time. Some people also looking after cattles of high altitude grazing variety, coming down from higher reaches. In the month of October, after harvesting their crops and vegetables the people along with their cattles of low altitude grazing variety, coming down to their main settlement unit of Lachen (altitude about 2865 m.). Since their permanent settlement unit introduce as tourist spot where cattles movement cause filthy environment due to cattles dung and urine. Thus, the animal rearer and herder who intend to rear their cattles in the permanent settlement unit, keep their cattles within the cattle shed. Other rearer and herder like to keep their cattles at temporary settlement unit Temchhi and its adjoining areas (near permanent settlement unit). This system is maintained by family level as instructed by their traditional Gram Panchayat (called as *'dzumsa'*). Ultimately, at the end of November, the animal rearer and herder come down to their temporary settlement units of Rabum, Latung and Denga area (altitude about 1676 m.) for grazing their cattle. In this way, the animal rearer and herder along with their cattle move up and down from one place to another keeping in search of grass and natural fodder availability in mind. They are also concerned with conservation of forages as much as possible by way of leaving the grasses to some extent to rejuvenate and be available for their cattle in next season. Thus for grazing these people adhere to cyclic grazing pattern on their own keeping in tune with the nature for optimal use of natural resources.

The second type of animal rearing and herding extended within high mountain valley (altitude about 4267 m.) for grazing of high altitude variety of yak, sheep and goat. They rear these cattles for milk, milk products, meat and wool. Male yaks are also used for carrying luggage on high to higher altitude areas. Generally, during the month of May to July, yak, sheep and goat graze on the high mountain valley (altitude about 4267 m.) of Thangu, Chopta valley and its surrounding areas. Those rearer and herder have agricultural land in these areas they also take part in agricultural activities at this time. During the month of August - October the animal rearer and herder along with their cattles move upward i.e. at Byamji and its adjoining areas (altitude about 4572 m.). Those animal rearer and herder have agricultural land in these areas also engage in agricultural activities at this time. November – February the high altitude cattle graze on the higher mountain valley (altitude about 4876 m. – 5486 m.) of Muguthang, Gurudongmar, Tsolamu and its adjoining areas. During this time snow covers the meadows. Simultaneously, heavy wind blow in these areas and grasses are found under the snow. Due to severe cold climatic condition the animal rearer and herder also provide supplementary food to their yak like – salt, 'ata', oil-cake etc. In these higher altitudes and severe cold areas those who rear and herd high altitude variety of yak, sheep and goat, they are called as *'dokpa'*. In these areas they built their temporary settlements, with stone, tin, yak-skin, polythin sheets for protection from severe cold situation. However, with the decrease in temperature cold increase, they reside under the ground for safe and comfortable living. During the months March to April, the cattle rearer and herder come down with their cattles as per the availability of grasses for their cattles. Ultimately, they move further down to Thangu and its adjoining areas (altitude about 4267 m.) in the month of May. Those rearer and herder have agricultural land in these areas they stay for a period upto month of July and also take part in agricultural activities at this time. Here they cultivate crops and vegetable like – potato, radish, cabbage, spinach, etc. with the help of other family members. These family members come from their main settlement unit and joined with them. In this way, the high to higher altitude animal rearer and herder along with their cattles move up and down from one place to another place in search of grasses and natural fodders. Through this system they also preserve grasses and natural forages to some extent for further growth of natural feeds for their cattle in next season.

Beside agriculture and animal rearing and herding, the people also depend on other economic activities as their primary and secondary occupations. Now the economic activities as their primary occupations are shown in table 2(b).

Table 2(b) Lachen: Distribution of Primary occupation

Economic Activity	*Total*		*Male*		*Female*	
	No.	*%*	*No.*	*%*	*No.*	*%*
Agriculture	39	26.35	31	20.95	8	5.40
Animal rearing and herding (low altitude grazing)	32	21.67	4	2.70	28	18.97
Govt. service	20	13.55	17	11.53	3	2.02
Animal rearing and herding (high altitude grazing)	13	8.80	12	8.12	1	.68
Petty shop	9	6.06	2	1.35	7	4.71
Hotel / lodge business	7	4.71	5	3.36	2	1.35
Hotel / lodge business cum petty shop	7	4.71	5	3.36	2	1.35
Religious performer (Lamahood)	6	4.04	6	4.04	-	-
Weaving	5	3.36	-	-	5	3.36

Economic Activity	*Total*		*Male*		*Female*	
	No.	*%*	*No.*	*%*	*No.*	*%*
Jeep driving	4	2.70	4	2.70	-	-
Daily labour	3	2.02	3	2.02	-	-
Contractor business	2	1.35	2	1.35	-	-
Painter	1	.68	1	.68	-	-
Total	**148**	**100**	**92**	**62.16**	**56**	**37.84**

Table 2(b) reveals that 148 persons of both genders are engaged in different type's primary occupation of which 62.16 per cent are males and 37.84 per cent are females. The highest percentage i.e. 26.35 per cent of both genders is engaged in agriculture. 21.67 per cent of both genders engage themselves in animal rearing and herding (low altitude grazing) within low to high mountain valley, 13.55 per cent of both genders engage in Government service, 8.80 per cent engage themselves in animal rearing and herding (high altitude grazing) within high to higher mountain valley. Between two to seven per cent people engage themselves in different activities like – petty shop, hotel / lodge business, hotel / lodge business cum petty shop, religious performer (Lamahood), weaving, jeep driving and daily labour. Less than two per cent people are engaged in following economic activities like – contractor business and painter. In this table some economic activities are directly and indirectly related with tourism activities, such as – petty shop, hotel / lodge business, hotel / lodge business cum petty shop, jeep driving.

The economic activities as their secondary occupation are shown in the table 3(b).

Table 3(b) Lachen: Distribution of Secondary Occupation

Economic Activity	*Total*		*Male*		*Female*	
	No.	*%*	*No.*	*%*	*No.*	*%*
Agriculture	55	27	7	3.38	48	23.62

Economic Activity	*Total*		*Male*		*Female*	
	No.	*%*	*No.*	*%*	*No.*	*%*
Agricultural labour	41	20.12	27	13.22	14	6.90
Animal rearing	39	19.14	15	7.34	24	11.80
Porter (related with trekking)	26	12.80	26	12.80	-	-
Daily labour	11	5.50	11	5.50	-	-
Handicraft works	9	4.50	6	3	3	1.50
'Dzo' keeper / yakman (related with trekking)	8	3.94	8	3.94	-	-
Milk business	3	1.50	2	1	1	.50
Wood cutting	3	1.50	3	1.50	-	-
Carpentry / masonry	2	1	2	1	-	-
Petty shop	2	1	1	.50	1	.50
Tourist guide	2	1	2	1	-	-
Cook (related with trekking)	1	.50	1	.50	-	-
'Phedangma / jhakri' (priest cum medicine man)	1	.50	1	.50	-	-
Total	**203**	**100**	**112**	**55.18**	**91**	**44.82**

Table 3(b) reveals that 148 persons of both genders are engaged in different types of secondary occupations of which 56.76 per cent are males and 43.24 per cent are females. The highest percentage i.e. 55.43 per cent people of both genders are engaged in agriculture. 15.53 per cent people of both genders engage in animal rearing and herding (low altitude grazing), 10.85 per cent people (i.e. male) are engaged as daily labour. Between 2 per cent to 5 per cent people engage in different economic activities like – weaving (female), hotel / lodge business (both genders), petty shop (both genders) and Lamahood (male). Below 2 per cent people are engaged in following economic activities, such as – porter (male), *'Chhang'* i.e. liquor of millet selling (female), musician (male). In this table, some economic activities are directly or indirectly related with tourism activities, like – hotel business, petty shop, and porter.

Tourism Related Economic Activities

It has stated that tourism in KBR area is spreading through Lachen for its scenic beauty and altitudinal variations. It is also an entry point to go for trekking within the core area of Biosphere Reserve of course with permission of the concerned Forest department. However, people of this studied village are benefited by way of engaging in tourism related (directly and indirectly) economic activities which are shown in table 4 (b)

Table 4(b) Lachen: Tourism related Economic activities:

Economic activity	*Total (M+F)*		*Male*		*Female*	
	No.	*%*	*No.*	*%*	*No.*	*%*
Porter	26	51	26	51	-	-
Handicraft works	9	17.64	6	11.76	3	5.88
'Dzo' keeper / yakman	8	15.67	8	15.67	-	-
Tourist guide	3	5.89	3	5.89	-	-
Jeep driving	2	3.92	2	3.92	-	-
Petty shop	2	3.92	1	1.96	1	1.96
Cook	1	1.96	1	1.96	-	-
Total	**51**	**100**	**47**	**92.16**	**4**	**7.84**

Table 4 (b) reveals that 41 persons of both genders are engaged in tourism related (directly and indirectly) economic activities of which 63.41 per cent are males and 36.59 per cent are females. The highest percentage i .e. 36.58 per cent people (male 12.19%, female 24.39%) are engaged in petty shop. Hotel/lodge business has been taken by 31.71per cent people (male 24.39%, female 7.32%). Next, 17.07 per cent people (male 12.19%, female 4.88%) are involved in hotel/lodge business cum petty shop. Zeep driving has been taken by 9.76 per cent males. The lowest percentage i.e. 4.88 per cent males are engaged as porter in connection with trekking tourism.

PEOPLE'S ROLE IN ECONOMIC ACTIVITIES

Dubdi

The role of people is to be understood in order to see the differential situation and the underlying factors in performing different kinds of human activities in the sphere of economic activities. It is observed that there is a gender related specialization and aptitude in carrying out the economic activities while the children though they are not supposed to do the work but have to do the work in terms of assistance in compelling situation. These differential situations are discussed herewith.

The male persons prepare land for cultivation with plough or spade and fork *('kanta')*. Those who have plough, they cultivate the land of other people also. After tilling this soil, they plant crops and vegetables and also engage themselves in harvesting with the help of adult female family members and sometimes with other villagers also. Those who have excess amount of crops and vegetables they sell in the market. The males also involve themselves in animal rearing. Nine male members are joined in Government service. Beside these, the working males are engaged in different economic activities, like – agricultural labour, daily labour, wood cutting, milk business, carpentry and masonry. They also take part in some other economic activities which are directly and indirectly related with trekking and tourism, like *'dzo'* keeper locally called as yak-man, porter, tourist guide, cook, jeep driving and handicraft works. In case of handicraft works some adult males are weaving different types of baskets, mat, cattle shed, etc. made of bamboo splits which are used for their own purpose and also for sell. Beside these there is a blacksmith who makes different types iron implements for sell to the villagers and other people. Sometimes, tourists also purchase different types of handicraft items from the shop of handicraft at Yuksam market. Few males are engaged as priest cum medicine man locally called as *'phedangma / jhakri'*. There is Gurung person who adopts Buddhism and practicing as Lama for religious purpose. However, male members also collect fuel wood for cooking and collect fodder for their animals.

The women remain involved in all types of household activities. They mainly devote in animal rearing and help in agricultural activities. Sometimes, they till the soil with spade and fork *('kanta')*. They help their male members at the time of plantation and harvesting. Sometimes, the adult female members also work as agricultural labour to support their family income. They rear different types of cattles for milk, milk products, meat and wool. Poultry birds are also reared by them for egg and meat. Some women practice traditional handicraft work i.e. weaving of mattress / blanket, locally called as *'rarhi'*, made of sheep wool used for their own purpose and also for sell. Few of them engage in their petty shop, milk business, etc. Two females are joined in Government service. However, the females also collect fuel wood for cooking and collect fodder for their cattles.

Children of both genders are sent to school for their education. But due to economic problems and unwillingness some of the children drop out from school after some years. However, children assist their parents in various activities like – collection of fuel wood, fodder and look after younger, cattles, poultry birds, etc. sometimes; they also assist in agricultural operation.

Lachen

The role of people is to be assumed to observe the differential situation and basic factors for executing different types of economic activities. It is seen that there is a gender related specialization and intension to do the economic activities whereas the children are not supposed to do the work but bound to do the work in terms of assistance in compelling situation. These different types of situations are discussed herewith.

As land is the main source of economy, the adult male members are mostly engaged themselves in agricultural activities. They prepare land for cultivation with plough or spade and fork. After tilling the soil they plant crops and vegetables and also take part in harvesting with the help of their female family members and sometimes with other villagers also. Those who produce huge amount of crops and vegetables sell their products in the market. They also engage themselves in animal rearing and herding related with high altitude or low altitude grazing for supplement their income. Seventeen male members are joined in Government service. Some of them learn Lamaism and employ as Lama/ monk for religious purpose. They also engaged as daily labour in connection with agriculture, road construction, building construction, etc. Some of them also take part in tourism related activities (directly or indirectly) like – hotel/ lodge business, petty shop, hotel/lodge business cum petty shop, porter, jeep driver, etc. Few of them engage as contractor business, painter and musician for their livelihood. The male members also collect fuel wood for cooking and collect fodder for their cattle.

Adult female members engage themselves in all types of domestic works. They take part in agricultural activities along with their male members. Sometimes, women till the land with spade and fork. They also involve themselves at the time of plantation and harvesting to help their male members. In case of animal rearing and herding related with low altitude grazing, the female members are involved themselves along with their male family members. In case of other type of animal rearing and herding related with high altitude grazing, few females are engaged along with their male family members. However, they rear different types of cattles for milk, milk products, meat and wool. They also rear poultry birds like – hen for egg and meat. They weave blanket from the wool of high altitude sheep, goat and yak and also weave carpet by colored threads for their own purpose and also sell to the other villagers who have no looms or who have no knowledge about weaving. Three female members have joined Government service. Some females take part in tourism related activities (directly or indirectly) in absence of male members like – hotel/lodge business, petty shop, hotel/lodge business cum petty shop. Few of them engage in selling *'chhang'* (liquor of millet). The female members also collect fuel wood for cooking and collect fodder for their cattle.

Children of both genders go to school for their education. But those who do not intend to go to school or have economic problems drop out from school after some years. The children of both genders also help their families in different activities like – collection of fuel wood and fodder, look after younger, cattle and poultry birds. Sometimes, they also help in agricultural activities.

ECONOMIC AND SOCIAL RELATIONS: INTER AND INTRA COMMUNITY LEVEL

Dubdi

The inter and intra community relation has been developed following the cultivation of land on share or lease basis. Those who have no agricultural land or little agricultural land, take agricultural land on share or lease basis under the locally prevailing system called *'adhiya'* or *'kut'* / *'byaji'* respectively. This system is more common among the Nepali communities. Some Bhutia and Lepcha people also have given out the agricultural land to Nepali people on share or lease basis. In *'adhiya'* system crops produce is divided in two equal halves to be shared by the tenant and the landowner. The 'kut' system is a lease system on yearly basis. In this system, tenant gives out fixed amount of crops to the land owner. The 'byaji' system is also a lease system on yearly basis. In this system tenant has given out fixed amount of cash to the landowner. The 'adhiya' system is also practised in case of rearing of cow, goat, pig, 'dzo', etc. Those people are unable to purchase these cattles but have capacity to rear or those who have few cattles, they brought cattles from their neighbours on share basis, called as 'adhiya' which varies for different cattles. This system depends on contract between the rearer and the owner. As for example in case of cow in 'adhiya' system the first issue keeps the rearer and the owner will get the second issue of the cow. In 'adhiya' system of pig and she-goat, the kiddies are divided into two equal halves for rearer and owner. In case of male pig and he-goat, meats are divided into two equal halves for rearer and owner. Incase of 'dzo' i.e. a hybrid male animal, the rearer earn money through 'dzo' which is used for trekking tourism. The total earning amount is distributed between owner and rearer. Such as, if the rearer keep two 'dzos', the rearer get money from one 'dzo' and owner get money from other 'dzo'.

A recent phenomenon is also observed in respect of providing service on reciprocal exchange. As for example, one 'Kami' (blacksmith) family who lives in the house of a 'Limbu' family in lieu of providing service i.e. repairing or supplying iron items. This kind of inter community relation has been observed. In case of marriage, communities are endogamous and their *'thars'* (clans) are exogamous. But marriage with in the different communities is also reported due to love marriage.

Lachen

It has reported and observed that in Lachen village inter and intra community members provide service in lieu of service. In some cases they provide service instead of ration, food and money. As for example,- one person provide service to other persons in construction of houses or in agricultural operation in lieu of getting some kind of service. It has also reported that those who have few cattles or those cattles rearer and owner are busy in different economic activities have given their cattles to the moving animal rearer and harder instead of ration, food or some money. These kinds of inter and intra community relations are locally called as *'byaro'*. Marriage within the same community is the common practice but marriage within different communities is also reported due to love marriage. In case of death, any kind of social support and financial help also been observed among them.

PEOPLE PERCEPTION: BIOSPHERE RESERVE

Dubdi

Due to restrictions in Biosphere Reserve, generally people can not enter into the core and buffer area for their livelihood or graze their cattles. But in case of trekking tourism, tourists along with porter, tourist guide, 'dzo' keeper / yak-man, cook enter into the core and buffer area with permission of Forest department and also give entry fee for this purpose. Previously the local people collected fuel wood, timber, etc. from forest. But at present, they may get fuel wood, timber of fallen trees from restricted areas through royalty in Forest department. Beside this, they also get fuel wood and timber from their surroundings. However, plantations are done on the upper portion of 'Dubdi' village by the local Forest office and Eco-development committee. table no. – 5 (a) show the views about Biosphere Reserve of 70 persons on both genders.

Table 5 (a) People Perception: Biosphere Reserve

No. of respondents	*Favour biosphere reserve*		*Against biosphere reserve*	
	No.	*%*	*No.*	*%*
70	61	87.15	9	12.85

Table 5 (a) shows that 87.15 per cent people favour Biosphere Reserve and 12.85 per cent people against of it. The reasons for favouring Biosphere Reserve are given below –

- Due to restriction of Biosphere Reserve, the forest is safe. Therefore, the medicinal plants and other plants grow safely which will good for them.
- If forest is safe, they will get fresh air, water and good rain fall.
- They also get fuel wood and timber of fallen trees through royalty in Forest department.
- The forest also protect from land slide.
- Natural flora and fauna as well as healthy weather attract tourist.

The reasons against Biosphere Reserve are as follows –

- Due to rules and regulations of Biosphere Reserve, cattle can not graze in the core and buffer areas. Therefore, it is not possible for them to rear more cattle.

- The people can not collect fuel wood from the cores and buffer areas of Biosphere Reserve. Generally, they get fuel wood from their surroundings which are not sufficient for them. Among the people of Dubdi village, 92 per cent families depend on fuel wood and 8 per cent families use fuel wood along with L.P.G connection. Moreover, due to lack of supply of L.P.G. on regular basis the dependence of fuel wood is most common.

Lachen

Due to restriction of Biosphere Reserve area, generally people can not enter into the core and buffer area for their livelihood. But in case of trekking tourism tourists along with porter, cook, yak, enter into the restricted areas with permission of Forest department. Previously, they used to collect fuel wood and timber from forest and grazed their cattle without any restrictions. But at present they face many obstacles to grazing their cattles and collect fire wood and timber except through royalty in forest department, they get fixed amount of timber and fuel wood of fallen trees which are not upto the mark to rum family. In this way the gaining of status as Khangchendzonga Biosphere Reserve imposes some restriction on smooth collection of fuel wood and timber. Regarding Biosphere Reserve, view is taken from 54 persons of both genders. Table 5 (b) give the detail –

Table 5(b) People Perception: Biosphere Reserve

No. of respondents	*Favour biosphere reserve*		*Against biosphere reserve*	
	No.	*%*	*No.*	*%*
54	18	33.33	36	66.67

Table 5 (b) reveals that among the 54 persons of both genders, 33.33 per cent people favour Biosphere Reserve and 66.67 per cent against of it. The reasons for favouring Biosphere Reserve are as follows –

- Due to Biosphere Reserve forest is safe and they keep the mountain eco-system fresh and balance by way of leaving oxygen and preventing soil erosion. Thus, it also protects the area of landslide.
- Tourists come here to see the scenic beauty of forest.

- If cattles graze in large number the forest will be destroyed.

The reasons against Biosphere Reserve are as follows –

- The villagers settled here for a long time and somehow, their livelihood depends on forests. But after declaration of Khangchendzonga Biosphere Reserve in the year 2002 they collect fuel wood and timber from their surroundings. Except this, they also get fixed amount of fuel wood and timber of fallen trees instead of royalty in Forest department. Fuel woods are required for cooking and to survive in this cold climatic area. As the fuel woods are not sufficient for them they also use kerosene and recently 77 per cent families have L.P.G. connection. But due to irregular supply of L.P.G. they have to depend on fuel wood.
- After declaration of Khangchendzonga Biosphere Reserve, cattles can not graze in the restricted areas. Therefore, they face problem regarding cattle rearing.

PEOPLE PERCEPTION: DEVELOPMENT OF TOURISM

Dubdi

It has already been stated that the study village is known for its antique Dubdi monastery, whereas tourism is mainly extended through Yuksam i.e. adjacent to Dubdi village. Thus, the local people of the Dubdi village are more or less benefited. The impact of tourism is also seen on society and culture. Here table no. – 6 (a) shows the views about tourism of 70 persons on both genders.

Table 6(a) Dubdi: People Perception on Development of Tourism

No. of respondents	*Favour Tourism*		*Against Tourism*	
	No.	*%*	*No.*	*%*
70	70	100	-	-

Table 6 (a) shows that 100 per cent people of both genders favour tourism. The reasons for favouring tourism are as follows –

- During tourist season, villagers get employment opportunities in connection with trekking, like – porter, 'dzo' keeper / yak-man, tourist guide, etc.
- Villagers also earn money by selling their vegetables, fruits, milk, milk – products, handicraft items, etc.

- Jeep driver, petty shop keeper, is also benefited during tourist season as they earn more money.

Lachen

As it has already been stated that tourism holds its importance through out Lachen which is a gate way to initiate trekking. It is reported that local people of the studied village are more or less benefited. Thus, the impact of tourism is seen on society and culture. Regarding tourism, views are taken from 54 respondents of both genders. Table no. 6(b) gives the detail

Table 6 (b) People Perception: Development of Tourism

No. of respondents	*Favour Tourism*		*Against Tourism*	
	No.	*%*	*No.*	*%*
54	52	96.30	2	3.70

Table 6 (b) reveals that among 54 persons on both genders, 96.30 per cent people favour tourism and 3.70 per cent against of it. The reasons for favouring tourism are as follows-

- During tourist season, hotel / lodge owner, petty shop keeper, jeep driver, etc. are benefited as they earn more money.
- Villagers also earn income through sale of their crops, vegetables, milk, milk products, fly-brush (made of yak tail), etc.
- Local people also get some employment opportunities.
- If the hotel / lodge owner earn more money, the poor people may lend money from them in their necessity.
- The local people can interact with tourists of different places.
- Due to tourism, villagers will try to keep the village clean as per system of their Gram panchayat.

The reasons against tourism are as follows –

- Only hotel / lodge owners, petty shop keepers, zeep drivers are benefited but poor people have no such opportunities for income.
- Generally, people of the main road side have opportunities to earn something during tourist season.
- In tourist season local transports are sometimes used for carrying tourists. Therefore, local people face the problem of transport.

CONCLUSION

The people of Dubdi and Lachen villages have kept themselves engaged in agricultural activities. In Dubdi village people practise terrace and hill slope cultivation. In this village agriculture is of mixed type but production from agriculture is not so much. Animal rearing including poultry birds also support their livelihood. As the village is situated in fringe set up, the people partly depend on forest. After declaration of Khangchendzonga Biosphere Reserve, people are restrained to utilize the forest resource to a large extent except for fuel wood as per their use. Grazing facilities are stopped in core zone area. Simultaneously, trekking in connection with tourism inside Khangchendzonga Biosphere Reserve has also created some new economic vocations. However, the villagers try to adjust themselves in new situations and practise different types of activities along with agriculture as their primary and traditional occupation. Thus, in these changing situations diversification in economic activities have been found in the village economy.

In Lachen village agriculture is of mixed type but main produce remains potato. The people depend on animal rearing and herding which is of two types based on altitudinal variation and varieties of animals. They also rear poultry to support their livelihood. Due to tourism local people are benefited to sell their crops, vegetables, milk, milk products, meat, egg, etc. In tourist season hotel / lodge owner, petty shop keeper, jeep driver, etc. at better prices and earn more money. Simultaneously, some people are also engaged as porters related with trekking tourism. Due to rules and regulations of Khangchendzonga Biosphere Reserve people can not utilize the forest resources as fuel wood, timber and restricted movement of their cattles happens inside the Biosphere Reserve area in the event of prohibition. The people of Lachen have gradually started depending on tourism related economic activities in addition to their traditionally uphold agriculture, animal rearing and animal herding. In this changing situation most of them have adopted some diverse economic activities while retaining their primary and traditional occupations as well.

ACKNOWLEDGEMENTS

At the outset, I convey my thanks to Dr. V.R. Rao, Director–in-Charge, Anthropological Survey of India, Kolkata for launching this project and involving me in this study. I am obliged to Dr. Ramesh Chandra, Deputy Director (C), An. S. I., NWRC, Dehradun for helping me in finalizing this report for which my indebtedness to him remains for ever. I am thankful to Dr. D.B. Mandal former Deputy Director (C), An. S. I. for giving suggestion in this work. Thank is also due to Dr. A. K. Singh, former Senior Human Ecologist, An. S. I. for going through the script and giving valuable suggestion in this work. I also express my thanks to all the informants, field assistant / interpreter and local people of Dubdi (West Sikkim) and Lachen (North Sikkim) villages for all sorts of cooperation.

5

Traditional Art, Craft and Performing Art: A Study in Khangchendzonga Biosphere Reserve of Sikkim Himalayas

Krishna Basu

INTRODUCTION

India is a land of multi-ethnic communities who have always been associated with their traditional culture signifying rich heritage. The art, craft and performing art are important components of culture, through which one's own potential or traditional knowledge can be reflected to the outside world. In reality, craft has remained a part of human activities, both manual and technical, concerned with one's feelings, emotions and expressions for creativity. The position of art, crafts and performing art interweaves various aspects of human society. It is used by humans to record progress in their quest for mastery, on the dominion of nature by using methods of indigenous knowledge.

The art is representing the sense of relationship between men and use of technical methods and application of machines and industry along with tradition and belief. Art is articulated in a variety of ways like drawing, painting, carving, weaving, body decoration, music and dance etc. Art also helps control the human behaviour. Poetry, folksongs, drawing, sculpture, music etc. all have their effects on man's emotions and sentiments. Art is pleasant social control, its influence is universal. Folksongs derive importance in every society. Music invariably makes human tendencies refined. Community feeling is enhanced by communal singing and dancing. It is well established that painting is a medium for expression of unique moods and sentiments, frustrations and fulfillments or accomplishments of the individuals. It is spirit of a people and an environment that determine the dominant trend in painting, whether it becomes saturated with the sense and geometrical pattern of architecture or of sculpture or of music. Painting has its source of inspiration in the senses, desires and feelings of the individual, but its resources are equally if not more variegated than those of sculpture.

The term "craft" is derived from the Anglo-Saxon word 'craft', meaning "strength, skill or cunning", in contrast to "art", which usually implies an intention of producing beauty or pleasure. Anthropologists prefer to use "technology" to refer to the processes of manufacture and "material culture" for the artifacts themselves. Since crafts include all activities that produce or modify objects by manual means, with or without the use of mechanical aids, such as looms or potter's wheels, the range of study is very broad. There is an equally wide range of social forms within which the craftsmen operate. In an other sense, "craft" is synonymous with "guild", commonly used as a term of class ascription and role delineation in contemporary sociology, and is applied to occupational associations. Within this meaning the status of craftsmen differs by culture, epoch and craft.

To understand relationships between art and culture such monographs as Bunzel's – *The Pueblo Potter* (1929), O' Neale's Yurok-*Karok Basket Weavers* (1932), and Adair's – *The Navajo and Pueblo Silversmiths* (1944) analyze the integration of craft activities with the structure of living societies, the economic base of the crafts and their social functions. The roles of the craftsmen, and the value systems that may be expressed through them; these monographs are, accordingly as pertinent to art historians, aestheticians and psychologists as to anthropologists. (Encyclopedia of Social Science, 1972. Vol. 3 & 4).

"Clay craft is probably the earliest of man's creations. The potter's wheel seems to be the first machine which man invented; to use the power of motion for a productive purpose" (Chattopadhyay 1975:3). Craftsmanship is also observed in stoneware, metal ware, lacquer ware, textiles, embroidery, basketry, mat weaving, cane articles, leather work, glasswork, mask, puppets, toys and dolls, horn, coconut shell, conch shell, etc. Craft is 'art or skill' or 'a manual art' and a craftsman is some with a knack, or aptitude for his trade, an acknowledge skill at it (Dark 1978:34). "In the craft world, however, there is no hiatus between service ability and aesthetics. One may say that in good craftsmanship the two are identical, for while the article is useful it would also be beautiful in appearance and joy giving" (Chattopadhyay 1975:1). Crowley (1972:430) writes "The term 'craft' derives from the Anglo-Saxon craft, meaning 'strength, skill or cunning' in contrast to 'art' beauty or pleasure.

Selection of the Study

The Anthropological Survey of India in its 10th Five year Plan Project undertook a detail study on "Cultural Dimension of Tourism" which was reoriented as "Man in Biosphere" project. Under this project the survey decided to study the Biosphere reserves, out of 14 biosphere reserve the Khangchendzonga Biosphere Reserve is one of them in Eastern Himalayan Region. For the purpose of our study I have chosen my topic on "Traditional art, craft and performing art: A Study on Khangchendzonga Biosphere Reserve of Sikkim". The inhabitants of KBR mainly live in buffer zone and they are used to biosphere resources to fulfill their needs. The biosphere resources like forest, hills, rivers, and streams as well as the natural resources play vital role in their socio-cultural, religious as well as in tourism industry.

Yuksam Village

Yuksam has a historical significance in the history of Sikkim. '*Yuk*' mean monk and '*sam*' mean three, which literally means 'meeting place of three monks' was the first capital of Sikkim. The modern history of Sikkim started from Yuksam with the consecration of the first king 'Chogyal Phuntsog Namgyal' in the year 1642 AD. According to legend, Gyalwa Lhatsun Chempo, a follower of the Red Hat Sect came to Sikkim in the 17th century to establish Buddhist monarchy.

Yuksam has been considered the "Lhakhang" or altar for offering to the Khangchendzonga deities. The seven holy lakes surrounding Khangchendzonga, that is: *Khechepelri*, *Karthok*, *Tso*, *Bar Cho*, *Marpu*, *Phuchokarpu*, *Ka Bur Latso*, *Sume Ten Tso* and Dafuk *Yam Tso* are the seven offering bowls to the Khangchendzonga deities. Every landscape of highland, middle land and low land, every river, stream, cave and big trees, deities are worshipped with great devotion by the Sikkimese. The area is also the base for trekking up to the Dzongri area that lies on the edge of the Khangchendzonga national park. The picturesque hills are covered with thick broad-leaved forest of oak, birch, maple, chestnut, magnolia, rhododendron, silver fir, ash, and alder. The people mainly maintain their livelihood within the harsh prevailing ecological conditions. On the basis of these ecological conditions they have developed traditional knowledge, beliefs and tool and technique as per their requirements. The type of art, craft, painting, dance and music play a vital role to maintain their livelihood. The object art and craft, dance and music carry some social value and symbolic meaning to cope up with their life style, which reflects their socio-economic and religious life.

Dzongu

Dzongu is situated in the North District of Sikkim. To save the Lepcha community the then Maharaja of Sikkim made a portion of North Sikkim as a reserve for the Lepcha and this is known as *Dzongu*. *Dzongu* is situated along the valley of the river *Talung* and western part of the *Tista*. The *Talung* river comes from the Khangchendzonga region and joins the *Tista* river, near Mangan, the district headquarters of North Sikkim. The area extends from 88°17′E to 88°31′E and 27° 22′N to 27°34′N (approx). The area, situated north of *Phichu* (*Chu* mean river), a small tributary of *Tista*, is known as upper *Dzongu* and the area on the South of this river is known as lower *Dzongu*. The settlement area of the upper *Dzongu* extends from 1219 – 2000 m. and lower *Dzongu* from 914 – 2000 m. above sea level. Above that level the area is covered by forest, and people go there for hunting and gathering of forest products. The density of population is more in lower Dzongu than that of upper Dzongu because the Lepchas fully depend on agriculture i.e. the settlement has grown up in the lower valley of the *Talung* upto 2000 mts.

Lachen valley

The word Lachen means high pass and the inhabitants of high pass call themselves as "*Lachenpa*". The high pass is situated at a height of 9600ft and located 29km from the Chungthang Sub-division office. The road continues to wind up to Chopta valley at a dizzying 13,200ft, and extends up to Gurudongmar Lake, the last point at 17,200ft. The place is famous for expedition sides gearing up to begin the Green Lake Trek or up the Khangchendzonga hill. The caravan trail to Tibet was a lot easier from Lachen than from Lachung so this was the route preferred by traders. But after the Chinese occupation of Tibet in 1959, this trade route was shut. With the Chinese aggression of 1962, several roads connecting the border areas were hurriedly constructed for mobilization of troops, and one among them was between Lachen with Gurudongmar. The Lachen has been privileged with the benefit of a highway leading to one of Sikkim's most sought after tourist place known as Gurudongmar.

OBJECTIVE OF THE STUDY

It was aimed to conduct the study with following objectives to provide understanding about:

- The role of art, craft and performing art in the society and their traditional method of craftsmanship.
- The focus on inherent social value of art, craft and performing art before and after tourism.
- The economic importance of traditional art, craft, and performing art in tourism industry.
- The perception of the local people regarding biosphere reserve and existing influence of tourism.

METHOD USED

The field investigations were carried out in the territorial identity of *Yuksum*, *Dubdi*, *Tsozo* and *Khecheperli* revenue villages of West Sikkim and also in the high altitude of *Lachen* valley and reserved area of *Dzongu* belonging to the North of Sikkim.

The data collection was done by using anthropological methods. Secondary source of data were used whenever necessary. However, much was rallied upon data collected from the Handicraft Board of Training Institute at Gangtok.

THE PEOPLE

Lepcha

Lepchas are said to the original inhabitants of Sikkim. It has yet not been established, as from where the Lepchas are originally from, though some theories indicate that the Lepchas came from the border of Assam and Burma. Other views speak of the Lepchas having migrated to Sikkim from Southern Tibet. The Lepchas are identifying themselves as "*Rongkup*", meaning the children of *Rong*. The literal meaning of *rong* is 'hill'. According to different scholars they belong to one of the Naga tribes or are associated with the Jimdars and Mech in their eastward migration from Nepal. Some scholars have found similarities between the Lepchas and tribes in Arunachal Pradesh. Some others contend they are related to the Khasis in Meghalaya (Halfdan Siiger, 1967). The Lepchas themselves are convinced that their home has always been the legendary kingdom of Mayel, in the vicinity of Mt. Khangchendzonga. The fact is, most Lepcha clans claim to have mythical connections with this particular mountain peak which they worship as their deity. Their cultural activities would be based in the name of God, or religion, or the ruling ideology of the moment. On the other hand, the work of art e.g.

a mural, painting, carving, a piece of architecture, a poster, a distinctive style of dress, etc. depicts their cultural impressions. The value of art, craft, and performing art, all play a vital role for their sustenance in harsh ecological conditions which also revolve round the surrounding ecology. The Lepcha are peaceful and nature worshipping people. There is an air of mysticism in their lives and rituals. The Lepcha *(Dzongu)* folklore is very rich. The well-known deities of the Lepchas are *Itbumoo, Rum, Itbu Debu Rum, Kongchen Konglo* and *Tamsang Thing* etc., and the famous festival is *Namsoong*. The *Boongthing* is the local priest and he performs ceremonies to invoke the deities seeking their benevolence.

Bhutia

The term *'Bhutia'* community is derived from their original habitat *"Bhot"* (Tibet) and consist of some sub groups: The Drukpas are people from *Drukul /Bhutan* (Thunder, Dragon); the Chumbipas are people from the Chumbi valley (eastern Tibet); the Dhopthapas are inhabitants of Dhopta, a place in south Tibet; the Thomopas or Do-mu-pas, inhabitants of *Do-mu*; the Lachenpa, people of the Lachen valley in Sikkim, and the Lachungpa, the people of the Lachung valley in north Sikkim, are also Bhutias.. According to the History of Sikkim by Maharaja Sir Thutob Namgyal and the Maharani Yeshay Dolma, the migration took place continuously in many ways and through different routes, from the northern and western passes of Sikkim. The Bhutias are spread over in the four districts of Sikkim, but their main concentration is in north Sikkim. They live in hilly terrain of high altitude and cold climate, where there is high rainfall with medium snowfall and high humidity with dense forests. They speak language like Bhutia, among themselves, and the script used is Tibeto-Burmese.

The Bhutias economy depends on pastoralism, dairy farming and agriculture. During the summer season people of Lachen and Lachung go to higher altitudes, to graze their animals. During winter, they come down to the lower altitude with their animals, and practise cultivation, cardamom being their principal cash crop. While some of them are in service. Land still remains the major source of income for these people.

The Bhutias are Buddhists by religion. Their chief deity is the tutelary galaxy of Buddha and Bodhisattvas, followed by the guardian deities, including local deities, family deities, village deities and Khangchendzonga. Most of the deities are identified with mountains, lakes and forest. In the Bhutia religion, the monastery or the '*gumpa*' plays a major role. The important festivals of the Buddhists of Sikkim are the Tibetan New Year, the *Sagadawa*, the *Pang-Lhabsol*, the *Losoong*, and the *Lhabab-Duchen*. In different Buddhist festivals, they have their distinctive functions in the form of dances, songs and gatherings, which are of socio-economic and socio-religious significance. Their tradition maintains that making images of the deities is a pious act, leading to salvation. There are eight auspicious signs, in painting, carving or sculpture. The *Tashi-Tagye* is a popular theme of Bhutia art. These eight symbols, considered auspicious in Mahayana Buddhism, are intimately associated with the life and teaching of the Buddha. The Bhutia women play a vital role in socio-economic life of the people. The women are mainly involved in different type of activities: carpet making and making woolen garments. Besides, the female folk also participate in the dance, music, during the festivals and functions The Bhutias are famous for their weaving, wood carving and '*thanka*' painting. These hand-woven rugs, carpets and blankets are exquisite. Marriage in a Bhutia family is arranged through negotiations by the paternal or maternal uncle of the boy who goes to the bride's place. The important festivals observed by the Bhutia community include *Losoong*; *Pang-Lhab-Sol*, worship of the guardian deity, Khangchendzonga; *Kagyat* dance or mask dance and *Saga Dawa*, the blessing of the spirits.

Nepalese

The Nepalese are said to have come from Nepal in the middle of the nineteenth century. To-day they are the dominant community of the Sikkim. The Nepalese can be broadly divided into the Magars, Murmis, Tamangs, Gurungs, Rais, Limbus, Damis, Kamis, Bahuns, and Chhetries etc. The Nepalese are both Hindu and Buddhists by religion. Some of them have also adopted Christianity. The major festivals of the Hindu Nepalese are Dasain, Teohar, Makar Sankarti, and Baisakhi etc. The Nepalese male in traditional attire is generally robed in a long double breast garment flowing below the waist and a trouser known as "*Daura Suruwal*". The female are usually attired in a double breasted garment with strings to tie on both the sides at four places, shorter than the Daura and is known as "Chow Bandi choli". The economic life of the Lepchas and Nepalese are mainly dependant on cultivation and trading. The Lepcha and Nepalese are mainly cultivators and produce different seasonal crops like cereals and millet crops, paddy, wheat, *jawar*, *bazjara*, *maize*, *ragi*, etc all cultivated in terraced hillsides. Pulses like *arhar*, gram, *khesari*, *mug*, *masur*, *urud*, etc., are also grown. Fiber crops like raw cotton, jute, sun hemp, etc; oil seeds like sunflower, soybean, ground-nut, rapeseed mustard, etc are cultivated. Sikkim is one of the world's main producers of cardamom, locally called '*elainchi*'. Besides, the agriculture, Lepcha male members are mainly involved in bamboo and cane craftsmanship. On the other hand, a sizeable numbers of Lepcha and Nepalese women are involved in different types of carpet weaving and especially Gurung women weave blankets, locally known as *rari,* from sheep wool.

The festivals of Sikkim can be said to belong to two religious streams (i) the Lepcha-Bhutia and (ii) Nepalese. During their worship the Bhutia and Lepcha people perform different types of dances, and play music, which is related to their socio-religious values. The women folk of all the three communities are very adept in carpet, blanket and woolen garment making. The male members of the Lepcha are experts in bamboo craft making thereby fulfilling their social mode of domestic needs. However, the impact of tourism industry has spawned a growing demand for all crafts objects along with greater need for dance and music, all playing a crucial role in the tourism industry.

POPULATION OF STUDIED VILLAGES

The studied villages are namely: *Yuksam, Dubdi, Khechipelri* and *Tsozo* village of West Sikkim. The area is mainly dominated by the Lepcha, Bhutia and Nepalese people. The *Yuksam* revenue village is categorically divided into fourteen numbers of hamlets like *Mangsaboong, Dosthang, Ramgyathang, Ingtang, Tinting, Sabse, Gechen colony, Topshing, Khengte, Gophadara, Yuksum Bazar, Nubgaon, Kopche, and Tsoka.* The *Yuksum* revenue villages consists of 359 nos households. The *Dubdi* revenue village consists of 74 nos of household. It is divided into two hamlets *Choong* and *Mangtaboong* respectively. Out of 74 households, 39 households belong to *Choong* and 35 households are under the *Mangtaboong* hamlets.

Only the hamlet of '*Tsoka*' of Yuksam village is located in the core area of KBR consisting of seven households. The *Tsozo* village belongs to *Khecheopelri* Block which consists of two hamlets i.e. *Lethang* and *Tsozo* hamlets. The *Tsozo* hamlet consists of 47 households and the *Lethang* hamlets comprise of 34 households. All the hamlets belong to Lepcha people. The total number of households of *Khecheopalri Gumpha* is 17. Out of 17 households, 15 are of Lepcha and 2 two of Bhutia households respectively.

Table 1. Village wise population distribution at Yuksam-Dubdi, Khechepalri-Tsozo of West Sikkim

Sl. No.	*Name of Village*	*Name of hamlets*	*Households*	*Total Popu. (approx)*
1.	Yuksam	Tsokha-Khyangte	87	892
2.	Do	Yuksam-Ramgyathang	91	1019
3.	Do	Ting-Ting	97	786
4.	Do	Mangsabung	83	787
5.	Dubdi	Choong-Mangtaboong	79	746
6.	Tshozo	Tshozo-Lethang	89	802
7.	Khechepalri	Khechepalri-Gumpha	14	48
	Total		540	5080

The table shows, population figure of the study villages of West Sikkim. The total study villages are seven numbers, which consists of 540 numbers of house holds. The total number of population is 5080, which is comprising of the *Tsokha-Khyangte* hamlet, the population are 892, the *Yuksam-Ramgyathang* hamlet the population figure are 1019, the *Ting-Ting* hamlet the population are 786 (Halfdan Siiger, 1967), the *Mangsabung* hamlet the population figure are 787, the *Choong-Mangtaboong* hamlet is comprising of 746 population, the *Tshozo-Lethang* hamlet is comprising of 802 numbers population and the *Khechepalri-Gumpha* the population figure are 48 numbers accordingly.

Dzongu is administratively divided into six Gram Panchayats . Out of these, four Gram Panchayats belong to upper *Dzongu* and two to lower *Dzongu*. The upper Dzongu Gram Panchayat falls under the biosphere reserve. The Gram Panchayats of upper Dzongu are: (a) *Barfok – Lingdon* Gram Panchayat, (b) *Sakyong – Pentong* Gram Panchayat, (c) *Tingbung* Gram Panchayat, (d) *Lingthem-Lingdem* Gram Panchayat. The Gram Panchayat of lower Dzongu are: (a) *Lum – Gor Shangtok* Gram Panchayat and (b) *Hee-Gyathang* Gram Panchayats.

Upper Dzongu

The Upper Dzongu area comprises of four numbers of Gram Panchyat i.e. *Barfok-Lingdong, Sakyong-Pentong* G.P. *Tingvong* G.P. and *Lingthem-Lingdem* G.P. Unit. The table shows ward wise population and household distribution of the Gram Panchayat.

Table 2 : (A) *Barfok-Lingdong* Gram Panchayat

Sl. No	*Name of Ward*	*Population*	*Household*	*G.P*
1.	Lower *Lingdong*	454	80	*Barfok-Lingdong*
2.	Upper *Lingdong*	267	44	Do
3.	Lower *Barfock*	222	37	Do
4.	Upper *Barfock*	153	24	Do
	Total	1096	185	

(B) *Sakyong-Pentong* Gram Panchayat

Sl. No.	*Name of Ward*	*Population*	*Household*	*G.P.*
1.	*Lower Lingzah*	219	37	*Sakyong-Pentong*
2.	*Upper Lingzah*	111	22	Do
3.	*Bay-Tolung (TolungGumpha)*	85	16	Do
4.	*Pentong*	152	24	Do
5.	*Sakyong*	150	25	Do
	Total	717	124	

(C) *Tingvong* Gram Panchayat

Sl. No.	*Name of Ward*	*Population*	*Household*	*G.P.*
1.	*Tingvong*	282	45	*Tingvong*
2.	*Namprick*	162	30	Do
3.	*Linko*	130	22	Do
4.	*Kusung*	149	30	Do
5.	*Nung*	172	25	Do
	Total	895	152	

(D) Lingthem- Lingdem Gram Panchayat

Sl. No.	*Name of ward*	*Population*	*Household*	*G.P.*
1.	*Salim-Pakel*	136	25	*Lingthem-Lingdem*
2.	*Safo-Liching*	147	25	Do
3.	*Leek*	132	29	Do
4.	*Panang*	204	35	Do
5.	*Pasingdong*	429	67	Do
6.	*Lingthem (Sofel Gumpha)*	374	66	Do
7.	*Lingdem*	274	46	Do
8.	*Laben*	92	17	Do
	Total	1788	310	

The Upper Dzongu comprises of four numbers of G.P. units i.e. *Barfok-Lingdong* G.P., *Sakyong-Pentong* G.P., *Tingvong* G.P. and *Lingthem- Lingdem* G.P. Unit. The *Barfok-Lingdong* G.P consisting of four numbers of ward. The total numbers of house holds are 185 and the population figure are 1096 numbers respectively.

The Sakyong- *Pentong G.P.* comprises of five numbers of ward. The total numbers of populations are 717 and the house holds are 124 numbers accordingly.

The Tingvong G.P. comprises of five numbers of ward. The total populations of the G.P. are 895 members and 152 numbers of house hold accordingly.

The Lingthem- Lingdem G.P. comprises of eight numbers of ward. The total populations of the ward are 1788 numbers and 310 house hold are respectively.

It may be mentioned that only upper Dzongu is described here ignoring details of lower Dzongu as it falls out side the purview of biosphere area.

Lachen Valley

The population figures of the Lachenpa as per census reports show that the people have gradually increased in their numbers. The population figures of Lachen valley is here considered since 1971 census as because the area was ruled over by the dynasty of King System. The people are mainly herdsmen and traders and engaged in agriculture and horticulture.

Table 3

Year of Census	*Population*
1971	799
1981	919
1991	1640
2001	2923

The population figure of Lachen valley was collected from Department of Census and it shows that the population figure gradually increasing in number.

ROLE OF ART, CRAFT AND PERFORMING ART IN THE SOCIETY

Products of craft- artifacts and performing art play an important role in socio-cultural and religious life of the people. At the same time after getting in touch with tourism industry the objects of art, craft and even performing art play an economic role in the society.

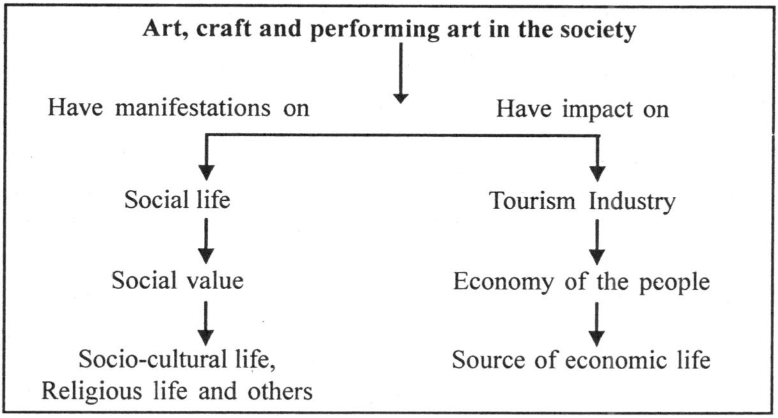

Schematic representation of art, craft and performing art.

The diagram shows how the artifacts and performing art have two way roles, on one side these are manifested in social and cultural aspects and on the other have impact on economy and tourism. Artifacts made of bamboo, wood and cane fulfill social as well as domestic needs of the people at cultural level. At the same time the artifacts also play an important role in the field of socio-cultural life as well as religious life of the local people. After introduction of tourism industry to the area, the local artifacts and performing art have become more inevitable components which are popular or attractive for the tourists. The nature of involvement and response by the local people in the cycle of tourism has its fallout as a new dimension of economic life.

Resource Availability

The land of Sikkim is rich in bio-diversity. Since the area is tropical and alpine, the flora and fauna is unique in its diversity. The lower mountain slopes are abundant with lush green bamboos. The area is rich in bamboo which is raw material for bamboo based crafts. There are some 20 varieties of bamboo available which give raw material in plenty. Cane and ferns also add to the resource material. Some of them are *Gyasi*, *Pareng*, *Po*, *Polam/Bhalu*, *Malyu* or *Muli* bans, *Malingo*, *Gope*, *Parmek*, *Pasang*, *Pasi*, *Kurthak*, *Bling-malo, Purmum, Rim*, *Rui-yung*, *and Ru-bang* etc. Chap, Tuni, Okhar (wall nut) etc., type of wood is generally used by the people for making craft items. The northern valleys are draped with wild cherry, oaks, chestnuts, pines, and white magnolia. The higher altitudes are abloom with a carpet of rhododendrons and medicinal plants also. While yaks and sheep are popular in the higher reaches, other livestock that are cattle, pigs, sheep, goats and poultry etc. The vast majority of the trees and shrubs in Sikkim are evergreen. It is estimated that the actual number of species of flowering plants and ferns is nearly four thousand. As far as the fauna is concerned the usual estimate has about eighty-one species of mammals. The rich potential strength of the physical environment helps them in sustenance. The people, in course of maintaining their life-style easily procure the raw materials from their physical surroundings.

Type of Bamboo, Wood and Cane

The Lepcha and Nepalese are famous for their art and craft making. Three types of wood are generally used, which is locally known as *tooni* (toona celiata), *'rani chaap'* (Macalia Exelsa) and *'Okhar'* (Walnut). The craftsmen use *Pareng, Muli bans, Chaiya, Bhalu, and Malingo* types of bamboo for making crafts items. The bamboo and cane are also used in construction of bamboo bridges, dwelling, domestic furniture, fences, gates, baskets, wind instruments, flutes, whistles etc. Besides these, the new generation after getting some training from crafts institute make decorative items like flower boxes, flowers, pen stand, photo frames, baskets, dust bins, tea pots, trays, mats, hats and tumblers etc. Given hereunder is the description of the major bamboo crafts making process, techniques and its uses in socio-cultural life as well as in the field of tourism.

Table 4 : Crafts of West Sikkim

Crafts of West Sikkim

Place	*Community*	*No. of Families engaged*	*Nature of Work*
Choong	Chetri, Gurung and Subba	16 families.	Rarhi (blanket) weaving and Bamboo making.
Mangtaboong	Subba	12 families.	Bamboo work
Dosthang, Topshing Kopche Gechen colony	Lepcha women	18 families.	Rarhi (traditional blanket), burkason (traditional cushion) and lukuni (traditional coat).

Place	*Community*	*No. of Families engaged*	*Nature of Work*
Yuksum Bazar	Bhutia women	7 families	Den or Dalaicha weaving (carpet)
Tsozo and Tinting	Lepcha and Bhutia	6 families	Pelung work
Ramgyathang	Lepcha	8 families	Bamboo work, jhola, (side bag) Tafu (Traditional weighing mechine) etc.
Lethang	Lepcha	10 families	Doko, Bow and Arrow, Tafu. Talung Phurlung etc.
Mangsaboong, Khengte, Gechen colony.	Subba	11 families.	Wood and Bamboo work.
Pemyangse and Dubdi Monastery	Group of Lamas	7/ 8 members.	Chaam (mask) performer.
Yuksam bazaar, Lethang, Tsozo, Ramgyathang.	Local people	9 girls, 6 boys and 3 women.	Songs and dance related to different festivals.
Gangtok	Age old persons and Instructor's of different sections	Formal and Informal interviews both the official and local people.	Artistes of Thanka, wood carving, handloom, mask and traditional paper maker etc.
Gangtok	Lepcha, Bhutia, Nepali and Tibetan	Attended Pang-Lhab-Sol festival Programme	Perform traditional dance and songs.
Yuksum	Singapore team	Attended cultural exchange Programme	Perforform Dance Programme

The above table shows the nature of work performed by the multi-ethnic people of *Yuksam*. They are divided categorically on the basis of their nature of work. It is observed that, people of west Sikkim are mainly involved in bamboo craft, wooden crafts and handloom weaving. The wooden and bamboo crafts are mainly the domain of men. On the other hand, the handloom work or weaving work is mainly performed by the women. In the *Choong* hamlets, 10 families are involved in *rari* making, of which seven are from the Gurung community and three are from the *Chettri* community, six families are into bamboo crafts. In the *Mangtaboong* hamlet, 12 families are engaged in bamboo work. In the *Dosthang*, *Topshing*, *Kopche* and *Gechen* colony 18 Lepcha families are involved in weaving work. In *Yuksam* bazaar, seven Bhutia females are involved in woolen work. In the *Tsozo* and *Tinting* hamlets altogether six Bhutia and Lepcha families are engaged in bamboo work. In the *Ramgyathang* hamlet eight families are busy in bamboo work. In the *Lethang* hamlets, 10 Lepcha families are mainly involved in bamboo work. In the *Mangsaboong*, *Khengte Gechen colony*, 11 families are engaged in wooden and bamboo work. In the Pemyangse and Dubdi monastery, eight members perform mask dance on different religious occasions and tourist places. A dance troupe consisting of 18 members perform dances in different festivals. All the art, craft and dance, music objects are inter-linked with the socio- economic and religious life of the people. To-day some of these object is more popular in the tourism industry.

Crafts of Dzongu

The people of Dzongu village are mainly involved in different types of art crafts and performing arts in their socio-cultural and religious life. Table 5 given below highlights various craft works done by these people.

Crafts of Lachen

The people of Lachenpa remain involved in crafts and weaving. In the field of weaving remains domain of women. The men do thangka painting and mask making. The table-6 highlights numbers of family involve in different craftsman work and weaving in the Lachen valley. The weaving item is divided into different categories. It was found that the 10 families are involved in making *Chuktuden*, nine families make

Table 5

Sl. No.	*Place*	*Hamlet*	*No of families involved*	*Pursued by*	*Nature of work*
1.	U.Dzongu	Tingvong	5 families	Men	Lepcha cap, Bow& arrow, Dhal (Layap), Kung Ladey (wooden thali),
2.	Do	Lingthem	4 families 2 families	Men, Women	Murrah, Pelung, Po-chung (traditional rice plate), Tin-gyip (Jhola), Doko
3.	Do	Lingdem	3 families	Men	Po-potek (musical instrument), Wookdu (fishing net), Kung Tukchim (wooden handi)
4.	Do	Namprick	4 families 2 families	Men Women	Traditional Lepcha cap, Hunting cap, Dhal(Layap), Doko, Tingyip (Jhola)
5.	Do	Nung	4 families	Men	Bow and arrow, Pun-tang (musical), Rudom (cane box), Sung (traditional weighing instrument)
6.	Do	Linko	2 families 3 families	Women Men	Thokro, Tingyip (Jhola) Pelung, Tuk-sheor (traditional strainer), Tung-hee
7.	Do	Lingzah	4 families	Men	Tung-buk (dotara), Cup (Tokpu), Po-potek (musical instrument)
8.	Do	Lingdong	3families	Men	Samokthyaktuk, Papri, Tongbu (milk container),
9.	L. Dzongu	*Hee-Gyathang*	3 families 6 families	Men, Women	Modern type of bamboo work, Thumji (traditional carpet)

Chuktu. In the rock making process 15 families are involved. Eight families do *thumji* (carpet) making. The traditional dress known as *Nambu* is made by only four families; eight girls of the village do the work of *Kharu* making. The wooden mask, works are done by men. The thangka painting is prepared by only two families and male members only allow do the work. The women are also related in the different type of woolen dress and only three families have engaged themselves in the work. The carry bag is locally known as *Jhola* make by three families. The *Jhuma* is made from the yak hair. prepared and sale it out side. The men are mainly involved in the work.

Table 6

Sl. No.	*Place*	*No. Families involved*	*Division of Labour*	*Nature of work*
1.	Lachen	10 families	Female	Chuktuden
2.	Do	9 families	Female	Chuktu
3.	Do	15 families	Female	Rock
4.	Do	8 girls	Female	Thumji (carpet)
5.	Do	4 families	Female	Nambu (traditional dress)
6.	Do	8 girls	Female	Kharu (Carpet with waste product).
7.	Do	2 families	Male	Wooden Mask
8.	Do	2 families	Male	Thanka painting
9.	Do	3 families	Female	Cap, Knee cap, sweater of Rabbit wool
10.	Do	9 families	Female	Jhola
11	Do	-	Male	Jhuma (chamor)

The study has highlighted the role of art, crafts, and performing arts of the Lepcha, Bhutia and Nepalese of West and North Sikkim. Accordingly the implementation of the objects, dance and music is classified in following manner as given below:

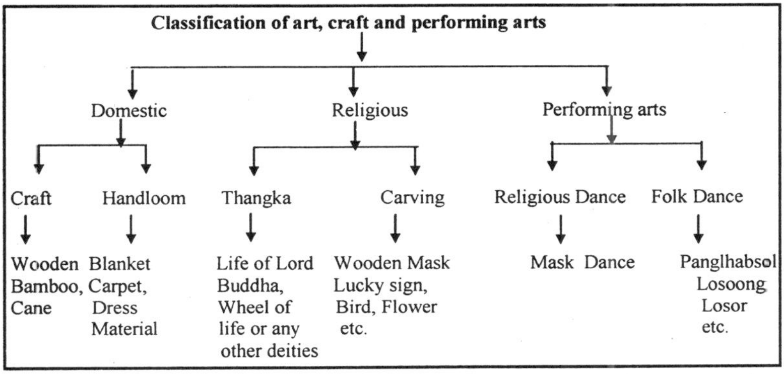

The above stated diagram is classified into domestic, religious and performing arts categories respectively. The respective category clearly mentions the function of each. The objectives are divided into two categories i.e. art and craft and handloom items. The craft items are generally used for domestic purpose and mostly made by using wooden, bamboo and cane material. The handloom craft category has also been segregated into three sub categories which comprise blanket, carpet and traditional dress material.

The art of religious category has been further divided into three categories, namely- Thangka painting, woodcarving and mask making. The artists or craftsmen collect resource material from the surrounding areas and give it the final shape using tools and their indigenous skill and knowledge. The third category considered all the performing arts, both religious dance and recreational dance items. During the religious festivals or recreational functions both male and female participants perform the dances on different occasions including social function. The dance troupes perform dance as part of the merry making.

CRAFT ITEMS (BAMBOO AND CANE ITEMS)

Lepcha hat

The Lepcha people generally use two types of hats namely *'papri'* and *'samokthyaktuk'*. *Papri* is an ordinary hat used during fieldwork, hunting, and fishing occasion. *Samokthyaktuk* hat represents the status and position of the person concerned in the Lepcha society. The kings and the village chief's generally use this hat having different designs like sun, moon and tails of birds on the front of the hat. The bamboo and cane is the major raw material for making the hat. The craftsman choose young bamboo for making hat. But in case of cane they prefer to use mature cane for its longevity. To examine maturity of the cane, they use traditional knowledge i.e. body of the matured cane usually becomes white in colour naturally. Besides, they also use *Po-pali* (yarn from large bamboo*), Poyong Pali* (small pieces of bamboo yarn), *Rukup* (cane), *Kungcho* (vegetable dyes, majeto), *Tongzer long* (stone: like glass), and *Kafer lop* (wild leaves) *Nombongong-fo- tuk- seem* (bird tail feather), *Pugu reep* (one kind of flower) and *Mongyung tukseem* (peacock feathers).

The hat consists of five layers - the inner one being a rough structure of the hat, locally known as '*Shambu-sop*' for which they generally prefer *chaiya bans.* The second stage is "*Kafer lop*" leaves, used for threshing purpose. The third stage is '*pugu reep*' using local flowers and the fourth stage is placement of mica stone on the hat and the final stage to make designs on the main part of the hat. The design is locally known as '*Eee- Mik*'. In Lepcha language '*Somok*' means the name of designs used in the craft. '*Somok*' and spider web like design on the top portion of the hat is called '*Sundyong soong*'.

Pelung

This is a round shaped air tight container locally known as *pelung*, which is used for storage purposes. It is used for preserving food items over long periods. These containers are of different sizes like small, big and medium types. The *Pelung* is prepared from bamboo and cane splits, locally called as '*pali*'. Cane or bamboo is cut into sections, from one knot to the other knot. These pieces are cut into thin splits and such splits are thereafter dyed with natural colors obtained from a locally available natural indigenous creeper called *'Majeto'* [Rubia cordifolia Roxb. ex Fleming (Rubiaceae)]. These splits are then dried within the household, usually in the kitchen and not in the sun as the people believe that the sun would make the colors to appear faded. These splits are woven together which is then soaked and boiled for some time making it easy to give it the required round shape. Two *'Pareng'* bamboo strips are used to hold the contraption together giving its final shape. The craftsmen usually choose old and matured *Gope* (cane,) *Chaiya bans*, *Pareng bans* (bamboo) *Majito* is a creeper, which is used for coloring purposes. The complete making and giving it a final shape of a Pelung usually requires five to six days. Cost of pelung is varying according to the size Rs. 300 to Rs. 500. The male members generally do the work.

Doko/ Tungjung

This is a traditional basket made out of bamboo and cane, used for carrying domestic items. In Nepali language it is called *doko* and it is square in shape, but in Lepcha it is called *Tung-Jung* and it is round in shape. It is also used for carrying agricultural crops and to preserve domestic items. It is conical in shape and generally 2 to 3 feet in height. The upper part of the Doko is one and half feet in diameter and the lower base is half feet square in shape. The craftsman first makes long bamboo splits, which is 1 cm. in width. The weaving starts from the lower part of the basket, gradually going upwards by weaving cris-cross pattern as per the requirement of the basket. The upper part of the *doko* is tied with the bamboo or cane in a round shape for longevity of the container. Then a strip of tree bark (locally called '*Argali*') is tied on both the sides and middle part of the *doko* as carrying belt. This belt is generally supported on their forehead at the time of carrying luggage. It takes 2-3 days to get final shape.

Phurlung / Tungdong

Phurlung is a bamboo basket and used for domestic purposes. It is generally rectangular or oval in shape. In Nepali language it is called *phurlung* and in Lepcha *tungdong* or *phintuk*. The craftsman makes bamboo splits locally known as *Pali*, which is generally 1/2 cm in breath and one meter long. The craftsman then weaves a criss-cross pattern or as per requirement. The upper part of the Phurlung is generally two inches in height, two feet long and the weave is usually very thick and tied with a round shape bamboo split. It is generally used for to kept or washing for vegetables and fish at the time of cooking. The male members are engaged in the work. The cost of Phurlung is locally Rs 100/ to 200/, which is depending upon the size of the basket but the tourist is changed higher rates.

Nunglo/ Talung (Winnoing fan)

Nunglo is a winnowing fan, used for domestic purpose of separating the grain from husk. It is generally two types in shape- one is U shaped and the other is round shaped. This is mainly used for cleaning rice and other cereals. To make a Nunglo the craftsmen first choose young bamboo one or two year's old, make thin bamboo splits and thereafter weave in criss-cross manner to get the finished product the nunglo. After finishing the weaving part of *Nunglo,* the craftsmen make a bamboo split which is one inch in width for border of the *Nunglo* and tie it with the help of cane split to the upper part of the implements. The people of Sikkim generally used *Pareng* bamboo for bordering due to long lasting and weaving part mainly used *chiaya bans*.

Konkro

It is an implement made of bamboo mainly used for new born baby-as a cradle. The *konkro* is generally rectangular in shape. It is one meter long and 35 cms in height. The *konkro* is made by *pareng* and *chaiya* types of bamboo. The weaver selects one year old bamboo and makes splits from the bamboo with in seven days after cutting. The lower part of the *konkro* is made of bamboo woven plate and the upper part of the *konkro* is tied with round shaped small bamboo pieces and tied in a zig–zag pattern. Finally upper part of the implements makes a boundary shape with the help of one inch bamboo or cane split. The male members generally make the implements. Konkro is also used by trekking party for carrying trekking materials.

Mandro

This is a traditional bamboo mat, which is used mainly for drying food grains like maize, millet, phaphor etc. In Lepcha language it is called '*Talu*'. The size of the *Mandro* is generally 2.5 m by 2 m. The craftsman first makes bamboo splits which are generally 2.5 mts long with little thickness as the splits are very thin in nature. The craftsman then weave the '*Mandro*' in a criss-cross pattern as per required measurement. To give its final shape, end part of the splits are banded and fixed with the *Mandro* and stitch with the help of jute round the boundary. To make a '*Mandro*' it requires about 7 - 10 days. Generally the craftsman use *Muli and Chaiya* bamboo which is locally available. The male member is involved in the work.

Chitra

This is used as roof sealing utensil. It is also another type of traditional bamboo mat, which is prepared from *Pareng* and *muli* bamboo. The people believe that the *Chitra* mat prepared by good quality of bamboo last for more than seven - eight years. It is used for house wall and roof or sealing purposes. Besides it's also used drying for cardamom, cowshed and goat shed roof, locally known as *Mendak*. The process of *Chitra* making is same as that of *Mandro*.

Po-chut–Pehip

Po-chut is a drinking country liquor pot made of bamboo. The pot is generally 30 cms in height having 5-6 cms diameter. The craftsman uses two year mature bamboo to make the pot. The making of *pochut*, involves steps that the bamboo piece is separated from main bamboo one knot just before the next knot of the bamboo. After cutting the bamboo, the craftsman chisels out the upper part of the bamboo with the help of a knife and inner part of the bamboo is scooped out with the help of a long chisel. The bamboo pot is now dried for a few days with the help of kitchen smoke to give final shape. It is also observed that sometimes the craftsman decorated the outer body of the pot with the help of silver. People use pipe for drinking, it is locally known as *Pehip.* The people generally used two types of pipe, one made from cane; locally known as '*Puyung pehip*' and other made from bamboo, locally known as '*po-pehip*'. '*Po*' means bamboo in Lepcha language.

Dhungro

It is a wooden mug used to drink '*chhang*' (country liquor) mainly by the Bhutia people. Outer wall of the mug is decorated by the silver plate and using Dhungro carries some status symbol for the Bhutia people. Now-a-days some people use aluminum plate also for the decoration as economic device. The craftsman generally preferred local wood like Siris [Albizzia stipulate (A. marginata) (Mimosaceae)], Okhar (Walnut) [Juglans repia Linn. (Juglandaceae)] etc. First the craftsman selects a round shaped 30 cms height and 5 cms diameter wooden piece. Thereafter, he gives a round shape from the centre point to less than 1 cm from the end of the wooden piece. This will be the upper part of the *dhungro* and from the lower bottom to 3 cms height of the wooden piece mark a cross mark where the base of the *dhungro* will be fixed. Now, with the help of chisel, the craftsman scoops it out from the top to reach the mark at base level. After finishing scooping it out, they color it and some times put an aluminum or silver ring on the outer part of the *dhungro.*

Dalo

Dalo is traditional household pot used for storing grains. It is generally made out of *pareng* bamboo. The making process of *dalo* is the same as that of *doko* but shape is sometimes square and round.

Thumse

It is conical shaped bamboo basket, like a *doko* with a difference that its walls are pasted with mixture of cow dung and local mud and then it is kept for drying from sunlight for long lasting. This is used for domestic purposes. Nowadays trekkers use it for carrying kitchen materials during their trekking. The making process of *Thumse* is as same as *doko* implements.

Phuru

This is a small traditional wooden bowl, used for domestic and as and when necessary for performing religious functions. For making *phuru*, the craftsman generally prefer locally available wood known as *Dude*. The craftsman selects wooden pieces of which 10 cms approx thickness. They make a round shape from the centre point to three cms just before the end of the wooden pieces. A three cms round strip is then set it as the border of the bowl. Finally the craftsman scoops out the inner part of bowl as per measurement. Today the *phuru* wooden bowl is an attraction for the tourists because of its small size and shape to be kept as show piece.

Chongshli and Dabroshli

This is a bamboo made traditional bow locally known as *Chongshli.* The bow is generally one and half meters long and the thickness in the middle part of the bow is nearly 5 cm, whereas the end of the bow is gradually slimmer. The rope used for stringing of the bow is generally from the tree bark or bamboo or cane splits. After finishing the work, the craftsman usually keeps it for a few days for smoking. It is believed that the process of smoking helps to protect the product from insects and increase the longevity of the bow. It is used for hunting purposes.

Dabroshli

This is a traditional arrow made from bamboo stem. The bamboo stem is generally 35 cms long having an iron triangle shaped plate tied with cane splits at the end of it and at other end of the arrow generally bird feathers are pasted to give direction while oncharge. As tradition for preparing bow and arrow bamboo material is cut during the period of dark moonlight nights to protect the implements from any damage caused by insects.

Po-Chung

It is a rice plate made of broad bamboo splits which are generally 10 cms wide and a quarter cm thick with the length as per the requirement. The craftsmen generally prefer to use the *Bhalu* (in Nepalese) or *padang* bamboo as raw material to make this item. The craftsman generally selects very young bamboo preferably less than one year old. They split out bamboo round wise. First the craftsmen draw a circle and the bamboo splits are set accordingly one after another. At the time of cutting the splits it is cut approx 3 cms extra from the main drawn circle. Then, the craftsman makes a round shape of the bamboo splits on the basis of previous circle. Now the round shaped splits are put on the base of the plate and stitched together with the cane splits. Some times they also use local gum for pasting purpose instead of weaving. Men and women both do this work.

Tingyip (Jhola)

Tingyip is a traditional carry bag, used for marketing and to carry the belongings while on short visits. Earlier, it was made from the bark of *Sisnu* tree but now the Lepcha prepare it from wool and cotton mixture colorful threads which are available in the local market. It is mainly used for carrying domestic items. In Lepcha it is known as *Tin-gyip* and outsider it called jhola. *Tin-gyip* is very popular among the tourists. The local price of the bag varies from Rs. 150 – Rs. 200 per bag.

Layap (Dhal)

Layap is a self protect cane made traditional shield used by the Lepcha people. In the early days at the time of war the army men used the implements. This is made by thin cane in round shape. The craftsman selects matured cane to make a round shape of it with the help of stitching one after another row as per the requirement. After making the Layap the artisan used smear resin and local color on it for preservation as well as decoration of the implements. Presently the item is rarely available and is used only as token of symbol. It is made by the Lepcha men.

Cup *(Toku)*

Toku is a bamboo made tea pot which is made from '*po*' and '*gyasi*' type of bamboo. The craftsman generally prefers to use two years mature bamboo. The craftsman selects or cuts the bamboo having two knots and finally the upper knot is separated and a lower knot is used as the base of the tea pot. The craftsman finally smokes the contraption and makes designs on the body of the cup. One handle is fixed on the body of cup that is made of cane and tide with thin cane split. Today, the craftsmen make different designs on the body of the cup. It is very popular in the tourist people. Male and female are engaged in the work.

Tung-shit/Tuk-sheor

The *Tung-shit* is a bamboo made round shaped implement used for domestic material filtration. In Nepali language it is known as '*Chappani*'. The Lepcha people generally use it as *Chi* or *Chhung* strainer. It is made by *chaiya* bans. The size of Tung-shit vary as per requirement. The artisan makes a bamboo net with the help of thin bamboo split. Finally upper part of the implement makes a circle shape and tide with wide bamboo split with the help of cane thin split.

Po-potek

This is a long musical instrument i.e. flute, locally called *po-potek* by the Lepcha and made of *Pareng* bamboo. During the festival and function the people used this flute. The length of the *Po-potek* is generally 50 cms height and inner part of the flute is three cms in diameter. The flute is having nine holes. Each and every hole is related to different function. Finally the artisan make it decorated and dry it by kitchen smoke to save it from insect.

Sutchang

Sutchang is another type of musical instrument of the Lepcha and made of *pareng* bamboo. The people used this instrument mainly during their festival.

Pun-tang

Pun-tang is also a musical instrument of the Lepcha i.e. flute which is made out of *Gope* bamboo.

Tung-bam

Tung-bam is bamboo made cylindrical traditional *chhang* pot, which is used for carrying liquid *chi* or *chhung,* during the harvest season. It is generally used by the people in the morning time carrying *chi* or *chhung* liquor for the field labor. This is generally 48 – 50 cms long an10 cms in diameter. Depending on size of bamboo the artisan selected one knot to another knot of the bamboo. The upper part of the bamboo knot is cut of from the main body of the bamboo.

Tung-kyung

Tung-kyung is a big size bamboo pot, used for during honey collection. People generally preferred *Padyang* bamboo in Lepcha and *Bhalu* in Nepali for making *Tung-kyung*.

The craftsman preferred mature *Padyang* bamboo for making *Tung-kyung* pot and considered one knot to another knot from the main bamboo. This type of bamboo species is very healthy one from the other variety of bamboo. The final shape of pot is open of upper part. For carrying purposes they used cane rope as a belt.

Cho-chok

Cho-chok is a traditional tea strainer; preferably *chaiya* bamboo is used for making this implement. The craftsman makes thin bamboo splits and weaving criss-cross wise bamboo net as per requirement (like an iron net). Finally make one grove (half inch) on ***Cho-chok*** in circle shape and tide bamboo net. In the same way handle of the ***Cho-chok*** also decorated upper part of the net and make handle of the implement.

Tung-buk

Tung-buk is a traditional wooden made musical instrument of the Lepcha people. It looks like a Sitar. It is made out of '*Soham Kung*' wood, which is available in the high altitude area. The instrument is divided into three parts viz- (a) *Thang-thi* upper part of the instrument on the area having five wooden knot which is setting with iron string or cattle fur. (b) *kuju-ki*, the middle part of the instrument, (c) *Am-nem* is lower part of the instrument.

Star

Star is a modern decorative bamboo made object. The bamboo star is prepared by using thin bamboo splits. The craftsman first makes thin bamboo splits that are generally half inch wide and length as per requirement of the object. Secondly, one cylindrical bamboo pot is selected that is 6 inches in height and 2 inches in diameter. Now the craftsman makes designs of flower shapes with the help of thin bamboo splits and puts it on the bamboo cylinder. Finally, it is made to look colorful with the help of local herbal and modern color. It is more popular in the tourism industry and also used as a domestic decorative item. Male and female both are engaged in the work.

HANDLOOM ITEMS

Sikkim has a very rich heritage in handloom woven artifacts. Today, the Sikkimese handloom artifacts are very popular in the market. The women folk are generally involved in weaving their own household requirement like *rari* (blanket), *dalaicha or den* (carpet) and making traditional dress materials of *thokro* etc. The Lepcha traditionally weave in lion looms. In addition, with the introduction of modern technology, which has infused a new lease of life in the form of table-mats, purses, cushion covers and other dress materials. Now-a-days new designs in handloom are also being incorporated to keep pace with the market demand. The raw materials used are mainly sheep and cotton yarn. It is purchased mainly by local people who use it to make traditional dresses, carpets, cushion covers etc. The new addition of bags, purse, cushion covers and table napkins etc., are very popular among the tourists.

Carpet (*Dalaicha / Den*)

Carpet weaving is a traditional cultural expression of the state of Sikkim. The process of carpet making is hand-knotted and woven in fixed vertical looms which are kept standing with the support of a wall. The carpet art and designs are normally of birds, snow-lions, eight lucky signs, flowers etc. Though it is a traditional activity, very few families follow it as a part of family tradition. The present problem faced by the weaver is local marketing system. The products are used mainly as covers to chairs, sofa-sets and those used for covering beds or Dee wan. Instead of the traditional carpet these items do have good demand in the local market.

Carpet weaving by a Bhutia woman

The carpet making process:

The carpet making process involves following stages -

(1) The white colour cotton *yarn* is set vertically on the main wooden frame. This process is locally known as '*taan*' setting, which consists of 120 lines of cotton *yarn,* set on both sides for standard size of carpet making.

(2) The weaving process begins according to the design which is drawn on graph paper. Before starting weaving they make rolls of cotton or woolen thread on a wooden frame.

The weaver usually prefers different colored wool to make designs on the carpet (locally called *woon*). At the time of weaving they preferred double line wool for making knots with the cotton *yarn*. They take cotton *yarn* in both sides (front and back.) for making knot and after that they cut the wool with the scissor. In this way they make carpet and after that the weaving process goes on and wooden hammers called '*fong*' are used to beat the woven wool into place for tightening and giving final shape of each and every round weaving.

(3) After weaving, the weaver cut the threads for giving final shape with the help of scissors. The female folk are mainly involved in the work.

Local market rate of carpet at Yuksam

Carpets are expensive item in the local market. The cost structures of carpets are various sizes and use is given below:

Items	**Cost**
Sofa cover (two pieces) is 2′ length and 2′ breadth	Rs. 750.00
Sofa cover (one piece) is 5′ length and 2' breadth	Rs. 3000.00
Bed cover one piece is 6′ length and 3′ breadth	Rs. 5000.00
Car cover one piece is 18" length and 18″ breadth	Rs. 650.00
Car cover one piece is 18" length and 15″ breadth	Rs. 517.00
Sofa one piece is 2′ length and 2′ breadth.	Rs. 950.00

Carpet rate of Lachen (*Thumji*)

Size	**Cost**
3′ × 6′	Rs. 3400.00
2′ × 5′	Rs. 2000.00
2′ × 2′	Rs. 750.00
18″ × 18″	Rs. 425.00
18″ × 15″ (size)	Rs. 417.00

Local Blankets Made at Yuksam- Dubdi

The women of Yuksam- Dubdi are mainly engaged in different types of blanket making nature of work. The type of blanket divided into three categories i,e *Rari* ,*Burkason* and *Lukuni*. This is made by Sikkimese sheep wool locally known as *woon*. The raw material is i.e. coarse sheep wool mostly available in west Sikkim. The sheep are sheared of their wool twice in a year, in the months of March-April (*Chaitra-Baishak*), and September –October (*Bhado-Ashaj*). The average yield of wool from mature sheep *(bhera*) is arround 200 gms and 700 gms.

Blanket (*Rari*)

Rari is a prepared by the Gurung community. The process of *Rari* making, requires different steps. The raw wool is washed and boiled with soap. It is thereafter dried in the sunlight and the black (*kalo*) color wool is separated from the white (*Sheto*) wool. After this, the wool is carded, with a brush locally called '*korna'*. In earlier times they used a '*dhanu'* (bow with wooden block) for carding instead of a brush. This process of carding of wool is locally called *'peuri'*. Next, they make a single strand of wool by using the charka in traditional way; this is called '*dhago'*. After that, they make single thread or double thread rolls as per the requirement. This process is locally known as '*Lauri'*. After the spinning process is over, the yarn is not given any other color; only natural colours, i.e., black and white is retained for final use and design.

Process of weaving:

Before starting the weaving, the weaver collects '*woon'* (wool) from the '*bhera'* (sheep). Then the collected '*woon'* is boiled in hot water with detergent powder. The boiled and washed '*woon'* is then dried in the sun. Thereafter, the dry wool is carded with the help of a brush. In earlier, they used a bow (*dhanu*) for cleaning the wool. Before starting the process of weaving, first they fix the structure or frame of the weaving loom (locally called *kath*) that is generally made of wood or bamboo..

(1) The weaver sets the single line thread *dhago* for making '*taan*'. This consists of two bamboo poles. One pole is fixed to the wall of the house, which is the upper part of the *'taan'*, locally called '*bhari kath'*. The other part is fixed with two wooden poles (locally known as '*khuta*') embedded on the floor of the house. The artisan starts her weaving work from the side. This bamboo pole is locally known as '*torso kath'*.

(2) The process of weaving is generally to weave one thread after another with the help of loom. This process of weaving is locally called as '*chitre'* design, the weaver also makes different types of designs, when the process of weaving takes in two threads at

the time of weaving; this process of weaving is locally known as '*mandre*'. Another process of weaving is to weave very thin thread one after another this process is locally known as *gidre,* but this process is not applicable for making blanket due to less quality. The women folk are generally involved in this work because the male members go to the high altitude area for sheep rearing.

(3) After completion of *rari* the artisan cut it into two parts and set it together to make one piece. After that they prepare starch in hot water by mixing corn flour in a big bowl. Then they put this starch on rari in three intervals and beat it with wooden hammer/ stick for mixing the starch properly to fill the gaps in the rari, if any. Male member are generally involved in this work.

Unit of measurement

The people follow traditional measurement for rari weaving which is as given below-

Length = 7 bita

Breadth = 5 bita (60 pair Dana)

1 bita = 1′ (12"); this represents the distance of 1 bighat (distance between tip of thumb to tip of middle finger) + back length of middle finger.

1/2 bita (adhi) = 6" it means distance of eight fingers.

Length of the rari is kept usually at 2.25 mts.

Making process

(i) '*Taan*' making – it means after preparation of '*dhago*' they set it into the bamboo frame according to their requirement. One bamboo is in the upper part and another one is in the lower part. After setting the '*dhago*' for weaving, one dhago is locally called '*dana*'.

(ii) They follow two types of weaving process. One is called '*chitre*' and another one is called '*mandre*'. At the time of '*chitre*' weaving they follow single thread weaving and at the time of '*mandre*' weaving they follow double thread weaving. For weaving following instrument are used:

'*Take-2*': made of bamboo, flat type. One '*take*' is used in the upper part of the taan and another '*take*' is used in the lower part of '*taan*' i.e. in the weaving part.

Nak-Tipne - This is a thin bamboo rod which is necessary at the time of weaving to facilitate the weaving process. One *'nak-tipne'* is used at the time of *chitre* and two is necessary for *mandre* weaving.

Pho-2: It is used for straight weaving of *rari*, setting it at one thread gap i.e. one after another in this manner. One is upper part and another one is lower part.

Tom – 1: It is used for tightening the thread.

Burkason

Burkason is a traditional blanket having *chitre* design. *Phurka* is u shaped single thread in both side of the *burkason* and it is placed 4 to 6 inches in gap. In *Burkason* sometimes they follow temple design and sometimes square design. They follow square design 15 cms inches in gap, black and white accordingly. In local language they refer to the square design as '*kosh*'. Only two natural colours black (*kalo*) and white (*sheto*) are used and its price in market is Rs. 750.

Lukuni

It is a traditional dress material of Gurung community. Weaving process is same as *rari* and *burkason*. This *lukuni* is prepared by the lamb wool and it is very fine quality of wool use for making dress. At the time of weaving they follow *chitre* design and use only one colour i.e. black. *Lukuni* is very costly and it takes much time to make it.

Cost of Craft Items

The artifact produced reaches the market through the middle man. The maximum numbers of artifacts are available in the Gangtok market but in case of Yuksum, Dzoungu and Lachen area buying facilities is not up to the mark. The ultimate result is the producers are deprived from as per skill of labour charge. Here some of items rate given below as per Gangtok market price.

Local market rate of blanket at Yuksam

Items	*Cost*
Rari (Mandre design) -	Rs. 2500.00
Rari (chitre design) –	Rs. 1500.00
Burkason (For sofa),	Rs. 950.00 – Rs. 1000.00
Lucuni (coat material) –	Rs. 4000.00

Traditional Blankets at Lachen:

The following are the different types of blanket prepare *by the Bhutia women at Lachen:*

(a) Rock (b) Mezae (c) Gnyapo (d) Chuktu and Chuktuden

The Lachenpa people are popular for warm colorful blankets weaver, which is made from sheep wool, locally known as '*phe*' and *yak* wool, locally known as '*khulu*'. Two types of sheep wool is available in Lachen area, one is white variety, good quality, very soft and fine, locally called *Phe* and another variety is mixed with black and white, these variety is coarse type and poor quality, locally known as *khiluk*. The *phe* is Rs. 150/ kg and *khiluk* is Rs. 110/ kg in the local market. The *phe* and *khulu* is collected once in a year, preferably in the month of May.

After cutting the raw wool it is washed with soap and dried in the sun light. Before preparation of blanket the washed wool is brushed with the help of a carder brush and actually it is half brushed, this process is locally known as *pheshak.* After that they fully brushed and they make separate rolls of the wool, this process is locally known *as chukre,* this process is usually done for two to three days. The next process is spinning the yarn by a wooden instrument called the '*phang*'. It requires the process to hold the yarn manually by hands. This process is locally called '*phechu*'. The next stage is locally known as '*khekheo*', it means the woolen thread is made into round shaped balls. The fourth or last stage is '*Thigo*'*:* After the spinning process is over the yarn is given color. Chemical dyes or natural dyes like walnut bark, *shungay*, *majito* and *chucha* are used to produce different colors.

It is also observed that previously they also used '*dhanu*' for carding of raw wool. The preparation of handloom work is done exclusively by the women folk. Different types of blanket are found in the Lachen valley. The types of blankets are popularly known as '*mezae*', '*rock, chuktu*, *Gnyapo* (used for carrying children) and are normally woven out of sheep wool. Beside these type of blankets they also prepare *Chuktuden* (sofa covers) and *Chuktu* (bed cover) usually made of sheep wool, but now -a -days they prepare it out of commercially available sweater wool, locally known as *pindo.*

Unit of measurement of blanket

Length = 5 Dyum

Breadth = 1 Dyum (120 line)

1 Dyum = this represents the distance of horizontal expansion of both hands.

1 Dyum = 4 chhyu

1 Chhyu = 1 hat

1 Hat = 2 tha (bighat)

1 Tha = 1 bighat (distance between tip of thumb to tip of middle finger)

Generally lengths of *rock/ mezae* always consider on the height of the male member approximate 6-7 feet's. Rock is very useful than other blanket and it is one piece blanket. Previously they prefer to use vegetable colour, recently use chemical colour.

Raw materials

The people of Lachen generally make blanket, locally called *rock* or *mezae* from sheep wool (*phe*), yak wool (*khulu*), commercially available sweater wool (*pindo*) and cotton yarn (*geu*).

For rock – 3 kg. *phe* and 2- 2.5 kg *Pindo* (wool)

Mezae—sheep wool (phe) and cotton yarn (geu). Generally consist of 5 pieces, one piece is approx 1 ft. breath and 5ft length.

Instruments used for making blankets are mentioned below along with its used for the work

1. Thishing - 1, wooden frame, main structure of the rock or mezae.
2. Sompo - 2 / 3, small bamboo frame where woolen thread is there
3. Tom - 1, wooden and bamboo made, just like a comb
4. Kathap - 4, wooden made, like a gear of a car
5. Judi - 2, upper and lower wooden part of Thishing
6. Simji – 1, seizer, use for cutting purpose.
7. Neka – 4, bamboo made, supporting to Tom

Mezae and Gnyapo

This is also one type of traditional blanket, but making process is something different. Rock is making in large frame and it is a single piece of blanket. Gnyapo is use for carrying child.

Chuktu / Chuktuden

This is prepared on small wooden frame, locally known as *thishing*. It is making mainly by the sweater wool, locally known as *pindo* and sheep wool, locally known as *phe*. No cotton yarn is used for making *chuktu* and *chuktuden*.. The women folk use their traditional knowledge at the time of making *Chuktu / Chuktuden*.

They use instrument like *sompo, tom, kathap, neka, simji* etc at the time of making. Chuktu is use for bed cover and it is standard size joined by five pieces. Chuktuden is use for sitting purpose mainly on sofa, locally known as *dinty* and it is only single piece, sometimes two pieces joined according to the size of sofa.

Local rate of blanket at Lachen

5′ × 7′ = Rs. 1500 – Rs. 1700. The Lachenpa people recently sell it to the army men.

Natural Vegetable Dyes

Local name	*Botanical name*	*Parts of plants used*	*Month when available*
Chucha	Rhubarb	Roots	October
Majito	Rubia Cordifolia	vine	May-June
Shungay	Symplocos Racemosa	Leaves	May-June
Taga/ Okhar	Juglan Regia	Bark, fruit	October
Halhaley	Rumex nepalisis	Leaves androots	May- June

Many plants are used for coloring. The plant products are locally available. The process of the dyeing techniques follow what these people learnt from their forefathers coloring clothes, shawls, hats, and woolen yarn for carpets or blankets. The people use different parts of plants and shrubs such as roots, barks, fruits, leaves and vines to produce different colors. Of late, it has become easier to use chemical dyes to create consistency in colors. Now-a-days, natural or vegetable dyes have become popular and its products have a niche market.

WOOD CARVING

Wood carving is an ancient form of art practised by the people of Sikkim. The objects are of different types viz *Choktse* (carved table), *bakchok* (Square table), wooden mask's, decorative screens, lucky signs, altars, lamp stands and other decorative items. These items usually covering a typical traditional design like the dragon, birds, flower, phoenix etc. Three types of wood are generally used for woodcarving namely '*toon'i* (toona celiata), *'rani chaap*' (Macalia Exelsa) and *'Okhar'*

(Walnut). The craftsman chooses the wooden piece and does the art work giving it the desired shape . After seasoning and making it smooth by sand-paper very fine chisels and tools are used to carve out the designs. The carved pieces are then assembled together and are ready for a coating of paint or polish.

MASK

Mask making is another ancient crafts of Sikkim. Masks are usually made of wood and clay. Clay mask is made by mixing with the fibers of jute, cotton or handmade paper pulp. All the ingredients should be mixed in the right proportion. Face masks in wood or clay of different Gods, Goddesses and animals of universe are made and worn during religious festivals and dances. The wooden mask is worn by people, mainly Lamas during festivals, religious ceremonies and dances of: *Gutor Chaam, Losar, Dubchen, Tsechu* puja etc. Different masks are used for different ceremonies. The wooden mask may depict screnes, partly reflecting anger or have animal expressions. Now-a-days, they are also used as wall hangings.

According to the artisan Lamas of Sikkim monasteries, characteristically there are four kinds of masks:

(i) Masks with serene expression (*Ziwa*),

(ii) Masks with mixed expression of serenity and anger (*Simzimatrau*),

(iii) Masks with angry expression, *Tro* (wrathful) and

(iv) Masks with animal expressions (*Gonen-Tshog*).

Unlike torma sculptors, thangka or mural painters, mask-makers are not found in every monastery. This is because all the monasteries may not have mask-dance ceremony. In Sikkim only a handful of monasteries arrange Lama–dance where wearing of mask is considered necessary. Hence, the art of mask-making is taught and practiced only in those monasteries where the resident lamas have to take part in dance. Wooden masks are carved out of tough light wood, known as '*Zaru Shing*' (*Zaru* wood) which is mostly found in the high altitude areas of Sikkim like Lachen and *Champ* and *Tunni* wood of West Sikkim.

Clay mask making

Masks are usually made of wood and clay mixed with the fibers of jute, cotton or hand made paper pulp. All the ingredients should be mixed in right proportion. The dough of this mix is cut into small pieces with the help of a chopper and again kneaded with hand. A locally available herbal glue (pin) is added to the dough to bind the ingredients. The dough is then flattened with a roller pin which is again pressed with a hot iron to smoothen the surface so that cracks can not develop afterwards. Next a sheet of wet handmade paper and a thin fabric is spread on the top and bottom of the flattened dough. This is again pressed with an iron. When the dough is partially dry, saw-dust of red sandal wood mixed with 'pin' is smeared on the dough so that the surface of the mask is textured. After this, the artist has to give the right shape of the mask. The masks are usually made larger than the standard size of human face so that they can be fitted on any person during dance. Dancing masks also contain lesser amount of clay so that they are not too heavy. Such masks have larger proportion of paper pulp or fiber. The masks are invariably painted with bright hues of red, green, blue, yellow and black.

Mask (Khangchendzonga)

Mask (Mahakal)

Wooden mask making

To make masks craftsman of Lachenpa generally use *Phentup*, *Khyasem*, *Zuru etc*, wood. In Lepcha language the mask is known as '*Bob*' and Bhutia people called it '*chaam*'. Face masks in wood or clay of different Gods, Goddesses and animals are made and worn according to religious festivals and dances. Different type of masks like faces of gods, animals and birds in different colors are made: each of these carry some significance. The guardian deity Khangchendzonga is red in color,

God Dapla is white in color, *Gumpu / Mahakal* is black or blue in color. The animal face like tiger is of black and yellow color, Snow lion is of white and blue color, Ox and Yak is of black color and the Deer is of yellow and black color.

The craftsman selects one meter height circular wooden piece, locally known as '*Dhum*'. The wooden log or '*Dhum*' is divided into half vertically and this is locally known as '*Thumphi*'. The craftsman then draws rectangular geometric lines, on the wooden log with the help of charcoal. The rectangular wooden log is divided into two halves vertically in the central position, and this is locally known as '*Thikchay*'. Similarly, in the horizontal axis also it is divided into four parts equally, each part is locally known as '*Chay*'. The craftsman then starts work from the lower part of the diagram, which is locally known as '*Yaku*'. This space is mainly used for making the lips, locally known as '*Mali*'; teeth, the '*Sho*' and beard the *Jaro*. The second space is used for making nose, the '*Nha*' ; eyes, the '*Menok*' and finally the ears, the *Amchok*'. The third space is used for making a third eye on the forehead, locally known as '*Yeshaychen*'. The fourth space is for making the crown the '*Thurdhmo*'. Finally, the craftsman colors it as per traditional norms. For the use of colors on the mask they observe some restrictions. The Khangchendzonga mask is in red colored. The *Dapla* mask is colored white and the *Gumpa* mask colored by black and blue colors. The face of the tiger mask generally uses black and yellow colors. The face of ox and yak mask use black color.

Local market rate of wood carving at Yuksam

Items	*Cost*
Mask –	Rs. 2000.00
Chokchi (only charge) –	Rs. 2000.00
Dragon (Polish) –	Rs. 280.00
8 Lucky sign (painting set) –	Rs. 580.00
8 Lucky sign (polishing set) –	Rs. 480.00

Local market rate of wood carving at Lachen

Items	*Cost*
Chokchi –	Rs. 1050.00.
Dragon (medium size)–	Rs. 280.00
Lucky sign set (painting) -	Rs. 480.00
Lucky sign set (polish) –	Rs. 380.00
Mask with painting	Rs. 2500 – 3000

THANGKA PAINTING

There are three types of 'thangkas':

(i) The first one depicts the life of Buddha, his birth, his disillusionment with life search for enlightenment and his understanding of life.

(ii) The second one is representing the Buddhist beliefs of life and death.

(iii) The third one consists of tools for meditation or as offering to the deities.

Thangka painting plays a vital role in the religious life of the Bhutia people. The painting is considered as one having auspicious value in the society. These paintings normally depict life sketches of gods and goddesses in different forms. They may depict the life of Lord Buddha, goddess *Drolma* (Tara), a wheel of life or any other deity. The central figure in a Thangka is always a Buddha or any other deity or bodhisattva of Mahayana Buddhism. The Thangka also has a religious and spiritual significance as a sacred object of the people. The Lamas and their followers firmly believe that the 'thankas' are equivalent to or even more effective than the idols of the deities in bringing happiness and blessings to a person, family or institution.

'Thankas' are painted on cloth or on the wall. They are rolled up for transportation or storage and then unrolled for display.

The preparation of the painting surface

The painter creating 'thangka' scroll paintings he proceded through six clearly defined steps:

(1) The preparation of the painting surface.

(2) Establishment of a design on that surface by means of a sketch.

(3) Laying down the initial coats of paint and that was followed by;

(4) Shading

(5) Outlining.

(6) Finishing touches.

Units of measurement

In Thangka painting there are two main units of measure: small units *('cha chung')* and large units (*'cha- chen'*). Except in one special proportional class there were always twelve small units to every large unit. A rough piece of cotton is stretched on a wooden frame and it is made smooth by applying it with a mixture of chalk and glue. The cotton frame is dried and it is polished with a shell (conch).The craftsman then draws the outline on the cotton pieces vertically and horizontally with the help of black or red colors. They depict images of different gods, goddesses and philosophies related to Buddhism. It is made mostly by Buddhist priests and monks. Today, commercialization has helped this art form to spread among a larger group of people. During painting, the people also maintain variation of colors and that has a lot of significance: White stands for serenity; golden for the birth or life, enlightenment and paro nirvana; Red for the intensity of passion- both love and hatred; Black for anger; Yellow for compassion; Green for consciousness. In the olden times almost all colors were natural pigments derived from different minerals. For example blue pigment to colour sky, water and other blue features was derived from azurite, while the green pigment to colour landscape features was derived from malachite. Native vermilion and cinnabar were used to colour orange and bright red. Yellow ochre, white chalk or calcium compounds and carbon blacks were used to colour the features in yellow, white or black. Black ink was derived from soot and glue. Finally, gold dust was used to get the color 'gold'. The craftsman generally uses stone colors and vegetable dyes together with gold dust and gold thread is used for the tapestry. The paintings are bordered with rich silk and brocade with heavily engraved silver knobs at either ends at the lower half of the Thangka. The work is carried on very carefully for even minute details of the ornamentation must be attended to before coloration. To make a mistake in the measurements of the body given in the iconographical manuals is considered to be a great sin. Sometimes other monk/lamas also remain present, whose duty is to read aloud prayers while the artist is at work and so intense is the religious atmosphere that surrounds the creation of painting, that the face of a Buddha or a Bodhisattva is preferably drawn only on certain auspicious dates. Throughout Tibet, the 15th and 30th of each month (of the Tibetan Calendar) are considered auspicious and the artist would usually draw the features on the 15th day of the month and colour them on the 30th day.

Technique of Thangka painting

The cotton-wooden frame is locally known as '*Reze*'. The craftsman now has drawn lines on the cotton frame which is locally known as '*Cha*'. The 13 numbers of horizontal lines (*Cha*) is drawn on the frame and the measurement for each is equal. Similarly, the craftsman has drawn three lines vertically. First, one is drawn to divide the frame equally in two halves, with a center point, by drawing one line vertically. Secondly, the measurement is taken from the centre point to the end of the frame and divided equally and a line is drawn on both sides of the frame. The total number of 13 horizontal lines is the main geometric measurement of any. Thangka painting. The painting is considered from top of the frame, line space one and two is considered for making the head, which is locally known as *Tue*. The 3rd and 4th lines are considered for making the face, which is locally known as *Shea*. The 5th line is considered for the neck which is locally known as *Ke*. The 6th, 7th, 8th and the 9th lines are considered for making the body which is locally known as *Kuju*. The line numbers 10, 11, 12 and 13 are considered for making the lower parts of the body which is locally known as *Thi*.

The second stage of the drawing considers the three numbers of vertical measurements, where the craftsman draws the nose, eye and mouth etc. The centre vertical line is allocated to drawing the nose, eyes and chin of the body. Accordingly the artist makes the drawing with the help of two or three vertical lines for the eyes, mouth, ear etc. After compilation of the drawing, the craftsman uses painting and finishing touches. Finally it is mounted on silk. In older Thankas the mounts were of simple dark blue silk or cotton, as is evident from many fifteenth and sixteenth century Thangkas that have retained their original mounts.

After the colors are dried, the painter has to scrape the whole painting to attain a smooth surface; the thick layers of paint are scraped with a sharp knife. After scraping, the thangka is dusted thoroughly. Finally, the painting is mounted on silk or Chinese brocade or a finely embroidered material and attached to the rolling rods which are attached at the top and bottom.

Rate of *thangka* painting varies from Rs. 100 to150 for ordinary painting while original thangka may cost Rs. 5000 and above.

1. Thangka (trainer) – Rs. 100 to 1500
2. Original Thangka – 5000 +

DANCE

Dance and performing art is part and parcel of life and culture of the people. Though their livelihood depends on forest, hill and rever etc for the welfare of individual or community they appease different types of god and goddess. During this occasion or function the people also perform different type of dance, which is related to nature base, socio-cultural life and religious life also. Here the Lepcha, Bhutia and Nepali do perform diverse type of dance and performing art in different situation to save their community as well as individual.

The religious type of dance based on nature revolve based and around the Buddhism faith where as on the other hand folk dance is related to marriage, birth, love affairs or any other folk base etc.

Guru Rimpoche's Trungkar Tshechu -On this day, the Buddhists pay homage to the master who first blessed Sikkim as a whole land. The guru is believed to have firmly established Buddhism in Sikkim and introduced his form of tantric Buddhism to the Himalayan kingdom after vanquishing the "*demons*" obstructing the growth of dharma in Tibet. This day commemorates his victory over these demons and the devout believe that the virtues accrued by recitation of mantras on this day are two-fold.

Saga-Dawa festival is considered as the holiest of holy Buddhist festivals. On this occasion, the people perform different stages of Lord Buddha lives went through: birth, achieved enlightenment and passed away attaining Nirvana. Three important events are celebrated in the festival of Saga Dawa. The three-fold auspicious day falls on the full moon day of the 4th month of Buddhist lunar calendar, usually around the end of May. During the occasion the people perform songs, dance etc.

Lhabab Dhuechen festival is performed for the descent of Buddha. Dhuechen means festivals, *Lha* means heaven and *Bab* means descent. *Pang-Lhab-Sol*. Legend has it that the mother of Lord Buddha Maha Maya did not live long after his birth and took rebirth in *Trayastrimsa* or the haven of the thirty Gods. After attaining enlightenment, Lord Buddha through spiritual power came to know about the whereabouts of his mother and at the age of forty one ascended to the heavens along with thousands of his followers. Lord Buddha stayed in heaven for three months during which he delivered sermons to his mother and other celestial beings. Lord Buddha had left behind on earth one of his disciples, Maudgalyayana as his representative. This disciple and other devotees of the lord could not bear the long separation and longed to hear his preaching, Maugalyayana, who possessed miraculous powers, was exhorted to go up to the heaven to request the Lord to return back to the earth. The Gods were not willing to let Lord Buddha return back to earth but Maugalyayana suggested that as the earthly beings did not have the powers to visit heaven, the celestial beings could come down to the earth to attend his preaching. Lord Buddha finally relented and descended to the earth at a place called Sankasya along a triple ladder that was prepared especially for the occasion by Viswakarma, the God of machines.

Pang-Lhab-Sol' festival is unique for the Sikkim people. The festival is held from the 15th of July and continues till the end of August. It was popularized by the third Chogyal of Sikkim Chakdor Namgyal. The festival also marks the signing of the treaty of blood brotherhood between the Lepchas and Bhutias by Khye Bumsa and Tetong Tek when the local deities were invoked to witness the occasion. The word '*Phang*' means witness. In this festival the snowy range of Khangchendzonga is worshipped for its unifying powers. Buddhist monks perform rituals and prayers in the name of the Khangchendzonga deities. The monks and devotees go all the way up to *Dzongri 'Dhapla Gang'* to offer prayers and rituals to the deities for good harvest; freedom for the whole country and world free from disease, hunger, famine, war etc. On the day, the guardian deity is portrayed by masked Lama dances as a fiery red-faced deity with a crown of five skulls, riding a snow lion. To lighten the mood of the spectators, jesters called "*Atchars*" play antics during *Chaams*. The third Chogyal of Sikkim, Chakdor Namgyal is credited for choreographing the *Pang-Lhab-Sol* dance performed by monks on this day.

Drukpa Tsheshi festival is performed by the Buddhist people, on occasion when the Buddha first turned the wheel of dharma. The festival is held on the 4th day (tsheshi) of the 6th month (drukpa) of the Tibetan calendar around July or August every year. The festival celebrates the Buddha's first preaching of the four noble truths to his first five disciples in a park at Sarnath. The first is the noble truth of suffering. The second noble truth is truth of the origin of suffering Karma and Delusion and their causes. The third noble truth is the cessation of the suffering or the attainment of nirvana. The fourth noble truth is the truth of eight fold path leading to nirvana. The day falls on the fourth day (*teshi*) of the sixth Tibetan month (*drukpa*). On this day, people also enjoy yak races.

Bumchu festival is celebrated at the monastery at Tashiding in the month of January or Feburary. The word '*Bum*' means 'pot or vase' and *Chu* means 'water'. During the festival, the pot containing the holy water is opened by the lamas of the monastery. The level of water in the pot foretells the future for the forthcoming year. They believe that if the water is full up to the brim, it foretells a year in which peace and prosperity will prevail. If the water is over the brim and is spilling over, it signifies a year with natural disasters and flood, it prophesies bloodshed and disturbances. If the water level is low or almost dry it signifies famine. A part of the holy water is distributed amongst the gathering of the devotees and the pot is replenished with river water and sealed at the end of the festival to be opened only in the next festival.

Beside festivals they perform religious dances like *Chaam* which is performed prior to *Losoong* and *Rolchaam* (cymbal dance), *Tshamche* (animal headed mask dance), *Shyak* (dance of horned animals), *Namding* (dance of winged animals), *Thakshobalap* (dance of the beasts of prey), *Hdur* (skeleton dance), *Shanag* (black hat dance), *Thoma Tshoglen* (dance of wrathful deities) and *Shawa chaam* (stag dance). The dances symbolize the exorcizing of the evil spirits of the year and the welcoming of the good spirits of the New Year. They also essentially represent the victory of the good over evil.

***Losar* (*Lo*-year, *sar*- new)** festival is celebrated mainly during the Tibetan New Year. It is celebrated in the month of February. On this day the youth perform Yak dances and threw '*Sampa*' as a way of greeting and welcoming the New Year with shouts of "*tashi delek*". The people enjoy with their brocades, jewelry, songs, dance and picnics.

Namsoong is an indigenous festival of Lepchas. It is celebrated as a mark of welcoming the new year of the Lepchas which begins from the first day of first month (*Kurnyit Lavo*) of the year which continues for seven days. It is celebrated all over Sikkim.

Losoong is performed during the harvesting season at the end of the tenth month of the Tibetan year. As it falls on the 11th month of the Tibetan calendar, it is not the real New Year but it is in fact an agricultural New Year when rice and grains are plentiful and the weather is moderate. Before *Lossong*, a ceremony called *Gutor* is performed by monks in the monasteries. The people pray for a good harvest and even better prospects for the next crop. During the festival the people perform the Chaam dance at the monasteries. The dance symbolized the exorcizing of evil spirits of the year and the welcoming of the benevolent spirits for the New Year. The people also participate in archery competitions as a mark of the festival. The men become Gods during the festival and don attires with mystical symbols. The '*Kagyed*' (eight teachings of the Guru) dance forms an important part of the Gutor ceremony and is held on the 28th day of the 11th month at the monasteries. The other religious dances or *chaams* that are performed prior to *Losoong*, are :

Rolchaam (cymbal dance), *Tshamche* (animal headed mask dance), *Shyak* (dance of horned animals*), Namding* (dance of winged animals), *Thakshobalap* (dance of the beasts of prey), *Hdur* (skeleton dance), *Shanag* (black hat dance), *Thoma Tshoglen* (dance of wrathful deities) and *shawa chaam* (stag dance).

SONGS RELATED TO FESTIVAL OF KBR PEOPLE

Being hilly people, living close to nature and having traditional culture these people have a variety of folk songs to be sung on different accasion of socio-cultural life. The songs reflect their relevance to festivals on worship of nature and form part of amusement. Some songs are given below.

Song concerning Namsung festival : This song is sung on New Year's celebrated by the Lepcha. 'Fan 'signifies a typical local bird from the Himalayas. The arrival of this bird signals the start of the New Year and is celebrated with pomp and gaiety involving lots of community singing and merry making on a high ground near the village

Nam fan fosa bhyum
Sut din ba nam al a-sa

Kaido Lenchho bhyum
Ung tuk chat Glure jam

Kuinu Kurthak rang re zang
Lenchho re Kaisa Layang

Sam rang ting na chho Layang
Ung byun a Padang Ka

Ado tin dak go soseo false
Ung nu selbo seo

Love song : This is sung by young males who are unsuccessful in love and sing to console themselves. Despite fresh mountain air and freshness in the surroundings, with springs flowing in gay abandon, nothing is appealing because of the unrequited love. This song is usually sung on social occasions.

Num rhedum dosa nimre
Sick mut La dar dar dinam de

Som muriun sak muriun
Lenchho re na ae

Tik layang sa aphang phing re
Lenchho re ting gyun bu- non –de

Som muriun sak muiun
Som muriun sak muiun
Lenchho re na – ë

Kungsa long la - ë
Jekla dinon de
Rebum la phalla dinon de

Kubum munin tunon la
Kubum munin tunon la
Susa som a re

Love song : This song is sung in the evening, just before dusk. The lover is usually in a reminiscent mood recalling the pleasant and good times spent together and the glorious time spent with each other:

Anam chimbu na ga na samica
Yuba ë susala sum nang ka

Tusa - sa ribur bur non de
Surong abido sap non de

Kakku fosa simla fo
Thing nhula sorang lum non de

Anam chimbu na ga na samica
Yuba ë susala sum nang ka

Tosho kang e yet agna
Ang Keung ka bhyum a-re

Kang - e – yet agna thing them bu
Ha non ung keung ka

So rang la bhyum a-re do thure zang
Sibipo ha kusum lik- re – zang

Marriage song - During marriages function both the unmarried males and females members are enjoying:

Din bole anam din bole
Rong sa abryang kaden bole

Sing Ling Kung Sa fo-sap-re
Nam Ling song sa tham sap re

Din bole anam din bole
Rong sa abryang kaden bole

Kung ka timbu Kung chang rip
Fuling song sa khap chang re

Din bole anam din bole
Rong sa abryang kaden bole

Mali bigu phiu – nieu - ö
Yam ka nong song gyuni – ä

Din bole anam din bole
Rong sa abryang kaden bole

Panzing long ô don magat
Kaium yagna don magat

Bhutia song in praise of nature : During the period of offering to nature based function the Bhutia people perform different type of songs:

Tseche tseche la yu yu
Khangri chemu rong rong

Denzong gyap ke tensang la
Khangchendzonga tak che

Phula khangri karpo
Syaba kengal tangdhok

Syaba kepa men bay
Lungpa kepa Enbay

Meaning : Look up in the hill, there is many mountains. In behind of Sikkim there is a mt. Khangchendzonga. All the mountains were cover by white snow. In that peace of Mountains there is animals, all that animals were very happy, because the land itself is very peaceful.

Song for Loosong festival-

So lo denzong la cheke jang lhari

So lo ya-la Phensang nangki uorbu Ya la sa

So lo ghurwa la me pe phenta-sang

So lo ya la serte tengla slyu ye yala so

So lo phula ne khangri karpu-la

So lo ya la kanchen yala zenga taksu Yala so

So lo kor kor la ney che kor ye

So lo yala jel jel chorten jel ye Yala so

So lo chorten la jel way mehla di

So lo yala yunje kencha mana yala so

Meaning: Our Sikkim is so precious. In our Sikkim we will find many precious things which are not found in other places. There are many beautiful lands, many hills, many wild animals, many beautiful mountains etc. The Sikkimese people were very honest. They were blessed by the Guru Rimpoche. They believed in almighty, they always do puja at their home.

Nepali song-

Lai bori lai, lai bori lai - 2 times

Gao ko keti sabai lai

Baisako nakli ghumao da

He la ma garchhan hami lai

Lai bori lai, lai bori lai, lai bori lai

Kambar ma patuki kasera

Nakali chhalama basero

Jilke lai deyada moskin the

Hami lai degda jhoskin the

Lai bori lai, lai bori lai, lai bori lai.

Gao bhari thuli

Jhal dhoka thune

Ajkal ko keta utaolo hun

Dhuri ma Basero ka rong la

Deo ung sai chhori harang la

Lai bori lai, lai bori lai, lai bori lai.

Bari bhari dol lai, dol la chha

Pahila janchho bhanne, hal la chha

Lai bori lai, lai bori lai, lai bori lai.

Meaning – This Nepali song is very rhythmic this song is usually sung on social occasions both the unmarried males and females members enjoy it.

IMPACT OF TOURISM

The role of art, craft and performing arts are very close to their day to day life. The objects and performing art bear mode of social value in the field of socio-economic and religious life. Due to impact of tourism the Sikkim occupies a special position in the tourism industry. The art, craft and performing art fulfill the tourist demand and its gradually popularized by the tourists. On the other hand, the craftsman, the performer is generating a new form of economy in the light of tourism industry.

Artifacts related to Tourism and its economic value

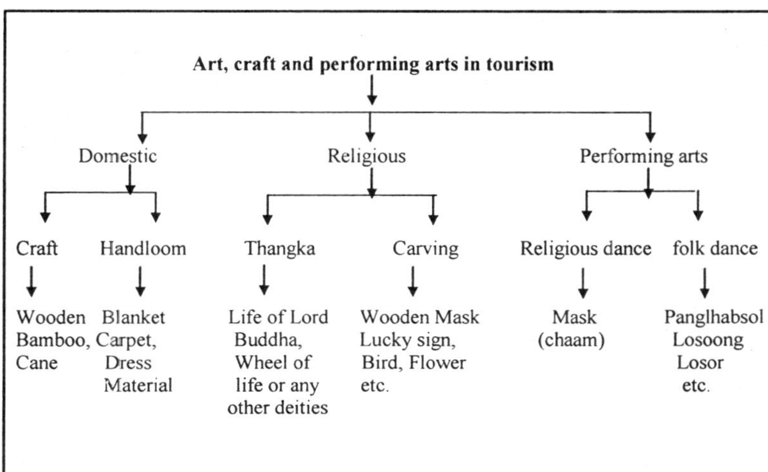

Art and crafts artifact and performing art play a vital role in the tourism industry. In the case of Yuksam area the art, crafts artifacts, dance and music are very popular among the tourists. The artifacts like bamboo, wood and cane items have great demand in tourism. Likewise weaving items viz, carpet and blanket also play a very important role in the field of tourism. In case of Lachen valley the art, crafts artifacts and dance music items are not so flourishing in the tourism industry. Due to lack of tourism facilities objects like art crafts and performing art do not get popular among the tourist people. Now the local people are trying to open the crafts stalls and crafts museum in the Lachen area with the help of local traditional political system i.e. the *Pipon* System. In case of Dzongu, the area being restricted for outside people due to the administrative problem, the tourism industry cannot be popular. After the observation of field situation the above diagram shows numbers of items and dance and music are very close to tourism industry. The crafts items like wooden, cane and bamboo making items like bamboo cup, tea tray, flower top, etc. are very close to the tourism industry. The handloom items are different type of blanket, carpet and *chuktuden/ chuk-tu.* To day it's also observed that the female are very close to *jhola* making.

IMPACT OF BIOSPHERE RESERVE

In case of Yuksam and Lachen valley, the area is surrounded by the reserved forest area. The local inhabitants like Lepcha, Bhutia and the Nepalese are very close to the forest based resources and economy. The forest resources are used as food items, shelters, fuel, and raw material for making implements or craft items, medicinal plants and place for tourism, especially trekking. Besides, the people are not allowed to catch fish in the nearby rivers and streams, though this is what they had always practiced since the early days. It is also observed that due to reservation, the people face problem in sheep rearing for giving poses problems. The people are those adversely affected in getting sheep wool of quality and in quantity. Besides, the raw materials for craft items like, bamboo, wood, plants to be used as dyes for coloring wool and other articles are collected from the forest area. Thus the raw materials and food resources of KBR region are very inter –linked with the people.

However, with the declaration of the area as a biosphere reserve, the people do not have easy access to the forest area. They are dependant now on the whims and fancies of the forest authorities. The forest department issues permits in favor of the local people once in a year. Additionally, due to lack of communication and transportation facilities, the people experience huge delays in procuring raw materials. The end result is that the people are not convinced with the forest department and vice-versa.

One of the objectives of the tourism industry is to help develop the economic condition of the local population with more participation in the related activities by the local people. In this context the tourism development Programme is considered important in two ways 1. the government provides more infrastructure facilities for the development of tourism; and 2. local people have more opportunities for enchasing the base products and traditional abilities like art, crafts, dance and music etc. However, in the course of study it was observed that the people like Lepcha, Nepalese and Bhatia's are very close to the tourism industry. As is the case in most places of the world the contact situation is governed by the people through the beauty of their art, crafts and performing arts. The present system in place regarding tourism and its economic effect has had very little impact and the people are not satisfied at all. There is an apparent gap between the producer and sales counter. In the present chain of economic system it is the middle man who controls the marketing system. It is also observed that even today the contact system exists i.e. the middle man supplies the raw materials to the weaver or the craftsman and in exchange the weaver or craftsman got cash or kind. If the middle man supplied materials for four blankets, after completion of the work, the weaver got the due of only one blanket. Similarly, the trainer or the students of the training centers, during their training period produce different types of products but they do not get any consolidated amount for their effort, but only the inadequate scholarships. There is a shortage of sufficient Govt. initiation for the producer to sell their production of art and craft reasonably well. Due to this breakdown of the economic system the local people or the producers are not satisfied with the present scenario.

CONCLUSION

Sikkim is a landlocked Indian state nestled in the Himalayas. Sikkim situated in an ecological hotspot of the lower Himalayas amidst the grandeur of the mountain peaks, lush valleys, fast flowing rivers and an invigorating climate, Sikkim leaves an indelible impression upon the minds of tourists. The Buddhist monasteries perched on the lofty mountains of Sikkim showcase the rich culture and heritage. The land embraces some ancient cultures which have remained geographically and culturally distinct. These cultures are expressed in their vernacular art which, in contrast to international art, represents both place and culture of rich heritage. Vernacular art mirrors historical and geographical forces and it provides insight into social aspirations, and thereby is important in understanding social behaviour. Most aspects of the art forms of painting, dance, music, embroidery, architecture and sculpture are regionally distinct. The Sikkimese culture finds expression in its beautiful art and craft. On the other hand the woolens carpet with the dominating dragon emblem and eight auspicious signs; wood carvings, Lepcha handlooms in traditional designs and rich colors for clothes, bags, linen and accessories; leather jackets and handbags, articles of homemade paper, Thangka (religious scroll paintings) and Sikkimese Dragon Jeweler make a fascinating collection of handicrafts, inspired by an age old culture.

In the light of tourism industry, the role of art, crafts, dance and music play an important role in the life of the Lepcha, Nepalese and Bhutia communities. The objects are a lifeline of the society and carry some social and religious values of the communities. The artifacts fulfill their modes of needs in the field of socio-cultural, economic and religious life also. The ecological backdrop is responsible for the development of tools, techniques and indigenous knowledge for the human society. The people like Lepcha, Nepalese and Bhutia are also dependant on their nearby surroundings. The people accordingly developed art, crafts, dance and music for their survival. All these are related to their life-de passage and socio-religious life. The types of crafts and products fulfill their socio- cultural and economic life. Besides, the wood carving (eight lucky signs), painting items (thangka) are very close to the religious life of the people. On the other hand, the mask dance, music and songs are very much co-existing in their religious and recreational life.

With the introduction of tourism to the area, the traditional artifacts carrying social values and religious values have been transformed to economic values. It is a new dimension, a source of economic development of the inhabitants of the people of Kanchendzonga Biosphere Reserved area. The place Yuksam is very popular with the tourist people. However, due to lack of infrastructure facilities, the tourist face different type of problems connected with: accommodation, guide and transportation etc. The place Dzongu is declared as restricted zone, as a result the tourists are not allowed in to the area. A similar situation exists in Lachen of north Sikkim, where due to the international border the tourists do not get easy access to the area.

Keeping all the above stated facts in mind, following observations are made to increase the effectiveness of the tourism industry in KBR area.

- To lay emphasis on availability of more ethnic cottages for tourist accommodation instead of 'pucca' buildings, as a means of greater cultural exchange and insight into their ethos.
- To involve the local youth as guides for the tourists instead of outsiders as tourist guides.
- To institute a controlled market system for local arts and crafts with the government or N.G.O's playing the role of facilitator.
- To popularize the local and healthy ethnic food habits by putting up stalls.
- There is need to improve the present available transportation system.
- Finally, the implementation of any development Programme should be done without tinkering with the pristine ecological conditions.

ACKNOWLEDGEMENT

I am greatly indebted to Dr. V. R. Rao, Director–in–Charge of the Anthropological Survey of India for giving me an opportunity to work on the National Project "Cultural Dimention of Tourism: Khangchendzonga Biosphere Reserve". I am indebted to Dr. Debabrata Mondal, (Ex Deputy Director), Eastern Regional Centre, Anthropological Survey of India, Salt Lake, as well as the core member of the project for his valuable suggestions during fieldwork. I am grateful to Dr. A. K Singh (Ex Senior Human Ecologist), Anthropological Survey of India, ex-coordinator of Man in Biosphere for his valuable suggestions and co-operation. I am also grateful to Dr. Ramesh Chandra, Deputy Director of North West Regional Centre, Anthropological Survey of India, and Dehradun for his guidance in finalizing the report. I am indebted to Dr. K. Chakravorty, Head of Office, Eastern Regional Centre, Anthropological Survey of India, for her co-operation in preparation of report.

I have been immensely benefited from my colleagues, in the Anthropological Survey of India, Kolkata.

I am also thankful to authority of different Department, the people of Lachen valley, Dzongu and Yuksam-Dubdi of West and North Sikkim, who helped me a lot from the core of their heart to facilitate the study.

6

Impact of Tourism: A Case Study of Khangchendzonga Biosphere Reserve of Sikkim Himalayas

Amitava Dinda

INTRODUCTION

In examining the impact of tourism, anthropologists have often devoted to writing ethnographic accounts of how tourism has affected host communities in a wide range of societies. In general, anthropologists have conceptualized tourism as determining the fate of hosts in many ways, such as whether they will develop economically or not, whether they will derive sense of pride or shame about themselves and their traditions, or whether they will have incentives to protect or destroy their environment. Rarely scholars have opined about the effects of tourism on local communities in positive sense substantially. At the level of the local economy, anthropologists have learnt that tourism has caused many kinds of havoc. For one, wage labor opportunities created through tourism are taken to be disrupting subsistence economy of small producers. Ethnographic case studies from host destinations around the world show that wage labor introduced through tourism raises the opportunity for subsistence activities. The disruption of subsistence activities was not necessarily a problem in itself, but it became a problem when the flow of tourists was reduced, and people left with no economic alternatives for sustenance. Unfortunately, this was (and still is) a relatively common phenomenon because the tourism industry is especially prone to boom-bust cycles. In addition to economic development, intercultural contact and the changes that result from it have been an especially pervasive theme for studying impact of tourism on any society. An early example came from testing as how acculturation occurs when urban tourists representing 'donor culture' interact with host society acting as 'recipient culture'. It is a matter of worry that tourism may cause hosts to forget their past or 'lose their culture' as they adopt the new lifestyles and mannerism that they learn from outsiders in the process of interaction. In this view, tourism can lead to a kind of 'cultural dependency' or 'cultural decadence' in which local people gain economic benefits. Loss of 'identity' occurs in this scenario as there is likelihood that the local economy improves and local community begin to imitate tourists behaviour pattern boasting to be superior in every way. Many early studies concerned with the social and cultural impacts on tourism highlight the costs rather than seeking a more balanced approach. Keeping these in view, the present study on 'impact of tourism' has been conducted in KBR in Sikkim to understand the socio-cultural and economic factors related to tourism that create impact on the life and culture of the people living around KBR or vice versa. The KBR extends in North, South and West district of Sikkim. It is situated between 27°15′ to 27°57′north latitudes and 88°02′to 88°40′east longitudes.

It is widely known that the journey from Stockholm to Rio de Janeiro forced the civilized society to launch for United Nations Educational Scientific and Cultural Organization's (UNESCO) Man and Biosphere (MAB) programme in 1970. The basic objective of this programme is to minimize man-nature conflict and to protect and conserve the biosphere wherever it is possible in its pristine ecosystem. It also suggested the sustainable development of human population living in and around biospheres and tried to establish a linkage between biodiversity and cultural diversity" (Singh and Patil 2007). KBR is one of the fourteen Biosphere Reserves known for its unique biodiversity, and effectiveness as a conservation unit.

In Biosphere Reserves, eco-tourism takes place in a controlled manner. "There is a growing demand for eco-tourism and a demand for nature towns, despite a minimum of marketing and promotion. Six in ten tourists stated natural areas as very important reasons for their decision to travel. However, potential benefits of eco-tourism, both economic and environmental, are yet to be realized. The vast majority of parks are not in a position to gain financially from tourism because they do not provide adequate means for tourists to spend money. Most parks lack trained guides, interpretative information, entrance fee systems and basic infrastructure such as visitor centers. Significant opportunities to bring money into the park and to provide employment for local population are missed. Another lost opportunity is the education of visitors. Tourists experiencing a natural area directly are more apt to become involved in conservation if informed about the issues. Unfortunately, most parks do not have the personnel or programmers to educate tourists" (Modi 2001). Yuksam and Lachen of KBR (study area) are the important ecotourism spots of Sikkim in India. Besides ecotourism and religious tourism as Buddhist monasteries are important attraction for tourists.

Chawla states that "The study of tourism is complicated. There are large data availability and measurement problems and no thorough theoretical framework exists. There is not even agreement on the definition of tourism. The actual assessment of social and cultural impacts appears to be the lack of a logically structured impact classification" (Chawla 2003). The World Tourism Organization (WTO) states that tourism is "the activity of people who travel to places outside their customary surroundings and stay there for leisure, business or other purposes for no longer than one year without interruption" (WTO as cited in German Federal Agency for Nature Conservation, 1997). Tourism can be perceived as an opportunity to satisfy certain needs such as social prestige, sense of accomplishment of having seen places and relaxation etc. There is a psychological driving force behind tourism. An important feature of the tourism industry is its contribution to the national integration and creation of harmonious social and cultural environment. It also encourages respect for and preservation of monuments and heritage properties. It is accepted fact that besides preservation of biological diversity in the promotion of arts, crafts, and culture and bring about prosperity and sustainable development without much investment should also be helped. Modi opined that "The heritage of historical and valuable cultural objects is not the exclusive possession and responsibility of a single nation. Cultural treasures are of great interest to people all over the world. The challenge: how best can we preserve and develop there cultural assets that they can sustain a continuous and lasting process of tourism development. The international conference on Cultural Tourism in Jakarta in 1992 opened on this note. It was emphasized that the global community has led to the development of 'global cultural patterns'; that tourism has 'socio-cultural influences' on both the tourists and their host communities and with the advancement of knowledge on tourism, 'the debate has shifted from costs and benefits' to the recognition that 'both positive and negative impacts can simultaneously co-exist'"(Modi

2001). Affeld viewed that research on the social and cultural impact of tourism falls into three different categories, it had been concerned with:

1. The tourist: Such research has stressed the ramifications of the demand for tourist services and the motivations, attitudes and expectations of tourists;
2. The host: This research has emphasized on aspects of the offering of tourist services. It is concerned with the inhabitants of the destination area, the labour engaged in providing services and the local organization of the tourist industry; and
3. Tourist-host interrelationships: This research has been concerned with the nature of contacts between hosts and guests and with the consequences of these contacts (Affeld 1975).

While discussing about the impact of tourism Fox states that "The social and cultural impacts of tourism are the ways in which tourism contributes to changes in value systems, individual behaviour, family relationships, collective lifestyles, safety levels, moral conduct, creative expressions, traditional ceremonies and community organizations" (Fox, W. 1990). On interaction between the tourists and hosts, Sutton says "The tourist-host encounter in which one or more visitors interact with one or more hosts is staged within a network of goals and expectation" (Sutton 1967). UNESCO (1976) opined "the tourist-host relationship is characterized by four major features which are as follows:

1. its transitory nature;
2. temporal and spatial constraints;
3. lack of spontaneity; and
4. unequal and unbalanced experiences.

Growing animosity to tourism is not confined to the socially and economically deprived, but has also been expressed by politicians, academic, and even some businessman. Past reluctance to measure the shortcomings of tourism because of its economic benefits is fast disappearing. Resentment tends to be highest in what Jafari termed that 'tourist magnetic' areas, where tourism is the principle source of income and all activities become oriented to accommodating tourist demand, which may be limited to a short season (Jafari 1974). Although livelihood of residents may be derived from the visits of tourists, they view the approaching season with mixed feelings and value the off-season as only permanent residents remain present during off- season period. The physical presence of tourists in the area, the demonstration effect, resource control by the outsiders and encroachment in employment, all these make local people baffled. Added to this, the effect of tourism is also felt on moral conduct of the people specially in areas like prostitution, crimes and gambling etc. Mc Naught presents a strong case for positive role of tourism in that perhaps the best explanation of apparent demonstration effect is the simplest: 'tourism accelerates changes already underway' (Mc Naught 1982). While discussing on demonstrating effect of tourism Mathews opines that the demonstration effect encompasses daily patterns of consumption. Emulating the visitors the residents may adopt new clothing styles, begin eating and drinking imported food and beverages favoured by the tourist or aspire to obtain the transistor, radio, camera and other material goods so casually displayed by the tourist. Inability by the local to emulate the visitor, if so desired, may lead to a greater awareness of poverty, envy, frustration and consequent ill-will towards the visitor or to his compatriots who have been more successful. At the same time, fulfillment of the desire for more imported goods may have significant adverse economic effects. This is not a one-way process however, for on their return hours, tourists may, for example retain a taste for food and drink experienced abroad and seeks out ethnic restaurants or food stores. The view that tourism is a new form of colonialism and imperialism is one extreme perception of tourist development and its effects (Mathews 1977). In Christopher Holloway's words, tourism is largely psychological in its attractions (Holloway 1985). The psychology of the attractions of tourism is determined by the evolving culture and mores of the society which generate it. It has also been argued that competitive advantage in serving the tourism consumer of the future (whom Martin and Mason 1987 have described as the 'thoughtful consumer' and whom Henley Centre for Forecasting have described as Added Value Seekers) will be gained not by quality assurance systems alone, but by an instinctive passion for service, which is psychological in its nature as are the satisfaction of the tourists it serves. Smith defined cultural tourism as the absorption by tourists of features resembling the vanishing lifestyles of past societies observed through such phenomena as house styles, crafts, farming equipment and dress (Smith 1977). Ritchie has defined that cultural tourism as an element in the attractiveness of the tourism regions. The isolated twelve elements of culture which attract tourists to particular destinations have been delineated as follows: 1. handicrafts; 2. language; 3. traditions; 4. gastronomy; 5. art and music, including concerts, paintings and sculpture; 6. the history of region, including its visual reminders; technology which is used; 7. the types of work engaged in by residents and the technology which is used; 8. architecture, giving the area a distinctive appearance; 9. religion including its visible manifestations; 10. educational systems; 11. dress; and 12. leisure activities (Modi 2001). The early work of Nunez documented the interaction between Mexican villagers and urban tourists, noting rapid and dramatic changes in economic and political structures, land use patterns, and value systems. The acculturation theoretical framework is common to those pioneering studies and too many that have been undertaken subsequently. Anthropologists studying acculturation argue that when contact takes place between two cultures, it is usually the dominant culture influences the other one. These studies have the underlying assumptions that cultural change:

1. occurs primarily in the indigenous society's traditions, customs and values rather than in the visiting group; and
2. it leads to a gradual homogenization of cultures, in which the local identity is being assimilated into the stronger visiting culture (Modi 2001). Nunez states acculturation theory asserts that when two cultures come into contact for any duration, each becomes somewhat like the other through a process of borrowing (Nunez 1978). Borrowing is by no means symmetrical and is largely influenced by the nature of contact, the socio-economic profiles of interacting individuals or groups and the numerical differences in the populations.

While evaluating the issue Lea put much emphasis on economic impacts that out weighs other consideration in most assessments of tourism development of the third world (Lea 1997). Derecognizing the negative impacts of tourism linked with sustainable development, Robinson foresees tourist's desire for a participatory expertise in a distinctive and often remote natural and or cultural environment (Robinson 1997). Bezbaruah opines that the impact of tourism is often underestimated to the fact that tourism activity generates substantial amount in personal spending, business receipts, employment, income, and government revenue (Bezbaruah 2002). Pant attests that substantial benefits can be reaped from the impact of tourism specially for economic advancement, local development educational development, preservation of culture, tradition and natural environment and contribution to develop sustainable tourism (Pant 2003). Chawla states that "Tourism emerges as the largest global industry of the 20th century. In the new millennium global economy will be governed by Technology, Telecommunication and Tourism. Tourism has potential to create the maximum number of jobs. According to an assessment, in India alone, 100 million additional jobs will be created by the Tourism industry in the next 25 years. It helps to earn valuable foreign exchange. There has been rat race among the developed and developing countries to expand tourism indiscriminately, which has resulted, in severe cultural and ecological damages to the host country" (Chawla 2003). While substantiating on the impact of tourism, Raina and Lodha have estimated a dyadic principle of impact comprising socio-cultural parameter preserves folk traditions, cultural properties, art or history and it encourages education and training of human resource, contact with outside world, speedy knowledge and rediscovery of lost traditions. On the other hand, the economic factor creates job opportunities for unskilled / semiskilled people, foreign exchange, and diversification; and it improves infrastructure development, regional development, and standard of living (Raina and Lodha 2004).

"Tourism in Yuksam-Dzongri-Goechha La trekking trial was operative even before 1960 and tourist flow suddenly increased after 1990 due to relaxation in government rules (Rai and Sundriyal 1997). In 1998, about 1482 tourists came to Yuksam exclusively to trek in the high mountains. Additional 1379 visitors comprising of mountaineering trainees used this trek in 1998. Travel groups involve large number of support staff to organize the trek. Mostly, local travel agents from Gangtok and adjoining Darjeeling district of West Bengal organize the trekking. Domestic (resident) tourists without involvement of travel agents from Gangtok and adjoining Darjeeling district of West Bengal organize their own trek. Besides visitors, communities staying in the surrounding areas are also exploiting the natural resources of Khangchendzonga National Park by livestock grazing and extraction of fuel, fodder and timber" (Maharana et al 2000).

"The tourist season at Pelling is from 15th September to 15th December and from March to May. However Khangchendzonga Festival at Pelling, celebrated in October every year is one of the important occasions for increasing tourist flow at Yuksam. The domestic tourists are from West Bengal, Maharashtra, Delhi, Rajasthan, Karnataka, Tamil Nadu, Andra Pradesh, Orissa, Punjab, Hariyana, Uttar Pradesh and Assam. Most of the domestic tourists are from West Bengal. The foreign tourists visiting these sites are from England, Germany, United States of America, Sweeden, France, Australia, Italy, Holand, and Israel. The problems faced by tourists at Pelling are internet, All Time Money (ATM) Banking, road condition, health, shopping centres, money exchange facility etc. The tourist flow in Pelling from March to August,

2006 is 2998 and 28,352 for international tourist and domestic tourist respectively" (Tourist Information Centre, Pelling 2006).

"Although monetary valuation of natural ecosystems is difficult, such valuation helps to draw attention to their importance and highlight conservation needs, especially in developing countries. The recreational value of Khecheopalri, a lake situated in the West District of Sikkim state, India, which has recreational, biodiversity and sacredness values, was assessed. The demand curves function for recreation increased with decreases in travel cost and distance for Sikkimese visitors" (Maharana et al 2000).

Yuksam is the only settled village on this trail, with 11 settlements and 274 households with a total population of 1572. The last northern most hamlet of Yuksam village with nine households (Tibetan refugees) is located 16 kms. away from Yuksam at Tshoka on the trail to Khangchendzonga with a total population of 59 people. The most dominant ethnic group in Yuksam village is the Limbu followed by the Bhutia, Lepcha, Nepali and the Tibetan refugees. Most of them pursue traditional agricultural livelihoods while some are involved in tourism related activities in recent years. About 110 persons are involved as porters for tourist trek, eight families have lodges / hotels, 25 families rear Yak / Dzo to provide pack animals and 6 individuals are trained as local guides (Maharana et al 2000). "Before formation of Sikkim states in 1975 local pilgrims generally visit Yuksam, Khecheopalri and its adjoining areas. In 1981-82 foreigners are allowed to visit Yuksam. The sudden increase of tourists in Yuksam started from 1995 - 96 due to problematic situation in Kashmir" [Khangchendzonga Conservation Committee (KCC) 2006].

The present study refers to the area specially the KBR under the geographical and administrative entity of Sikkim, which is coterminous with the neighbouring countries of Nepal, Bhutan and China. Mountain Khangchendzonga lies on the north-west of Sikkim. Like many other states of India, Sikkim is a multi-ethnic, multi-lingual and multi-cultural state. There are Buddhists, Hindus and Christians co-exiting happily. Sikkim has three main ethnic groups: the Lepchas who were the original inhabitants of the state; the Bhutias who migrated from Tibet in the seventeenth century and the Nepalese whose migration from Nepal started in the nineteenth century. The most important resource of Sikkim is land controlled generally by individuals and terrace cultivation is reported as main stake of these communities. Hunting and gathering, shifting cultivation and settled cultivation were traditional occupations which have declined.

For the present study, the KBR has been selected where the prime focus has been to understand the impact of tourism. Since not many studies have been done earlier, the efforts has been made to undertake empirical study as well as to understand the concept of development in the light of developmental initiatives undertaken by the government and non-government agencies. The perception of the tourists *vis-à-vis* the local people have also been taken into consideration to understand the cognitive dimension of tourism that lies in the minds of the local inhabitants.

SIGNIFICANCE OF THE PRESENT STUDY

The people of Sikkim mainly sustain on its ecological set up and accordingly have adopted different types of economy that are related to their immediate environment.

The total gamut of the study duly considers the facets of sustainable development where impact of tourism is a part. Sustainable tourism is 'envisaged as leading to management of all resources in such a way that economic, social and aesthetic needs can be fulfilled maintaining cultural integrity, essential ecological process, biological diversity and life support systems'. A clear distinction should be made between the concepts of ecotourism and sustainable tourism: the term 'eco-tourism' itself refers to a segment within the tourism sector, while the 'sustainability' principles should apply to all types of tourism activities, operators, establishments and projects, including conventional and alternative forms. To understand the factors responsible for the impact of tourism in a particular locale, management is necessary to coordinate and synchronize the development of different sectors to balance competing and sometimes conflicting claims on the same limited resource base, to maximize the positive impacts of tourism development and to minimize its adverse effects. A well managed tourism at all levels is essential for achieving successful tourism. Some of the benefits of tourism management that have a direct bearing on the impact of tourism are:

1. Establishing the overall tourism development objectives and policies.
2. Development of tourism in a way that the natural and cultural resources are conserved for future.

3. Optimizing and balancing the economic, environmental and social benefits of tourism with equitable distribution of these benefits to society, while minimizing possible problems of tourism.
4. Providing the framework for effective coordination of the public and private sector efforts and investment in development tourism (Dinda 2007).

MAJOR OBJECTIVES:

Through the present study it is attempted to understand the following objectives: -

1. To understand the ecological background of the said area as a direct bearing force on the sustainability of the local people and others in each tourism sector.
2. To understand the economy that has involved people in managing tourism activity and its sustainability in each sector of tourism in relation to the tourists *vis – a – vis* other sectors of economy.
3. To understand the tourist's information in relation to the people involved in tourism and the local people.
4. To understand the socio-cultural and economic factors related to tourism that creates an impact on the life and culture of the people of KBR or vice versa.

Further, through the present study, it is also attempted to look into the following:

1. How far the exogenous factors of tourism have a direct bearing on the life and culture of the people of KBR.
2. How far the endogenous elements / matrix of socio-cultural and economic parameters have helped these impacts or it has resisted the impacts.

METHOD

The work was undertaken in order to have some basic and preliminary information about the present status of impact of tourism which prevailed in KBR and its adjoining region in Sikkim. For studying impact of tourism in KBR, the two main locales comprising of Yuksam, Tshoka, Khecheopalri and its adjoining areas in West District; and Lachen, Thangu, Gurudongmer and its adjoining areas in North District were selected. It is important to mention that Tshoka is the only inhabited hamlet of Yuksam – Dubdi Gram Panchayat lying in the core zone of

KBR. Both the Yuksam – Dubdi Gram Panchayat and Similarly Lachen village are in the fringe area of KBR. For gathering first hand information, structured schedule on tourists (total 204 schedules - 100 in Yuksam and 104 in Lachen covering both domestic and foreign tourists) were canvassed with a view to cover tourists profile in brief besides understanding the impact of local culture on tourists during their short stay there. The schedules on tourists were randomly canvassed in different locales – such as Yuksam and Khecheopalri in West district; Lachen, Thangu and Gurudongmer in North district. About 50 case studies, 25 each from the two study locations were also carried out. The local people were selected from different sectors of tourism such as hotel, restaurant, travel agent, shop, and guide and also from different ethnic background such as Bhutia, Lepcha and Nepali. Educational and religious backgrounds were also considered. People were also interviewed regarding environmental pollution such as land, water and air pollution. Impact of tourism has also been studied in the sphere of economic activities, material culture, political structure and religious life of the local communities. Major emphasis had been laid on the spheres like – change of economic activities; birth, marriage and death rituals; change of food habits; use of modern household utensils and electronics items; change of language and way of talking; change in community relationship; change of kinship terminology; change of dress; change of awareness about education; change in art, music, dance and folk songs. While gathering new experiences, indigenous knowledge out put, criminal activities, corruption, prostitution and drugs (PADS), gambling, damage of cultural norm, erosion of values in daily life and local politics, changes in religious activities; illegal transportation of forest products etc were also looked into. The study was conducted on a comparative basis to assess impact of tourism prior to 1995-96 with post 1995 – 96 (as tourist flow increases after 1995-96) in case of Yuksam. In case of Lachen the situation prevailing prior to 2003 – 04 was compared with post 2003 – 2004 situation (as tourist flow increases after 2003 – 2004). The present field work was carried out in the months of August- September and November- December, 2006 in Yuksam areas and in the month of May – June, 2007 in Lachen areas.

FRINGE VILLAGES

The villages are located in the altitude zone of 5000 – 9000 feet in West and North Sikkim. These villages consist of about 4,042 households having a total population of 16,013 (Census of India, 2001) of which about 75% are tribals. They are mostly subsistence level farmers, residing in these remote villages, adjacent to the Khangchendzonga National Park (KNP). Tshoka the only Tibetan hamlet of Yuksam – Dubdi Gram Panchayat has eight households and is located inside the KNP. The total area of KNP is 2619.92 sq. kms. of which 1784.00 sq. kms and 835.92 sq. kms. as core and buffer zones respectively (Department of Forest, Government of Sikkim 2006).

Table 1. Household and Population Structure of Fringe Villages of KNP

Revenue Block (West Sikkim)	*Households*	*Population*
Dubdi	69	402
Yuksam	364	1951
Tsozo	89	476
Khachodpalri	114	556
Meli	116	623
Melliaching	109	589
Topung	52	286
Singrangpung	47	227
Nambu	146	859
Kongri	71	442
Labdang	80	456
Dhupidara	76	493
Narkhola	82	510
Mangnam	64	380
	1,479	**8,250**
Revenue Block (North Sikkim)	*Households*	*Population*
Lachen	1609	2923
Shipgyer	166	695

Revenue Block (North Sikkim)	*Households*	*Population*
Tung	52	201
Lachen Forest Block	12	32
Salim Pakel	132	615
Lingthem	210	1161
Lingdem	97	542
Tingbong	164	1001
Lingzah-Tolung	80	397
Sakyong-Pentong	41	196
	2,563	**7,763**
Total	**4,042**	**16,013**

Source: Department of Forest, Government of Sikkim 2006.

The households details and population of the villages lying in the fringe of KBR are given in Table-1. Dubdi (household - 69, population – 402; Yuksam (household – 364, population – 1951), Khecheopalri (household – 114, population – 556); and Lachen (household – 1609, population – 2923) are revenue blocks under the present study.

The Lepcha villages were mostly inaccessible, with narrow paths through ravines and steep hillsides leading to them. Gradually the bridle – tracks are being replaced by motor able roads; the cane and bamboo made shift bridges are being substituted for by ones made of steel; educational institutions are being opened in the most remote villages. All these changes, no doubt, are bringing benefits in their wake, but they are also disturbing the balance within the ecosystems to which, for centuries, the Lepchas were so finally tuned.

THE PEOPLE

The population of, Yuksam, Khecheopalri and its' adjoining areas of West District, Sikkim consists mainly of the Nepalese, the Lepchas and the Bhutias. Of these, the Nepalese who themselves have a conglomeration of different ethnic groups, are the largest in number. The population of Lachen and its adjoining areas consists mainly of the Lachenpas i.e. Bhutias.

The Lepcha

The *Rongkup* ('children of *Rong'*) as they call themselves, are said to be the earliest settlers of Sikkim. There has always been controversy regarding their origin. In fact most Lepcha clans claim to have mythical connections with particular mountain peaks, which they worship as their deity and from which the clan is believed to have originated. Thus the mountains Simvo, Siniolchu, Kanchanjan find prominence in Lepcha culture.

Some philologists believe that the language belongs to the Tibet – Burman family while others have found its roots in the Austro – Asiatic family. The basis for these differing contentions has been due to similarities between the Lepcha language and the languages spoken by the Kharis, Mizo and tribes of Arunachal Pradesh. The life of the Lepchas is always mingling with the nature. They have developed an intuitive relationship with their environment. The Lepcha folk dances, songs and folk tales reflect this wonderful synthesis with the natural world.

The Lepchas are said to have embraced Buddhism since the 17th century onwards. There are the *'rum'*, the benevolent spirits or god – like deities and the '*mung'* the malignant spirits. These *mungs*, the Lepchas believe, reside everywhere, in the trees, bushes, rocks and rivers. Occasionally they possess human beings and bring illness and misfortune. The daily lives of the Lepchas, their religions and healing ceremonies are based in an effort to propitiate these *mungs* with ritual sacrifices and incantation. The *bongthing* and the *mun* hence play a significant role in the traditional family. The *bongthing* is a sort of priest, an exerciser and a healer.

The Bhutias

The Bhutias are considered to be mainly the descendants of the early settlers from Tibet and Bhutan who accompanied the ancestor of the first Chogyal, Phuntsog Namgyal. The early Bhutias and three distinctive social classes, the aristocracy, the quasi – aristocrats i.e. those who belonged to the leading Bhutia families who were land holders and had special powers conferred on them by the rulers and were called Kazis, and the commoners. When the monarchy was over these social distinctions also lost their relevance. Like the Lepchas and the Nepalese, the Bhutias are also agriculturists.

Tibetan Buddhism plays a dominant role in shaping the Bhutia society. The monastery and the monk work as the pivot around which their daily lives revolve. Every household ritual, marriage, birth, death ceremonies and agricultural rites are conducted by the monks from the *gompas*, which have a place of prominence in all the Bhutia and Lepcha villages. The faith generated by Buddhism is total and the devotion of the loyalty to the monastery and the monk is equally impressive. This relationship gives the Bhutia culture its dynamism and enduring quality. The prayer flags, the prayer wheels and the *chortens* are as much a part of their lives as faith in reincarnation and an almost obsessive desire to collect merit.

From every Bhutia family usually one male member enters the monastery and leads life of a monk. Bhutia villages, like the Lepchas, support these monasteries through regular donations. Till recent times the monks were considered the intellectual elite of the Bhutia society and education was the sole preserve of the monasteries. Today social status is no longer equated solely with monk hood and white collar jobs as well as government appointments have become equally attractive vehicles of social mobility. The Bhutia society is therefore, undergoing a subtle change. But the Bhutia culture has managed to retain its sense of pageantry and colour given to it by the very nature of the religion that sustains it. The monasteries are the main repository of Bhutia culture and the main social events are the festivals held in these monasteries.

Like the Lepchas and the Nepalis, the Bhutias are fond of their *chaang* – a preparation of fermented millet. It is served in bamboo containers (called *tongba*) with hollowed bamboo pipe. This drink may be called the state drink of Sikkim. It has become an indispensable part of Sikkimese ceremony, whether religious or social.

The Bhutias are famous for their weaving. The hand woven rugs, carpets and blankets from Lachen, Lachung are proof of this skill. All Bhutia art forms are derived from their Buddhist spirituality. They have produced *Thangka* painters. The Bhutia craftsmen are known for intricately carved statues objects of worship etc.

The Nepalis

The Nepali community of Sikkim is itself a mélange of diverse ethnic groups such as Magars, Murmis, Tamangs, Gurungs, Rais, Limbus, Damais, Kamis and the Chettris. The early Nepali settlers were brought by the British who needed labour force to work in the tea gardens of nearby Darjeeling. Government legislation prohibited the Nepali population settling in North Sikkim and most of the Nepali population, even today, is concentrated in the East, West and South Sikkim. The Nepalese with their drive and diverse skills made singular contributions to the development of Sikkim. Today many of them occupy important positions in the government. A large number are employed in professional jobs but the majority has remained farmers. The majority of the Nepalese population is either Hindus or Buddhists, with small minority converted to Christianity. The legacy of Hindu – Buddhist traditions tempered with tribal beliefs gives the Sikkimese Nepali culture a vigor and colour no less impressive and exotic than that of the Bhutias and the Lepchas.

The Hindu Nepali population of Sikkim follows the pattern which governs the Hindus living in other parts of India. However a parallel religion indigenous to the Nepalese co-exists with their Hindu beliefs. They practice a form of shamanism and the '*Jhankris*' have an important function in the Nepali society. This is the *Jhankri*, who by profession can be a tailer, a grocer, a carpenter or any common man, but who through a special calling has the power to exorcise evil spirits and witches ('*boksas' and 'boksis'*), which dwell in the forests and streams and cause illness or being misfortune.

Agriculture

In recent years the paddy fields have been transformed into large cardamom cultivation areas in agro forestry systems. Still, in many areas, a wide variety of agricultural practices are recorded from the region. The low land agricultural fields practice maize as the major crop followed by finger millet, buckwheat and variety of vegetables. Some hamlets in Yuksam - Dubdi Grampanchayat also practice wheat cultivation along with other vegetables. In high elevation area (Tshoka hamlet), potato is the major cash crop followed by cabbage, along with variety of other vegetables such as beet, raddish, carrot, beans and a number of green vegetables. Fruits like Guava, Pears, Banana, etc. are available here. Three decades ago, the villagers used to grow a wide variety of crops such as rice, maize, pea, *bajra,* cereals, green vegetables etc. but now they have slowly diverted to large cardamom because of its high economic value requiring low manpower.

Livestock

Income of the people mostly comes from composite source of agriculture, horticulture, tourism and animal husbandry. Livestock rearing was mainly done to produce milk, meat, manure, cheese and to use as pack animals along the trekking corridor. They rear cows, sheep, pigs and fowls for their subsistence livelihood. It is found that in some tourism potential areas, pack animals such as *dzo* and horse are widely used. A considerable number of *dzo*, yak and horse are also recorded from some part of the valley [*dzo* (7%), yak (3%), horse (1%), and pigs (15%)]. Livestock rearing seems to be dependent on farm size, family size and income. The collected data on livestock reveal field experiences that more number of sheep belongs to Gurung community, and yak and *dzo* to Tibetans and Bhutias [Khangchendzonga Conservation Committee (KCC) 2002].

Food Habits

The staple food of the local people is pulses, rice and vegetables with occasional inclusion of beef, pork, chicken, mutton and fish in their meals. Local delicacies include Stinging Nettle Soup *(Sisnoo ko Jhal)* Fiddlehead Fern (*Ningro*) with local cheese (*Churpi*), Fermented Mustard Leaf Soup (*Gundruk ko Jhol*), Mushroom (*Chaou*), Corn Porridge (*Dhendo*), Roasted Barley Porridge (Tchampa) taken with Sikkimese Tea (*Solja*). *Momo* along with soup is a very popular Sikkimese delicacy. Noodle with soup (*Thupka*) is readily available in most of the local restaurants. Sikkimese Tea *(Solja)* or Salt Butter Tea is made from tea leaves, butter and milk. Traditional warm beer (*Chhang* or *Tumba*) is made by fermenting millet using yeast (*Morcha*) and sipped from a bamboo or wooden container using a bamboo pipe.

Dress

The traditional dress of the Lepcha men is called *gada.* It consists of a long, beautiful striped cloth loosely worn down to the knee leaving one or both arms free. The *trouser* which reaches up to the calf only is called the *phomu.* Women wear the *dumdyan,* a full length robe, held at the shoulders by a pair of brooches and fastened at the waist.

The Bhutia costume for both sexes is called the *po-kho*, whereas that worn by women is called the *mo-kho.* Underneath the *kho,* a man wears a double-breasted, high-necked shirt, the *tson-ta-ti*, and pants (*gya-ton*).

The traditional costume of Nepali men consists of the *daura* and the *suruwal.* The *daura* is a knee-length doubled shirt, fastened at four points across the body by a string of cloth called the *tuna.*

Languages

Three major languages spoken in Sikkim are Nepali, Bhutia, and Lepcha. Due to the overwhelming presence of the Nepalese, Nepali has since long become the lingua franca of Sikkim.

TOURISM IN KBR

The key players in the ecotourism business are the governments at Central and State levels, the local authorities, the developers and the operators, the visitors and the local community. Each one of them has to be sensitive to the environment and local traditions and follow a set of guidelines for the successful development of tourism. In addition, non-governmental organizations and scientific / research institutions also have to play a key role in the development of eco-tourism. Each one of them has a set of standard operational guideline in eco-tourism (Bezbaruah 2002).

The administrative in charge of Khanchendzonga National Park (KNP) in KBR is Join Director, Department of Forest, Government of Sikkim. Department of Tourism, Government of Sikkim has also offices at Yuksam and Lachen. Lachen Police Check Post is an important office regulating tourism in a strict way as it is a border area. Indian Military has performed prominent role in promoting tourism in Gurudongmer Lake. Khangchendzonga Conservation Committee, an NGO, has played an important role in promoting eco-tourism in Yuksam. Lachen Tourism Development Council is newly constituted local body.

Land and Tourism Potential of Yuksam

The area of KNP extends from 27°29′4″ north latitude and 88°9′18″ to 88°15′ east longitude. The park bordering with Nepal occupies about 25 per cent of the total geographical area of Sikkim with an elevation ranging from 1829 to 8586 meters. The KNP in the Eastern Himalaya was notified by the Sikkim Government in August, 1977 and was later expanded to 1784 sq. kms. in May,1997. This park lies between the lowland of Yuksam (1780 meters) Khangchendzonga (8586 meters). The accessible trail, better known as Yuksam – Dzongri-Goche-La is about 45 kms. long in distance that extends from the temperate to Alpine zones and covering areas such as Sachen, Bakhim, Tshoka, Phethitang, Dzongri Base camp, Thansing etc. Its diverse tropical mixed broad – leaved forest, sub-alpine conifer – rhododendron forest, alpine meadows, cascading streams, sacred lakes, a wide variety of birds and flowering plants and panoramic view of the world's third highest mountain – Mt. Khangchendzonga – are a few among the tourists delight. The trail leads to Goecha La, which provides a panoramic views of Mt. Khangchendzonga surrounded by Mt. Pandim, Mt. Kabur, Mt. Narsing and many other snows capped mountain. The KNP lies along the extensive forest areas with many pristine patches of forests. Tshoka and

Dzongri are situated on at the ridge lifted out from Onglathang and Tey-Gyap-La valleys. Two rivers flowing through these valleys namely Prek Chu and Rathong Chu nurture two main tributaries merging into the River Rangeet, which is one of the two main rivers of Sikkim. On 7th February 2000, the Ministry of Environment and Forests, Government of India notified KNP as a Biosphere Reserve with a total area of 2192 sq. kms. The newly notified KBR area includes the settlements of Bakhim, Thsoka, Karjee, Gangyap, Labdang, Khecheopalri, Chong, Dubdi and Yuksam in its southern periphery, within the conservation area. While other settlements such as Sakyong, Chungthang, Menshithang, Lachung, Monguthang and Lachen are located in its northern periphery.

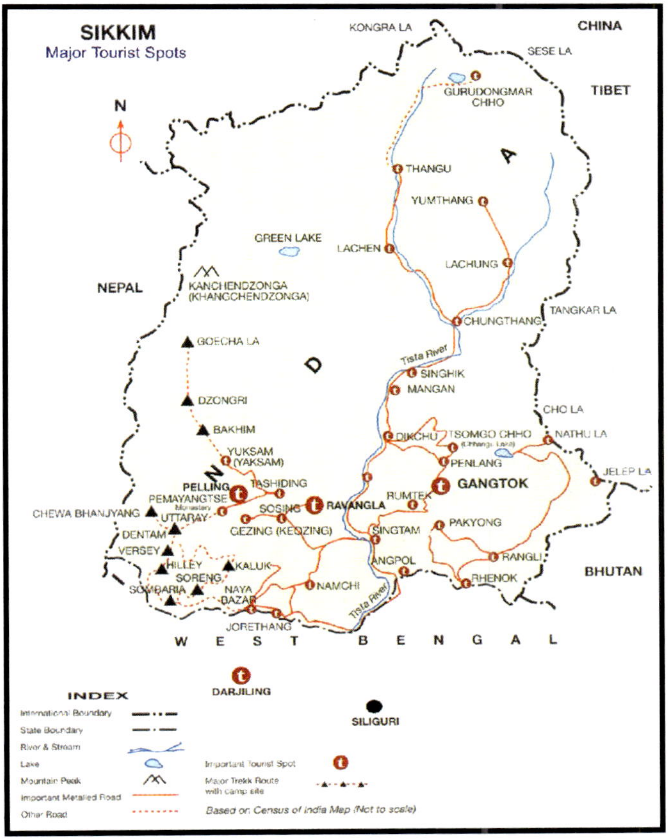

Places of Tourist Interest in Yuksam, Khecheopalri and adjoining areas.

Pemayanatse Monastery, Pelling, Khecheopalri Lake, Yuksam, Dubdi Monastery, Khang-Chen-Dzonga water fall, Rabdentse Ruins, Sanga – choling Monastery, Singshore Bridge / Uttarey, Rangit water world, Tashiding Monastery, Kongrt – Labdang, Varsey, Soreng, Rinchenpong – Kaluk Hee Beermiok, Dentam, Sirijonga Yuma Manghrm Mortam, Sirijonga Fooku and wadhan (cave), Limboo cultural centre, Tharpu etc. are the tourists spots of West Sikkim.

With the establishment of the first Buddhist monastery at Dubdi near Yuksam, Buddhism was introduced into Sikkim and was a State Religion until Sikkim became a part of India in 1975. A stone throne shaded by a 300 years old Cypress tree still stands here today. A foot-print on stone in front of the throne is said to belong to Lhatsun Namkha Jigme (follower of Padmasambhava, Nyngmapa sect) and is worshiped by the Sikkimese people. Opposite this throne is the Norbugang *Chorten* [stupa], which contains soil and water from all over Sikkim, Norbu Gang is the oldest *chorten* built in Sikkim and is believed to contain conch shell, hair and cloth of past and present Buddha and also contains cloth of Maha - Maugdalayana and Sariputra (two disciples of lord Buddha). It also contains left foot shoe of Lord Padma Sambhava and hair of Khandu Yashe Chogay (consort of Lord Padma Sambhava). Thus Yuksam, the first capital of Sikkim occupies an important place in Sikkimese history and the history of modern Sikkim starts from here.

Dubdi monastry, the oldest Buddhist monastery in Sikkim is located on the top of a hill about an hour's walk from Yuksam. Dubdi translates to 'Hermits Cell' and was founded by Gyalwa Lhastun Namkha Jigme in the year 1701. There are two monasteries at Dubdi, and the smaller

Dubdi Monastery at Yuksam.

Gurudongmar Lake in North Sikkim.

one is dedicated to the protector deities of the region. The people of Yuksam offer offerings of newly harvested food crops every season to thank these deities for their blessings. Kathok and Khecheopalri are two important lakes in this area. Khecheopalri known as, 'wishing lake' is one of the most sacred lakes of Sikkim. It is believed that Khecheopalri Lake was originally at Yuksam. However the people made it unpopular by dumping carcass of donkeys, dogs and other animals, polluting the lake and hence destroyed its sanctity. It annoyed the deities of Khecheopalri Lake and hence shifted to the current location at Khecheopalri. On the 15th day of the first month of the Tibetan calendar, a big *puja* is organized by the monk of Khecheopalri Monastery and the community of Khecheopalri village in order to propitiate the lake deities to avert disease, natural calamities and personal harm.

Sikkim is also known as '*Demazong*' by the Sikkimese people, which translates to "hidden valley full of treasure, fruit and flower". It is considered as a sacred land blessed by the Saint Padma Sambhava. '*Neysol*', describes that the whole region around Khangchendzonga [The mountain of five magnificent treasures] has hidden treasure or '*ters*' which will be revealed in the course of time. In the month of August during Panglhabsol festival, Buddhist monks perform rituals and prayers in the name of the Khangchendzonga deity. The monks and the devotees go all the way upto Dzongri 'Dhaplha Gang' to offer prayers and rituals to Khangchendzonga deities for good harvest and to free the whole country and world from disease, hunger, famine, war etc. There are all together 109 existing large and small lakes in Sikkim regarded sacred by the Sikkimese people. No one dares to pollute these lakes and all the streams and lakes are considered as holy. Besides the Khangchendzonga area, there are four holy caves in the four directions of Sikkim viz, Lhari Nying Phu in North direction, Dechen Phu in West direction, Khandu Sang Phu in South direction and Bas Phu in East direction. Out of these four holy caves, the cave of Lhari Nying Phu and Dechen Phu are in remote corners and amidst forest. These areas are religiously protected. Therefore any large-scale disturbance by human beings in this area is not allowed. It is feared that any such act will destroy these hidden treasures and harm the people themselves.

Since the whole region surrounding Khangchendzonga is regarded as very sacred, Yuksam is considered to be a 'Lhakhang' or altar for offerings to the Khangchendzonga deities. The seven holy lakes surrounding Khangchendzonga viz, Khecheopalri, Kathok Tso, Bar Cho Marpu, Phu Cho Karpu, Ka Bur La Tso, Sume Ten Tso and Dafuk Yum Tso are the seven offering bowls to the Khangchendzonga deities. Every landscape of highland, middle land and low land and every river, stream, cave, big trees are believed to have guardian deities *(yullha, Zibda)* of their own and therefore during the morning ritual in every monastery, these deities are worshiped with great devotion.

Gandak Sempa Chempo established a Monastery at the holy place of Dhakar Tashiding (the elevated glorious white rock). The site of the monastery at the high promontory between the junction of the Great Rangit and the Rathong River is believed to have been miraculously raised up by Saint Padma Sambhava.

The Khangchendzonga Trekking Trail

Yuksam the first capital of Sikkim, has 11 settlements with a population of about 2500 persons. It is a trail head for Dzongri, Thangsing, Goche La and Khangchendzonga Base Camp in West Sikkim. The tourist trekking corridor extends over a distance of over 26 km from Yuksam to Dzongri at the elevations ranging from 1780 m to 4000 m. One settlement with 7 households is located on the trail at Tshoka (3000 m). The Department of Forest, Environment and Wildlife, Government of

Sikkim is the sole authority responsible for management and protection of the reserve. Along this trekking trail, there are camping sites at Sachen, Bakhim, Tshoka and Dzongri.

Tourism Potential of Lachen

At Chungthang where the route dissects, one curls up to Lachung a good 18 kms. up hill while the other move up to another highland village, Lachen. Negotiating 29 kms. up crazy spurs, the Lachenpas (i.e. the Bhutias of Sikkimese origin) lives sprawled upon an easy spread of land sitting on an incredibly high hill. No wonder the old folks had called it Lachen meaning high pass. The road then continues to wind up to Chopta valley at a dizzying 4,023 meters and then in at Gurudongmer Lake, the last point at 5,243 meters. At Lachen anyone could bump into expedition groups either relaxing or gearing up to begin the Green Lake Trek or the Khangchendzonga expedition. In the old days this must have been a similar camping site for those great caravan trains trundling up towards Tibet or descending down to Gangtok.

The caravan trail to Tibet was a lot easier from Lachen than from Lachung, so this was the route preferred by the traders. It is believed by the local people that this village might have got significance for being on the trail just like that of neighbouring Lachung. But after the Chinese occupation of Tibet in 1959, the trade route was closed and with the Chinese aggression of 1962, several roads connecting to the border areas were hurriedly built to facilitate military operations and one such road run between Lachen and Gurdongmer. The aftermath of the Indo-Chinese hostility came as a blessing in disguise for the area. Lachen was privileged with the benefit of a highway leading to one of Sikkim's most exquisite tourist site, Gurudongmer, a chance for a slice of the pie in the state's travel trade.

Lachen village is typically traditional and retains its age old practice of the "*Dzumsa*" (traditional village council). Here people still raise yaks and keep migrating with their herds. Tega revealed that his family still owns 250 yaks. It is the head of a family who becomes the 'Khepo' meaning a member of the *Dzumsa*. Community service is still prevalent and each 'Khepo' is required to offer his physical services. Even yak migration and slaughter is only undertaken when the '*Dzumsa*' appropriates the dates. "It is usually by November end that around 300 yaks are slaughtered and its meat preserved for consumption throughout the year.

Lachen's monastery is called 'Ngodup Choling'. Preserved within its chapel are centuries old statues brought from Tibet. Its annual '*Chaoim*' (musk dance) is held in its grassy courtyard, and is an auspicious event for the people.

Deep down in the gorge as the Lachen chu rushes along, you could try interpreting this rivers song. Somebody, sometime on a lazy afternoon or a sleepless night memories of Lachen will surely rush back with the river's song.

Places of Tourist Interest at Lachen

'Lachen' meaning the Big Valley is situated at an altitude of 2987 meters. It takes about six hours to reach here by road from Gangtok. The village is said to have been blessed by the Goddess "Domai Rhee". The title *Lachenpa* is used by all the original inhabitants of this valley though they are Bhutia of Sikkimese origin. Restricted Area Permit (RAP) or Protected Area Permit (PAP) are needed for those visiting Lachen and other nearby sites. Foreign tourists are allowed to go up to Lachen only. The best season for visiting the Lachen valley is from in early March to middle June, a time when valley enchants the flower lovers. Mere the tourist spots are worth visiting are as follows -

Thangu

Thangu is located 30 kms. from Lachen at an altitude of 3962 meters. Tree lines disappear at Thangu and then start the alpine zone. It is a small picturesque hamlet. Thangu is regarded as the base camp for the Thangu – Muguthang – Chorten – Nyimala – Green Lake Trek.

Chopta valley and Muguthang

Chopta valley just a 20 minutes drive from Thangu. It provides one of the few accessible places in Sikkim where one can actually walk over the frozen rivers. Muguthang (4572 meters) is well known for its famous annual yak race festival.

Gurudongmer Lake

Gurudongmer is one of the highest lakes which lies in the north side of Khangchendzonga and is encircled all around by snow-capped mountains. Conspicuously the sacred lake freezes during winters but only in part. This Cold desert is one of the most attractive spot on way to Gurudongmer Lake.

Green Lake

Lachen – Green Lake Trek is considered as one of the most beautiful trek in the region. Green Lake is exotic water body green in colour. The peaks of Simvo are a short distance. At the base of the Khangchendzonga is the Zenu Glacier full of a sea moraines, rocks and boulder and debris created by moving ice scrapping the mountainside – a veritable natural pulveriser. Once in a while the distant thunder of avalanches can be heard resounding in the emptiness. The glacial snow peaks surround the region on either side of the valleys. The landscape transforms into a snowy desert.

Chungthang

Chungthang lies at the confluence of the Lachen chu and the Lachung chu. From Chungthang the road bifurcates for the Lachen and Lachung valleys. The spot worth visiting at Chungthang is the rock on which legend has it, Guru Padmasambva rested and the imprint on it is said to be his footmark. It is said that here Guru Padmasambva had sprinkled a handful of grains and paddy grows here ever since as blessing of the Guru.

Lachen – Dzumsa System

The local governance system of Lachen valley is unique. This system is called the *Dzumsa* system. It literally means the "gathering place". It is the traditional institute in-charge of administering and organizing activities within a given territory (Lachen and Lachung). as well as to the general council of villagers composed of household heads. This system of self-governance was initially established during the first half of the 19th century in order to provide structure and cohesion for these societies and their activities. During the reign of the erstwhile kings of Sikkim, the Dzumsa and the Pipon (village chief) were recognized pro administering these local areas. In the year 1970s, when the Indian Government initiated the reorganization of Sikkim's administration and introduced the Panchayatraj system, the new system was not imposed in Lachen and Lachung, and but the Dzumsa continued as officially recognized system which continues to function even today.

Tourism At Yuksam

Tourists of different types such as explorers, adventurers, cultural tourists, expedition's troop, trainees of Himalayan Mountainairing Institute, pilgrims, scientists, students of both domestic and foreign visit Yuksam, Khecheopalri and its adjoining areas. Unique flora and fauna along with Himalayan unique natural ecosystems attract adventurers, explorers, expedition's troop and others to visit KBR. A section of people sustain with the help of running hotel, restaurants, shops (Eco-Development Committee out let for promoting locally hand made artifacts, woolen goods etc.), and tour operators; involved as guides and porters, etc. jobs. In this way eco-biological set up of Khangchendzonga has influenced in shaping 'tourism based culture' at Yuksam. Though the numbers of trekkers is low in KBR area at Yuksam, the Government of Sikkim tries to maintain trekking paths throughout the year with the help of local people. The local people protect the natural forest from the devastation of fire. The local people have form a non-government organization named Khangchendzonga Conservation Committee (KCC) which creates awareness about conservation among common people. The local people strongly believe in Khangchendzongaas their sacred deity. They have full faith in stone worship. Hence the local people do not want to disturb mountainous range for constructing any type of hydroelectricity project. In this way eco-biological and cultural factors of KBR have influenced in shaping the tourism though in a limited way at Yuksam.

The local people are depended on traditional agriculture besides transhumance activity (yak and sheep grazing) and occasional gathering of roots, tubers and medicinal plants. After declaration of Biosphere Reserve in 2000, forest department imposed certain rules and regulations on gathering and grazing in certain parts of the reserve area. Limited trekkers' movement in Yuksam does not show much impact in nearby areas except the economic benefit. The Bhutias who are traditionally traders are now involved in tourism as there is no scope for them to follow traditional occupation. Following the Bhutias, the Nepalese also got involved in tourism sectors such as hotel, travel agents, restaurant and others. The Lepchas are however lagging behind in terms of their involvement in tourism in major way except as porters.

The Lachenpas, i.e., the Bhutias are traditionally dependent on agriculture, transhumance activity (Yak, sheep and cattle grazing) and occasional gathering of roots, tuber, medicinal plants etc. They were a trading community. Bamboo (locally known as *chowa*), natural colours (locally known as *majito* and *geetha*), wood plank (locally known as *singlep*), etc. items were traded with Tibet. Generally goods were transported by yaks and they use horses. Sheep wool, sheep meat, blanket, carpet, red salt (locally known as *tsa*), etc. were brought from Tibet to Lachen as trading material. Trading season was for five months from April to August. The Lachenpa also carried food and other items to defense persons with the help of Yak and horse. After Chinese aggression in 1962, this type of trading was stopped. The Lachenpas were also engaged in collection of Minor Forest Produces (MFP) occasionally. Such MFP collection included *Dhup* (incense) locally known as *sang* (a type of incense resin, having present value of Rs. 40/ per kg.), *jatamashi* (a type of incense resin), *chhimto* (a type of incense resin), a type of medicinal plant (locally known as *kurki*, available near glacier, selling at Rs. 80/ per kg) etc. A section of local people have yaks (cost around Rs. 17000/ per yak, use for its' meat, skin, tail with hair, milk, ghee, *chhurpi*, etc.), sheep (cost around Rs. 1100/ use for its' wool, meat, etc.) etc. are source of income for local people. Declaration of Khangchendzonga as Biosphere Reserve and subsequent imposition of ban on collection of forest produces has posed problems to these people. Forest Department has also declared ban on yak and sheep grazing in the reserve area. The above mentioned factors acted as causal factors pushing people to orient themselves for some other professions. Metal road from Gangtok to Gurudongmar via Lachen is now open for tourism purpose. The tourist flow in Lachen has increased in recent years (2003-2004). Some of the Lachenpas have their property at Chungthang and at Gangtok also. Their background of being traders and also above-mentioned circumstances led them to get involved in tourism industry.

Generally the travel agents of Gangtok and Darjeeling book the hotels / lodges both at Yuksam and Lachen for the tourists as package. They carry rice, vegetables, fish, drinking water etc. from Gangtok along with cooks and helpers to facilitate tours of tourists. Tourists generally reaches in evening at Yuksam and Lachen after completing day's journey. Next day, trekkers at Yuksam generally leave for Tshoka while those at Lachen visit Gurudongmer lake.

Tourist Flow:

The tourist flow as recorded by the Department of Forest, Gechhen Check Post, Government of Sikkim at Yuksam shows that most of the tourists are from West Bengal, Maharashtra, and Madhya Pradesh. Peak tourist season is October and May while lean tourist season is January and from June to August (Table 2).

Table 2: Domestic Trekking Tourist Flow

Domestic Trekking Tourist Flow from Yuksam 2005													
State / Organization	*Jan*	*Feb*	*Mar*	*Apr*	*May*	*Jun*	*Jul*	*Aug*	*Sept*	*Oct*	*Nov*	*Dec*	*TOTAL*
Maharashtra	3	0	0	43	33	0	0	0	36	18	0	0	**133**
West Bengal	17	35	15	52	153	14	3	0	5	285	85	157	**821**
Haryana	0	0	0	0	0	0	0	3	0	0	0	0	**3**
Kerala	0	0	0	0	0	0	1	0	0	0	0	0	**1**
Uttaranchal	0	0	0	0	0	0	0	0	0	10	0	0	**10**
Andhra pradesh	0	0	0	0	8	0	0	0	0	0	0	0	**8**
Karnataka	0	0	0	11	0	0	0	0	0	10	0	0	**21**
Madhya Pradesh	0	0	52	5	39	0	0	0	0	0	0	0	**96**
Sikkim	0	1	0	8	1	0	0	0	0	0	8	6	**24**
Punjab	0	0	0	0	0	0	0	0	0	1	0	0	**1**
New Delhi	0	0	0	1	4	0	2	0	0	4	0	11	**22**
Tamil Nadu	0	0	1	2	2	0	0	0	0	6	0	0	**11**

State/Organization	*Jan*	*Feb*	*Mar*	*Apr*	*May*	*Jun*	*Jul*	*Aug*	*Sept*	*Oct*	*Nov*	*Dec*	*TOTAL*
Jharkhand	0	0	16	0	2	0	0	0	6	0	0	11	**35**
Manipur	0	0	0	0	0	0	0	0	0	0	0	21	**21**
Uttar pradesh	0	4	0	0	16	0	0	0	0	0	0	0	**20**
Meghalaya	0	0	0	0	3	0	0	0	0	0	0	0	**3**
Defence service	0	18	0	0	0	0	0	0	0	0	0	0	**18**
Total	**20**	**58**	**84**	**122**	**261**	**14**	**6**	**3**	**47**	**334**	**93**	**206**	**1248**

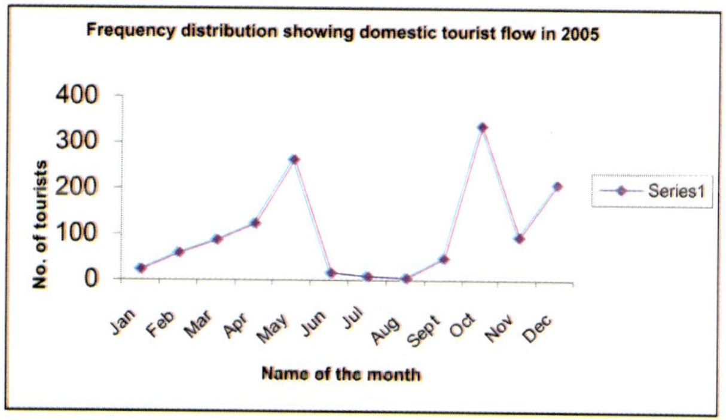

Source: Department of Forest, Gechhen Check Post, Government of Sikkim and Frequency Distribution prepared by the author.

Table 3: Domestic Trekking Tourist Flow

Domestic Trekking Tourist Flow from Yuksam 2006													
State	*Jan*	*Feb*	*Mar*	*Apr*	*May*	*Jun*	*Jul*	*Aug*	*Sept*	*Oct*	*Nov*	*Dec*	*TOTAL*
Sikkim	0	4	6	0	32	0	0	4	13	7	16	0	**83**
West Bengal	0	5	132	135	121	0	0	2	145	229	77	0	**845**
Haryana	0	0	2	12	0	0	0	0	0	0	0	0	**14**
New delhi	0	0	1	0	5	0	0	0	0	11	3	0	**20**
Gujarat	0	0	2	4	0	0	0	0	0	0	0	0	**6**
Karnataka	0	0	0	35	17	0	0	0	5	14	0	0	**71**
Assam	0	0	0	63	0	0	0	0	2	8	0	0	**73**
Maharashtra	0	0	0	15	53	0	0	0	0	16	0	0	**84**
Tamil Nadu	0	0	0	0	1	0	0	0	0	0	0	0	**1**
Jharkhand	0	0	0	0	0	0	0	0	22	0	0	0	**22**
Mizoram	0	0	0	0	0	0	0	0	0	1	0	0	**1**
Meghalaya	0	0	0	0	0	0	0	0	0	0	0	2	**2**
Total	**0**	**9**	**143**	**264**	**229**	**0**	**0**	**6**	**187**	**286**	**96**	**2**	**1222**

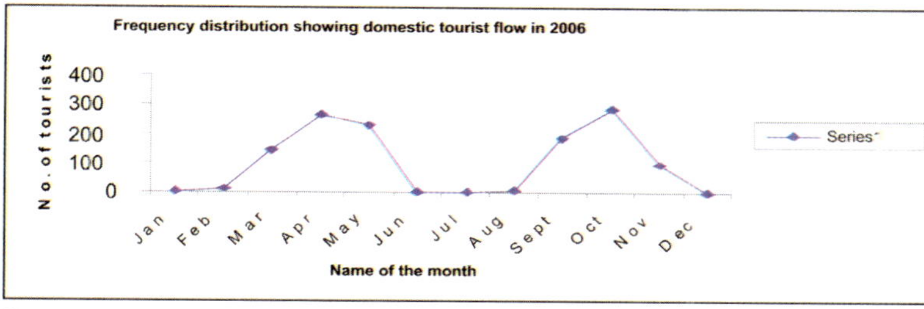

Source: Department of Forest, Gechhen Check Post, Government of Sikkim and Frequency Distribution prepared by the author.

Most of the trekking tourists are from West Bengal. It appears from the tourist records that the peak tourist season for domestic tourists in 2006 was October, April and May. Lean tourist season was December to February (Table 3). From the above tables, it is clear that tourists from many states of India visit Yuksam.

The tourist records of 2005 shows that most of the foreign tourists visiting Yuksam are from U.S.A., U.K., Australia, Germany, Netherland, France and Switzerland respectively up to 12th April to December, 2005 (Table 4).

Table 4 : International Trekking Tourist Flow

International Trekking Tourist Flow from Yuksam 2005 (12/04/2005 to Dec 2005)

Country	*April*	*May*	*June*	*July*	*Aug*	*Sept*	*Oct*	*Nov*	*Dec*	***Total***
Equador	0	0	0	0	0	0	1	0	0	**1**
Australia	27	12	0	0	0	20	20	44	34	**157**
Korea	0	0	0	0	0	1	0	1	0	**2**
Canada	15	22	1	0	0	2	9	7	0	**56**
Hungary	0	0	0	0	0	1	7	0	1	**9**
Germany	16	4	0	0	0	11	78	34	3	**146**
Mexico	0	0	0	0	0	1	0	1	0	**2**
Austria	1	1	0	0	0	3	5	5	0	**15**
Jordon	0	0	1	0	0	0	0	0	0	**1**
Switzerland	13	7	1	0	0	9	39	20	2	**91**
Malaysia	0	2	0	0	0	0	7	2	0	**11**

Country	*April*	*May*	*June*	*July*	*Aug*	*Sept*	*Oct*	*Nov*	*Dec*	***Total***
France	27	17	1	0	0	5	55	24	0	**129**
Poland	0	4	0	0	0	2	4	4	1	**15**
U.S.A	49	26	14	0	0	4	83	48	7	**231**
Singapore	0	5	0	0	0	3	12	12	11	**43**
Thailand	4	0	0	0	0	0	1	1	0	**6**
Indonesia	1	0	0	0	0	0	0	0	0	**1**
U.K.	34	45	7	1	0	9	80	48	4	**228**
Greece	2	0	0	0	0	0	0	0	0	**2**
Nether-lands	19	23	0	1	0	1	68	28	2	**142**
China	0	3	0	0	0	0	0	2	0	**5**
Italy	4	1	1	0	0	9	19	4	0	**38**
Russia	0	13	0	0	0	0	0	0	0	**13**
Belgium	6	3	0	0	0	8	17	21	0	**55**
Denmark	0	6	3	0	0	0	7	6	0	**22**
Ireland	2	3	0	0	0	2	0	0	0	**7**
Spain	1	17	0	0	0	0	26	10	0	**54**
Israel	4	4	2	0	0	1	11	12	3	**37**
Brazil	1	2	0	0	0	0	0	0	0	**3**
S.Africa	1	0	0	0	0	0	0	0	1	**2**
Japan	19	0	1	0	0	0	0	3	0	**23**
New zealand	9	1	1	0	0	1	3	3	0	**18**
Sweeden	3	2	0	0	0	2	40	12	0	**59**
Czeck Rep	1	16	0	0	0	2	21	3	0	**43**
Norway	2	2	0	0	0	0	3	0	0	**7**
Lebanon	2	0	0	0	0	0	0	0	0	**2**
Finland	0	0	0	0	0	0	1	0	0	**1**
Portugal	0	0	0	0	0	0	2	1	0	**3**
Lithuania	0	0	0	0	0	0	2	0	0	**2**
TOTAL	263	241	33	2	0	97	621	356	69	**1682**

Source: Department of Forest, Gechhen Check Post, Government of Sikkim.

Table 5. International Trekking Tourist Flow

International Trekking Tourist Flow From Yuksam

2006 (Up to Nov 2006)

Country	*Jan*	*Feb*	*Mar*	*Apr*	*May*	*June*	*July*	*Aug*	*Sept*	*Oct*	*Nov*	*Total*
Japan	1	0	0	1	14	0	0	0	0	1	1	**18**
Korea	0	0	0	1	0	0	0	0	0	0	0	**1**
S. Africa	0	0	0	5	2	0	0	3	0	0	2	**12**
Czec Republic	0	0	0	4	10	0	0	0	0	25	16	**55**
France	2	0	22	18	18	0	0	1	3	63	41	**168**
Mexico	0	0	1	0	0	0	0	0	0	0	0	**1**
Canada	0	6	13	10	7	0	0	4	0	16	7	**63**
Belgium	0	0	14	2	0	0	0	0	0	4	8	**28**
Germany	0	1	8	19	10	0	0	0	7	91	29	**165**
Brazil	0	0	1	0	0	0	0	0	0	0	0	**1**
Netherlands	2	1	0	40	8	0	0	0	3	97	24	**175**
Newzeland	0	0	0	0	3	0	0	0	0	7	9	**19**
U.K.	5	4	34	111	65	0	0	0	4	103	31	**357**
Argentina	1	0	0	0	0	0	0	0	0	0	0	**1**
Poland	0	0	5	5	7	0	0	0	1	7	10	**35**
Denmark	0	2	5	3	6	0	0	0	0	1	0	**17**
Ireland	0	0	3	9	1	0	0	0	2	1	6	**22**
Hungary	0	0	0	1	0	0	0	0	0	1	2	**4**
Australia	2	3	21	39	35	0	0	0	8	17	19	**144**
Taiwan	0	0	0	0	2	0	0	0	0	0	1	**3**
Russia	0	0	2	6	7	0	0	0	5	24	6	**50**
Singapore	0	0	0	13	1	4	0	0	0	11	0	**29**
Indonesia	0	0	0	0	1	0	0	0	0	0	0	**1**
Switzerland	0	0	6	14	18	0	0	0	4	29	7	**78**
Estunia	0	0	0	0	0	0	0	0	0	0	6	**6**
Israel	0	0	13	16	12	0	0	0	7	15	9	**72**

Country	*Jan*	*Feb*	*Mar*	*Apr*	*May*	*June*	*July*	*Aug*	*Sept*	*Oct*	*Nov*	*Total*
Ukrain	0	0	0	10	0	0	0	0	0	0	1	**11**
U.S.A.	0	1	48	63	36	0	0	0	8	75	28	**259**
Spain	0	0	3	12	4	0	0	0	0	20	0	**39**
Romania	1	0	0	0	0	0	0	0	0	0	1	**2**
Sweeden	0	0	9	9	1	0	0	0	0	4	15	**38**
Phillipines	0	0	0	0	0	0	0	0	0	4	0	**4**
Italy	0	1	0	3	2	0	0	0	0	19	3	**28**
Thailand	0	0	0	0	0	2	0	0	0	0	1	**3**
Austria	0	0	0	3	4	0	0	0	0	14	8	**29**
Finland	0	0	0	5	1	0	0	0	0	0	2	**8**
Portugal	0	0	0	0	1	0	0	0	0	0	0	**1**
Norway	0	0	1	1	4	0	0	0	0	0	0	**6**
Slovakia	0	0	0	5	4	0	0	0	0	0	0	**9**
Malaysia	0	0	0	8	0	0	0	0	0	0	0	**8**
Total	14	19	209	436	284	6	0	8	52	649	293	1970

Source: Department of Forest, Gechhen Check Post, Government of Sikkim.

While comparing the Table 4 and 5 for two years i.e., 2005 and 2006, it is seen that there is increasing inflow of tourist (17 per cent) and most of foreign tourists were from U.K., U.S.A., Netherlands, Germany, and Australia respectively up to November 2006. Foreign tourists were very much less in case of Korea, Indonesia, Finland, Portugal, Argentina, Romania, and Jordon.

About 50 domestic tourists were interviewed in 2006 (Table-6). Among surveyed 50 domestic tourists, 50.00 per cent, 14.00 per cent, 12.00 per cent, 8.00 per cent, 6.00 per cent, 6.00 per cent, and 4.00 per cent tourists are from West Bengal, Jharkhand, Delhi, Maharashtra, Uttar Pradesh, Tamil Nadu, and Goa respectively.

Table 6. Sex wise Domestic Tourists in 2006

Sl. No.	*State*	*Male*	*%*	*Female*	*%*	*Total*	*%*
1.	West Bengal	18	36.00	7	14.00	25	50.00
2.	Delhi	4	8.00	2	4.00	6	12.00
3.	Jharkhand	4	8.00	3	6.00	7	14.00
4.	Uttar Pradesh	3	6.00	0	0	3	6.00
5.	Goa	2	4.00	0	0	2	4.00
6.	Maharashtra	3	6.00	1	2.00	4	8.00
7.	Tamil Nadu	2	4.00	1	2.00	3	6.00
	Total	36	72.00	14	28.00	50	100.00

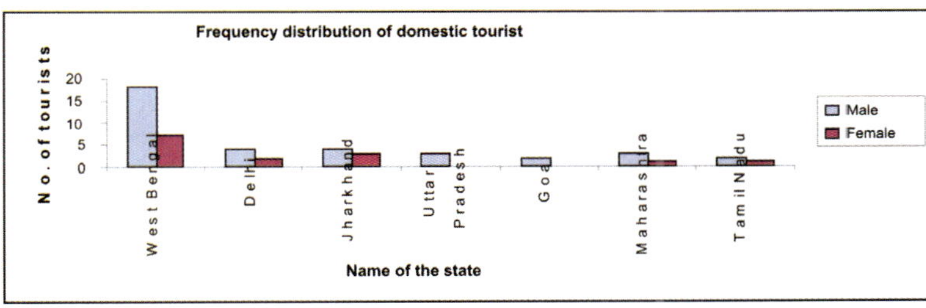

In order to find out the flow of foreign tourist about 50 foreign tourists were interviewed. Of the total interviewed tourists, surveyed, 18 per cent tourists are from United Kingdom. Each 12 per cent are from France, U.S.A., and Canada respectively. About 10 per cent are from Germany. About eight per cent tourists are from Singapore. Each four per cent tourists are from New Zealand, Netherlands, Argentina, and Nigeria. Each two per cent tourists are from China, Russia, Israel, Italy, Finland and Australia respectively. From the above tables, it indicates that the percentage of female domestic tourists is less (28 per cent) while in case of foreign tourists, females are higher in percentage (60 per cent) compare to their male part.

Table 7: Sex wise Foreign Tourists in 2006

Sl. No.	Name of the Country	Male		Female		Total	
		No.	%	No.	%	No.	%
1.	**Asia**						
	1. China	1	2.00	0	0	1	2.00
	2. Russia	1	2.00	0	0	1	2.00
	3. Singapore	1	2.00	3	6.00	4	8.00
	4. Israel	1	2.00	0	0	1	2.00
2.	**Europe**						
	1. Germany	2	4.00	3	6.00	5	10.00
	2. United Kingdom	3	6.00	6	12.00	9	18.00
	3. France	2	4.00	4	8.00	6	12.00
	4. Newzealand	0	0	2	4.00	2	4.00
	5 Netherlands	1	2.00	1	2.00	2	4.00
	6. Italy			1	2.00	1	2.00
	7. Finland	1	2.00	0	0	1	2.00
3.	**North America**						
	1. U.S.A	3	6.00	3	6.00	6	12.00
	2. Canada	3	6.00	3	6.00	6	12.00
	South America						
	Argentina	1	2.00	1	2.00	2	4.00
4.	**Australia**	0	0	1	2.00	1	2.00
5.	**Africa**						
	1. Nigeria			2	4.00	2	4.00
	Total	20	40.00	30	60.00	50	100.00

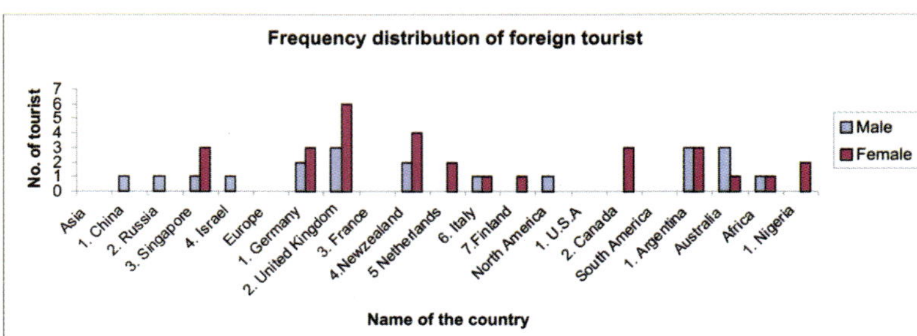

Tourism at Lachen

Tourists of different types such as adventurers, pilgrims, expedition's troop, scientists and students of both domestic and foreign origins visit

Lachen, Thangu, Gurudongmer and its adjoining areas. Unique flora and fauna along with Himalayan unique natural ecosystems attract adventurers, explorers, expedition's troop and others to visit Lachen and adjoining areas of KBR. A section of people sustain them by running hotel, restaurants, shops; working as tour operators, guides, porters, etc. Though the numbers of trekkers are less at Lachen, the Government of Sikkim always maintains trekking paths throughout the year with the participation of the local people. The local people protect the natural forests from fire. In view to protect healthy environment, the local people protested against constructing a hydroelectricity power project at Lachen. Tension between government and local people of Lachen lasted for a long period on this account. The Lachenpas of this area strongly believe in Khangchendzonga as guardian deity. They worship all most all elements of nature like stone, tree, water body, hills etc. Hence the local people do not want to disturb mountainous range by constructing any type of hydroelectricity power project. In this way eco-biological and cultural factors of KBR have influenced in shaping the tourism though in a limited way at Lachen.

Tourist Flow at Lachen

In order to assess the tourist inflow data on tourist vehicles passing through Lachen Police Check Post from October 2006 to May 2007 were relied upon as no such records were available otherwise (Table 8).

Table 8. Tourist vehicles passing through Lachen Police Check Post from October 2006 to May 2007

Month	*Numbers*
January 2006	10
February 2006	23
March 2006	59
April 2006	135
May 2006	93
June 2006	13
August 2006	18
September 2006	26
October 2006	91
November 2006	87
December 2006	27
Total	582

Frequency distribution showing flow of Tourist Vehicles passing through Lachen

Police Check Post

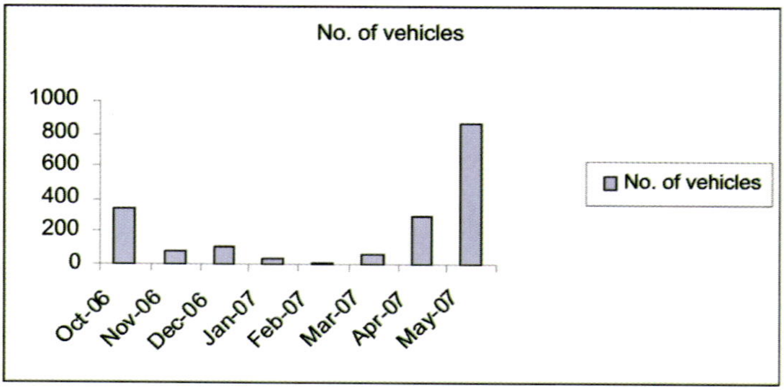

Source: Lachen Police Check Post and frequency distribution prepared by the author.

On an average each vehicle carries seven tourists. Around 12,700 tourists have visited Lachen in two peak seasons of the years 2006 and 2007 i.e. from October, 2006 to May, 2007.

As regards foreign tourists, it is observed that around 582 foreign tourists visited Lachen in 2006. April, May, October and November were peak months for foreign tourist (Table 9)

Table 9: Foreign Tourist flow in 2006 at Lachen

Month	*Numbers*
January 2006	10
February 2006	23
March 2006	59
April 2006	135
May 2006	93
June 2006	13
August 2006	18
September 2006	26
October 2006	91
November 2006	87
December 2006	27
Total	582

Frequency distribution showing month wise foreign tourist flow in 2006 at Lachen

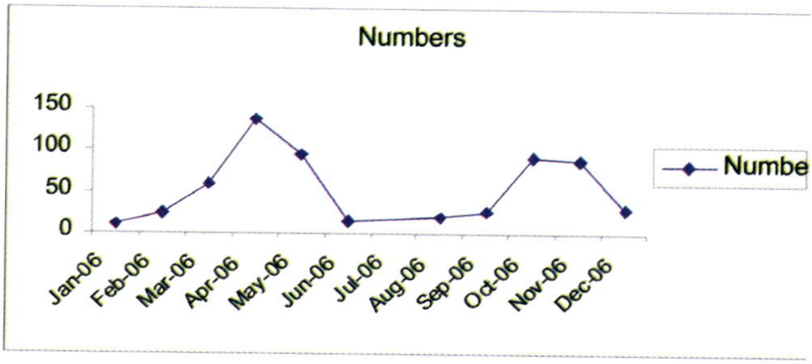

Source: Lachen Police Check Post and frequency diagram prepared by the author.

Table 10: Foreign tourists flow from January 2007 to May 2007 at Lachen

Sl. No	*Name of the hotel/lodge*	*Owning Community*	*Year of Establishment*
1.	Hotel Dzongrilla	Bhutia	1992
2.	Hotel Wild Orchid	Do	1995
3.	Hotel Tashigang	Do	1997
4.	Hotel Pemathang	Do	1999
5.	Hotel Dragon	Do	2003
6.	Hotel Yangrigang	Do	2004
7.	Hotel Demazong	Do	2005
8.	Hotel Arpen	Nepali	1991
9.	Kabur Lodge	Do	2000
10.	Hotel Narshing	Bhutia	2004
11.	Hotel Sherpa	Do	2006
12.	Hotel Blessing	Do	2006

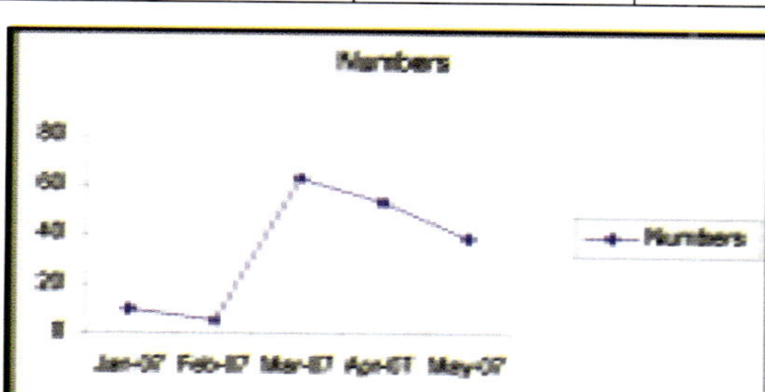

Source: Data collected at Lachen Police Check Post and frequency diagram prepared by the author.

With regard to foreign tourist flow in 2007 from January to May, 2007, it has been observed that the foreign tourists flow is higher from March to May in 2007 (Table 10).

The author has interviewed 102 domestic tourists in 2007. The details are given below in the Table 11.

Table 11: State wise surveyed domestic tourist at Lachen

Sl. No.	*State*	*Male*	*%*	*Female*	*%*	*Total*	*%*
1.	West Bengal	54	52.94	6	5.88	60	58.82
2.	Maharashtra	13	12.75	1	0.98	14	13.73
3.	Andhra Pradesh	5	4.90	1	0.98	6	5.88
4.	Sikkim	5	4.90	0	0	5	4.90
5.	Gujrat	3	2.94	0	0	3	2.94
6.	Tamil Nadu	3	2.94	0	0	3	2.94
7.	Rajashtan	3	2.94	0	0	3	2.94
8.	Assam	2	1.96	0	0	2	1.96
9.	Orissa	1	0.98	0	0	1	0.98
10.	Uttar Pradesh	1	0.98	0	0	1	0.98
11	Jharkhand	1	0.98	0	0	1	0.98
12.	Madhya Pradesh	1	0.98	0	0	1	0.98
13.	Bihar	0	0	1	0.98	1	0.98
14.	Kerala	1	0.98	0	0	1	0.98
	Total	93	91.17	9	8.82	102	99.99

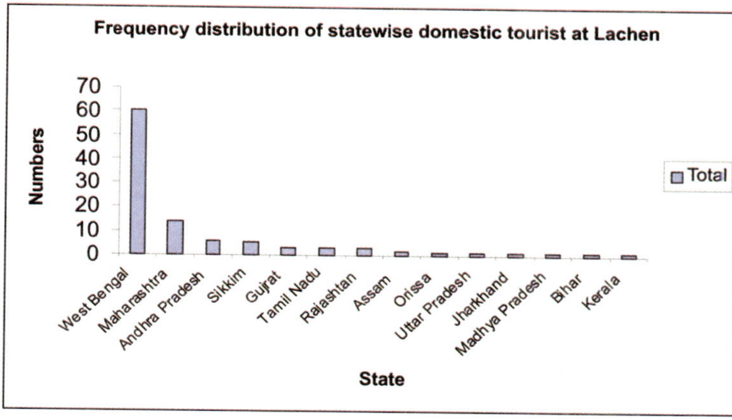

Tourists at Lachen check-post.

A view of hotels at Lachen.

Most of the tourists interviewed are from West Bengal. Others are from Maharashtra, Andhra Pradesh, Sikkim, Gujarat and so on. Two foreigners from France were also interviewed during the field work. They had desired that the foreign tourist should also be allowed to visit Thangu and Gurudongmer.

Tourists generally start their journey from Yuksam on or around 7-00 a.m. so that they can reach at Thoska in the evening and take rest in right. In case of Lachen also, tourists also perform their journey early in the morning around 5-30 a.m. so that they can visit Gurudongmer before wind begins blowing strongly. Here time is an important factor in every type of trekking. Therefore, the hotels as well as home stay owners try to maintain time schedule of trekkers and provide them early morning tea and snacks. Generally the shops are opened in the early morning to facilitate the trekking troops to get their necessary daily provisions - rice, vegetables, fruits, bread, kerosene oil, etc. The travel agents collect these fresh items with help of their team members, cook, porter, guide, etc. In the mean time travel agents ready the pack animals Dzo for the journey. All of them show good discipline, commitment, and trust for the trekkers in this adventurous journey. Tourists interact with the guides, porters, cooks and others on the way to Thsoka, Gochala and Dzongri and also display keen interest to know about the local people and their economic condition, food habits, dress, religion, political structure, life cycle rituals, arts, crafts, music and dance, cooking etc. In this way interaction between tourists both national and international and the local communities go on.

Whenever any land slide takes place on way to Yuksam and Lachen, it disrupt the transport of local people as well as the tourists

Tourism linkages with local Institution at Yuksam and Lachen

Khangchendzonga Conservation Committee (K.C.C.), monastery and local panchayat are the main organizations have direct contact with tourism.

Khangchendzonga Conservation Committee

K.C.C. is a community based Non-Government Organization based in Yuksam It comprises of representatives from different communities and stakeholders involved in tourism enterprises. It works for conservation of natural and cultural resources to mitigate negative impacts with skill development programmes, awareness campaigns, monitoring of natural resources along with advocacy for appropriate policy changes. K.C.C. also supplies kerosene stoves to each trekking group to avoid use of firewood inside biosphere reserve. They create awareness among tourists about not to drop polythene packets in the trekking trail. K.C.C. has opened home stay facility for tourists in different hamlets of Yuksam – Dubdi gram panchayat. During November – December, 2006, the school children from Singapore visited Yuksam and they visited Yuksam – Dzongri trail organized in collaboration with K.C.C. The troop participates in creating awareness among local people about the importance of biosphere reserve. They had also identified the different trees with name plates. K.C.C. also manages garbage disposal in such areas flourishing as the tourism.

Monastry

"Monasteries in Sikkim are of three kinds viz – (a) Tak –phu, literally a rock – cave or cave heritage; (b) Gomp, literally "a solitary place" or monastery proper; and (c) the so called "gompas" founded in or near villages. The latter are, as a rule, merely temples (hla-khang) with one or more priests engaged in ministering to the religious wants of the villagers" (Gazetteer of Sikhim, 1973). Most of the tourists visit monasteries and observe its paintings, symbols and rich cultural heritage. People of the monastery and monks perform sort of a role of social leader and encourage local people to participate in the activities related tourism to improve their economic condition.

Panchayat

Local *panchayat* along with K.C.C. make efforts to spread awareness about conservation among local people, garbage management, etc.

Pipon and Lachen Tourism Development Committee, school and monastery at Lachen play positive roles in promoting tourism.

Pipon and Lachen Tourism Development Committee

Pipon has authorized Lachen Tourism Development Committee to do work along with UNDP for the growth of tourism in the region. Making pucca footpath, providing street light along the road, maintenance of drainage system, keeping the area clean, etc. are some of the works being carried out by this organization.

Tourists' Perception about Tourist Places and the People

Domestic tourists viewed that local people were friendly, peace loving, pleasant, well dressed, colourful in nature, had respect for their religion, etc. Some of the domestic tourists viewed that knowledge of utilizing agricultural land at local level was very unique as land remained scarce. Foreign tourists also opined similarly that local people were very friendly, peace loving, had respect for their religion, religious symbols, cultural norms etc. They were trust worthy and careful about their attire. Very few foreigners have privilege to see the daily life of local people, feel spirituality and respect for life. Some of them eat traditional food. Some of them expressed views about the local peoples' concern for the environment. Home Stay facility at Yuksam was a unique experience to the tourists. Some of the foreign and domestic tourists opined that people should not built high rise *pucca* building at Yuksam.

Contrary to this, some of the foreign tourists expressed their view about the problems of tourism at Yuksam such as:

(i) poor maintenance of trekkers' hut;

(ii) poor toilet facilities,

(iii) garbage problem,

(iv) shortage of camping site during peak season,

(v) shortage of drinking water, etc.

Some of the tourists opined that entry permission for trekking inside the reserve should be at Yuksam also.

Most of the tourists viewed that Gurudongmer Lake is unparallel to any high altitude tourist spots.

Problems identified by tourists at Lachen are as follows:

(i) land slide at Gangtok – Lachen road

(ii) food quality

(iii) cheating by the travel agents (travel agents of Mumbai, Delhi, Kolkata, Gangtok and other places) as they collects huge amount for accommodation in hotels room rent while room rents are comparatively lower at Lachen etc.

Some of the tourists were of the opinion that the there should be facility of providing oxygen at Gurudongmer Lake on payment basis as it is high altitude location. Tourist Information Centre should be at Lachen. Some of the foreigners opined that they should be allowed to visit Thangu and Gurudongmer lake and should also be allowed to go for trekking. Some of them expressed that the local people have little knowledge about garbage management at Lachen.

Local Peoples' Perception about Domestic and Foreign Tourists at Yuksam and Lachen

One local Bhutia lady doctor appreciated "tourists sense of

admiration, their sense of enthusiasm to know more about local culture and value what we have here with us". Domestic tourists are well behaved, but not so disciplined and generally fail to stick to time schedule unlike foreign tourists. Local people acquire knowledge about different communities of the area, their food habit, dress, language, life style, etc. Foreign tourists are well behaved, disciplined, soft spoken, gentle, maintain time schedule for visiting any place, and have penchant for cleanliness. Foreign tourists spend more than domestic tourists. Foreigners generally use the term *namastay* when they meet with the local people. They try to gather information on matters related to sacredness of the land, panchayat system, Buddhist religion, home stay, *Dzumsa* system (local political organization), etc. from the locals.

IMPACT OF LOCAL CULTURE ON TOURISTS

Tourists visiting Yuksam can be put into two categories. One category comprises of those tourists who do not go beyond Yuksam. At Yuksam they visit Norbugang, Kathok lake, Dubdi Monastery and enjoy beauty of mountain and falls. The other category comprise of those tourists whose main purpose is trekking from Yuksam – Dzongri to Gochala. In both cases tourists do not stay for longer period at Yuksam. The climatic condition throughout the year is not congenial for tourists to visit local peoples' houses. Hence, it is most impossible for tourists to interact with local people frequently. However the impact of local peoples' culture on tourists does carry some impression.

Tourists visit monasteries, wheel of life, Eight Lucky Signs, Prayer Flags, chortens etc. Monastries and many buildings in Sikkim are richly decorated with symbols and icons. These symbols are painted or embossed on the walls or on *Tankas*. These paintings may depict the life of Buddha or some Tibetan saint, the wheel of life or a deity surrounded by lesser deities. The wheel of life is one of the purest Buddhist emblems. This emblem can be seen at the entrance of almost all monasteries. This emblem is also widely depicted on Tankas or religious scrolls. The Eight Lucky signs are called as Tashi Tagye in Tibetan. These auspicious signs are intimate with life and teachings of Buddha. These eight lucky signs manifest themselves in paintings and in the form of carvings on furniture and can also be seen on the walls of buildings.

The prayer flags can be seen almost anywhere in Sikkim - on hill, or building tops – an integral part of the landscape of Sikkim. These flags have prayers inscribed on them. Chortens or stapes dot every nook and corner of Sikkim, chortens are normally found concentrated around monastries. In old times, the *chortens* were built as relic holders but now they are erected in memory of Lord Buddha or some Buddhist saint. The Prayer wheel is a religious implement on which holy mantra is inscribed and which is held in the hand and rotated with the motion of the wrist. Some of the tourists draw symbols of the Buddhist rich religious heritage. They express about the richness of the Buddhist religion.

The comparatively high paid tourists of Yuksam stay at Tashiding hotel. Tashiding hotel arranges cultural dance for tourists by engaging people of Gechhen colony of Yuksam. The group performs the Nepali, Lepcha and the Bhutia dance. It, in turn, revives lost cultural traditions. Tourists also enjoy it. The rich cultural heritage of the local people creates an impact on the tourists.

The tourist flow is increasing day by day in Yuksam. It, in turn, adds to accumulation. In such a remote place, the local people are aware about garbage management through K.C.C. They generally use fire for destroying garbage. The local people have a plan for transporting garbage to a distant place if the government authority provides them vehicle. The local people have put posters "not to throw plastic or any garbage in paths and trekking route". It creates awareness among tourists about cleanliness and garbage management.

Tourists witness monastries, buildings, wheel of life, eight lucky signs, prayer flags, *chortens* etc. Monastries and many buildings in Sikkim are richly decorated with symbols and icons. These eight lucky signs manifest themselves in paintings and in the form of carvings on furniture and can also be seen on the walls of buildings at Lachen. The prayer flags, *chortens*, prayer wheel, etc. are witnessed by the tourists at Lachen. They express about the richness of the Buddhist religion. Tourists enjoy *gompha* dance (locally known as *chham*), *khabju* (locally known as *day* for removing evil spirits from house) and different festivals at Lachen. Tourists also observe blanket and carpet making and sometimes also interacts each other.

IMPACT OF TOURISM ON ECONOMY

The increasing tourist inflow has led local people to get engaged in a variety of professions. Tourism offers a number of new employment opportunities such as owning hotel / lodge / restaurant / shop, working as tourist guides, porter, working as travel agents, attendants in hotel / lodge and restaurant, etc. in Yuksam and Khecheopalri area and also in Lachen and its' adjoining areas. To some extent it has impacted the traditional economy of the area.

There are 75 hotels, eight restaurants and six travel agencies at Pelling, one of the entry points for the tourists. Some of the tourists from Pelling visit Yuksam. Trekkers generally reach Yuksam directly from Gangtok and Darjeeling. There are 12 hotels / lodges at Yuksam. Community wise hotel / lodge owners with year of establishment are given below:

Table 12: Community wise Hotel / Lodge at Yuksam

Sl. No	*Name of the hotel / lodge*	*Owning Community*	*Year of Establishment*
1.	Hotel Dzongrilla	Bhutia	1992
2.	Hotel Wild Orchid	Do	1995
3.	Hotel Tashigang	Do	1997
4.	Hotel Pemathang	Do	1999
5.	Hotel Dragon	Do	2003
6.	Hotel Yangrigang	Do	2004
7.	Hotel Demazong	Do	2005
8.	Hotel Arpen	Nepali	1991
9.	Kabur Lodge	Do	2000
10.	Hotel Narshing	Bhutia	2004
11.	Hotel Sherpa	Do	2006
12.	Hotel Blessing	Do	2006

Of the hotels / lodges owners, about 67 per cent are the Bhutia and about 33 per cent are the Nepali. About 17 per cent hotels / lodges came up before 1995. Two new hotels were coming up at Yuksam during the field visit period. There are altogether 102 rooms available in Yuksam which can accommodate 208 persons. Mountain lodge, Norling Café and Restaurant cum lodge, Himalayan Cafe cum lodge, and another lodge without name do their business in Tshoka. Most of the hotels have no fixed room rent.

Table 13: Hotels / Lodges at Lachen

Sl. No.	*Name of Hotel / Lodge*	*Year of Establishment*
1.	Gurudongmar Lodge	1997
2`.	Hotel Sonam Palgey	1998
3.	Bayel Inn	1999
4.	Lachen Tourist Centre	1999
5.	Twins Peak Lodge	1999
6.	Hidden Hill Lodge	2002
7.	Hotel Snow Peak	2002
8.	Sonailchu Lodge	2002
9.	Green Lake	2002
10.	Hotel Doma Ray	2004
11.	Juniper Mountain Resort	2004
12.	Mount Pandim Lodge	2004
13.	Without name (Owner Bandhu Lachenpa)	2005
14.	Lichen Khangri Lodge	2005
15.	Bichung Lodge	2005
16.	Shangrilla Retreat	2006
17.	Tsopta Valley (now stopped)	2006
18.	Tso Lahmit	2006
19.	Without name (Owner-Pema_Lachenpa)	2006

With the tourist flow increase at Lachen, number of hotels / lodges has also increased. About six lodges have taken on contract by peoples who stay at Gangtok and are non Lachenpa. Hotel Tashidekh is situated at Chhaten near Lachen proper. Four hotels / lodges are at Thangu proper three lodges are at Chopta valley proper. The rent for double bedded room varies from Rs. 250/- Rs. 600/-. Four new lodges are coming up in the heart of Lachen. Most of hotel / lodges are run by family members. All these hotels / lodges have nearly 30 persons deployed as staff who attend to the needs of tourists and cook food as per their demand viz. Bengali, South Indian, North Indian, Western etc.

Home Stay

Besides hotels / lodges, K.C.C has introduced home stay facility among 12 villagers. 'Home stay' is a unique system. Here the tourists stay along with owners of the houses and thus get an opportunity to interact directly with the local people. It, in turn, and get to know about their life style, food habit, customs, religion, etc. with limited communication capacity. In Khecheopalri, there are four home stay units while there is no home stay facility available at Lachen.

Restaurant

There are five restaurants at Yuksam. Three restaurants are owned by the Bhutias while one each by a Nepali and a Bihari family respectively. Gupta Restaurant is comparatively bigger one. Yangrigang hotel also has as restaurant facility.

Table 14: Details of Restaurant at Yuksam

Sl. No	*Name of the Restaurant*	*Owning Community*	*Year of Establishment*
1.	Gupta Restaurant	Bihari	1992
2.	Yak Restaurant	Bhutia	1996
3.	Norling Restaurant	Nepali	1997
4.	Gamgrogamt Restaurant	Bhutia	1997
5.	Tashinam Restaurant	Bhutia	1998

Most of the restaurants are opened after 1996. They serve North Indian food, South Indian food, Bengali food and different types of Chinese food as preferred by different foreign tourists. Most of the restaurants serve food as per tourists' desire. In Khecheopalri, one petty restaurant serves food for the tourists.

Shops

There are 40 shops at Yuksam including government fair price shop, grocery, vegetable, general stores, liquors, shoe, pan (betel leaf) etc. belong to Nepali, Bhutia, and Lepcha communities. Besides these, a finance company named SIDHE Private Company is also doing their business. One Lepcha lady runs a petty pan shop near Norbugang. Most of the pan shops are run by the Bhutia women. Five shop owners are from Motihar district (3), Sitamari district (1) and Patna (1) of Bihar state. One shoe shop owner is from West Bengal. There is one government Community Information Centre (CIC). It has few computers along with internet and photocopying facilities.

Table 15: Details of Shops at Yuksam

Sl. No.	*Type of Shops*	*Owning Community*					
		Nepali	*Bhutia,*	*Lepcha*	*Behari*	*Bengali*	*Total*
1.	General stores	4	5	0	2	0	11
2.	Grocery	6	2	0	1	0	9
3.	*Pan* (Betel Leaf)	5	2	1	1	0	9
4.	Vegetable	2	1	0	1	0	4
5.	Ready made Garments and gift items	0	2	0	0	0	2
6.	Foot Wear	0	1	0	0	1	2
7.	Tea	0	1	0	0	0	1
8.	Liquor shop	1	0	0	0	0	1
9.	Travel Agency	0	1	0	0	0	1
	Total	18	15	1	5	1	40

Most of the groceries shops are of the Nepali people. General stores are owned by the Nepalis and the Bhutias. In general stores they sell items like mineral water, cold drinks, biscuits, etc. Most of the *pan* shops are owned by the Nepalis. Generally the ladies run the *pan* shop. Ready made Garments and gift shops are exclusively of the Bhutias. Only one liquor shop is there whose owner is Nepali. Among six shops, three shops are of the Bhutias (one *pan* shop and two grocery shop), two *pan* shops are of the Nepalis and one pan shop is of the Lepchas.

There are 21 shops at Lachen proper. Out of these, three are petty tea stalls. One tailoring shop belongs to a Jadav family of Bihar. Other shop owners are from Lachen itself. Shops are mixed in nature. Grocery, liquor, stationary, gift items, etc. are sold in these shops. Blanket (locally known as rok), small carpet, *chamar* (articles used for *pujas* locally known as *juma*, made from Yak hair), woolen cap, cap made from Rabbit wool etc. are items in few shop.

Travel Agency

Travel agencies are one of the important components of tourism industry. Only one permanent travel agent for local route is available at Yuksam. The permanent route, distance, and number of vehicles plying on those routes are as follows :

(i) Yuksam to Gangtok (only two vehicles, 130 kms.)

(ii) Yuksam to Gerethang (only four vehicles, 64 kms.)

(iii) Yuksam to Gyalshing via Pelling (four vehicles, 35 kms.).

Besides these ten vehicles, which are regularly plying on these routes, 18 other available on hire vehicles are also operating there for tourism purpose. Of these 18 vehicles, seven vehicles each are owned by the Nepalis and the Beharis respectively. The remaining four vehicles are owned by the Bhutias. Most of the hotel owners have linkages with the travel agents/agencies of Gangtok like Alpine Etoss, Namgyal Trekks and Tours, Marcopolo Tours and Travels, Khangri Truss Trekks, Sikkim Holiday Travel Agent, Bayal Trekks, Sinoilchu Tours, Altitude Tours and Travels, Himalayan Explorer, Wisdom Tours and Travels, etc. Besides these, some of travel agents from Darjeeling are also operating tours at Yuksam. Most of the domestic and foreign tourists visit Yuksam with the help of these travel agents of Gangtok and Darjeeling. Travel agents generally bring with them all the required items including ration, vegetables, etc. They only use hotels of Yuksam for their temporary night halt before leaving for trekking and after returning from trekking. It takes four days to trek to Dzongri, five days to Dzongri - La –and eight days to Go-Cha-La from Yuksam including return.

Only two vehicles for local route ply between Lachen and Chungthang. Besides these vehicles, 22 vehicles are available on hire. The Lachenpa are the owners of these vehicles. Most of the hotel owners have link with the travel agents/agencies of Gangtok. Some of these are Marcopolo Tours and Travels, Khangri Trvels, Omega Travels, Tempo Travels, Zimbale Tours and Travels, Khangsharp Tours and

Table 16: Use of Tourist Attendants by Domestic Tourists in 2005

	Jan	*Feb*	*Mar*	*Apr*	*May*	*Jun*	*July*	*Aug*	*Sept*	*Oct*	*Nov*	*Dec*	*Total*
Guide	4	6	6	17	35	1	2	1	8	38	17	7	**141**
Porter	4	3	4	49	83	1	5	5	19	108	30	30	**341**
Pack Animal	3	15	28	35	90	0	0	0	24	153	17	9	**374**
Total	**11**	**24**	**38**	**101**	**208**	**2**	**7**	**6**	**51**	**299**	**64**	**46**	**857**

Table 17: Use of Tourist Attendants by Domestic Tourists in 2006

	Jan	*Feb*	*Mar*	*Apr*	*May*	*Jun*	*Jul*	*Aug*	*Sept*	*Oct*	*Nov*	*Dec*	*Total*
Guide	0	1	15	24	31	0	0	1	12	51	10	0	**145**
Porter	0	2	64	58	63	0	0	4	60	113	32	0	**386**
Pack Animal	0	0	102	104	65	0	0	0	104	27	57	0	**459**
Total	**0**	**3**	**181**	**186**	**159**	**0**	**0**	**5**	**176**	**191**	**99**	**0**	**990**

Travels, etc. Most of the domestic and foreign tourists visit Lachen with the help of travel agents of Gangtok. Travel agents generally carry all the items including ration, vegetables, etc. necessary for trekking. They use hotels of Lachen as their night halt only.

These travel agents have their own tourist guides to be provided to the tourists. There are about 26 local tourist guides in Yuksam, besides few more as casual guides. Each 13 tourist guides of Yuksam are Nepali and Bhutia. These tourist guides do not get job regularly. In Khecheopalri one gentleman and one lady of the Bhutia community serve as tourist guides. Local tourist guides generally earn about Rs. 250 per day from domestic tourists and Rs. 400-500 from foreign tourists. Local tourist guides prefer to do work with the foreign tourists as remuneration is attractive. Besides, they also get huge amount of tips in cash and also in kinds like dress, shoes and other items. Local trekking guides also mention about some problems such as (i) tourism department deducts Rs. 10 from guide for each day i.e. for nine days trekking they deduct Rs. 90 (ii) tourism department does not widen the route of trekking.

Use of tourist attendants in the form of guide, porter and pack animal by domestic tourists in 2005 and 2006 are as follows in tabular form.

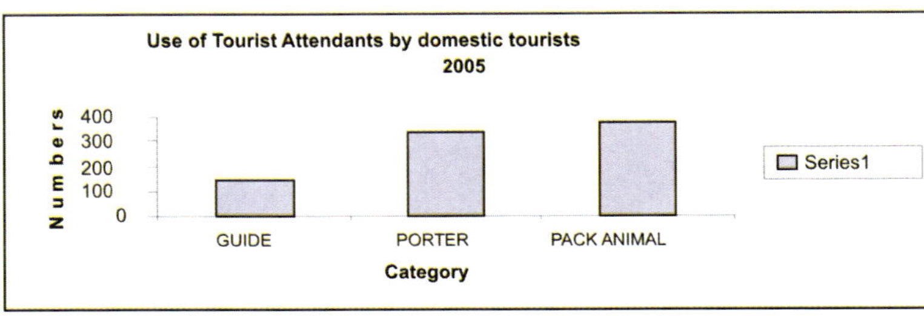

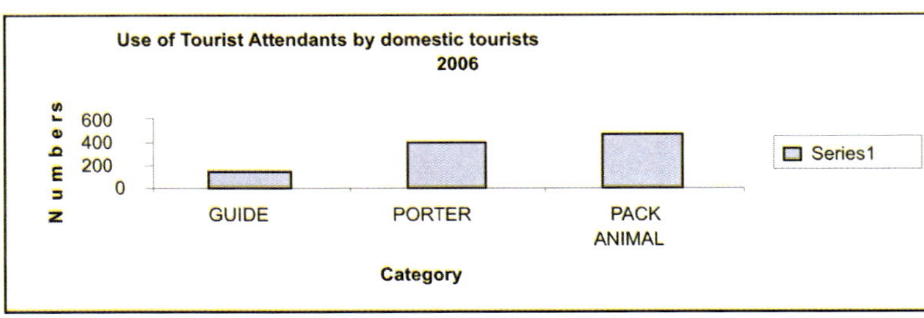

Source: Department of Forest, Gechhen Check Post, Government of Sikkim 2006.

Table: 18 Use of Tourist Attendants by International Tourists in 2005

Use of Tourist Attendants By International Tourists 2005										
	April	*May*	*June*	*July*	*Aug*	*Sept*	*Oct*	*Nov*	*Dec*	*Total*
Guide	67	48	8	1	0	39	135	100	23	**421**
Porter	280	220	27	5	0	97	433	198	65	**1325**
Pack Animal	234	231	18	0	0	86	591	280	64	**1504**
Total	**581**	**499**	**53**	**6**	**0**	**222**	**1159**	**578**	**152**	**3250**

Table: 19 Use of Tourist Attendants by International Tourists in 2006

Use of Tourist Attendants By International Tourists 2006 (Up to NOov 2006)											
	Jan	*Feb*	*Mar*	*Apr*	*May*	*June*	*July*	*Aug*	*Sept*	*Oct*	*Nov*	*Total*
Guide	6	9	60	196	69	2	0	4	18	128	80	**572**
Porter	10	25	165	295	214	4	0	20	67	528	161	**1489**
Pack Animal	6	19	154	342	245	4	0	0	32	511	94	**1407**
Total	**22**	**53**	**379**	**833**	**528**	**10**	**0**	**24**	**117**	**1167**	**335**	**3468**

Source: Department of Forest, Gechhen Check Post, Government of Sikkim, 2006.

In trekking operations carrying luggage such as tent, beddings, tour items, drinking water etc., large number of porters, pack animals and pack animal operators are required. Nearly 700 persons were engaged as guides and about 550 persons as porters for trekking for a period of at least five days in 2005 and 2006 respectively in such an interior place.

Details of use of tourist attendants in the form of guide, porter and pack animal by international tourists in 2005 and 2006 are given in Table 18.

About 1750 persons and about 2050 persons respectively in 2005 and 2006 were engaged as guides and porters during trekking for at least five days except pack animal operators in such a remote place where means of subsistence is so hard. Majority of the porters are the Lepachas. Similarly, pack animals (Dzo) providers are mainly the Nepalese. More numbers of tourist attendants are required in case of international tourists than domestic tourists.

In context of Lachen, the situation is a little bit different. There tourist guides are few in number as the number of trekking parties are also less and same is organized mostly by the travel agents. These travel agents have their own guides, or sometimes even vehicle drivers also act as guides to facilitate tourists.

Porters are a necessary component of tourism. In Ramgyathang hamlet, there are seven Lepchas acting as porters. They are in the age group of 18 - 31 years. In Lethang hamlet, there are four porters. Most of the porters are Lepcha of different hamlets. The Bhutias, Nepalis, and the Lepchas of Dubdi, Ting Ting, Gachhen, Topsing, Gerethang, Gumphadera and Dosthang hamlets of Dubdi – Yuksam grampanchayat do the job of porters. The porters rate is Rs. 120/- per day with food. Trekking agents of Gangtok and Darjeeling have their own porters. Hence, local porters have limited scope to remain interested to do their job with foreign tourists rather than domestic tourists as former pay better amount of wages along with tips and sometimes also in kind like dress materials, shoes, walking sticks, etc. Foreigners are generally not bothered about food during the trekking. Same is the case with domestic tourists also except few. In the perception of the local people, foreigners are disciplined, soft spoken, aware about do's and don't of biosphere reserve. The domestic tourists, on the other hand, do not show much concern to know about 'dos' and "don'ts" of Biosphere Reserve. Most of the domestic tourists generally do not follow tour timings and other guide lines of trekking. Only domestic tourists are allowed for trekking at Lachen. Foreigners are not allowed to visit Thangu and Gurudongmer. Cooks play important role in tourism specially trekking and adventure tourism. In each trekking team, cook, helpers are necessary. Nepalis are good cook. Most of the cooks accompanying the trekking team are from Nepal and Bengal.

Maintenance of trekking path

Large number of people remains involved in maintaining trekking paths throughout the year under different local contractors. The Lachenpas do the maintenance of paths at Gurudongmer under local contractors.

Foreigners feel interested in having Cycle Tour in Hilly roads. There is one Cycle Tour agent each at Lachen and Lachung to serve such interested tourists.

IMPACT OF TOURISM ON SOCIO-CULTURAL LIFE

Tourism has helped the local people in changing their life style, consumption patterns, habits, transformation of values etc. which are as follows -

Local people specially young people of Yuksam get attracted by the tourists' clothing, eating habits and their spending patterns. Tourist guides, porters, shop owners, hotel / lodge attendants and others have direct contact with tourists.

Change in consumption patterns

Contact between hosts and tourists leads to change in consumption patterns of the people. This is caused due to increased income levels. If a tourist is rich and successful in the eyes of the host, the consumer may try to follow the formers' behaviours and consumption pattern. Copying tourists' food, the local youths of Yuksam area have started eating pickles, salads, spicy food, etc. in their daily food, though this trend is recent and in limited manner.

Impact on habits

Family members of a hotel owned by the Bhutia were found to be imitating their behaviour while interacting with the tourists. They use English language and accent as per visiting tourists' during interaction. They start their day with morning tea and "good morning". The girls who know better English take lead in interacting with tourists and come forth during breakfast, launch and dinner time. The hotel attendants do their individually assigned jobs. Generally the local people sleep for more hours and get-up early to attend tourists leaving for trekking or departing from their hotel. By this way, the local people have conditioned themselves to acquire the sense of timings and sense of discipline.

Transformation of values

Due to contact with the foreign and domestic tourists, the young people of Yuksam have imitated many of their modern traits. Often erosions in moral behaviours are attributed to tourism. Such development includes prostitution, drug addiction, alcoholism, gambling and petty crimes. While discussing about prostitution, alcohol and drugs (PADS), a mild form of alcoholism is there at Yuksam. Due to cold climate at high altitude, the local communities are generally used to take local drinks. But after the introduction of foreign liquor in the wake of tourism, the situation has changed a little bit. Some of the porters, guide and pack animal operators spend a large part of their payment, which they get from their respective travel agent or hotel used on drinks. The local people who can afford also take foreign liquor.

Modernization of attitudes amongst the young people of Lachen arises due to contact with young domestic and foreign tourists. Negative developments of moral behaviour such as alcoholism are found more among young people.

Increasing of self respect

Tourism is highly related to the service sector. People can work in the service industry without looking their self esteem. A section of local people have earned money by involving in tourism and as a result, increase their self respect both in case of Yuksam and Lachen.

Impacts on non-material culture

Tourism in Yuksam also gives rise to old art forms, mixed with Kali, Shiva, Durga, Ganesh, etc. images. Commercially produced art forms without any significance are sold to the tourists. This kind of fake arts indirectly affect local art forms.

Impacts on material culture

Impact of tourism has been felt on the material culture of the KBR people. Traditional cooking wares and utensils are now used mainly as source of income by them in the local market. The traditional material cultural items have been replaced by modern crockery, non-stick pans, pressure cookers, gas stove, electric heater etc.

High rise building has no place in the traditional Lepcha, Bhutia, and Lachenpa society. But now multi storied hotels have come up and many more are likely to come up. This, coupled with an often high level of building may lead to complete alternations of the local scenario.

Due to tourist flow vegetables such as French bean, radish, pumpkin etc. are being cultivated as per tourists demand though in limited way by the local people. Banana, guava, etc. are cultivated in limited manner and are important sale fruit items for tourists at Yuksam. Vegetables such as French beans (locally known as *thaku*), radish (locally known as *lapu*), peas (locally known as *sashe*), mustered seed leaves (locally known as *chhena*), lettuce (locally known as *chhapati*), cabbage (locally known as *golgobi*), onion (locally known as *ochom*), etc. are cultivated as per tourists demand by the Lachenpas. Head Lama (locally known as *Dorjelepon*) of the gompas instruct them about agricultural calendar, religious and other activities of life by seeing their records.

The seasonal workers from West Bengal such as Bengali mason, carpenters are engaged in works related to constructing hotel, lodges, etc. at Yuksam and Lachen.

Language Behaviour

Terms of address have been changed due to tourism at Yuksam. Young children of the Bhutia use *pappa* or *daddy*, *amma* or *mummy* instead of using *pala* and *amla* (in Bhutia language) respectively. In case of Lachen, young children of the Lachenpa use *apa* instead of using *pala* (Tibetan) for father and *amma* instead of using *ama* (in Tibetan language) for mother.

Impact of tourism is clearly visible in Yuksam *Bazar* area only and not in interior part of the different hamlets of Yuksam – Dubdi grampanchayat.

ENVIRONMENTAL IMPACT

Dependence on fuel wood for energy is causing serious deforestation problems in trekking corridor and forests adjacent to settlements. The total fuel wood consumption including cooking, water heating and other purposes ranged from 1.02 Mgy by the pack animal porter to 2264 Mgy' by local communities. The demand for fuel wood is estimated to be 2434 Mgy' against production of 21769 Mgy' for the entire trekking corridor (Maharana et al 2000). The consumption pattern varies with season. KBR reports somewhat similar situation in this regard.

Fuel wood consumption is still there for trekking tourists as well as for others staying in hotels where cooking is done by using fuel wood. Uses of fuel woods for tourism and personal purposes have been observed both at Yuksam and Lachen. Increase of tourist flow creates pressure on biosphere reserve in terms of increasing usage of fuel woods. Accumulation of garbage is another major negative aspect of tourism for environmental conservation point of view. Garbage is problem for local villagers. However, at Yuksam efforts are being made by the Garbage Management Committee towards disposing all the garbage and waste material raised on account of tourism recently. The committee takes up the healthy environment campaigning by displaying leaflets, banners and posters etc. making people aware of maintaining healthy environment.

CASE STUDIES

Case –I

Tenzing Gyatso Bhutia aged 54 years, resident of Yuksam Bazar area and also owner of Yangrigang Hotel, had expressed his view about flourishing tourism. He was also in service a few years back. The local people are depended on traditional agriculture besides transhumance activity (yak and sheep grazing) and occasional gathering of roots, tubers and medicinal plants. After declaration of Biosphere Reserve in 2000, forest department imposed certain rules and regulation on gathering and grazing in certain parts of the reserve area. The flow of trekkers and other tourists had increased in the post 1995-96 period due to disturbances in Jammu – Kashmir problematic. Besides, beautiful mountain peak, sacred lakes and its natural surroundings of Yuksam are factors which attract tourists to Yuksam. Limited trekkers' movement in Yuksam does not show much impact in nearby areas except economic benefit. Only few local people are acquainted with English language and that too because of their interactions with the trekkers. Basically the Bhutias are traditionally traders. Later the Bhutias are involved in tourism as there is no other way for subsistence. Following the Bhutias, the Nepalis are also involved in tourism sectors such as hotel, travel agents, restaurant and others. The Lepchas are always lagging behind in terms of their involvement in tourism except as porters.

Case - II

Azo Kesang aged 81 year, Ex-headmaster of Lachen School expressed his view about trading from British period as well as his experience about flourishing tourism. The Lachenpa were traditionally depended on agriculture, transhumance activity (Yak, sheep and cattle grazing) and occasional gathering of roots, tuber, medicinal plants etc. They were a trading community. Bamboo (locally known as *chowa*), natural colour (locally known as *majito* and *geetha*), wood plank (locally known as *singlep*), etc. items were carried from Lachen to Tibet. Generally goods were carried by yaks and they used horse as their transport. Sheep wool, sheep meat, blanket, carpet, red salt (locally known as *tsa*), etc. items were carried from Tibet to Lachen. Trading period was from April to August. The Lachenpa also used to carry food and other items for defense personnel with the help of Yaks and horses. After India – China war in 1962, this type of trading was stopped. Then the Lachenpas were depended on forest produces and occasional job of trekkers. Occasionally people also used to collect and sell some of the forest produces like *dhup* (incense) locally known as *sang* (a type of incense resin, Rs. 40/ per kg.), *jatamashi* (a type of incense resin), *chhimto* (a type of incense resin), a type of medicinal plant (locally known as *kurki*, available near glacier, Rs. 80/ per kg) etc. A section of local people have yak (cost around Rs. 17000/ per yak, use for its' meat, skin, tail with hair, milk, ghee, *chhurpi*, etc.), sheep (cost around Rs. 1100 use for its' wool, meat, etc.), *Kasturi* of Musk deer (cost around Rs. 15000/ - Rs. 20000/), etc. are source of income for local people.

Forest Department, Government of Sikkim had declared ban on collecting forest produces after declaration of Khangchendzonga Biosphere Reserve as reserved area in 2000. Forest Department, has also declared band on yak and sheep grazing in the biosphere reserve area in 2005. It has created problem between Forest Department and the Lachenpa. These above mentioned factors have driven them to get engaged in some other profession. Metal road from Gangtok to Gurudongmar via Lachen was opened for tourism purpose. Due to problematic situation in Kashmir, the tourist flow in Lachen has been on increase.

A section of the Lachenpas has their property in Chungthang and also at Gangtok. Their trading background and also above mentioned situation help to them get involved tourism. Azo Kesang also informed that the tourist flow had increased from 2003-2004.

Generally the travel agents of Gangtok book the hotel / lodges at Lachen. They carry rice, vegetables, fish, drinking water from Gangtok along with cook and helpers. Tourists generally come here at evening. Next day morning they visit Gurudongmer, come back by afternoon and then same day leave Lachen for other destinations.

Case - III

Mitali Ayyangar aged 23 years resident of Mumbai, Maharashtra was a trekking tourist. They were three persons in the team. She was basically a student and enjoyed trekking. For her Sachen was an area located on high altitude; mountain ranges were wild and adventurous one; snowy peak of the Khangchendzonga during sunrise and sunset were inexpressible in words; the beauty of plants was unparallel and the local people were peace loving, trust worthy, hardy and had respect for their religion. She appreciated about the rustic beauty of the area. She enjoys home stay and traditional food.

Case -IV

Jason Lisinski aged 36 years; resident of Ontario, Canada is a trekking tourist. He had visited Yuksam – Dzongri along with his friend for five days. He had expressed about his feelings of adventurous journey, desolateness, unique smell of the forest etc. He had also informed about the problems of trekking such as accommodation in trekkers hut, medical facility, toilet, camping site, garbage management etc. He was very much happy in staying in home stay. For him, the local people were peace loving, friendly, deep faith in Buddhism.

Case –V

Samir Gajjar aged 33 years resident of Gujrat had visited Lachen, Thangu and Gurudongmer along with his family members. He opined that Lachen – Gurudongmer journey was adventurous one. Varieties of trees attracted tourists' attention. Cold desert before Gurudongmer Lake were wonderful. Gurudongmer Lake was unparallel. He also expressed about the problems of Lachen based tourism such as (i) providing oxygen at Gurudongmer, (ii) land slide, (iii) cheating on room rent by travel agents of Mumbai, Delhi, Kolkata and other areas, (iv) food, (v) garbage etc. He found the Lachenpas as hardy and peace loving people having faith in Dzumsa system and Buddhism.

Case - VI

Pema Gyalsing Bhutia aged 42 years; resident of Yuksam Bazar is owner of the Hotel Wild Orchid. The year of establishment of the hotel is 1995. He opined that before 1995 the tourist inflow was very less except trekking troops. After Jammu- Kashmir disturbance, the tourist inflow had increased in Yuksam. Trekking tourists, both foreign and domestic, stay in his hotel. For him the hotel business is profitable one. He has ten rooms. He viewed that increasing tourist inflow has given rise flourishing business in hotel as well as restaurant, shop, travel agency and other sectors.

Case –VII

Chhangma Lachenpa aged 30 years resident of Lachen is the owner of Juniper Mountain Resort. He viewed that the tourist inflow has increased year by year at Lachen. He has relation with the travel agencies of Gangtok such as Khangri Travels, Chhojung Travels, Omega Travels and others. He along with two employees and family members run the hotel. He considers it a profitable business as there is no other alternative means of subsistence. He also expressed about the problems of tourism such as (i) room rent they receive is low as it is on commission basis with the travel agencies (ii) land slide (iii) span of visit at Lachen is only one day (iv) short span of tourist season etc.

Case - VIII

Madan Gurung aged 24 years of Topsing hamlet of Yuksam- Dubdi grampanchayat belongs to Nepali community. He is a tourist guide. He opined that a section of local people have benefited through tourism. He has no agricultural land. He is basically XII standard student. He generally acts as tourist guide for the foreign tourists as he gets more amounts of rupees. For the Yuksam – Dzongri trip (five days) he receives more than two thousand five hundred rupees besides trips. He is happy with his profession. Mr. Gurung also informed about the problems faced during trekking such as (i) Uneven camp sites not suitable for pitching of tents (ii) need of more trekking huts at Tshoka and Dzongri (iii) unhealthy toilet and garbage site (iv) need for mattress, blankets etc. for the porter, cooks and helpers.

Case – IX

Kinzong S. Bhutia aged 28 years; assistant secretary of Khangchendzonga Conservation Committee (KCC), a renowned Non-Government Organisation (NGO) and an energetic Bhutia is resident of Yuksam Bazar area. He is very much busy in his NGO activities besides attending national and international seminars. He has gathered lot of practical experiences in conservation by while attending the training programme in different reputed institutions. He is actively engaged in ecotourism activities by creating awareness about restrictions of Khangchendzonga Biosphere Reserve.

While discussing on impact of tourism on local people he has admitted that the local people are engaged as tourist guides, cooks, involved porter and pack animal operators besides very few people are engaged in hotel business, home stay while few are also working as travel agents, shop owners etc. He has mentioned that most of the local boys engaged as porter have even not completed their secondary education. He has also mentioned that the involvement of local people in ecotourism is less compared to those from outside the area. Most of the tourists visiting Yuksam, Dzongri-trail come through the travel agents of Gangtok, and Darjeeling. He has pointed out a problem between local and outsider related to hiring involving porter, cook and dzo. He has also mentioned about change of material culture such as use of small trekking torch light on forehead, spoon, cup and saucer instead of *batuka*, non stick cooking pots, pressure cooker, heater, gizzard, walking sticks, etc. Use of pickles, salads etc. are the recent introduction in their food items. He has mentioned about change in dress and style among young generation such as use of half pant, cap and specs, hair styles etc. Married Bhutia women generally do not wear their traditional dress i.e. *bakhu* in Yuksam Bazar. He has also informed that Bhutia young folk of *bazar* area use *pappa* or *daddy*, *amma* or mummy instead of using *Pala* (i.e. father) and *Amla* (mother) respectively.

Case – X

Camelees Lepcha aged 50 years primary school teacher is resident of Lethang village. He belongs to the Lepcha community. He is very much aware about impact of tourism.

He has mentioned that the local people are benefiting by involving them as porters, cooks, owners of pack animal in tourism. He has also admitted that the involvement of local people of Yuksam and its adjoining areas are less than the outside people of Gangtok, Darjeeling and other areas. The Lepchas are generally involved as porters in tourism. He also has mentions about the change in material culture such as use of spoon, cup, saucer, etc. has been found only among the service holders' and porters' families. Change in crop production i.e. staple crop to cash crop such as vegetables, fruits has been found though in limited manner. He has also informed that young and aged people are having feelings of bitterness and frustration due to non fulfillments of their desires though on the other hand they find tourists spending as per their desires.

Case – XI

Mohan Gurung, Ex-minister Government of Sikkim aged 55 years is resident of Yuksam – Dubdi panchayat. He belongs to Nepali community.

While discussing the impact of tourism he has rightly pointed out that the involvement of people of Yuksam and adjoining areas is less than the outside people. He has suggested that Pahungry should be developed. Road should be built for visiting Chong village so that local people could benefit through such activities as home stay, porters, guides and cooks. He has informed that wooden crafts such as *doko*, peling etc; bamboo crafts such as *phurlung*, bamboo flower etc; woolen blankets (locally ferwed as *rarhi*) made from sheep's wool and prepared by Gurung people of Nepali community etc. are the product of tourism. Tourists purchase *thangka* painting. Images of Hindu gods and goddesses such as Shivju, Durga, Kali, etc., are newly introduced item in *thangka* painting. He has mentioned that local people try to learn English language. The terms lime Hello, Hai, Namastay etc., are being frequently used by the local people of Yuksam Bazar. *Chowmin*, *parota* (made of wheat), bread etc., are the new food items learnt from tourists through interaction with them. Use of half pant, cap, specs, long hair etc., denotes changes in dress and style among young generation. Use of spoon, cup and saucer instead of *batuka* etc., are the changes in material culture. He has admitted that there is change in crop production i.e., from staple crop to cash crop such as French bean, radish, pumpkin etc., This change in crop production is due to demand from tourists though being cultivated in limited way.

Case – XII

Dorjee Lachenpa aged 56 years is resident of Lachen village. He belongs to Bhutia community. He knows a lot about the locality and also about tourism. He has mentioned that trekking group consisting of both domestic and foreign tourists had participated in Khangchendzonga Expedition from Lachen since around 1987. Later government had stopped Khangchendzonga Expedition as Khangchendzonga is sacred mountain to local people. Tourism was not so much prevalent at that time as it is now-a-days. He is of the opinion that tourism does not have any significant social impact on the society except the fact that many people engage themselves as porters during trekking. He has also mentioned that tourists in batches have been visiting Lachen, Gurudongmer and its adjoining areas since 2003-2004.

Case –XIII

Azu Dorjeelopen aged 89 years; teacher of *Gumpha* School is resident of Lachen village. He belongs to Bhutia community. He has vast experience about his community. While discussing on impact of tourism, he has mentioned that since around 1987 limited of trekkers both domestic and foreign had visited the Lachen, Green Lake, Chopta Valley and its adjoining areas. He has also informed that actual flow of tourists have started since 2003-2004. According to him, flows of the

Bengali tourists have been on rise due to militancy in Jammu-Kashmir. Sikkim is a peaceful state. During the time of Chhogyal king horse was used as transport. Now cars are used for transport. The standard of living of the people has improved after government of India took over Sikkim as their territory in 1975. During their early days they put on dress made of natural such as bark fiber. Now they use dress made of artificial material. Due to interaction with tourists, people have learnt to speak a bit of English too.

CONCLUSION

The tourist flow in Sikkim and to KBR area has increased from 1995-96 and 2003-04 in case of Yuksam and Lachen respectively. Domestic and foreign tourists visit both Yuksam and Lachen. Moreover it is observed that most of the domestic tourists are from West Bengal. Foreign tourists though in a limited number are from all parts of the globe. In tourism economic, environmental and socio-cultural impacts are not reflected independently; but have their cumulative effect. Economic impact of tourism at Yuksam and Lachen is clearly visible in the sphere of changing occupation from traditionally land based activities to professions like owning hotel / lodge, home stay, restaurant, shop, travel agency etc., besides jobs as tourist guides, porters, cooks, daily wages in maintaining trekking path and road and so on. A section of Bhutia, Nepali and few outsiders from Bihar do good business in these areas. The Lepchas mainly work as porters at Yuksam. About 67 per cent and 33 per cent hotel owners are the Bhutia and the Nepali respectively. About 45 per cent, 37.50 per cent, 12.50 per cent and each 2.50 per cent shop owners are Nepali, Bhutia, Bihari, Lepcha and Bengali respectively. About each 39 per cent and 22 per cent travel agency owners are Nepali, Bhutia and Behari respectively at Yuksam. From the study it emerged that about 1250 persons were engaged as guides and porters by domestic tourists in 2005-06, and about 3800 persons were engaged as porters and guides by foreign tourists. Some 1407 pack animals were used for carrying luggage by the tourists in 2005-06. In Lachen all hotel except six lodges are running under contract pattern by non Lachenpa people, though owned by the Lachenpa people. Similarly at Lachen all shops are owned by local people but for one tailoring shop whose owner a Jadav family hails from Bihar. Despite the fact that travels agents are locally available both in case of Yuksam and Lachen, most of the tourists get their visit organized by the travel agents operating from Gangtok in Sikkim and even from Darjeeling in West Bengal.

A negative aspect of tourism is seen in terms of feelings of bitterness and frustration among the local youth and also the aged people in villages under study. It partly results from the fact that they find the affluent looking tourists attired in different clothing with different eating habits and their lavish spending behaviour which smacks of better economic level of the tourists as compared to the local people. This has resulted in changing pattern of consumption of daily food among local youths of Yuksam and Lachen villages as they try to copy the tourists' behaviour in these areas. With regular contact with the tourists, the hotel attendant have learnt few English words and its pronunciations following tourists accent and use it while interacting with outside tourists but only a limited extent. Hotel and restaurants of Yuksam and Lachen prepare foods as per tourists' desire such as Bengali, North Indian, South Indian, Western etc. Interestingly Bhutia girls and women of Yuksam are seen changing their dress style copying from the tourists. Now Bhutia men can be found dozed with foreign liquor. In language aspect, tourism has made some changes in case of terms of address, changing pleasantry and welcoming words as the local people have started using language of tourists coming from different background. It is note worthy that with the flourishing of tourism, traditional *thangka* painting which usually carried picture of Lord Buddha in form or other, are now accommodating deities like Kali, Shiva, Durga, Ganesh etc., Images which are commercially produced are often to detract tourists' attention from real cultural expressions of the local population. *Thangka* painting, woolen blanket, drum, wooden crafts, etc. are the sale items in different shops at Yuksam. *Chammer* (hand fan made from Yak hair to be used for gods), blanket, small carpet, rabbit woolen cap, woolen cap, etc., are sale items of Lachen. With more and more tourists visit these tourist sites, sale of above items has increased and others lead to mass production as a consequence and in the process, significance of traditional culture loose their identity. Buddhist monks of *Gompas* inspire local people for involving themselves in tourism so that local people can have better earning. Cultivation of French beans, radish, pumpkin, banana, guava, etc., has gone up to meet demand of tourists at Yuksam and Lachen. By this way, the endogenous factors have been helped with flourishing tourism. Local people have full faith in nature worship what the Lamas follow in Lamaic Buddhism both in case of Yuksam and Lachen. The Lachenpas act as per instruction of the Head Lama of the *Gompas* for agricultural activities, religious and other spheres of life. *Gompas* along with *Pipon* controls their livelihood in all activities of daily life in case of Lachen. Though the tourists of different religious background visit Yuksam and Lachen, there is no such impact on the local peoples' religious life. High rise building both in Yuksam and Lachen may change the local scenario. Seasonal workers such as Bengali mason, carpenters are needed for infrastructural development such as roads, hotel / lodge, restaurant, shop, etc. and these are responsible for making local scene different way.

Tourists enjoy natural beauty of mountains, water falls, wild life, and greenery of Khangchendzonga both at Yuksam and Lachen. It gives mental pleasure to the tourists. Mixing of tourists and local people at Yuksam is not possible frequently due to short span of stay of tourists at Yuksam. Most of the tourists stay at Lachen for a night only. So, it is not feasible for them to interact with the local people as tourists visit monasteries to see, wheel of life, eight lucky sign, etc. of Buddhist religion expressing their richness of the religion. Tourists observe dances of the Bhutia, Nepali, and Lepcha performed by dancers of Gechhen colony at Tashiding hotel at Yuksam and it, in turn, get glimpse of local cultural traditions. Sometimes tourists also witness festivals of Buddhism at Yuksam and Lachen. Most of the tourists opined that local people of both Yuksam and Lachen are well behaved, peace loving trust worthy, having respect for their religion, having knowledge of utilizing agricultural land as land is scarce here and so on.

As part of tourism local people acquire knowledge about sense of timings and of discipline from the tourists' daily activities. Local people acquire knowledge about different communities of their own country as well as foreign countries and about their life styles, cultures, etc. Foreign tourists are well behaved, disciplined, soft spoken, knowledge about cleanliness and so on. Foreign tourists spend more than domestic tourists. Hotel owners of both Yuksam and Lachen are eager to enhance more number of foreign tourists. Tourists acquire knowledge about sacredness of the land of Khangchendzonga, *Dzumsa* system, richness of Buddhist religion, etc. from the locals.

While discussing on the impact of tourism, a visible impact of tourism have been seen on their economic life, specially during tourist season in Yukasam and in case of Lachen. On the contrary, the social impact of tourism does not show much dent on the life and culture of the local people both in case of Yuksam and Lachen. Impact of tourism is observed mostly in Yuksam *Bazar* (market) area and not in interior part of villages. Tourists are overwhelmed by the natural beauty of the mountains, streams and forests. They also derive about the eternal peace from solitude and serene atmosphere of this holy land by witnessing the influence of Lamaic Buddhism.

ACKNOWLEDGEMENTS

The author is grateful to Dr. V.R. Rao, Director-in-Charge, Anthropological Survey of India for giving me the opportunity to do field work in Sikkim. The author is thankful to the Dr. Kakali Chakraborty, Head of Office, Eastern Regional Centre, An. S. I. and Dr. D.B. Mandal, former Deputy Director (C) and core member of the project for their guidance. The author is very much grateful to Dr. Ramesh Chandra, Deputy Director (C), North – West Regional Centre, Dehradun for his untiring effort for helping in finalizing the report. The author is also highly obliged to Dr. Arun Kumar Singh, former Senior Human Ecologist and former national coordinator of the project 'Man in Biosphere'. The author is also thankful to Dr. Sibir Ranjan Das, Anthropologist (C) for his valuable suggestion for preparing the report. The author is indebted to Dr. Sumit Mukherjee, Head Quarter, for preparing the tourist map of Sikkim. The author remembers Mrs. Dipa Saha for typing the manuscript of the report. The author is very much indebted to the people of Yuksam and Lachen; tourists; Department of Forest, Tourism and Police and other Government Departments, Government of Sikkim and Khangchendzonga Conservation Committee and other non government authorities. The author also acknowledges all team members of the project for their cooperation without which the work could not have been done successfully.

7

Growth of Urbanization in Yuksam: A Study in Khangchendzonga Biosphere Reserve of Sikkim Himalayas

Gautam Kumar Bera

INTRODUCTION

This year of 2007 creates a great milestone in the history of human civilization, similar in magnitude to the agricultural era and industrial revolution. For the first time in history, a majority of human beings will be living in vast urban areas, according to the United Nations, many in mega cities and suburban extensions, with populations of 10 million people or more. The *Homo sapiens sapiens* have become *Homo urbanus*.

As long as the human race had to rely on solar flow, the winds and currents, animal and human power to sustain life, human population remained relatively low and controlled keeping time with nature's carrying capacity. The tipping point was the exhuming of large amounts of stored sun, first in the form of coal deposits and then oil and natural gas from beneath the surface of the earth. Fossil fuels allowed people to create new technologies, which dramatically increased food production and manufacturing of goods and services. The unprecedented increase in productivity led to the runway growth of human population and urbanization.

No one is really sure whether this profound turning point in human living arrangements ought to be celebrated, lamented, or merely acknowledged for the record. That's because our burgeoning population and urban way of life has been purchased at the expense of the dwindling of the earth's vast ecosystems and habitats.

It's no accident that as we celebrate the urbanization of the world, we are quickly approaching another historic watershed, the disappearance of the greens and wildly. Rising population, growing consumption of food, water and building materials, expanding road and rail transport, and urban sprawl continue to encroach up on the remaining natures green lands pushing it to extinction olbiet slowly. Hence, in the great processed of urbanization we have perhaps increasingly separated the human beings from the rest of the natural world in a belief that we could conquer, colonize and utilize the rich heritage of the planet to ensure our complete autonomy and without dire consequences to future generations. In the next phase of human history, we will need to find a way to reintegrate ourselves back in to the rest of the living earth if we are to preserve our own species and conserve the planet for our future generations.

The Anthropological Survey of India, when took up the study of Khangchendzonga Biosphere Reserve in Sikkim, one of its objectives was to look into the growth of urbanization in relation to this Biosphere. As Yuksam happens to be the only urban like situation under Khangchendzonga Biosphere Reserve unhesitantly it was selected for the study purpose.

Yuksam is important for the study as it has too another angles to level at this was the first capital of Sikkim, where according to the historical records, the first Chogyal of the Sikkim kingdom was consecrated in 1641 A.D. by three learned Lamas. The evidence of the consecration ceremony is still intact in Norbugang Chorten in the form of stone seats and a footprint of the Head Lama on a stone.

Three major ethnic groups namely the Lepcha, the Bhutia and the Nepalese inhabit the Yuksam area. Historically speaking this region had originally been the domain of the Lepcha who are said to have migrated here from the hills of Assam or from South-East Asia around the 13th century. The Tibetans started migrating to Sikkim during the 15th century to escape religious strife among various Buddhist orders. From the available inscriptions on the back rest of the throne of Phuntshog Chogyal, the first king of Sikkim at Yuksam, scholars opine that three Lamas namely Sempa Chembo, Rinzing Chembo from the western and southern sides respectively and Lhatsum Chembo from Tibet in the north arrived at Yuksam and established the Nyingmapa order of Tibetan

Buddhism here. Scholars later gave the literal meaning of Yuksam as 'meeting of three great Lamas'. Phuntshog, the first of the Chogyals, possibly came from the east to seek his fortune in Denzong, the valley of rice. The three Lamas sprinkled holy water on his head from a nearby pond called *Katok Pokhari*, thus coronating him to become the 'Fountain Head of the Secular and Religious Powers'. After the establishment of the kingdom with its first capital at Yuksam, Sikkim derived its name from *Su Khin* meaning new house that is being constructed. Later Phuntshog Chogyal was conferred the title Namgyal who was succeeded by his son Tensung Namgyal in 1670 A.D. The new king shifted the capital from Yuksam to Rabdentse, near the present Gyalshing. Yuksam is the entry point of Khangchendzonga Biosphere Reserve and is treated as the base camp for trekking to different peaks of Khangchendzonga. It is also the gateway to adventure tourism in West Sikkim leading to popular destinations like Goechala, Sumer Lake, Dzongri, Chaurikhiang and so on and to Tshoka – the last village under the Khangchendzonga Biosphere Reserve inhabited specially by the Tibetans who were settled in that area about half a decade back by the then king of Sikkim.

With the historical backdrop mentioned above growth of urban like situation in Yuksam was seen in the light of development of a town from orthgeneticity to heterogeneticity where tourism has taken over all other pursuits. The advantage of selecting Yuksam as 'universe' for the present study is that the population size is small. Moreover, it is almost encapsulated in a common mode of social and economic interaction with lesser divergence in the wider economic and political network and so on. Further, these units are directly observable and immediately discernible. The basic objective of the present study was to look for a morphological contour of an entity along with the continuation of traditional cultural affiliation of people and their social commitment in the culturally rooted traditional customs. In addition to that it is theoretically assumed that the physical space has been confronting a constant change in terms of its land use patterns and constant demand of interaction with its hinterland. As a result there seems to be some kind of inverse relation between the physical space and the social space. It was, therefore, felt necessary to enquire into what happens when a space changes its character in terms of the basic mode of production and concomitant social relations. It was also necessary to know to what extent the orthogenetic development has retained its character or has it led to heterogeneticity. While understanding the work emphasis was laid on peripheral linkages, the social morphology of the area and various kinds of occupational shifts including some specific emerging problems like social disorganization and so on. In totality this has led to understand the culture of the place.

METHOD

The detailed investigation was undertaken through both individual and group interviews, and canvassing of schedule to bring into relief the various socio-economic, cultural and literary dimensions of the town and some changes that have taken place over the years. The sample of households was restricted to a manageable universe for direct and close observation. The first phase of fieldwork was undertaken for about a month in the month of September 2006, followed by the second round in November – December 2006 for another month. The study is based on data collected from some 260 persons of 67 households as per details given below:

The population figures covered under these areas are as follows:

Area	*Household*	*Male*	*Female*	*Total*
Kapchay	14	26	28	54
Yuksam Bazar	53	102	104	206
Total	67	128	132	260

KHANGCHENDZONGA BIOSPHERE RESERVE

Khangchendzonga Biosphere Reserve is situated in the North, South and West Districts of Sikkim with its boundaries between latitude 27°15′ and 2° 57′ North and longitude 88°02′ and 88°40′ East encompassing a total area of 2655.26 sq. kms. It has two core zones with total area of 1819.34 sq. kms. and four buffer zones covering an area of 835.92 sq. kms. lying at an altitude ranging from 1220 to over 8550 at mean sea level. It is bounded in the north by the Khangchendzonga (high altitude) National Park and Lungnak La (5537 meters) ridge; in the east by the Tista river; in the south by the various reserved forests of the South and West Forest Divisions of the state and in the west by the Singalila range that forms the international boundary between Sikkim and Nepal. It also touches a short stretch of international boundary with the Tibet Autonomous Region (TAR) of china in the north-west corner of the state.

The salient features of the Biosphere Reserve that are more or less in agreement with the international criterion are:

(i) it contains unique geomorphic features with some of the lofty picturesque and beautiful heights ranging from 5825 meters to over 8550 meters above sea level;

(ii) it is endowed with one of the highest ecosystems of the world encompassing glaciers and high altitude lakes;

(iii) it covers varying eco-clines from sub-tropical to arctic areas (1220-8550 meters) and several major north-south and west-south trans-boundary watersheds; and

(iv) it is of high religious significance where people consider mountains, lakes, rocks and caves as sacred and worship these for their posterity.

A total of 5,064 households, with a total population of 21,888 (Census of India, 2001) of which about 75% are tribals, live adjacent to the Khangchendzonga Biosphere Reserve. The villages are located at the altitude varying from 5000 – 9000 mtrs in West and North Sikkim. The fringe villages are located in the altitude zone of 5000 – 9000 mtrs in West and North Sikkim. A total of 4,042 households, with a total population of 16,013 (Census of India, 2001) of which about 75% are tribals live in the fringe villages. They are mostly subsistence level agriculturists, residing in these remote villages, adjacent to the Khangchendzonga Biosphere Reserve. Only the Tibetan settlement of Tshoka in Yuksam Revenue Block, which has eight households, lies inside the Khangchendzonga Biosphere Reserve.

Population of fringe villages under Khangchendzonga Biosphere Reserve

Revenue Block (West Sikkim)	*Households*	*Population*
Dubdi	69	402
Yuksam	364	1951
Tsozo	89	476
Khachodpalri	114	556
Meli	116	623
Melliaching	109	589

Revenue Block (West Sikkim)	*Households*	*Population*
Topung	52	286
Singrangpung	47	227
Nambu	146	859
Kongri	71	442
Labdang	80	456
Dhupidara	76	493
Narkhola	82	510
Mangnam	64	380
	1,479	**8,250**
Revenue Block (North Sikkim)	*Households*	*Population*
Lachen	1609	2923
Shipgyer	166	695
Tung	52	201
Lachen Forest Block	12	32
Salim Pakel	132	615
Lingthem	210	1161
Lingdem	97	542
Tingbong	164	1001
Lingzah-Tolung	80	397
Sakyong-Pentong	41	196
	2,563	**7,763**
Total	**4,042**	**16,013**

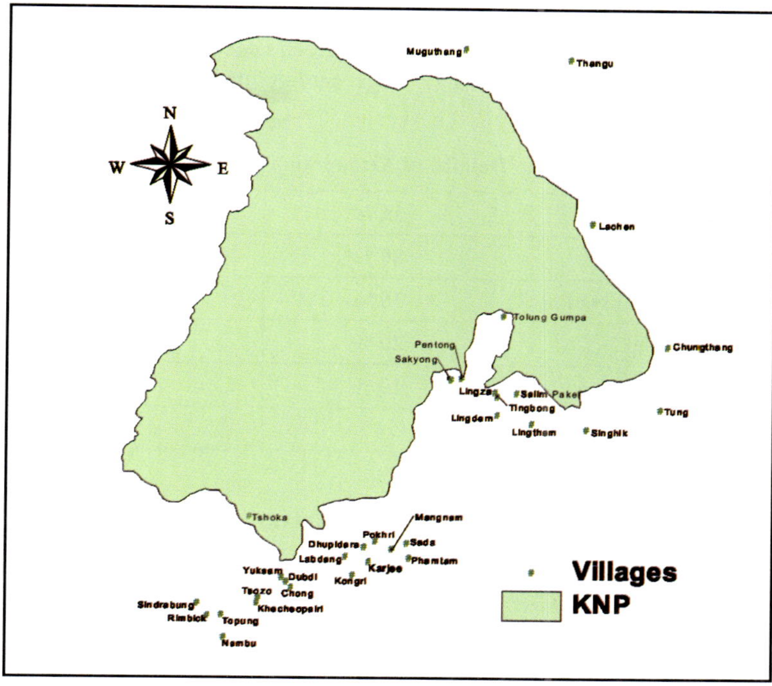

Khangchendzonga National Park and location of Villages

Map courtesy: Mr. J.B. Subba, DFO, KNP (North), Government of Sikkim.

Agriculture

In recent years the paddy fields have been transformed in to large cardamom cultivation areas in agro forestry systems. Still, in many areas, a wide variety of agricultural practices are recorded from the region. The low land agricultural fields practise maize as the major crop followed by finger millet, buckwheat and a variety of vegetables. Some hamlets of Yuksam also practise wheat cultivation along with the vegetables. In high elevation area (Tshoka), potato is the major agricultural product followed by cabbage, *bajra* along with a variety of other vegetables such as beet, radish, carrot and a number of green vegetables.

The major crops practised are cereals, vegetables (potato, cabbage, beans, radish, etc.), fruits (guava, pea) and maize. Potato is the major crop in the village for which the villagers prepare farm during December followed by sowing in January, weeding in April and finally harvesting in July. Three decades ago the villagers used to practise a wide variety of crops such as rice, maize, pea, cereals, green vegetables, etc. However, the practices slowly diverted to large cardamom because of its high value and low manpower.

Details of Occupation

Occupation	*Male*	*Female*
Agriculture	80 %	85 %
Cardamom cultivation	30 %	-
Cattle rearing	20 %	40 %
Labour in trekking	10 %	-
Business	-	15 %

Consumption of Energy

Fuel Wood	70 %
Kerosene oil	05 %
Liquid Petroleum Gas	20 %
Electricity	5 %

Livestock

Income of the people mostly comes from composite source of agriculture, horticulture, tourism and animal husbandry. Livestock rearing was mainly done to produce milk, meat, manure, cheese and to use as pack animals along the trekking corridor. The yaks are milked twice and a better part of the day is spent in churning the milk for butter and curding it for cheese (*churpi*). The fresh cheese is left to dry above the community fireplace. After dehydration for a couple of months it becomes stone hard, and is then sold as hard cheese (*supari*). Butter and hard cheese are the two main marketable items of this yak dairy trade.

Generally, almost all the families living in the village possess some livestock. They rear cow, sheep, pig and fowl for their sustainable livelihood. It is found that in some tourism potential areas, pack animals such as dzo and horse are widely used. In Yuksam Block the proportion of different livestock in the visited areas revealed higher number of cattle (26%), followed by goat (18%), sheep (7%) and pig. A considerable number of dzo (7%), yak (3%), horse (1%) and pig (15%) are also recorded from some part of the valley. Livestock rearing seems to be dependant on livelihood of the people and to the ecological niche. Data reveal that more number of sheep belongs to Gurung community, and yak and dzo to Tibetans and Bhutias. Most of the livestock, other than cows are of local variety.

URBAN LIKE SITUATION IN YUKSAM

However, sense of urbanization of Yuksam can be seen in the fact that it has some five wards as the Yuksam-Dubdi Gram Panchayat Unit comprises five **wards** that encompass sixteen **villages** in total. The names of the villages are given below under respective ward numbers. The village names have been spelt according to the local nomenclature as the people spell there.

Ward 1: Ramgaythang, Nubgang (Norbugang), and Yuksam Bazar.

Ward 2: Khengtay, Gaychen, and Tshoka.

Ward 3: Dubdi, Mangtabung, and Tshong.

Ward 4: Tingting, Doshtang, Eantang, and Kapchay.

Ward 5: Mansabung, Tapsing, and Sapsay.

Yuksam, the key door and the nearest human habitation to the Khangchendzonga Biosphere Reserve is situated under Yuksam-Dubdi Gram Panchayat. The village is developed due to influx of tourists for adventure trekking to Himalayan Range Khangchendzonga. Yuksam is situated in the West District of Sikkim with its boundaries between latitude 27°20′ and 27°30′ North and longitude 88°10′ and 88°25′ East at an altitude of 1742 meters above the mean sea level. The topography belongs to slope and slide plain with southwest aspect. Some perennial streams flow westwards to mix with Rathong Chu and some perennial streams flow downward to confluence with the same Rathong Chu. The temperature varies between 2°C (minimum) to 25°C (maximum) with an average temperature of 15°C. The average annual rainfall is 31.24 cms., and the number of rainy days is about 170. The humid factor ranges from 10% (minimum) to 75% (maximum) with an occasional history of hailstorm. The inhabited area is spread over with a sex ratio of almost 1:1. The literacy rate is 48%. Almost all the households (99%) are connected with electricity and about 15% households have telephone connection that, however, excludes mobile telephone connection. Throughout the day light medium vehicles ply on the fair road condition.

In Yuksam the area has an effective forest area of 5.90 sq. kms. The forest type includes Dense forest, Degraded forest, Barren forest and Land Slide forest all of which come under Tropical moist evergreen forest and Temperate broad leaf forest. The vegetation details comprise Top canopy, Middle stony and Grand flora. The density of the forest cover is of fairly dense type and of degraded type. The non-forestland consists of sandy and loamy mixed soil type where maize, millet, wheat, cardamom, potato and vegetables area grown. The cropping pattern is of mixed farming type where three annual crops are produced. The ratio of grain versus cash crop is 1:8. An area of 25 hectares comes under wasteland.

Yuksam, the first capital of Sikkim, is still a village or an agglomeration of villages. May be it is quite big in size but it has not yet attained the characters of a town despite being the fact that it has a remarkable glorified history of the past that has given birth to a sense of nationalism among its inhabitants and has also grown both in size and magnitude but not developed as per the criterion of the factors of urbanization. The foregoing discussion will provide a clue to understand the various facets of Yuksam as eventful characters that have grown over the years in this land.

Two areas under two different wards were selected for the study namely **Kapchay** and **Yuksam Bazar** since these two areas are the only localities that lie in close proximity of Yuksam proper and these have experienced the developmental measures that lead to the path of urbanization.

The ethnic diversity in Sikkim is represented by the Tibetan sobriquet *Lho-Mon-Tsong -Tsum*, meaning three original ethnic groups coexist in Sikkim since the days of its foundation in Yuksam in the seventeenth century A. D. The term *Lho* means south and it refers to the early Bhutia settlers who migrated from southern Tibet to Sikkim. The term *Mon* refers to foothills where Lepchas inhabit and the term *Tsong* refers to the Limbu community. However, influx of population belonging to the Nepali origin in the nineteenth century added more diversity to the ethnic mosaic of Sikkim.

The Lepcha, who call themselves 'Rong Pa', are believed to be the original inhabitants of Sikkim. They prefer their faith in Buddhism. The Bhutia, who came to Sikkim in the fourteenth century are considered as good traders and pastorals and own herds of yaks, cows and sheep. Their brotherhood bond with the Lepcha dates back to a century old tradition that is still observed as *Pang Lhabsol* festival. The *Tsong* call themselves *Yakthungba* and are popularly known as Subba or Limbu. The last group of people comprises the Nepali who migrated to this land quite late possibly in search of new occupational pursuits.

In Yuksam Bazar and Kapchay areas where the study was undertaken sixty-seven households were identified with the following ethnic groups. The Nepali population belongs to the Gurung and Chettri ethnic categories.

Distribution of ethnic groups

	Bhutia	*Lepcha*	*Nepali*
Kapchay	-	-	14
Yuksam Bazar	40	05	08
Total	40	05	22

The key events that make Yuksam a remarkable place under the Yuksam-Dubdi Gram Panchayat Unit are:

Sl. No.	*Year*	*Event*
1.	1641	Coronation of the king of Sikkim at Nubgang (Norbugang), Yuksam.
2.	1701	Foundation of Dubdi Monastery, the oldest monastery in Sikkim.
3.	1933	A major earthquake broke out when severe damage was done to Yuksam that included destruction of monasteries.
4.	1952	Government School started at Yuksam.
5.	1969	Tshoka village was settled by the then Chogyal of Sikkim.
6.	1972	Road construction to Yuksam was initiated.
7.	1973	Massive forest fire destroyed large areas of virgin temperate forest.
8.	1976	Opening of D.L. Pradhan Grocery shop, first shop at Yuksam.
9.	1978	Electricity arrived at Yuksam.

Sl. No.	*Year*	*Event*
10.	1980	First Lodge for the tourists opened at Yuksam.
11.	1986	Primary Health Centre started at Yuksam.
12.	1993	Panchayat house was built.
13.	1993	Private Nursery School started.
14.	1994	Rathong Hydro Electric Power Project started at Yuksam.
15.	1995	Weekly market on Sunday started.
16.	1995	Rathong Glacier started receding. Doodh Pokhari also started
17.	1996	Rathong Hydro Electric Power Project stalled for hurting ethnic and cultural sentiments.
18.	1997	Khangchendzonga Conservation Committee (KCC), a Non Governmental Organization is officially registered as a nodal agency to look after the welfare of Khangchendzonga Biosphere Reserve.
19.	2002	Telephone and Internet facilities arrive at Yuksam.

Education at Yuksam

In 1952 a small academic institution started functioning at Yuksam in the form of a Primary School which later got upgraded to the Secondary level under the patronage of the Government of Sikkim. It now functions as Government Secondary School. The total staff strength is 25 of which 19 are teachers belonging to the communities namely Subba (6), Bhutia (5), Lepcha (1), caste Hindus (1) and the rest belong to the Nepali groups. There are 6 non-teaching staffs. In total there are 317 students and the students belonging to the pre-primary class to the Vth standard are provided with the mid-day meal. The ethnic communities that enrolls their children in this school belong to Subba (mother tongue: Limbu), Bhutia (mother tongue: Bhutia), Lepcha (mother tongue: Lepcha), Gurung (mother tongue: Tamu) and the Nepali (mother tongue: Nepali). About 65 per cent of the students belong to the Subba ethnic origin. Nepali is the *lingua franca* of this region. The 1st language of the instruction is English, followed by mother tongue as 2nd language (Limbu, Bhutia,

Lepcha and Nepali) and Hindi (from IV th to VIII th standard). The primary students are provided with free textbooks, exercise books, school bag, raincoat, jersey, and uniform as a welfare measure by the State Department of Education, Government of Sikkim.

For higher education Yuksam students go to Tashiding (23 kms.) and Pelling (45 kms.). About 50 % of the passed out students pursue higher education at these places and most of them are Bhutias. Of late, a nursery school has also been started at the behest of the local community for imparting English education.

Health Practices

Since time immemorial the people of Yuksam depended on the traditional system of rural and folk medicine for curing ailments. Since it is an age-old practice mostly depending on herbal system of medicinal treatment it never waned out. About half a century back the Dalai Lama Foundation based in Dharamshala, Himachal Pradesh started functioning in this area with periodical visits of the *Amji* (doctor) who practise Tibetan System of medicine. In addition to that a few U.S. based doctors under the Himalayan Health Exchange Programme with their office in the state of Himachal Pradesh also contributed to the health problems of Yuksam people by making occasional visits. All these worked under the banner of a small dispensary, which witnessed dearth of experts in this discipline. In the wake of process of growth and urbanization occupying in Yuksam, in 1986 a Primary Health Centre (PHC) was opened under the patronage at the Department of Health and Medicine, Government of Sikkim. Currently it has only one non-resident (but local resident of Yuksam) medical professional with helping hands of three staff nurses, one lady health visitor, one compounder, one laboratory technician and nine non-medical staff. This medical centre has three sub-centres at Melliaching, Thingling and Tamatang, all lying in remote distances. There is a provision for residential accommodation in twelve government quarters for staff nurses and non-medical attendants. The Health Centre has also the facility of one Ambulance van and one Programme vehicle. The PHC has a provision of beds for ten non-communicable disease patients and one communicable disease patient in isolation bed.

From the available records of the PHC it is evident that the patients mostly suffer from pulmonary diseases that include tuberculosis also, liver problems due to the habit of alcoholism, varicose veins and hypertension problem specially among the tourism porters who carry loads on their back quite frequently, rheumatic heart problems, worm infestation due to frequent intake of animal protein and so on. The PHC also makes an arrangement for de-worming students and this programme is arranged at the school premises. From the month of May till August the frequency of both outdoor and indoor patients increase with high occurrence of Respiratory Tract Infection, diarrhoea and dysentery. The people having pastoralism as occupation quite often meet with accidental injuries and snakebites since they follow herds during grazing. As a case study, data on patients were collected from the PHC for the year April 2004 to March 2005, which suggested that during one year period some 1679 patients were treated at the Out Patients' Department, and 163 patients were admitted to the PHC for treatment of different ailments.

The PHC also has a Family Welfare Centre inside its campus, which looks into the matters related to family welfare scheme for promoting small family norms. It operates at two levels, one permanent measure through sterilization methods that include vasectomy for males and ligation programme for females; and the other providing temporary solution like provision for oral pills for females and barrier method like condoms for males and copper –T for females. It has been recorded that the frequency of visit to the PHC for promoting small family is more among women than their male counterpart. Hence, the PHC organizes quite frequently awareness programmes for promoting small family norms. Of late, they have been successful in their efforts and it was found that in the month of June 2006 there had been cases of male sterilization among 43 villagers living in and around Yuksam.

Financial Institution

In Yuksam there is no bank or other financial institution like insurance company. However, since 1999 a private finance company is under operation here in the name of SIDHE Pvt. Co. Ltd. with its headquarters at Gyalshing, the district headquarters of West District, Sikkim. It has total staff strength of three personnel working as Manager, Assistant and a Daily Deposit Collector. Since the nearest nationalized bank is located at Pelling, about 50 kms. away from Yuksam people prefer using this local finance company for making cash deposits. There is a system of personal account maintenance in this company and the customers are allowed to get loan in kind like cement, iron rod, consumer products, etc. paying an annual interest at the rate of 20 %. The cash deposits accrue a bonus at the rate of 10.5 % that can be received after the tenure of total maturity period. It has been observed that the Bhutia go for daily deposit to a great extent followed by the Nepali. The Lepcha, however, show less inclination for the financial deposit scheme.

Shops and Establishments

At Yuksam there are in total fifty shops and establishments excluding hotels and home stays. These include Post Office, Government Fair Price shop, travel agency, restaurant, grocery shops, vegetable vendor shops, liquor shop, general merchandise, pan and beetle shop, Gram Panchayat Office, Community Information Centre, Khangchendzonga Conservation Committee, Police Station, School, Tourism Office of the Government of Sikkim, Khangchendzonga National Park Office of the Government of Sikkim, Forest Guest House and Forest Range Office and so on.

There are in total eleven home stays and twelve hotels in Yuksam. Out of these twelve hotels, the Bhutia owns eight; the Nepali owns three; and the Subba owns one. The whole credit of owning and managing the home stays goes to the Bhutia community and the Khangchendzonga Conservation Committee (KCC) is also instrumental in promoting the system of home stays in tourist locations since it helps in a way the local community for reaping economic benefits.

Community Information Centre

Yuksam was connected with Telecommunication network and Internet facilities of the satellite system on the 9th day of April 2002 with the establishment of the Community Information Centre under patronage of the Department of Information Technology, Government of Sikkim and sponsorship from the Union Government of India. The National Informatics Centre looks after the Hardware system of the network. The CIC functions at the premises of the Yuksam-Dubdi Gram Panchayat office under patronage from the Department of Rural Development, Government of Sikkim. This Centre has opened up a new chapter in the history of development in Sikkim. It has not only minimized the geographical distance that one has to cover for doing formalities like procurement of application form for driving license, passport, permission letter for entering the Reserved Forest and so on from District and State Head Quarters but also it has extended its support system for enriching communication network at the global level. The beneficiaries of this Centre include people from all run of the society specially the students, teachers, porters, tourist guides, and even housewives. The CIC has also made arrangements in collaboration with the Indira Gandhi National Open University to run training courses, duly approved by the Council of Education in Sikkim, for students, teachers, Rural Development Assistants, forest guides, housewives and others. This interactive learning curriculum has put Yuksam in the communication map of Sikkim through the implementation of electronic system of academic learning. As a developmental measure it helps in eradicating the unemployment problem of the local area. Above all since Yuksam is a major place of tourist attraction for both domestic and international tourists the CIC stands as a nodal agency for providing communication network across the globe to the visitors who enter the Khangchendzonga Biosphere Reserve through this only gate of Yuksam.

Rathong Hydro Electric Power Project

The Rathong Hydro Electric Power Project was initiated in 1994 and the project work started smoothly. It was a major leap for Yuksam towards urbanization and industrialization. But it took a different course of direction as there was a massive landslide claiming several lives involved in the project. It was also associated with local ethnic and cultural sentiments since Rathong happens to be a sacred river for the local communities and the water of Rathong is used for *Bumchu* festival held on the 14th and the 15th day of the 1st month of the lunar calendar sometime in February or March every year. The local communities had apprehension that construction of Rathong Hydro Electric Power Project would affect the flow of Rathong water losing its sanctity forever. So the project was brought to the half in the year 1996. As a result a possible breakthrough in the developmental path of urbanization at Yuksam was deferred.

CONSERVATION SEQUEL TO URBANIZATION

The Khangchendzonga Conservation Committee, a non-governmental organization was established in the year 1997 at Yuksam that aimed at the conservation and preservation of the Biosphere Reserve falling under the jurisdiction of Khangchendzonga. It functions at the local level with mass awareness to protect the Khangchendzonga Biosphere Reserve at the global level. It is the only nodal agency that brings in to relief the code of conduct of the forest apart from the State Forest Department. It arranges its programmes at various levels in collaboration with several other non-governmental agencies like the Centre for Environmental Education, The Mountain Institute and so on.

Tourism as a resource

Tourism is the main resource base in Yuksam. The peak season of tourist arrival is April/May and October/ November. Both domestic and

Domestic Tourist Flow to Higher Altitudes From Yuksam 2005

State/Organization	*Jan*	*Feb*	*Mar*	*Apr*	*May*	*Jun*	*Jul*	*Aug*	*Sept*	*Oct*	*Nov*	*Dec*	*Total*
Maharashtra	3	0	0	43	33	0	0	0	36	18	0	00	133
West Bengal	17	35	15	52	153	14	3	0	5	285	85	157	821
Haryana	0	0	0	0	0	0	0	3	0	0	0	0	3
Kerala	0	0	0	0	0	0	1	0	0	0	0	0	1
Uttaranchal	0	0	0	0	0	0	0	0	0	10	0	0	10
Andhra Pradesh	0	0	0	0	8	0	0	0	0	0	0	0	8
Karnataka	0	0	0	11	0	0	0	0	0	10	0	0	21
Madhya Pradesh	0	0	52	5	39	0	0	0	0	0	0	0	96
Sikkim	0	1	0	8	1	0	0	0	0	0	8	6	24
Punjab	0	0	0	0	0	0	0	0	0	1	0	0	1
New Delhi	0	0	0	1	4	0	2	0	0	4	0	11	22
Tamil Nadu	0	0	1	2	2	0	0	0	0	6	0	0	11
Jharkhand	0	0	16	0	2	0	0	0	6	0	0	11	35
Manipur	0	0	0	0	0	0	0	0	0	0	0	21	21
Uttar Pradesh	0	4	0	0	16	0	0	0	0	0	0	0	20
Meghalaya	0	0	0	0	3	0	0	0	0	0	0	0	3
Defence Service	0	18	0	0	0	0	0	0	0	0	0	0	18
Total	20	58	84	122	261	14	6	3	47	334	93	206	1248

Domestic Tourist Flow to Higher Altitudes From Yuksam 2006

State	*Jan*	*Feb*	*Mar*	*Apr*	*May*	*Jun*	*Jul*	*Aug*	*Sept*	*Oct*	*Nov*	*Dec*	*Total*
Sikkim	0	4	6	0	32	0	0	4	13	7	16	0	83
West Bengal	0	5	132	135	121	0	0	2	145	229	77	0	845
Haryana	0	0	2	12	0	0	0	0	0	0	0	0	14
New Delhi	0	0	1	0	5	0	0	0	0	11	3	0	20
Gujarat	0	0	2	4	0	0	0	0	0	0	0	0	6
Karnataka	0	0	0	35	17	0	0	0	5	14	0	0	71
Assam	0	0	0	63	0	0	0	0	2	8	0	0	73
Maharashtra	0	0	0	15	53	0	0	0	0	16	0	0	84
Tamil Nadu	0	0	0	0	1	0	0	0	0	0	0	0	1
Jharkhand	0	0	0	0	0	0	0	0	22	0	0	0	22
Mizoram	0	0	0	0	0	0	0	0	0	1	0	0	1
Meghalaya	0	0	0	0	0	0	0	0	0	0	0	2	2
Total	0	9	143	264	229	0	0	6	187	286	96	2	1222

Use of Tourist Attendants by Domestic Tourists 2005

	Jan	*Feb*	*Mar*	*Apr*	*May*	*Jun*	*July*	*Aug*	*Sept*	*Oct*	*Nov*	*Dec*	*Total*
Guide	4	6	6	17	35	1	2	1	8	38	17	7	142
Porter	4	3	4	49	83	1	5	5	19	108	30	30	341
Pack Animal	3	15	28	35	90	0	0	0	24	153	17	9	374
Total	11	24	38	101	208	2	7	6	51	299	64	46	857

Use of Tourist Attendants by Domestic Tourists 2006

	Jan	*Feb*	*Mar*	*Apr*	*May*	*Jun*	*Jul*	*Aug*	*Sept*	*Oct*	*Nov*	*Dec*	*Total*
Guide	0	1	15	24	31	0	0	1	12	51	10	0	145
Porter	0	2	64	58	63	0	0	4	60	113	32	0	386
Pack animal	0	0	102	104	65	0	0	0	104	27	57	0	459
Total	0	3	181	186	159	0	0	5	176	191	99	0	990

International Tourist Flow to Higher Altitudes from Yuksam 2005 (12/04/2005 to Dec 2005)

Country	*April*	*May*	*June*	*July*	*Aug*	*Sept*	*Oct*	*Nov*	*Dec*	*Total*
Ecuador	0	0	0	0	0	0	1	0	0	1
Australia	27	12	0	0	0	20	20	44	34	157
Korea	0	0	0	0	0	1	0	1	0	2
Canada	15	22	1	0	0	2	9	7	0	56
Hungary	0	0	0	0	0	1	7	0	1	9
Germany	16	4	0	0	0	11	78	34	3	146
Mexico	0	0	0	0	0	1	0	1	0	2
Austria	1	1	0	0	0	3	5	5	0	15
Jordan	0	0	1	0	0	0	0	0	0	1
Switzerland	13	7	1	0	0	9	39	20	2	91
Malaysia	0	2	0	0	0	0	7	2	0	11
France	27	17	1	0	0	5	55	24	0	129
Poland	0	4	0	0	0	2	4	4	1	15
U.S.A	49	26	14	0	0	4	83	48	7	231
Singapore	0	5	0	0	0	3	12	12	11	43
Thailand	4	0	0	0	0	0	1	1	0	6

Country	*April*	*May*	*June*	*July*	*Aug*	*Sept*	*Oct*	*Nov*	*Dec*	*Total*
Thailand	4	0	0	0	0	0	1	1	0	6
Indonesia	1	0	0	0	0	0	0	0	0	1
U.K.	34	45	7	1	0	9	80	48	4	228
Greece	2	0	0	0	0	0	0	0	0	2
Netherlands	19	23	0	1	0	1	68	28	2	142
China	0	3	0	0	0	0	0	2	0	5
Italy	4	1	1	0	0	9	19	4	0	38
Russia	0	13	0	0	0	0	0	0	0	13
Belgium	6	3	0	0	0	8	17	21	0	55
Denmark	0	6	3	0	0	0	7	6	0	22
Ireland	2	3	0	0	0	2	0	0	0	7
Spain	1	17	0	0	0	0	26	10	0	54
Israel	4	4	2	0	0	1	11	12	3	37
Brazil	1	2	0	0	0	0	0	0	0	3
S. Africa	1	0	0	0	0	0	0	0	1	2
Japan	19	0	1	0	0	0	0	3	0	23
New Zealand	9	1	1	0	0	1	3	3	0	18

Country	*April*	*May*	*June*	*July*	*Aug*	*Sept*	*Oct*	*Nov*	*Dec*	*Total*
New Zealand	9	1	1	0	0	1	3	3	0	18
Sweden	3	2	0	0	0	2	40	12	0	59
Czech Republic	1	16	0	0	0	2	21	3	0	43
Norway	2	2	0	0	0	0	3	0	0	7
Lebanon	2	0	0	0	0	0	0	0	0	2
Finland	0	0	0	0	0	0	1	0	0	1
Portugal	0	0	0	0	0	0	2	1	0	3
Lithuania	0	0	0	0	0	0	2	0	0	2
TOTAL	263	241	33	2	0	97	621	356	69	1682

International Tourist Flow to Higher Altitudes From Yuksam 2006 (Up to Nov 2006)

Country	*Jan*	*Feb*	*Mar*	*Apr*	*May*	*June*	*July*	*Aug*	*Sept*	*Oct*	*Nov*	*Total*
Japan	1	0	0	1	14	0	0	0	0	1	1	18
Korea	0	0	0	1	0	0	0	0	0	0	0	1
S. Africa	0	0	0	5	2	0	0	3	0	0	2	12
Czech Republic	0	0	0	4	10	0	0	0	0	25	16	55
France	2	0	22	18	18	0	0	1	3	63	41	168
Mexico	0	0	1	0	0	0	0	0	0	0	0	1
Canada	0	6	13	10	7	0	0	4	0	16	7	63
Belgium	0	0	14	2	0	0	0	0	0	4	8	28
Germany	0	1	8	19	10	0	0	0	7	91	29	165
Brazil	0	0	1	0	0	0	0	0	0	0	0	1
Netherlands	2	1	0	40	8	0	0	0	3	97	24	175
New Zealand	0	0	0	0	3	0	0	0	0	7	9	19
U.K.	5	4	34	111	65	0	0	0	4	103	31	357
Argentina	1	0	0	0	0	0	0	0	0	0	0	1
Poland	0	0	5	5	7	0	0	0	1	7	10	35

Country	Jan	Feb	Mar	Apr	May	June	July	Aug	Sept	Oct	Nov	Total
Denmark	0	2	5	3	6	0	0	0	0	1	0	17
Ireland	0	0	3	9	1	0	0	0	2	1	6	22
Hungary	0	0	0	1	0	0	0	0	0	1	2	4
Australia	2	3	21	39	35	0	0	0	8	17	19	144
Taiwan	0	0	0	0	2	0	0	0	0	0	1	3
Russia	0	0	2	6	7	0	0	0	5	24	6	50
Singapore	0	0	0	13	1	4	0	0	0	11	0	29
Indonesia	0	0	0	0	1	0	0	0	0	0	0	1
Switzerland	0	0	6	14	18	0	0	0	4	29	7	78
Estonia	0	0	0	0	0	0	0	0	0	0	6	6
Israel	0	0	13	16	12	0	0	0	7	15	9	72
Ukraine	0	0	0	10	0	0	0	0	0	0	1	11
U.S.A.	0	1	48	63	36	0	0	0	8	75	28	259
Spain	0	0	3	12	4	0	0	0	0	20	0	39
Romania	1	0	0	0	0	0	0	0	0	0	1	2
Sweden	0	0	9	9	1	0	0	0	0	4	15	38

Country	*Jan*	*Feb*	*Mar*	*Apr*	*May*	*June*	*July*	*Aug*	*Sept*	*Oct*	*Nov*	*Total*
Philippines	0	0	0	0	0	0	0	0	0	4	0	4
Italy	0	1	0	3	2	0	0	0	0	19	3	28
Thailand	0	0	0	0	0	2	0	0	0	0	1	3
Austria	0	0	0	3	4	0	0	0	0	14	8	29
Finland	0	0	0	5	1	0	0	0	0	0	2	8
Portugal	0	0	0	0	1	0	0	0	0	0	0	1
Norway	0	0	1	1	4	0	0	0	0	0	0	6
Slovakia	0	0	0	5	4	0	0	0	0	0	0	9
Malaysia	0	0	0	8	0	0	0	0	0	0	0	8
Total	14	19	209	436	284	6	0	8	52	649	293	1970

Use of Tourist Attendants by International Tourists 2005

	April	*May*	*June*	*July*	*Aug*	*Sept*	*Oct*	*Nov*	*Dec*	*Total*
Guide	67	48	8	1	0	39	135	100	23	421
Porter	280	220	27	5	0	97	433	198	65	1325
Pack animal	234	231	18	0	0	86	591	280	64	1504
Total	581	499	53	6	0	222	1159	578	152	3250

Use of Tourist Attendants by International Tourists 2006 (Upto Nov. 2006)

	Jan	*Feb*	*Mar*	*Apr*	*May*	*June*	*July*	*Aug*	*Sept*	*Oct*	*Nov*	*Total*
Guide	6	9	60	196	69	2	0	4	18	128	80	572
Porter	10	25	165	295	214	4	0	20	67	528	161	1489
Pack Animal	6	19	154	342	245	4	0	0	32	511	94	1407
Total	22	53	379	833	528	10	0	24	117	1167	335	3468

international tourists visit the area for both historical reasons as well as adventure tourism particularly for trekking to higher altitude areas like Goechala, Sumer Lake, Dzongri, Chaurikhiang and so on and to Tshoka – the last village under the Khangchendzonga Biosphere Reserve inhabited specially by the Tibetans who were settled in that area about half a decade back by the then king of Sikkim. It is also considered to be the gateway to adventure tourism in West Sikkim. Data on tourist flow in this area were collected for the years 2005 and 2006 for both domestic as well as international tourists.

It is evident from the above eight tables that there have been influx of domestic tourists for both the years (2005 and 2006) from several states (16 and12 respectively) where West Bengal contributes the maximum followed by Maharashtra and Madhya Pradesh. There is an influx of local tourists too from the home state of Sikkim in 2006. In addition to that tourists from almost forty countries visited Yuksam and higher altitude areas of the Khangchendzonga Biosphere Reserve for both the said years where the U.S.A., the U.K., Australia, Germany, France and the Netherlands contributes the maximum. There is a tendency to engage local porters, tourist guides and pack animals from Yuksam proper, which in a way contributes to livestock rearing among local inhabitants as well as revenue earning. This gives a portrayal of local economy too justifying Yuksam as a place of resource base of tourism where Khangchendzonga Biosphere Reserve stands as the chief attraction with paramount importance. However, this avenue of tourism is restricted to a few months only when there is influx of tourists. It all starts from the month of March and extends till May after which there is a dull period for another three to four months. The next phase of influx of tourists starts in the month of September or October and it extends till December. This suggests in a way that tourism as an economic pursuit provides opportunity to the local people for only six months or so. Otherwise the rest of the months of the year are barren months as regards economic opportunity from tourism is concerned.

The uniqueness about Sikkim lies in the fact that the state never contributed to the factors of urbanization and as a result there were no urban centres in Sikkim even half a century back although there was hereditary monarchy since mid seventeenth century. Over these centuries the kingdom of Sikkim remained completely rural in nature though in later stages it came under the influence of the British during the colonial rule over India.

Many scholars opine today that Sikkim was purely rural from the beginning of the monarchy. Both indigenous communities as well as immigrants, over the centuries, practised rural mode of production agriculture, livestock rearing, hunting and food gathering as their principal economy. The Lepcha continued their age-old practice of hunting and food gathering as subsistence economy along with swidden cultivation. The Bhutia pursued their pastoral habit of livestock rearing and shifting cultivation. The Nepali immigrants practised settled agriculture and developed trade in their localities. On the whole, there was a reflection of subsistence type of economy with no surplus production. All these in a way affected the development of township in whole of Sikkim. Further the rulers of Sikkim quite frequently shifted their capital for some reasons or the other. One such was the fear of invasion of the Gurkha population from Nepal. These frequent shifting did not allow the capital places to form or transform into towns. The best example can be of Yuksam, which basically grew as an orthogenetic place but is still a big village commanding respect from a host of villages of neighbouring areas.

It was felt at the initial stages that there was a possibility of orthogenetic development of Yuksam with the presence of a number of monasteries both in and around Yuksam and the presence of *Katok Pokhari*, a sacred lake considered auspicious for fulfillment of wishes, hence called a wishing lake. But this did not happen so since the first capital of Sikkim was shifted within a few decades leaving behind Yuksam as an uncared place. It remained remote and untouched by visitors from outer world till the advent of tourism there and the place gained importance as the gateway of Khangchendzonga Biosphere Reserve. What both orthogenetic initiation and heterogeneticity could not do over centuries, advent of tourism in Khangchendzonga Biosphere Reserve brought into relief the development of Yuksam in only a few decades. Yuksam remains as merely a resource base for tourism as long as Khangchendzonga Biosphere Reserve commands respect from its visitors for its magic word, Khangchendzonga, the sacred mountain.

8

The Lepchas of West Sikkim: A Study in Khangchendzonga Biosphere Reserve of Sikkim Himalayas

Krishna Mandal

INTRODUCTION

Anthropological Survey of India under the 10th Five Year Plan has undertaken a national project, 'Man in Biosphere: Khangchendzonga Biosphere Reserve'. Under the project I have attempted to look into the aspect of the life and culture of the Lepchas of West Sikkim of Khangchendzonga Biosphere Reserve. For the study two villages called Lethang and Tsozo under Khechepudi block of West Sikkim were selected.

OBJECTIVE, METHODS AND TECHNIQUES

The objective of the study is aimed to highlight the life and culture of the Lepcha of West Sikkim. In order to achieve the stated objective the standard anthropological methods and techniques were used in the field. The participant observation method was employed as often as the opportunity allowed. Non-participant observation technique was used when the participation was not possible. For examples, a full participation was not possible at the time of their ancestral worship. Therefore, we had to satisfy ourselves with interviews and case histories. Most of the time the interviews were unstructured so as to allow maximum freedom to the informants for a spontaneous response. The descriptive technique has been followed in the presentation, supported by few quantitative data where possible. The data is checked and rechecked.

All categories of informants of both the sexes and of all age groups were interviewed for studying the various aspects of Lepcha culture. Besides, structured interviews, some open ended schedules were also tried in the beginning but these did not yield much results because of mass illiteracy and lack of comprehension of the people about the techniques of eliciting information. The genealogical method of collecting information was used though to a limited extent among the Lepchas. As they, in general could not recollect many events of the past, the method was not much insisted upon. I, however, could extract some general information regarding the migration of individual household as much about physical movement of the tribe. Informations have also been gathered regarding the marriage pattern and kin marriages, if there were any; their inheritance rules as regards the house and household possessions and also about the incidences of breaches of the tribal endogamy and clan exogamy.

The data was collected with the assistance of a Lepcha interpreter. The interpreter used to explain the intricate points in Hindi/English languages.

It would have been ideal to conduct the study residing in a village in the midst of Lepcha concentration but that was not possible for lack of any suitable accommodation. However, the investigator camped in the Yuksam tourist spot which is about 15 kms away from the village.

STUDY VILLAGE

The present study has been undertaken at the Tsozo revenue village which consists of two hamlets, i.e., Lethang and Tsozo hamlets under Khechupodi block in West Sikkim district which falls under Khangchendzonga Biosphere Reserve. All the hamlets belong to Lepcha people. The Lethang hamlet is situated by the side of a road which connects the two tourist spots namely Pelling and Yuksam. Pelling is situated at an altitude of 6100 meters. It offers a good view of the mountain ranges. Due to its locational advantages and scenic beauty tourists use to come to this place. The trek to Dzongri and to the base camp of the famous Mt. Khangchendzonga begins here. Lethang is the junction place which is at a distance of 15 kms. from Yuksam and 25 kms. from Pelling. The Tsozo hamlet is situated 1/2 km away from the Khecheopalri Lake and at a distance of 25 kms from Pelling, Khecheopalri lake is considered to be one of the sacred lakes of the state both by the Buddhist and the Hindus. There is motorable road from Pemayangtse right up to the lake area. As the hamlets are situated by the side of tourist spots, they will be influenced by tourism, and for this reason above mentioned hamlet were selected for study.

Lethang and Tsozo are situated more or less in same ecological condition 5400 meters from sea level. There are 33 families in Lethang hamlet and 41 families in Tsozo hamlet. The total population of the Lethang hamlet is 194, out of this male is 112 i.e. 57.73% and female is 82 i.e. 42.26%. The total population of Tsozo hamlet is 212, out of this male is 114 i.e. 52.53% and female is 103 i.e. 47.46%.

Table 1

A. Hamlet wise Lepcha population (LETHANG)

Hamlet	*Number of Families*	*Population*		
		Male (%)	*Female (%)*	*Total (%)*
Lethang	33	112 (57.73)	82 (42.26)	194 (100.00)

B. Hamlet wise Lepcha Population (Tsozo)

Hamlet	*Number of Families*	*Population*		
		Male (%)	*Female (%)*	*Total (%)*
Tsozo	41	114 (52.53)	103 (47.46)	217 (100.00)

The table shows total number of families in each of the hamlet and their total population including percentage wise males and females.

The Lethang hamlet is surrounded by the Rathong Khola river, Rungmoon river, Tofrock village and Khanchendzonga water falls. The Tsozo hamlet is surrounded by sacred Khechupodi lake, Rathong khola river, Thingling block and Dufuk cave. The area is rugged terrain, high altitude with steep slope and dense forest. The settlement pattern of both the villages is dispersed. Houses are in scattered position on the terraces. The shape of the houses are rectangular, roof is made of either corrugated tins or asbestos or sometimes thatched with straw. Floors of the houses are mostly wooden and about a meter high from the ground level. The plinth of the house is made of stone with mud. Walls are made of bamboo strips with thin layer of clay or cement plastered. These types of huts/houses were introduced by the Nepalese. Lepcha traditional huts are made of wood. But in those villages there is absence of any traditional huts of the Lepchas. For making the Lepcha huts large amount of wood is required specially six long wooden poles and due to declaration of the Biosphere Reserve the Lepchas can not collect large quantity of wood from the forest. Specialized person for making the huts is not available in Yuksam area. They built their huts with minimum quantity of wood and it is economical also. The lower space of the hut is used for storing firewood and keeping the piggery and poultry. A typical Lepcha hut consists of at least two rooms, one of which is used as kitchen (*thopsong*) and living room and the second as ceremonial room (*deong*) where rite de passage are formed. In the kitchen above the fire place is a drying ledge of woven bamboo hanging from the raftlers. In some huts there is a small and narrow store room, where maize and millet are kept to the bamboo ceiling to dry. Drinking water is available from stream, pipe water, etc. All the hamlets are electrified, most of the families do not have toilet facilities. They use wood as a fuel for cooking. They are all Buddhists except one person who is Christian residing in Lethang. There is one primary school in each of the hamlet. Yuksam is a nearest market place which is 15 km away from the Lethang hamlet and 25 km away from the Tsozo hamlet. From the Tsozo hamlet if one will walk for half km then he will find two teashops, one canteen for the tourists and one grocery/stationary shop.

HISTORY

It is important to know the early history of Lepcha as they are said to be the earlier inhabitants of Sikkim. "It is, however, commonly agreed that Sikkim did not have any strong centralized political power before 17th century. It is also accepted by all that the Lepcha, were the autochthonous people of the state who may have migrated from South-East Asia long back. Besides, it is commonly believed that Sikkimese Lepcha were in contact both with India and Tibet for a long time." (Sinha, A.C. 1975). No definite history is available as and when the Lepcha came to settle in this land of Sikkim; their main concentration especially in the Dzongu valley. They are also concentrated in the West district of Sikkim. Before the Chogyal dynasty, Sikkim was divided into small territories and each was governed by the *pano* or chief. The last Lepcha chief was Thub Athuk. After his death Lepcha chieftainship came to an end. "In the middle of the seventeenth century the kingship started in Sikkim with the advent of Namgyal dynasty. Phuntsog Namgyal, a descendant of Khye Bumsa, a Tibetan warrior became the first ruler of Sikkim by the grace of the lamas. It is said that Phuntsog was one of those Tibetans or the Khampas who had already migrated to Sikkim and settled at Gangtok at that time. As the lamas were the chief architect of the Namgyal dynasty all this happened with the prerogative of the lamas and in theocratic model of Tibet. A lot of monasteries were built in different parts of Sikkim. The main emphasis was given on the spread of Buddhism in this land. The early inhabitants came under the control of the Tibetans or the Bhutias. They had to symbolically surrender their land to the king and also embrace the new religion of their master." (Basnet 1974:15). The Nepali immigration started in Sikkim long after the Bhutia settlement. Though it was started in the middle of eighteenth century but the large scale immigration took place during the middle of the nineteenth century. Now-a-days the Nepalese are a numerically dominant population of Sikkim and the political structure bestows upon them. These Nepalese are spread all over the State and their cultural influence is clearly discernible among the other people of Sikkim.

Table II

A. Age-sex wise population distribution of Lethang

Age group	*Male*		*Female*		*Total*	
	No.	*%*	*No.*	*%*	*No.*	*%*
0 – 4	8		11		19	9.79
5 – 9	20		10		30	15.46
10 – 14	10		10		20	10.31
15 – 19	11		9		20	10.31
20 – 24	17		10		27	13.92
25 – 29	8		8		16	8.25
30 – 34	11		5		16	8.25
35 – 39	6		4		10	5.15
40 – 44	4		4		8	4.12
45 – 49	5		3		8	4.12
50 – 54	3		2		5	2.57
55 – 59	3		2		5	2.57
60 + above	6		4		10	5.15
Total	112	57.73	82	42.26	194	99.97

B. Age-sex wise population distribution of Tsozo

Age group	*Male*		*Female*		*Total*	
	No.	*%*	*No.*	*%*	*No.*	*%*
0 – 4	7		13		20	9.22
5 – 9	20		15		35	16.13
10 – 14	20		20		40	18.43
15 – 19	4		7		11	5.06
20 – 24	9		9		18	8.29
25 – 29	10		10		20	9.22
30 – 34	9		7		16	7.37
35 – 39	9		7		16	7.37
40 – 44	6		3		9	4.15
45 – 49	6		5		11	5.06
50 – 54	4		1		5	2.31
55 – 59	2		2		4	1.84
60 + above	8		4		12	5.53
Total	**114**	**52.53**	**103**	**47.46**	**217**	**99.98**

The above two table shows, in the Lethang hamlet in the 5 – 9 years of age, total member of males and females are highest (15.46 %) and in the Tsozo hamlet highest percentage (18.43 %) is seen in the age group 10 – 14 years of age. In the Lethang hamlet among the total population 194 (57.73 %) are male folks and (42.26 %) are female folks where as in the Tsozo hamlet, among the total population 217, (52.53 %) are male folks and (47.46 %) are female folks.

According to the table III, in the Lethang village unmarried male folks and female folks are highest (20 in number) and (11 in number) in the age group of 5 to 9 years of age and in the Tsozo hamlet unmarried malefolks and femalefolks are highest (20 in number) and (19 in number) in the age group 10 to 14 years.

In the Lethang hamlet among the total population 194, (38.66 %) are unmarried males, (23.19 %) are unmarried females. Again (17.53 %)

Table III.

A. Age – sex wise Marital distribution of Lethang

Age group	*Unmarried*			*Married*			*Widower/widow*			*Divorce/Divorcee*			*total*		
	M	*F*	*T*	*M*	*F*	*T*	*M*	*F*	*T*	*M*	*F*	*T*	*M*	*F*	*T*
0 – 4	9	9	18	-	-	-	-	-	-	-	-	-	9	9	18
5 – 9	20	11	31	-	-	-	-	-	-	-	-	-	20	11	31
10 – 14	10	10	20	-	-	-	-	-	-	-	-	-	10	10	20
15 – 19	11	9	20	-	-	-	-	-	-	-	-	-	11	9	20
20 – 24	11	3	14	6	7	13	-	-	-	-	-	-	17	10	27
25 – 29	6	2	8	2	6	8	-	-	-	-	-	-	8	8	16
30 – 34	5	1	6	6	4	10	-	-	-	-	-	-	11	5	16
35 – 39	2	-	2	4	4	8	-	-	-	-	-	-	6	4	10
40 – 44	1	-	1	3	3	6	-	1	1	-	-	-	4	4	8
45 – 49	-	-	-	4	4	8	-	-	-	-	-	-	4	4	8
50 – 54	-	-	-	3	2	5	-	-	-	-	-	-	3	2	5
55 – 59	-	-	-	2	1	3	1	1	2	-	-	-	3	2	5
60 + above	-	-	-	4	3	7	2	1	3	-	-	-	6	4	10
Total	75 38.66	45 23.19	120 61.85	34 17.53	34 17.53	68 35.65	3 1.54	3 1.54	6 3.09	-	-	-	112 57.73	82 42.26	194 100

B. Age – sex wise Marital distribution of Tsozo

Age group	Unmarried			Married			Widower/widow			Divorce/Divorcee			total		
	M	F	T	M	F	T	M	F	T	M	F	T	M	F	T
0 – 4	7	14	21	-	-	-	-	-	-	-	-	-	7	14	21
5 – 9	20	14	34	-	-	-	-	-	-	-	-	-	20	14	34
10 – 14	20	19	39	-	-	-	-	-	-	-	-	-	20	19	39
15 – 19	4	8	12	-	-	-	-	-	-	-	-	-	4	8	12
20 – 24	9	5	14	-	4	4	-	-	-	-	-	-	9	9	18
25 – 29	7	2	9	3	8	11	-	-	-	-	-	-	10	10	20
30 – 34	3	1	4	5	5	10	1	1	2	-	-	-	9	7	16
35 – 39	1	1	2	6	6	12	2	-	2	-	-	-	9	7	16
40 – 44	1	-	1	5	3	8	-	-	-	-	-	-	6	3	9
45 – 49	2	1	3	4	3	7	-	1	1	-	-	-	6	5	11
50 – 54	1	-	1	3	1	4	-	-	-	-	-	-	4	1	5
55 – 59	-	-	-	2	2	4	-	-	-	-	-	-	2	2	4
60 + above	-	-	-	3	1	4	5	3	8	-	-	-	8	4	12
Total	75 34.56	65 29.95	140 64.51	31 14.28	33 15.21	64 29.49	8 3.68	5 2.31	13 5.99	-	-	-	114 52.53	103 47.46	217 99.99

married male folks, (1.54 %) widower, (1.54 %) widows. In the Tsozo hamlets among the total population 217, (34.56 %) are unmarried males, (29.95 %) are unmarried females, (14.28 %) are married males, (15.21 %) are married females, (3.68 %) are widows, (2.31 %) are widower.

Table IV

A. Literacy and Educational level among the Lepcha (Lethang)

Literacy level	*Male*	*%*	*Female*	*%*	*Total*	*%*
Illiterate	24	12.37	29	14.95	53	27.32
Pre-primary (before class-I)	15	7.73	14	7.22	29	14.95
Primary (I – IV)	50	25.77	27	13.92	77	39.69
Secondary (V – X)	13	6.70	11	5.67	24	12.37
Higher secondary (XI-XII)	1	0.52	1	0.52	2	1.03
Graduation	1	0.52	-	-	1	0.52
Lamahood	8	4.12	-	-	8	4.12
Total	112	57.73	82	42.27	194	100%

B. Literacy and Educational level among the Lepcha (Tsozo)

Literacy level	*Male*	*%*	*Female*	*%*	*Total*	*%*
Illiterate	38	17.51	46	21.19	84	38.71
Pre-primary (before class-I)	12	5.53	20	3.22	32	14.75
Primary (I – IV)	37	17.05	19	8.75	56	25.81
Secondary (V – X)	10	4.61	18	8.29	28	12.91
Higher secondary (XI-XII)	1	0.46	-	-	1	0.46
Graduation	-	-	-	-	-	-
Lamahood	16	7.37	-	-	16	7.37
Total	114	52.53	103	41.45	`217	100.01

The table IV of the two hamlets shows that in the Lethang hamlet among the 194 souls 12.37% are male illiterates and 14.95% are female illiterates, where as in the Tsozo hamlet among the 217 souls 17.51% are male illiterates and 21.19% are female illiterates.

In the secondary level in the Lethang village 6.70% are malefolks and 5.67% are femalefolks where as in the Tsozo hamlet 4.61% are malefolks and 8.29% are femalefolks. Again in the Lethang 4.12% males have been studying in Lama school and in Tsozo, 7.37% males have been studying in lama school.

DWELLING

The Lepcha construct their new huts in the late autumn months (October – November) after gathering of the harvest. After the autumn the dates are auspicious and people have leisure time. Regarding selection of site people seek help of Lama who tells them about the good site. People believe that a good site is the one where the mountain is in the southern direction of the site and a slope below the site, stream on either side of the slopes and trees in front. Roads from east and north are considered good. Presence of hill should be in north and east side to avoid the chilly winds thus saving the occupants from harsh environmental conditions.

After selecting the site the Lama takes the sample of the soil of the site and offers *cherkem* – that is mixed grains floating in strained chi – which is thrown on the ground to gratify the devils who might have their abode in the neighbourhood and not to trouble the construction work of the site. After that the four corner posts and a centre post are set up. The house always starts from the east. So that they can get sun shine. Then the walls, flooring, ceiling, rafters and finally the thatch being built. After knowing the news that a house being built or repaired other Lepcha neighbours come to help spontaneously. People are engaged in house construction work. They are not given any wages but are served a meal at the end of the day.

The ceremony of *Tashichene* is observed to pacify the demons who are believed to live underground below the house or the demons may have inhabited the trees of which the house is built. After the completion of the house an ox is sacrificed by a Mun to all the gods, cut up the head, right foreleg and left hind leg are given to the carpenters who have worked on the house as their labour charges. A Lamaist ceremony with music and readings from the appropriate books is performed, at the end of which the chief Lama of the hamlet anointed the house pillars with blood, chi, liquor and butter. Then the pillars are stamped with a large cone made out of ground rice *Gettrs Thomu*. Finally all present throw rice mixed with flour at the pillars, shouting in as loud a voice as possible *Ta-shishu*.

View of Lepcha Settlement (Lethang)

In front of each Lepcha house is a field fenced with bamboo, it is called the garden (*sing*) and in it are raised various types of vegetables which they consume as food. Below every garden is a bamboo plantation, a small number of fruit trees like oranges, peaches, apples, pears, plums, etc. Animal manure is used in this garden. The rest of the land of the Lepcha household is scattered all over the surrounding areas where they cultivate millet, maize, cardamom etc.

Both men and women wear thin knee-length drawers and on the upper body a shirt (*Hanju*); men's shirts are slightly shorter. Over this women also wear a sort of bodice made out of a thin material. The traditional Lepcha dress was a thick piece of home woven striped material, fastened over one shoulder with a broach, belted at the waist with a sash and reaching to the knees. The colouring of this sash has certain significance, those of lamas usually being yellow and of laymen red or purple, though other colours are sometimes used.

Now women have completely given up this indigenous type of dress in favour of the Tibetan dress which consists of a coloured long sleeved under bodies and a dark sleeveless over dress, reaching half-way down the calves and fastened with buttoms. Women often tie up their hair with a head cloth. The original Lepcha head dress – a small sugar-loaf of women bamboo covered by a feather has been completely abandoned in favour of Tibetan hat decorated with coral beeds. Hats are only worn in ceremonial occasions.

The men's upper garment is called *Hanju* and lower garment is the *Halusural* and covered by *Dumpara* (shawl). Men also wear strings of coloured beads round the neck, ear rings (silver, coral) and a long knife called the *ban* or *payak* constantly worm by male members of all ages and ranks. Women wear the *Dumbeem*. They wear a full sleeve blouse and the boku (*itisko*). Women also wear colourful bead necklaces (*Lyak*), earrings (*Alurjer*), bangles (*kager*) and ring (*kukip*). Recently both men and women wear this type of dress.

Lepcha men and women are non vegetarians. They eat beef, pork, mutton and monkey (rarely). They eat all types of birds. In previous days they used to take *Kunchunjo* (prepared it by pounding maize), *mongjo* (prepared hand made bread by pounding millet), *kheching* (one type of fruit available in forest), *kuchak* (fruit) and *kuluck* (fruit) are available in forest. They also eat tubers of different wild yams. They consume root like *Mangur book, book chak, tungru book.* They eat Makki-*kunchang,* Gehu-*kuchar,* Millet-*mong,* cardamom-*renji,* Buckwheat bitter variety-*kuru,* Backwheat sweet variety-*kurhat,* Jinger-*hang,* Turmeric-*munga,* Beans-*timbi,* Pompkin-*Tingrit,* Cucumber-*sarat,* Orange-*chilium*. They eat Banana-*kurdum,* Jackfruit-*rumsupat,* Mango-*ambi,* Naspati-*naspati* as a fruit item. Their recent food items are: rice (*thamheu*), (prepare rice from makkai), potato (*Alubuk*) and vegetables (*shi bi, tin bit*) etc. They eat beef-*bik*, pork-*man*, chicken-*he,* mutton-*shar,* fish-*ung* and alcohol i.e. *mongchi*, which they made from (millet) at the time of marriage. In the off season they eat shoots like ferns, bamboo shoots and innumerable kinds of wild plants and tubers. As a cooking medium they use mustard oil-*kandangnum*, rapeseed oil, animal fat of pig, cow but traditionally they used to take boil food. Both men and women are fond of fermented liquor, locally known as *chi,* prepared from millet. They drink it in a bamboo container (*patheyot* or *thumba*) with a pipe (*pahive*). They take tea with butter and salt which they have adapted from the Tibetans. They also drink tea with milk and sugar. Use of pulses-*pergeing* in their diet has increased of late.

All ceremonial occasions among the Lepchas – birth, marriage, death, religious ceremonies are marked by the consumption of extra large quantity of food and drink. All though of secondary importance as far as diet is concerned domestic animals play a considerable role in the life and culture of the Lepchas. Nearly all the ceremonies of the *Mun* demand animal sacrifices; animals are essential for the socio-religious celebrations of birth, marriage and death. Most important animal is oxen. Goats and pigs are used exclusively for food and sacrifice.

LEPCHA SOCIETY

Clan (putse, ptso)

The Lepchas are divided into several exogamous patrilineal clans (putse, ptso). These are Aadeng puchubu, Soladimoo, Hemoo, Sandyangmoo, Kachobu, Palong singang, Tengzirmoo, Aadenbu, Sinkartabo, Lungdarmo, Bung moo, Samlingmoo, Singangmoo, Loksangmoo, Thinglobsam, Lookblumu, Tikkelmo and Karthakboo etc. They can not tell the total number of clans in their society (Gorer: 2005, Appendix – I pp. 438-39) has mentioned the clans like Jamyong ptso, Zumchyong ptso, Tamsang ptso, Paki ptso, Sakmi ptso, Aram ptso, Aram Pandjet ptso, Demik ptso, Kalong Kandong ptso, Lubdong Rabji ptso, Takpo ptso, Tseltelim ptso etc. However all the above mentioned clans which reported by Gorer are not present in the study hamlets. However in the Lethang hamlet the clans which are found namely - Singangmoo, Loksangmoo, Himu, Singdammu, Thinglobsam, Kabomoo. Again the Tsozo hamlet consists of clans like Samling Luksamu, Himu, Singdyangmu, Sangdengmu, Chadamu, Taso Luksammo, Adenpocho. The Lepcha belief that these clans have originated from some supernatural or legendary ancestors. The chief function of the *ptso* is the regulation of marriage and the prevention of incest. People of the same *ptso* are allowed to marry if they are separated by nine generations from a common ancestor. In the two hamlets no cases are reported who have married in same male or female *ptso*. Each ptso is under the guardianship of a certain supernatural being who is worshipped by all the male members of the *ptso*. Mun invoked the ptso supernatural for the benefit of the Lepchas. Every third year all the man of one hamlet assembled together and make a sacrifice of an ox as desired by the Mun followed by a feast.

The ptso supernaturals descend from father to son; women have their different supernaturals which descend from mother to daughter. Women supernaturals are propitiated by the Mun after sowing and harvesting. Special sacrifices are made in the case of illness and at the time of marriage feast. The supernaturals for women are *Ami rum* and *katong Fi*. Men's supernaturals are *Pong rum* and his wife *shing rum*. Mun worship these supernaturals for Lepchas long life, many children and prosperity.

The Lepcha clan names generally ends in 'Moo'. The word 'Moo' means dwellers of some village or locality from where they originally comes from.

Table V

A. Clan wise family (Lethang)

Sl. No.	*Name of the clan*	*No of families*	*%*
1.	Singangmu	1	3.03
2.	Loksangmu	23	69.69
3.	Singdangmu	4	12.12
4.	Himo	2	6.06
5.	Foknammu	3	9.09
Total		33	99.99

B. Clan wise family (Tsozo)

Sl. No.	*Name of the clan*	*No of families*	*%*
1.	Samling Luksommu	4	9.76
2.	Himo	13	31.71
3.	Loksangmu	12	29.27
4.	Singyangmu	1	2.44
5.	Singdangmu	2	9.09
6.	Namchomu	1	2.44
7.	Sadamu	1	2.44
8.	Chadamu	2	4.87
9.	Thing Luksangmu	3	7.31
10.	Thing Namcho	1	2.44
11.	Adenpochobu	1	2.44
Total		41	99.99

The data shows that in the Lethang hamlet (69.69 %) people represent the Loksangmu clan followed by Singdangmu clan (12.12%) and in the Tsozo hamlet highest concentration of Lepchas (31.71%) are found in the Himo clan, followed by Loksangmu clan (29.27%).

Family (Jathang)

The word *Jathang* reflects the Lepcha society. All the inmates of a house sharing economic responsibilities and related through kinship have been considered as a family. The family type of the hamlet is divided into nuclear, vertically extended, horizontally extended and other types. As per opinion of Lepchas, nuclear family consists of husband, wife and unmarried children. There are many incomplete families where any one of the three elements of the family i.e. husband, wife and children are missing, this type of family comes under 'other' type of family. Vertically extended families are those family where vertically three generations have been living together (who belong generation wise in ascending order from father-son-grandson). Horizontally extended family are those where families are extend through horizontally from father to his brothers.

A Lepcha Family

The following table speaks of the Lepcha family type.

Table VI

A. Type of family among the Lepcha of Lethang

Type of family	*Household*		*Male*		*Female*		*Total*
	No	*%*	*No*	*%*	*No*	*%*	
Nuclear	24	72.73	77	-	53	-	130
Vertically extended	7	21.21	29	-	28	-	57
Horizontally extended	1	3.03	4	-	1	-	5
Others	1	3.03	2	-	-	-	2
Total	33	100	112	-	82	-	194

B. Type of family among the Lepcha of Tsozo

Type of family	*Household*		*Male*		*Female*		*Total*
	No	*%*	*No*	*%*	*No*	*%*	
Nuclear	27	65.85	71	-	70	-	141
Vertically extended	6	14.63	22	-	20	-	42
Horizontally extended	4	9.76	14	-	10	-	24
Others	4	9.76	7	-	3	-	10
Total	41	100	114	-	103	-	217

Predominantly, the families are of nuclear kind in both the hamlet namely Lethang (72.73%) and Tsozo (65.85%) followed in order by the vertically extended (21.21%) in Lethang and (14.63%) in Tsozo. Nearly (3.03%) of the families in Lethang and (9.76%) of the families in Tsozo belong to the category horizontally extended. Lastly, (3.03%) families in Lethang and (9.76%) families in Tsozo belong to the other category type.

Table VII
A. Family size (Lethang)

Members of the family	*Household*		*Male*		*Female*		*Total*
	No	*%*	*No*	*%*	*No*	*%*	
One member	-	-	-	-	-	-	-
Two member	1	3.03	2	-	-	-	2
Three member	2	6.06	3	-	3	-	6
Four member	8	24.24	18	-	14	-	32
Five member	7	21.21	21	-	14	-	35
Six member	4	12.12	16	-	8	-	24
Seven member	2	6.06	10	-	4	-	14
Eight member	3	9.09	14	-	10	-	24
Nine member	4	12.12	20	-	16	-	36
Ten member	1	3.03	3	-	7	-	10
Eleven member	1	3.03	5	-	6	-	11
Total	33	99.99	112	-	82	-	194

B. Family size (Tsozo)

Members of the family	*Household*		*Male*		*Female*		*Total*
	No	*%*	*No*	*%*	*No*	*%*	
One member	2	4.87	1	-	1	-	2
Two member	2	4.87	2	-	2	-	4
Three member	5	12.19	10	–	5	–	15

Members of the family	*Household*		*Male*		*Female*		*Total*
	No	*%*	*No*	*%*	*No*	*%*	
Four member	3	7.31	7	-	10	-	17
Five member	12	29.26	30	-	25	-	55
Six member	5	12.19	17	-	13	-	30
Seven member	4	9.75	14	-	14	-	28
Eight member	6	14.63	24	-	24	-	48
Nine member	2	4.87	9	-	9	-	18
Ten member	-	-	-	-	-	-	-
Eleven member	-	-	-	-	-	-	-
Total	41	99.94	114	-	103	-	217

The table depict that in Tsozo most frequent number of family size is in five members family i.e. (29.26%) and in Lethang most frequent number of family size is in the four members family i.e. (24.24%).

Lepcha society is patrilineal, patrilocal and patriarchal in nature. The family is the strongest structural and maximum functional unit of the Lepcha. It is the most important and effective economic unit too. The members of an family always cooperate with one another and the responsibilities are shared by all the members jointly. The Lepcha society, they follow the patriarchal system. The head of the family i.e. the father remains supreme in the family. The words spoken by him or any decision taken by him remains beyond question. All the property both movable and immovable, belong to him. He may during his life-time dispose of some part or keep the whole property as he may consider best. After his death normally the eldest son inherit the family property including cattle and other assets, rights, duties and everything. Since the widow and daughters do not receive any share of land as they usually live with the eldest son of the deceased person, he gets an extra share of the property for their maintenance. In the event of a woman or group of women being left sole possessors of a property, they must acquire, either by marriage or adoption, a male who can inherit the property. Some childless couples adopt a son to look after them in their old age and to be their heir.

Daughters normally owned only animals which they took along when they got married. At times they could also own land as a source of income but this arrangement continued only till the time she got married. On getting married, even if it was within the village, she would lose all claim on the landed property of the family.

Whenever required, one family helps the other especially at the time of house building, marriage, death and other occasions whenever help is sought.

Avoidance relationship exist between mother-in-law and son-in-law, daughter-in-law and father-in-law, sister-in-law (y) BW and elder brother-in-law H(e)B etc.

Marriage

It usually involves some kind of formal ritual or ceremony before it is considered to exists, represents a union that is recognized and publicly approved by the other members of the Lepcha society. Married persons are expected to cooperate with each other and sometimes with other relatives in the maintenance of a household. Marriage involves ordinarily asset of cultural patterns that sanction parenthood and provide a stable background for the care and rearing up children. It is the major cultural mechanism involved in the formation of the household, the continuation of the family and the maintenance of relationship based upon kinship.

In Lepcha society, the contracting of marital bonds is not just a union of the two individuals only, it turns out to be an unbreakable tie and a solid link between the two clans. In Lepcha society, even after the death of the husband or the wife, the connection is never broken. The families and clans bind themselves in obligation to supply mutual nuptial requirements for those who are already bound, as well as for those of the generation who are still unattached. Among them even after the death of the husband, another person, who may be dead husband's brother is selected for the next husband of widow. Likely, after the death of the bride, from the brides family another girl will be picked up who will be the next bride.

For their marriage (*bree*) they follow community endogamy and clan exogamy. Now they have marital alliances with the Bhutias, Nepalese, but it is very few. In the Lethang hamlet two cases are reported where one Lepcha boy has married one Nepali girl and other Lepcha has married one Bhutia girl. In the Tsozo hamlet, four Lepcha boys have married four Bhutia girls and one Lepcha boy has married to a Nepali girl. According to their old custom the younger brother has to marry the widow of the elder brother. But it is now decreased. They make their marriage at very young age. The form of marriage is monogamy. There are three types of marriages, viz. 1. arranged marriage, 2. marriage by sororate and levirate, 3. marriage by service, (this is not in practice) now. There are two stages in a Lepcha marriage viz. 1. *Khachong* (betrothal), 2. *Bree* (marriage). Arranged marriage is known as *Ago-anit-wool-thambu.*

The rule of post marital residence is patrilocal. Most of the marriages are stable and divorce or separation is very rare. Not a single case of divorce is reported in the study hamlets. If a married couple is not agreeing to live together then *pibus* or *pamibus* (middle man) is appointed to attempt to solve the problem. For the bad temperament or the wife's refusal to work properly is the chief cause of divorce. If a woman runs away with other male persons, at that time the relatives of husband will come and bring her back or claim back the bride price. But if the wife is not satisfied with the husband, she will get compensation for this.

Among the Lepcha a man can marry the wife of his elder brother real or classificatory. Like this the woman can be inherited by all her husbands younger brothers, all the sons of her husband's paternal uncles and all the husbands of her elder sisters, real or classificatory. At the time of widow marriage previous marriage functions will be observed. If any divorce (*bretdangshang*) case is there, the children become liability of the father. Widow/widower/divorces remarriages are permissible. Regarding widower remarriage two cases are reported where the Lepcha widower have married Lepcha unmarried girls. Though widow and divorcee marriages are allowed but no cases are reported in both the two hamlets.

Kinship

The importance kinship is reckoned on the occasions of various customs observed during birth, marriages, deaths and festivals. Kinship is basically related to social approval. This approval is observable on social and cultural occasions such as phases of life and festivals.

Agnate and affinal relations

All the Lepcha belong to a family. For example if they consider an extended family then they will find, in this family there is one pair of husband and wife. They are affinal kin, which means they are united by marital ties, the relatives so related are called *affinal kin.* The affinal kin are not connected to each other through blood, which is the case with relatives of the second kin i.e. bond between parents and children, which are known as *consanguineous kin.* These relation are called agnate relations i.e. relations tied by blood. If there are grand parents in the family, they are also agnate kin. Similarly, if one of the sons in the family is married, his wife is affine. She is related to her husband and other members of the family through marital relations. Thus a family consists of agnates and affines. Kinship extends beyond the family also.

Kin are broadly divided into two categories: Kin from the side of mother and from the side of father. The kinship terminology and analysis of the kinship terms of Lepcha community is given in the following pages.

List of kinship terms

Sl. No.	*English terms*	*Terms of address*	*Terms of the reference*
1.	Father's – fathers – father	Thikung	Apa/Abo – baje
2.	Father's – fathers – mother	Nikung	Appasa Appa – Amma
3.	Mothers – mothers – mother	Nikung	Amma sa-Ama-Nikum
4.	Mothers – mothers – mother	Nikung	Amma sa-ama-Nikum
5.	Fathers father	Aājo	Appa sa Ajo
6.	Fathers father's elder brother	Batim	Appa sa-Aanom
7.	Fathers father's younger brother	Bachim	Appa sa ink kancha
8.	Fathers mother	Nikung	Appa sa Nikum
9.	Mothers father	Aājo	Amma sa Aajo
10.	Mothers mother	Nikung	Amma sa Aama

Sl. No.	*English terms*	*Terms of address*	*Terms of the reference*
11.	Father	Aabo, Aapa	Apa
12.	Father's elder brother	Bathim	Appa sa Aanom
13.	Fathers younger brother	Bachim	Amma sa Ing
14.	Fathers elder brothers wife	Mathim	Amma sa aan Tinba
15.	Fathers younger brother wife	Machim	Appa sa Ing Shali Le amu
16.	Father sister	Aaneu	Amma sa – Musongmu
17.	Fathers sisters husband	Aakku	Appa sa – Ingsa – Tidi
18.	Mother	Aamma	Aama
19.	Mothers elder brother	Aajong	Amma sa Aanom
20.	Mothers younger brother	Aajong	Amma sa – Ing
21.	Mothers brothers wife	Aaneu	Amma sa – Ingsa – Teyo
22.	Mothers elder sister	Matim	Amma sa Aanom
23.	Mothers elder sisters husband	Bathim	Amma sa Aamomsa Tidi
24.	Mothers younger sister	Machim	Amma sa Ingsa to yekub
25.	Mother younger sisters	Bachim	Amma sa Ingsa Tedi
26.	Husbands father	Aaphet	Abo
27.	Husbands mother	Aaneu	Ammake Tidi
28.	Wife's father	Aaphet	Appa sa Teuu
29.	Wife's mother	Gukma	Tenu sa Aamma
30.	Husbands mothers brother	Aajong	Amma sa aanam tedi
31.	Wife's mothers brother	Aajong	Amm sa Aanumsa Teoo
32.	Elder brother	Anam	Aanam Tinbu

Sl. No.	*English terms*	*Terms of address*	*Terms of the reference*
33.	Wife's elder brother	Anam fhet	Aanamsa Teuu
34.	Wife's elder sisters husband	Anam fhet	Aanamsa Tedi
35.	Husbands elder brother	Anam fhet	Aanamsa Teuu
36.	Elder sister	Aanam	Anam Timbu
37.	Wife's elder sister	Nom jukmu	Aanam Tinbusa Tedi
38.	Husband's elder sister	aanam jugm	Aanam tinbusa Tedi
39.	Husband's elder brothers wife	Aanam	Aanam tinbusa Teoo
40.	Sons wife's father	Bribo	Appasa-ingsa-aayeu
41.	Sons wife's mother	Brimu	Ammasa – Aakubsa – aai
42.	Daughters husband	Mijok	Teukub Miyok
43.	Daughters husbands father	Bribo	Teukub sha Meyok Aaphet
44.	Younger brother	Ing	Ing chimbu
45.	Wife's younger brother	Ing jong	Ingsa-teub
46.	Son	Tdhikup	Aakub
47.	Younger brothers son	Namkup	Aanumsa – aakubsa – aakub
48.	Elder brother son	Namkup	Aanumsa-aakubsa-aakub
49.	Husband elder brothers	Namkup	Aanumsa-aakubsa-aakub
50.	Husbands younger brother	Aajong	Ings – Niamsa – aanumb
51.	Brothers son (W.S)	Namkup	Aanumsa-aakub
52.	Elder sisters son	Namkup	Aanumsa – aakub
53.	Younger sister son	Namkup	Musing-musa-aakub
54.	Wife's elder sisters son	Namkup	Aanam – tinbusa – aakubsa-aakub
55.	Wife's youngest sister son	Namkup	Aausa-Ingsa-aakub

Sl. No.	*English terms*	*Terms of address*	*Terms of the reference*
56.	Wife's younger sisters husband	Muyok	Ingsa-aakubsa-Tedi
57.	Sisters daughters husband	Muyok	Ingsa-aakubsa-Tedi
58.	Elder sisters husband	Aajong	Aanam-tinbusa-tedi
59.	Wife's brothers son	Namkup	Aanamsa-teyugsa-aakub
60.	Husbands sister son	Namkup	Ingsa-teyubsa-aakub
61.	Daughter	Thukup	Teiyekub
62.	Younger sister	Musungmu	Ing-teeu
63.	Husband younger brothers wife	Ing	Ingsa-aanamsa-aub
64.	Husbands younger sister	Musung mu	Ingsa-tedisa-teyub
65.	Elder brothers daughter	Namkup	Aanamsa-teukub
66.	Husband elder brothers daughter	Namkup	Aanamsa-teukubsa-Meyok
67.	Wife's brothers daughters daughter	Namkup	Aanamsa-teukubsa-aakup
68.	Husbands sister daughter	Namkup	In-teyokubsa-aakup
69.	Wife's elder sister daughter	Kubjong	Aanam-tinbusa-aakubsa-Meyok
70.	Wife's younger sisters daughter	Nethe	Ingsa-teyokubsa-Meyok
71.	Younger sisters daughter	Nethe	Ingsa-teyokub
72.	Younger brothers daughter	Nethe	Ingsa-teyokub
73.	Husbands brothers daughter	Namkup	Tedisa-aanamsa-aakub
74.	Brothers daughter	Aanam	Aanamsa-teyikub
75.	Sons son	Tedikup	Aakubsa-aaakub

76.	Son's daughter	Namkup	Aakubsa – teyokub
77.	Mother brothers daughter	Namkup	Ammasa – aanangsa-teyokub
78.	Mother brothers son	Namkup	Ammasa – aanomsa – Aakub
79.	Husband	Tedi	Tedi
80.	Wife	Teyao	Teeu
81.	Son's wife	Niom	Aakubsa – Niom
82.	Brother son's wife	Niom	Aanamsa – aakubsa – Teyub
83.	Sister son's wife	Niom	Aanamsa – teukubsa – tedi
84.	Younger brothers wife	Niom	Ingsa-Aanamsa-Teuu
85.	Elder brothers wife	Aajong	Aanum-tinbusa-Liyamo
86.	Father sisters son	Kabjong	Aapasa-mosungmusa-Aakub
87.	Father sisters daughter	Kubjong	Aapasa-mosungmusa-teukub
88.	Widow	Teuubon	Teubon
89.	Widower	Teddibon	Tidibon
90.	Adopted son	Kupchok	kupchok

RITE DE PASSAGE

Birth (*aagek*)

The Lepcha think that a child's life starts from the baby's movement in the mothers' womb. At the fifth month when the baby is considered fully formed the expectant parents start observing the numerous pre-natal precautions. The pre-natal precaution is established by a Mun *pik-ing* both parents with a bunch of elephant grass in one hand and a live fowl in the other. They believe both parents are equally capable of influencing the child within the womb and a greater number of the precaution is to be observed. This is concerned with the work of the man more than a woman. To procure safe delivery a Mun will offer two chickens to *sormoong* (*deity*) in the seventh month of pregnancy. For consumption on the *thung bong fat* on the third day after delivery, about a month before delivery some specially strong *chi* (liquor) is given to the mother after a month. In the kitchen the mother gives birth to a baby. Any body who knows how to cut the naval cord, they do it with a small knife. At the time of delivery, if difficult situation arises then a *Mun* or L*ama* is called for their services. For the first three days of life, the baby is considered to be remaining in the womb of the mother and all the pre-natal precautions have to be observed. After giving the birth feast to the *thung-bong-fat* on the third day after the birth, the mother may go out side, if she thinks she is alright and ready for work. Invitation for the birth of a child is given only the females of the village. Four hens and one goat are sacrificed by the Bumthing if a male child is born. The invited females are treated with this feast. However no sacrifice is offered in case of female child. At the time of feast every guest is given three pots of special *chi* and a sufficient quantity of cooked rice. The child's horoscope is prepared by a Lama. In the horoscope sacred name of the child is written. Finally the child is given a name in keeping with the name of the day on which the child is born by Bumthing or parents of the child. After that the baby is given a tiny ball of pounded rice mixed with butter and after that a small bit of this mixture is given three times a day. As a food the mother of the baby takes ghee, chicken, mutton and beef. She does not take pork meat. The umbilical cord is cut by a Lepcha woman (*Majejungpo*) with the help of knife (*bank up*) or sickle. She gets hundred rupees, two bamboos and new clothes. Now it is changed and they use blade. For serious condition they take the patient to the Yuksam hospital, which is 15 to 20 kms. away from the two hamlets. Pregnancy is known as *Tobok-ka-aakub-boyam*.

Marriage Procedure

There are two stages in Lepcha marriage: 1. *Khachong* (betrothal), and 2. *Bree* (marriage). Khachong is actually the ceremony at which the formal gifts from the family of the groom to that of the bride are presented; these gifts are called 'the price of the bride'. When the gifts are accepted the groom has full access to his bride and the children born after khachong are considered as legitimate. When the marriage ceremony or *bree* has been performed, the wife and her children stay at her father's house. During this period the son-in-law will have to obey all the words by his father-in-law and he cannot protest for any thing. All the negotiations for the marriage are carried on by the paternal uncles or the maternal uncles of the boys' and girls' specially a paternal uncle who is older than father. All the things for marriage, is always made firstly by the boys *pamibo* (middleman) who acts under uncle's instructions. The middle man from boy's side visits girl's place and enquires about the middle man of the girl's side. Then the girl's middleman acts as an intermediary between the boy's *pamibo* and the girl's uncle.

Khachang - when the boy, choose a girl for marriage then at the first stage the boy has to pay a bride price in cash and kind. These are:

1. Half portion of the cow
2. *Chhang* (liquor) 40 kg or more, varies, prepared from millet
3. Roxy (local liquor), 70 to 80 bottles and have to give Rs. 10/- with every bottle to the girl's parents. 70 to 80 bottles amount to Rs. 700/- to Rs. 800/-
4. Khada, a piece of silk cloth for every respected person i.e. 70 to 80 in numbers

Persons like boy's father's elder brother, boy's uncle, elder brother of the boy, Village Panchayat Pradhan, middle man for the marriage (*Pamibo*) and the boy himself with the above mentioned things will go to the girl's house, if the boy likes that girl and then keeps the things in the house of the girl. The invitee villagers of the girl's side will come to their house and see the things brought by the boy's house. By placing the *Khada* (silken cloth) on the shoulder of the boy's and girl's, *Bumthing* (religious priest) will perform puja. After that the girl will be at the girl's house and boy's relatives and other persons will leave the girl's house. This is known as *Khachang*.

After one month of the previous incident i.e. (*Khachang*), the *pamibo* form boy's side, one aged person, elder brother of the boy or younger brother of the boy will visit girl's house. They will take with them one pig, 40 kgs *Chhang*, liquor 60 bottles, *Khada* (silk cloth) 60 in numbers with Rs. 5000/- in cash which varies time to time to the girl's house. All this procedure is known as *Nang Chang*.

Now the father-mother, maternal uncle of the girl will declare the date for marriage, which will be solemnized after one year, (depends on the economic condition of the boy). Marriage will be held at the girl's house. The boy's side has to give the below mentioned articles to the parent of the girl's, which are fixed at the time of meeting with the girl's parents, medium man and other relatives.

These are : Rs. 10,000/- in cash, chhang - three *fulrung* (40 kgs per fulrung x 3 = 120 kgs), liquor 70 bottles, rum one case (i.e. 12 bottles), beer one case (i.e. 12 bottles), one ox, silk cloth i.e. *Khada* 70 numbers, dress for the girl's, dress for the girl's mother. Female dress consists of: *Dumboon* – like sarees, *Tyago* - blouse, *Aaro* - for covering the head, *Nombrey* - belt and *Foorkup* - small type of sickle. Ornaments includes *Lyak* (Necklace), *Jyar* (earing), *Kagyar* (bangles), made up of gold only.

Lamas find an auspicious day for the marriage from their horoscopes. Marriages are taken place mostly after the harvest in autumn at noon, on the auspicious day. In the marriage there is a bridal procession when the members of the boy's party enter into the girl's house (temporary shed) the girl's middleman goes into the house with a ceremonial scarf for the groom's mother, then a ceremonial meal is given to the party. After this a number of long marriage formalities are observed. As a part of the wedding ceremony, Lamas play musical instruments for the whole day, burn incense and read out their books. Then the *Mun* sacrifices an ox to satisfy the gods and reads the sacred story which is all about the marriage. When the sacred story is completed then the bride and groom and the members of the both sides, are called to the Mun's alter. Mun's then advice the newly wedded boy and girl about the marriage life. Then the rest of the time passed by eating, drinking, singing and dancing. There is a competition of music (*a prey aaboun*) and dance (*aloke-achut*) between the boy's and girl's party. The newly married grooms stay for three nights in the bride's house. After that the bride will start for groom's house in the morning. Again, those accompany the bride and groom's are girl's uncle (*aaku*), girl's maternal uncle (*aajong*), younger brother or elder brother of the girl (*phamin*), father's sister (*aanu*), father's sisters husband (*batim*), father's elder brother's wife (*matim*) and elder persons of the village.

Reaching to the boys house the bride and groom will sit together, *Bumthing/Mun* will worship in the house. The villagers of the groom's side will offer rupees which varies Rs. 50/- to Rs. 200/- to the couple. During the final farewell the girl brings with her, all her private property (animals, harvested grains clothes, jewels etc.). The rituals for marriage which are cited above all are from those Lepcha who follow Buddhism. The boy's father appoints one *Mun* for worshipping and praying to the *agak alat run* (deity) for the well being of the new couple.

The rule of post-marital residence is patrilocal. Most of the marriages are stable and divorce or separation is very rare. If a married coupled is not agreeing to live together then *pibus* or *pamibus* is appointed to see and solve their problems. For the bad temperament or the wife's refusal to work properly is the chief cause of divorce. If a woman runs away with other male person, at that time the relatives of husband will come and bring him back and claim the marriage price. But if the wife is not satisfied with the husband, she will get compensation for this. According to the Lepcha tradition, by giving the bride price the husband's group purchases the wife. So, if the husband is no more, the wife is still the property of the husband's group and has to be married to another member of the same group without any communication from her parents. Again the wife has no right to refuse the man offered in the place of her dead husband. If it is not so, then the wife's group should give another woman as replacement of the women. Similarly, the husband should supply another man in place of him if he wishes to refuse the wife. Divorce cases are not reported in the field.

Death (Makharan)

When a person is dead, Lepcha do two things: first the dead man must be got rid of as thoroughly and second the danger of the devil that has caused death finding another victim in the society must be averted. They believe children and young people suddenly off from their life will be turned into malevolent spirits. Again from the older persons the less he is to be feared.

There are three methods of disposing of corpse, this may be burnt, buried or thrown into the river. According to the lamas horoscope, it is decided which method have to be followed. The Lamas and Muns are never buried, if it is rainy season then their bodies are immerged into the river. Young children are always thrown into the river. Laymen will be burnt or immerged into the river which depends on the Lamas horoscope. Traditionally, the Lepcha used to bury their dead but for Buddhism, cremation of the dead has become a common practice. Other than rainy season Lamas, Muns and Bumthing are buried facing Mount Khangchendzonga, the guardian deity of the Lepcha tribe. Lamas are called immediately after death to help the soul of the deceased, to reach to heaven. According to the lamas decision, the dead body is kept in the house which varies from one to forty nine days.

If a Lama dies then the corpse is tied to a pole with his back, the knees are bent up to the body and held by a length of cloth, the head is popped up with a stick and the hands are joined with the palm together as in prayer. After the first day of death the corpse is placed in a big copper pot. Infront of the corpse a table is placed on which three pots of water, two dishes of rice and a lantern are kept. Except this, another table is placed on which the liking food items of the deceased which he used to eat through out his life are kept. Every time they change the food which is taken by the members of the deceased house. This preliminary ceremony last for one, three or seven days, it depends on the economic conditions.

The corpse of a layman is kept in the same way but the hands are crossed on the breast and the head is allowed to flop. The body of the deceased is kept in a big basket. For the layman there is only one day's wait between death and burial, but in reality people will wait for three days. Presence of lama is must but at the same time Mun will perform the *sanglion. Sanglion* i.e. after death ceremony is observed by the Lepchas for the transportation of the soul to *Rumlyang*, the place of the Gods, to meet with the souls of Lepchas' ancestors. In the sonorous and tuneful chantings and invocations of the Muns, the *apil* (soul) is told that he has to cross the dangerous rivers to reach to the *Rumlyang.* In this occasion two bulls have to be sacrifice by the Mun for the offering to the gods and the demons in the name of the deceased. Many mounds of ice, millet for preparing the *chee* (liquor) and large quantity of vegetables are required for the Sanglion feast. Side by side Buddhist 'last rite' ceremony is also observed. All the cross leg seated Lamas chant the verses from the holy Buddhist texts. They beat the drums, cymbals and clarionate. A pyre must be prepared, before carrying out the body of Lama from the house for burial. A pyre consists of a square pile about seven feet high, with eight layers of wood for a man and nine layers of wood for a woman.

During carrying the dead body from the house to the burial place must be completed without a break. The body is placed on the pyre by facing towards Khangchendzonga. If the corpse has left a widow or widower a portion of the person's hair is cut off and burnt with the body. It is urgent that every piece of wood and bone must be burnt into ashes. A large quantity of butter, a big basket of rice and all sorts of other grains are burnt with the corpse. Lama then declares the ceremony as end by shouting. A pig or an ox is killed at the house and this is kept on the pyre as food of the corpse. After retuning home from the cremation ground the mourners have to step over fire and a knife which is kept infront of the main entrance of the deceased home to save them from the danger of the dead person. Some portion of the meat is taken back from the pyre and the same is distributed among the people those who have participated in the funeral ceremony. If the meat is exhausted the money is paid those who have not got meat.

After that the sacred books are read by lamas and Muns. The ashes of the dead body are burried and a memorial tomb, known as chorten is made. On the third day after the *Sanglian* a Moni Longtha (Mani prayer flag) is erected. On the twenty first day a second of such flag is erected and on the forty-ninth day a number of flags are erected. The invited members are offered with vegetarian food. A year after the death some more Mani prayer flags are set up and on that day a memorial ceremony known as *Lun-juk* is performed by lamas.

Bumthing and the Muns both of them act as a intermediaries between god and man. They are equally powerful as magicians, who can exercise demons and appease the gods through sacrifices. Pollution period for death is known as *tongnon.* According to the *Muns / Bumthing* they observe pollution period for thirteen days. Now according to the lamas they observe it for forty nine days.

The dead father and mother are carried in a basket by his/her son and wife is carried by her husband to the burial ground. With the friends and relatives of the deceased a Mun accompanies them. After reaching the burial place, the corpse is placed on the ground. The body is washed and anointed with the mixture of butter, cloves, camphor, then the bodies is wrapped by a new cloth. A seven feet circular grave is dug, a big stone is put at the bottom, the grave sides are lined with stones. Four ropes are placed against the four corners. The body is put into the grave sitting condition in the basket facing to the Khanchendzonga and at the top of the grave is placed a big flat stone. Then the Mun ceremonially washed his hands in a pot of chi (drink).

In case the dead body is disposed in the river before disposing the body is put into the water (river) offers *Cherken* the strained chi with grains floating in it for the supernaturals of the water. The basket is thrown into the river in such a way that the head should be downwards. In the case for a small child the body and the basket are thrown away without any type of ceremony. The body is thrown into the river without any gifts. At the time of disposal of the body the knees are fastened to the body by a cloth.

Status of Woman

Women have more important role to play in their society. Women are praised possession of families and as a recognition of the same, custom of payment of bride price is considered as a prerequisite condition for marriage. Women have roles in agricultural operations, animal husbandry, collection of fuel and fodder, in bringing potable water from the spring and in social and religious affairs. Woman feed and nurtures the animals but in any situation woman will not kill any animal. Women prepare the meal and distribute it in the family. Women prepare chief (drinks) also. Because of the difficult physical conditions and limited working seasons the male and female have to work hard for their existence. The women make equal contribution in agriculture fields and work as labourer. The women are seen working in the agriculture fields and in road construction almost on equal footing with men. This is an addition to their household duties. Woman can spin and weave. In spite of active participation in harvesting and productive functioning a woman is not independent for major spending. It is man sphere and she may or may not be consulted. Woman have not been given right to inherit the parental property. If there is no male child in a family then the property is distributed among the daughters. They can enjoy such properties even after their marriage. The female members are given the rights over pigs, fowls etc. of the family. They can sale these without prior permission of their guardians. Ten years back, they run the gram panchayat now it is not present.

In social matters the Lepcha woman enjoys considerable freedom of movement. She has a say in the selection of the mate provided it is in conformity with the marriage rules of the tribe. There is hardly any stigma with regard to divorce, remarriage of a divorcee or a widow. A greater degree of tolerance and social sanction prevails with regard to intimate relationship between a Lepcha maid and youth which may or may not lead to marriage. The lepcha women have a role in religious and ritual spheres also. In Lepcha religion women possessed by the *Mun* spirit can exercise demons and appease the gods through scarifies.

Household jobs like cooking, cleaning of house and rearing up children are done by woman. Marketing of goods and buying articles of daily necessity are done by both man and woman. A major extent to collection of roots, tubers, twigs, flowers, fruits and other eatable from forests are done by woman.

Some of the women contribute to the family income by breaking up the stones which is required for the construction of the road. Women have equal status with men. They have decision making powers.

ECONOMIC LIFE

Traditionally the Lepchas are hunters and food gatherers. Now a days they are primarily a community of land owning cultivators. However, a few of them are land less agricultural and non-agricultural labourers.

They practice terrace cultivation. There is only one type of land i.e. *Sukha land* (dry land). They mainly produce maize, millet, potato, beans, large cardamom, ginger, buck wheat, cauliflowers and leafy vegetables. They yield fruits, roots and tubers. Their cash crop is large cardamom though they like rice very much but due to high altitude rice does not grow there. Two male Lepcha from two hamlets are engaged in teaching profession in primary and high school but service is their secondary occupation, primary occupation is cultivation. People who have no agricultural land or very meager land cultivate the land as share cropper or lease holder. Very little amount of production they get from agriculture. When they get opportunity, 4 persons from Lethang and 3 persons from Tsozo worked as a guide and cooked during tourist season. It has happened in the last year. Femalefolk do household work. They sometimes engaged in labour work like agricultural labour, stone breaking for the construction of road and get Rs. 60/- per head for the construction work for the whole day. They also engage in rearing of domestic animals and collecting of fodder for the animals and fire wood for cooking. For breaking of stone, for the construction of road male folk get Rs. 100 per day if the work is available.

It is informed that the reciprocal ties among the Lepcha are fully legitimized through an institution called 'Lobo'. It is the networks of individuals involving reciprocal exchange of particular goods and services. Each family is involved in the 'Lobo' which include family members, friends and neighbours which is based on the working areas where they live. A person may be a member of more than one Lobo. In the Lepcha families where male members absent there the women can cultivate land with the help of neighbours and relatives. Share cropping locally called *adheya* is also present. In this tenancy land, agricultural implements, seeds and other things are provided by the land lord, only labour is employed by the tenant. The total produce is divided equally between the land lord and the tenants. This type of practice is applicable to each crop including cardamom.

Though the land is their primary economic resource but the yield from agriculture are not so good. When the area is declared as a biosphere reserve, from that time they cannot enter the forest like previous days and are not able to utilize the forest resources and cannot grazing their cattles in the forest. Again for tourism in the Khanchendzonga Biosphere Reserve some jobs are available for the local people of Lethang and Tsozo area. From that job they can earn money. The jobs are porter (related with trekking), guide and cook (related with tourism).

So in the tourist season very little impact of tourism is seen on their economic life. But only very few people have got this opportunity, as the Lethang hamlet and Tsozo hamlet are situated 15 kms and 25 kms away from the Yuksum Bazar. Impact of tourism is observed only in Yuksam Bazar area only. But there is no social impact of tourism on the life and culture of the Lepchas who are living in Lethang and Tsozo.

POLITICAL SYSTEM

The traditional authority structure of the studied hamlets is maintained by the Gaon Bura (*Keuing gyaan boo*) i.e the head of the village. In every hamlet there is a *Gaon Bura.* The name of the Gaon Bura of the Lethang hamlet is Norcho Lepcha. Criteria for the selection of the Gaon Bura is: he should be an aged person, have experience about the work, resident of the same village etc. The post previously was hereditary now it is by election. The panchayat of the two hamlet is known as Lethang Gaon Samaj and Tsozo Gaon Samaj. The panchayat consists of posts like president (*thidak*, one post), general secretary (*garnong*, one post), treasurer (*Judak*, one post and member i.e. *aangdo)*, one member from each house of the hamlet. Responsibility of the Gaon Samaj is to maintain law and order, peace on the social, economic and political matters. Every matter is settled under the leadership of the Gaon Bura. If some malefolk and femalefolk have illegal relationaship between them, then their case is settled by the Gaon Bura in the Gaon Samaj. The Gaon Bura imposes fine on the matter. As a punishment for quarrels the guilty person has to treat the villagers with two bottle drinks (*chi*) and Rs. 3000/- in cash which varies from time to time. In the agreement the guilty person has to write that afterwards he will never do this thing. If the Gaon Bura can not solve the above problem then he places the case to the Statutory Panchyat of the hamlet. Different roles of the Gaon Samaj members is given below :

President (*thidok*, controls all the villagers of the village) General Secretary (*Garnong*, he has to carried over all the activities related with the Gaon Samaj).

Treasurer: He collects Rs. 10/- as a fee from every family. If some body dies and there is no money in that deceased family then the treasurer provides money to the deceased family as a loan with the interest from his fund.

Members: (*Ongdu*) has to carryout the orders of the president and secretary. After the death of a person in the village he has to inform the Lamasc the villagers. Besides this he has to serve tea etc. to the villagers from the deceased family side.

SOCIO-RELIGIOUS LIFE

The Lepchas are adhered to two religious systems, Lamaism and the old Mun religion or Shamanism. Some of them are now Christians. The traditional Lepcha religion is known as Mun religion. For the Mun religion priesthood goes by manifestation or possession of a supernatural spirit. The Muns and Bumthing are considered by the Lepcha to be the media for communicating to the gods (*rum*) and devils or demons (*mungs*). The Bumthings ward off the evil spirits by appeasing them by offering animal sacrifices and other things. They are invited to officiate during clan /community rituals or even for worshiping the family deities. Their assistance is also invariably sought for curing sickness of individuals. The institution of Mun and Bumthing differs from Lamaism in that respect that not everybody can become a Mun or Bumthing like one can become Lama by undergoing training. In case of Bumthing or Mun, who gets possessed by the spirit only. "This is very important as the Bomthing symbolizes the upholder of the Lepcha traditional 'Lungten'. Lungten means the culture, custom, tradition and way of life which the Lepchas are also supposed to have been following from the very beginning of creation. The traditional values are all maintained through the mythological stories, parables, folklores etc. These the Muns and Bomthings are expected to know well for guiding the people". (Foning: 1987, p. 74)

The Muns are classified hierarchically as per their status. The pilden Muns are considered to be the most superior as they can communicate with the soul of the dead during *sanglyon ceremony*. Some of the Muns are thought to be evil doers who cause hardship to the people. They are known as *Mun-mook-Mun* there is another category of Muns called *Mun-Jyum-Mun*. They are a quite like the pildon Muns, except for that they cannot communicate with the souls of the departed. They can however, cure the sick by using herbal medicines. Tangli Muns are considered to be the custodians of Lepcha cultural tradition and are invited to recite folklores, legends, myths etc, during wedding or death ceremonies.

The Bumthing are considered more popular among them as their services are more frequently sought for, particularly during illness. They are believed to have powers toward of the malignant spirits and devils. The Bumthing are also sought for during weddings as they invoke the gods and goddesses for seeking blessings for the couple. Besides this, in the course of his various calls, moving from one place to another and meeting different people, he automatically gets all the information in the locality and outside. Thus he is an excellent medium or agent.

CASE HISTORY

Name of the informant	- Norcho Lepcha
Age	- 55 years
Education	- IV
Profession	- Head Gaon bura of the Lethang village and Bumthing of the same village.

The puja which is held yearly once in the Bumthing house known as *Rumphat*, in the month of December. There is no fixed date of the puja, according to the religious book they observe it. The puja lasts for 24 hours, starting from the morning of the day and continued upto next day twelve noon. The Lepchas who are suffering from various diseases, after the completion of the worship, Bumthing declares the name of the deity for the diseases. Bumthing worships inside the room of his house and observe fasting till the end of the puja. Bumthing worships the deity *lang-it-rum*. There is no photograph or idol for this deity. At the time of worshipping of that deity are offered are flower, any colour (*rip*), fish (*oou*), chhang (*chi*), sweet potato, sugarcane, Zinger, onion and ghee and incense (*samsing*).

The deity Mahakali or *Lang-it-rum* come to his body and after that Bumthing says the Lepchas about particular diseases. As a sacrifice ox is given to the deity. When Bumthing worship, the villagers give Rs. 5 or Rs. 10 to the Bumthing and then only they come to know about the disease from the Bumthing. At the time of uttering the name of the disease Bumthing shivers and beats the plate, with dance and brings the deity from the heaven to his house. After the completion of the puja the deity return to the heavens. The presented villagers are treated with ox meat.

The chief two female deities of the Mun are *It bunoo* and Nozyongnyu, they are also the chief Lepcha goddess. Mun ceremonies are performed for the benefit of individual households or groups of households. The first ceremony consists of an offering to the devils, called *rum*. The second ceremony performed by the Mun consists of offerings to the gods of Khangchendzonga. The services of the Mun are necessary throughout the life of every Lepcha. They must be present at all occasions like birth and marriage. They are the only priests at the time of death of Lepchas. The Buddhist Lepcha adhere to the Buddhist rituals but also practice the shamanistic and animistic conventions, (*Mun and Bumthing*). The malignant spirit (*mung*), they believe resides every where, in the trees, bushes, rocks and rivers. They belief in soul (*apil*) and heaven (*roomlyang*) and hell (*pharroom*). They worship the deities like:

1. Tung-kung-mit-river god
2. Timayarme-fire god
3. Midrummoo-forest god
4. Suchukroom-Sun
5. Labhoroom- Moon
6. Nerroom-cave
7. Doo-river and khechupudi lake
8. Hlo-hill

Except the forest god (*midrummoo*), they worship all the above deities in their houses and offer sacrifices like hen and goat to the deities. They worship ghosts like *mousam, mothen, yagit, aagit, mikhyam, somlogn, langrum, tangle-mir* etc. They observe ancestor worship.

Lamaism or Mahayana Buddhism is the other religious system. The villagers' religious life centers round the gumpha or the monastery. In their everyday life they worship lord Buddha. The Lepcha are converted to Buddhism (Lamaism) from the seventeenth century onwards (according to the field data). Later with the arrival of the Scottish and foreign missionaries, some Lepchas were converted to Christianity. But the Lepcha of the two study hamlets are all Buddhists except one person; he is Christian. In most Lepcha villages and households the Buddhist monastery and the monks play an important role, side by side a strong element of their old animistic tradition persists. The malignant (mung) spirit the Lepchas believe, resides every where in the trees in the bushes, rocks and rivers. The daily lives of the Lepchas, their religion and ceremonies are based on an effort to propitiate these mungs with ritual, sacrifices and incarnation. Lepcha have deities for the family, clan, village etc. Their regional deities are associated with Khangchendzonga (Chyu-rum-fat). They have many festivals with socio-economic and socio-religious significance. Among them conversion can be traced back due to poverty.

CONCLUSION

The Lepchas, living in the eastern part of the Himalayas, are believed to be inhabitants of undivided Sikkim. How and from where the Lepchas came to live in this Himalayan state, lacking historical records and are shrouded in mystery. Risley (1995: 27) mentioned that the oldest and perhaps aboriginal inhabitants of Sikkim were the Rong, who were popularly known by their Nepalese as the Lepcha. They are fair complexioned and medium statured people. They came in contact with the Tibetans and embraced lamaist Buddhism. Lepchas have their own language Rong-ring of Tibets-Burmese family. The Lepcha population is divided into a number of exogamous clans or *Putso*. They prefer adult marriage for both the sexes and prevalence of bride price which sometimes leads to high age at marriage.

Due to impact of tourism and contact with outsider and other neighbouring peoples some changes are noticed in their social-cultural as well as economic life. These are as follows:

Gorer, G: 1938 reported that the Lepchas used to live in traditional Lepcha houses. But at the time of field investigation, traditional Lepcha houses are not found. In lieu of traditional Lepcha houses they used to live in Nepali type of houses because for the declaration of Biosphere Reserve and imposition of various rules and regulation on forests by the Government, they are not in a position to collect large quantity of wood and various types of bamboos from the forest for constracting their traditional houses. Bamboos are required for house fencing, wall matting, pole, roof framing, house ceiling, thatching and roofing. After the declaration of biosphere reserve the Lepchas can collect limited quantity of wood and bamboos from forest by paying money to the Government. Again the carpenter who will build the Lepcha houses is very rare, even their presence is not reported in Yuksam area. For constructing Nepali type of house less quantity of wood is required and carpenters are easily available in the surrounding area.

The Lepcha have changed their food habits by mixing with the Bhutia and Nepalis. Again like earlier days they can not collect different roots, tubers from the forest due to imposition of various laws for entering into the forest for the declaration of Biosphere Reserve.

Introduction of ready made garment replaced the traditional dress of the Lepchas only two – three aged lady of the two hamlets wear traditional dress.

In early days extended family institutions contributed positively towards joint and organized endeavour in the hunting gathering fields, agricultural fields and it assured better stability securing to the family economy. Now nuclear families dominates over extended families.

In their marriage pattern inter community marriages are noticed. Like early days, (50 years ago), according to the field data, now they are no longer prefer marriage by services. There is a growing popularity of what is known as 'elopement marriage' *ago anit long tet thambu* in the village. As a result the traditional role of the middleman (*pamibo*) has considerably diminished. In most of the cases the young man and woman tend to choose their partners by themselves. This also means that age and appearance of the young people are gaining importance. The duration between engagement and marriage has also been considerably reduced today.

The instances of the man marrying a second wife while the first wife is still alive or the woman running away from the husband seen to be really a thing of the past. But the concerned villagers seemed unhappy about the custom of levirate or sorrorate marriages which are still insisted upon by the society and the people accept these merely as cultural practice.

The Lepcha economy has undergone some important changes, though they practice terrace cultivation but hunting is stopped and of dependence on forest has come down. For searching of jobs they have started migration from their place to different parts of Sikkim and outside of Sikkim to Kalimpong. After the declaration of the Sikkim Estate they have witness cash crop economy e.g. cardamom.

One of the most important changes that have come about in the last fifty years so is the opening of schools in the villages. The Lepchas have send their children to monastery to become a lama. The children are today in the schools and not in the forest or pastures though during the winter holidays they still take animals for grazing. Going to schools has changed the entire division of labour at the family level. Instead of the grown up children looking after their younger sibs they now go to high schools.

Going to schools itself has a lot of effect on their cleanliness distribution of worth, language used for reading and writing etc. Along with the history, geography, mathematics etc. They also learn new languages like Nepali, Hindi and English.

The Lepchas presiding deity Khangchendzonga is still worshipped by them with great reverence. The Lepchas embraced Buddhism. Side by side they have retained their *Mun Bumthing* tradition even after their conversion. One point is there that all the scriptures of the Buddhist text were written in Tibetan language and the Lepchas had a very little idea of this language. For this season the Lepchas perhaps retained their Mun-Bumthing tradition side by side along with the new faith of Buddhism. Their new faith perhaps was not quite enough to satisfy the needs of the people in the unpredictable climate of the Himalayas. Even today while initiating construction of a house the Lepchas follow some rituals with the help of a bumthing. A cock is sacrificed in the name of evil spirit on mung.

The present study shows some apparent changes in family, marriage, education, economy in the two study hamlets but no substantial or structural changes seems to have taken place in the last fifty years ago.

ACKNOWLEDGEMENT

The present research study carried out on the Lepchas of Khangchendzonga Biosphere Reserve who predominantly live in the tiny Himalayan state of Sikkim. I preferred to focus my study to understand the life and culture of the Lepchas who are a minority tribal group of the area.

I feel deeply concerned to owe my gratitude to Dr. D.B. Mandal, former Deputy Director of the Anthropological Survey of India and Dr. A.K. Singh, former Senior Human Ecologist, Anthropological Survey of India who inspired me to work among the Lepchas and guided me by providing valuable suggestions for fruitful work on that project.

My deep sense of gratitude is due to our Director-in-Charge Dr. V.R. Rao, Anthropological Survey of India, not only allowed me to complete the work but also provided all sorts of infrastructural facilities and logistic support.

I am also grateful to the Govt. officials of Sikkim those who are supported to us for carrying out the research work smoothly. The work would not have been possible without the extensive support from my Lepcha informants who always supported me whenever it was felt necessary.

It gives me immense pleasure in expressing my deep sense of gratitude to Dr. Ramesh Chandra, Deputy Director, Anthropological Survey of India, North West Regional Centre, Dehradun for guiding for finalizing the report.

I would like to thank Smt. Dipa Saha, Anthropological Survey of India, Eastern Regional Centre, Kolkata, for typing my manuscript.

9

Man, Nature and Spirit: A Study on the Lepchas and the Bhutias of North Sikkim in Khangchendzonga Biosphere Reserve

K.M. Sinha Roy

INTRODUCTION

Ecology plays a vital role in the society. The rhythm of life linking between man and nature is a common phenomenon all over the planet. The people specially the simple folk - the tribe- are dominated by their immediate ecology. In order to make their existence and survival easy, they worship different gods and goddesses of their own areas and derive satisfaction for their well being. The tribal people having direct dependants on nature fulfill their needs from the surrounding ecology.

Cultural ecology, one of the important current theoretical strategies subscribes to the view point that an intimate relationship exists between a culture and its surrounding environments. According to Marshall Sahlins (1969) cultures are human adaptations. In most its areas, latent as well as manifest, a culture assigns relevance to typical external conditions. And the arrangement helps survive the members of the group in terms of its practical requirements, and polity ideology. Human beings have sufficient capacity to adapt, to the ecology for the sake of their existence. According to the cultural ecologist, they search for adaptation of societies to specific environments. It is done on the plea that natural features, whether cognitive or through physical means, lead to changes in cultural milieu, and this necessitates a new kind of adaptation (Honigmann 1976). Steward feels that cultural ecological adaptations are responsible for distinctive cultural traditions (1969).

The Indian tribal situation enlightening, the world of spirits is also found to have a very close interaction with man, his social structure, and the natural environments. According to Vidyarthi, "nature- man-spirit complex" provides sharp tools in understanding and describing the cultural matrix of Indian tribes. Some studies have supported man - nature interaction. The study of Evans-Pritchard on Nuers is an excellent example where his reasoning is strictly ecological. But the idea of natural interaction between culture an environment is comparatively of late origin; Redfield (1955), Vidyarthi (1963), Thompson (1961), Wolf (1957) and Fried (1952). Some of their works prove that cultural ecology links emic phenomena with the etic condition of nature. The group structure and ideology are responsive to material conditions provided by ecology. Since the religious format can broadly be taken as part of culture and it presents an exhaustive account of socio-cultural-environmental phenomena in the case of Indian tribes; where the ecological variation, as broad as sea, forest, hills, plains, high altitudes etc., mark the Indian tribal scene, with deep rooted religious organization. The method of "cultural ecology" is of quite significance in exploring the tribal cultural nexus.

The belief system in the existence of supernatural powers is almost universal. Around the coordination certain day-to-day happenings like disease, death and the unexplainable, have led tribal people believing in spiritual world, other than the materials visible world, i.e., in the invisible sprit-world or supernatural power. They establish a kind of close relationship between themselves and this power by adjusting themselves to it in two ways, first by controlling or overpowering the spirit by enchanting or practicing some techniques and canalizing the power, for good or bad and secondly, by offering worship to propitiate the superhuman power for acquisition of things or objects desired. In the tribal religion magic is actually an integral part of their religion and magical practices may be included as a method of propitiation. Lowie also includes all forms of supernaturalism including magic in religion (1950).

The tribal religions in India have long been described as animistic. Animism is that exceedingly crude form of religion in which magic is the predominant element. It conceives of man as passing through a life surrounded by a ghostly company of power (powers), elements mostly impersonal in character, shapeless phantoms of which no image can be formed. Some of these are taken to be presiding over particular departments of life or spheres of influence. Thus we have spirit presiding over different diseases, undesired happens and in for seen curates. It is believed that spirits dwell in rocks, mountains, forest areas in trees, rivers and waterfalls, etc. These are diligently propitiated to ward off the dangers associated with their influence (Majumdar, 1961: 423 in J.chakraborty 1994). So these images were formed by the classical foreign and Indian ethnographers of the formulative period.

J. Steward presents his observation on Vidyarthi's book *The Maler: A study in Nature–Man-Spirit Complex.* Social structure elements like family, lineage and village community, the variety of supernatural attributes and the basic drives and anxieties, including those connected with survival of a people, are analysed in interrelatedness and interdependence. He explained that adoption of social arrangement for survival is, as part of the cultural ecology well explained. Steward argues that the study makes it obvious that the little traditions perpetuate in spite of certain links with the large society. Such persistence is attributed to the ecological condition and religion (Mann, 1981).

Ramesh Chandra, while dealing with study of "Ecology and Religion of the Kinner: opines that culture has a great bearing on ecology, especially through adoption. He picks up religion as major ingredient of culture, and argues that "Religion, both as a dogma and as a way of life helps maintaining a well adjusted plane with the ecology ; thus satisfying people to fulfill their requirements- in terms of (1) deriving remedial treatment to their problems, and (2) achieving psychological satisfaction. Ramesh Chandra has tested his hypothesis in his study conducted among the Kinner (which include Kanet, Badhi, Lohar, Koli and Nagaloo), a polyandrous community of North Western Himalayas. In three distinct divisions of his paper, Chandra starts with the ecological context, goes on to the description of people, and finally lands into religious attributes vis-à-vis their reciprocity to ecological setting (Mann 1981).

Sinha, R.K. in his study on "A Note on the Nature–Man–Spirit Complex of a Tribe (Pondo), his approached the complex of nature, man and spirit on the lines similar to the one adopted by L.P. Vidyarthi in case of the Maler. Interactions and interconnections between nature, man and spirit have thus been explored. Sinha also makes use of K.N. Sahay's model of interpreting change in the three cornered complex, in the light of forces of change around. The Pando are living in Surguja district of Madhya Pradesh. Their economy of food-gathering, hunting and basket-making is dependent on the forest around. He mad clear in his explanations that Pando life and culture have developed and flourished in the lap of nature.

The above references are taken into consideration as guiding research text for the present study conducted in north Sikkim in an around K.B.R. area. Further the coded studies add vehemently in providing understanding of nature, man and spirit nexus present context.

The origin of Lepcha religion *Siger* states that "it is complex and rather difficult because Tibetan Bon and Red sect Lamaism for centuries have influenced the religious practices of the Lepchas" (Silger 1956:45). Morris wrote on the basis of David Neel, that in the mountainous tracts of Sikkim, the so called Buddhist population is practically shamanist and they transmit the message of god, demons and the dead through their religious specialist (Morris 1938:115). The religious beliefs and practices of the Lepcha seem difficult because of the co-existence of two mutually contradictory religious traditions like the *mun-boongthing* and the Lamaist tradition to Tibet. The study has focused on how *mun-boongthing* tradition is associated with the Lepcha celestial life. On the other hand, the Lachanpa of Lachen valley, are very close to their natural surrounding. The harsh ecological condition governed series of belief systems-the belief systems allied with forests, hills, rivers and avalanche etc. Here the people of Lachenpa depend on gumpa or monasteries for easy existence and survival. The deities are related to mountains, lakes and forest, which is reflected to their socio- cultural, economic and religious life to maintain their sustainable existence.

The present study tries to bring into relief understanding of the interdependence among the Lepcha of Dzongu reserved area and Lachenpa of Lachen valley, who live in realities isolation, in such high altitude ecological condition, and how interplay of nature, man and spirit in the field of socio-economic and religious life in this harsh ecological niche takes place.

INTRODUCING THE STUDY

In the light of "Man in Biosphere: Khangchendzonga Biosphere Reserve" (K.B.R.), I selected the problem as understanding of nature-man- spirit –complex in K.B.R. region. The problem is interesting and worth explaining as the study area offers a situation of thick relationship-the people of Lepcha and the Bhutia with their surrounding (nature) and due to harsh and tough living condition adapts sense of worshiping various deities both malevolent and benevolent in the interest of peaceful living. The people protect their faith in spirit- complex through their religion.

In India, there are fourteen biosphere reserves, of which the Khangchendzonga reserve in Sikkim is under consideration to carry out a study on nature, man and spirit to K.B.R. The biosphere reserve cover parts of Khangchendzonga hills in Sikkim. The total area 2619.92 sq.km out of which Core zone is 1818.34 sq.km and Buffer zone 835.92 sq.km respectively. The transitional zone consists of twenty three revenue villages and one forest village (as enlisted by forest department). As per notification of forest department fourteen revenue villages under the west Sikkim and nine revenue villages with one forest village in north Sikkim. In the north Sikkim Bhutia and Lepcha people are major groups. The people are very close to biosphere resources for their survival. During their procurement of resources like fuel, food, raw materials and medicinal plants from the hill, forest etc., they develop series of belief system. Thus the belief system or supernatural power plays an important role every sphere of live and culture of the people.

AREA OF STUDY

The village Dzongu falling in the buffer zone of K.B.R is situated in north Sikkim. The Dzongu beyond the Talung river, there are a few Lepcha villages which although geographically outside Dzongu, form a part of it administratively. The inhabitants of these villages, e.g. the Tingbung people, are considered still more conservative than the people of lower Dzongu. The people are visiting the neighboring bazaar, selling their products to the local merchants and buying cloth, kitchen utensils, etc. In this way the life of the people is modified and new inventions are imported and adopted. The main spiritual influence in Dzongu has come with Lamaism and the missionary work undertaken by the Lamanist monasteries in many places e.g. Tingbung, or in Lingthem, studied by Gorer and Morris, the Lamas perform their ceremonies while the local Lepcha religion persons performed theirs. Some ceremonies may be performed by each group, while others are performed jointly. The study area mainly concentrated the upper Dzongu; the area is divided into two divisions. The lower Dzongu is identifying as revenue village and upper Dzongu is under the of biosphere reserved forest.

Dzongu is situated in the North District of Sikkim. The area consists of the Talung valley and western part of the Tista river. The area situated in 88°17′E to 88°31′E and 27°22′N to 27°34′N (approx). The settlement area and cultivated land are between 3,500ft and 7,500 ft above sea-level. Above that level the area is covered by forest and people go there for hunting and gathering of forest products. The density of population is more in lower Dzongu than that of upper Dzongu because the Lepchas fully depend on agriculture i.e. the settlement has grown up in the lower valley of the Talung up to 6600 ft. The Dzongu is divided into six Gram Panchayats Unit. The four number of G.P. units are belonging to upper Dzongu and having two Units, of the lower Dzongu. The Units are: (a) Barfok – Lingdong G.P. (b) Sakyong – Pentong G.P. (c) Tingbung G.P. (d) Lingthem- Lingdem G.P. The units of lower Dzongu are: (a) Lum – Gor Shangtok G.P. and (b) Hee-Gyathang G.P.

Upper Dzongu

The Upper Dzongu area comprises of four numbers of G.P. units i.e. Barfok- Lingdong, Sakyong- Pentong G.P. Tingvong G.P. and Lingthem-Lingdem G.P. Unit. Population details of these gram panchyat units are given below:

A. Barfok-Lingdong Gram Panchayat

Sl. No.	*Hamlet unit*	*Household*	*Population*		*Total*
			Male	*Female*	
1.	Lachen (non-Lama, public)	145	377	325	702
2.	Lachen (Lama)	15	35	23	58
3.	Chaten	11	25	23	48
4.	Thangu	4	12	8	20
5.	Zeema	2	7	5	12
6.	Yathang	1	4	2	6
7.	Rabom	4	10	7	17
8.	Dokpa (Lachenpa)	7	22	18	40
9.	Mangam	2	3	3	6
10.	Gangtok	10	16	15	31
	Grand total	201	511	429	940

B. Sakyong-Pentong Gram Panchayat

Sl. No.	*Name of Ward*	*Population*	*Household*	*G.P.*
1.	Lower Lingzah	219	37	Sakyong-Pentong
2.	Upper Lingzah	111	22	Do
3.	Bay-Tolun (Tolung Gumpha)	85	16	Do
4.	Pentong	152	24	Do
5.	Sakyong	150	25	Do
	Total	717	124	

C. Tingvong Gram Panchyat

Sl. No.	*Name of Ward*	*Population*	*Household*	*G.P.*
1.	Tingvong	282	45	Tingvong
2.	Namprick	162	30	Do
3.	Linko	130	22	Do
4.	Kusung	149	30	Do
5.	Nung	172	25	Do
	Total	895	152	

D. Lingthem- Lingdem Gram Panchyat

Sl. No.	*Name of ward*	*Population*	*Household*	*G.P.*
1.	Salim-Pakel	136	25	Lingthem-Lingdem
2.	Safo-Liching	147	25	Do
3.	Leek	132	29	Do
4.	Panang	204	35	Do
5.	Pasingdong	429	67	Do
6.	Lingthem (Sofel Gumpha)	374	66	Do
7.	Lingdem	274	46	Do
8.	Laben	92	17	Do
	Total	1788	310	

The Upper Dzongu comprises of four numbers of Gram Panchayat i.e. Barfok-Lingdong, Sakyong-Pentong Gram Panchayat, Tingvong Gram Panchayat and Lingthem-Lingdem Gram Panchayat.

The Barfok- Lingdong Gram Panchayat consisting of four numbers of wards. The total households are 185 and the population 1096 respectively. The Sakyong- Pentong Gram Panchayat comprises of five numbers of ward. The total populations 717 and house holds 124 accordingly. The Tingvong Gram Panchayat comprises of five numbers of ward. The population of Gram Panchayat 895 and 152 numbers accordingly. The Lingthem- Lingdem Gram Panchayat comprises of eight numbers of ward. The total populations of the ward are 1788 and 310 house hold are respectively.

LACHEN VALLEY

The Lachen is narrow valley situated in the western part of the North Sikkim. The valley is tired by the river *Lachen Chu* and its tributaries *Lasa Chu, Chhopta Chu, Kalep Chu, Zemu Chu, Tram Chu, Rabom Chu*, etc. The high pass valley is about 9600 ft high and from the Chunthang Sub-division office 29 km. The road continues to wind up to Chopta valley at a Dizzying 13,200 ft, and extend up to Gurudongmar Lake, about 17,200 ft high altitude. Lachen valley stands on a grassy and flat bush from the periphery of which rise with the pine clad mountains with their snowy peaks and black cliffs. The valley has moderately shallow, some-what excessively drained, coarse loamy soils on moderate steep slope (15-30%) with gravelly loamy surface, moderate erosion and slight stoniness. Lachen forest can be categorized as Himalayan Wet Temperate Forest. The mountain slope of Lachen is almost covered by the Silver fir. The numbers of trace like Quercus spp, Castanopsis triuloides, Acerspp, Machilus spp and Cinnamomum spp associated with shrubs Rosa, Rubus, Berberies and Viburnum. There are a few patches of pure oak (Quercus lamellose) which stands with other species such as Eurya, Viburnum and Symplocos and an abundance of mosses and epiphytes. Some species of Rhododendrons are also found in this region. The region preserves an astonishing diversity of wildlife. Yak and Horse are commonly used for transportation of goods in these areas. Blue Sheep's Sapi (Domestic Sheep) Kiang, Nayan, Tibetan Wolf, Tibetan Snowcock, Lammergeier, Raven, Golden Eagle, Ruddy Shelduck and some species of Deer are also often. The place is also famous for expedition side gearing up to begin the Green Lake Trek or the Khangchendzonga hill. The route was easier from Tibet to Lachen than from Lachung so this was the route preferred by traders. After the Chinese occupation of Tibet in the year of 1959, the trade route was close. With the Chinese aggression of 1962, several roads connecting the border areas were quickly constructed for mobilisation of troops, and one among them was between Lachen to Gurudongmar. Lachen was privileged with the benefit of a highway leading to one of Sikkim's most important tourist place known as Gurudongmar. The narrow strip of extended valley is covered with thick vegetations. Different species of rhododendron in different colors are found along the valley. The valley is also characterized by a number of hot springs, water falls, glaciers and glaciated lakes, such as Green Lake, Lhonak, Zemu, Gurudongmar, Chholhamu and Chhopta Lake. The Chungthang is situated at the junction of Testa and the Lachung river. It is sub-divisional head quarter of the Lachen valley. From the Chungthang onwards, northern Sikkim absolutely inhabited by the Bhutia population; though Chungthang itself has got a mixed population of Bhutia Lepcha and Nepali.

The population figures as collected from census department are available 1971 or before there is no such population records collected in the census department. The population considers as Chungthang sub-division, having the Bhutia as main consideration can be seen as given below:

Year of Census	*Population*
1971	799
1981	919
1991	1640
2001	2923

The Lachen valley is divided into two parts (i) lower or southern part (ii) upper or northern part. The lower part belongs to Lachen valley i.e. permanent settlement area. The upper part belongs to Thangu, which is used as agricultural and cattle meet area in summer season.

Household and Population
Lachen, 2007

Sl. No.	*Hamlet unit*	*Household*	*Population*		*Total*
			Male	*Female*	
1.	Lachen (non-Lama, public)	145	377	325	702
2.	Lachen (Lama)	15	35	23	58
3.	Chaten	11	25	23	48
4.	Thangu	4	12	8	20
5.	Zeema	2	7	5	12
6.	Yathang	1	4	2	6

Sl. No.	*Hamlet unit*	*Household*	*Population*		*Total*
			Male	*Female*	
7.	Rabom	4	10	7	17
8.	Dokpa (Lachenpa)	7	22	18	40
9.	Mangam	2	3	3	6
10.	Gangtok	10	16	15	31
Grand total		201	511	429	940

Lachenpa

The study area is concentrated ten hamlets of Lachen valley. The total hamlets are ten of which 201 nos, of house holds and 940 numbers are souls respectively.

OBJECTIVE OF STUDY

The Lepcha and Bhutia are inhabitants, of North Sikkim. Their socio-economic and religious life is deeply related to natural surrounding. On the basis of ecological condition they have developed a series of belief system keeping the focus of the study of man- nature- spirit aspects the study has been conduced with the following objectives to provide understanding on:

1. The peoples view about forests, hills and surrounding nature.
2. Mode of economic life and belief system.
3. Socio-cultural and religious life in relation to nature.
4. The role of traditional political system of the people.
5. The method of conservation on plants and animals with the natural ecosystem.
6. Inter-relationship of nature and world view of the people living in Khangchendzonga Biosphere Reserve.

METHOD

Under the project "Man and Environment: Khangchendzonga Biosphere Reserve", the present study has been conducted on the theme "Nature, Man and Spirit" of the Lepcha and the Lachenpa of North Sikkim. The study has followed the model enunciated by L.P Vidyarthi in his study of nature –man- spirit of the Maler. Considering similar ecological setting of North western Himalaya, of Ramesh Chandra's model on ecology and religion of the Kinner, Mountain Dwellers of north-Western Himalayas has been extensively used. During the field work conventional tools and techniques were used for necessary data collection, such as conducting household census, interview, case study and observation.

THE SOCIETY

Lepcha

The Lepchas are a Mongoloid people living in the Himalayas on the southern and eastern slopes of the Mount Kangchendzonga. The Lepchas identify themselves as "*Rongkup*", meaning the children of *Rong*. The literal meaning of *rong* is 'hill' and *kup* is "children" of the hill. The Lepchas themselves are convinced that their home has always been the legendary kingdom of *Mayel*, in the vicinity of Mt. Khangchendzonga. It is notice that; most of the Lepcha clans claim to have mythical connections with this particular mountain peak which they worship as their deity.

The economic life of the people is mainly based on land and forest. In the early days, the people were hunters and food –gathers and favored animal husbandry before they became shifting cultivators. Now-a-day, the main crops are cultivate rice, maize, millets, barley, oats and cash crops like ginger, potatoes, tomato, vegetables etc and fruits like orange. The Lepcha adhere to religious system simultaneously, viz. *Lamaism* and the old *Mun* religion or shamanism. In *Mun* religion priesthood goes by the possession or the manifestation of supernatural spirit. Lamaism or Mahayana Buddhism is the other religious system. The religious life of the village revolves round the Gumpa or the Monastery. This faith was based on spirits, which is malevolent and benevolent in nature with witchcraft and exorcism being very common. They worshipped the spirits of mountains, rivers and forests which co-existed so pleasantly with surrounding nature.

The life cycle rituals of the people are encircled and dominated by nature. The rite de passage, socio-economic and religious life of the people revolves round the surrounding ecology. The life cycle ritual activities of the people are based on the name of God or Goddess, which is related to river, hill and nature based. On the other hand, the people of upper Dzongu follow two types of religious path i.e. the traditional religion and Buddhism fold. The Lepcha are peaceful and nature worshipping people. There is an air of mysticism about their lives and rituals. The Lepcha (Dzongu) folklore is very rich with stories. The well-known deities of the Lepchas are *Itbumoo*, *Rom*, *Itbu Debu Rom*, *Kongchen Konglo* and *Tamsang Thing* etc., and the famous festival is *Namsoong*. The *Boongthing* is the local priest and he performs ceremonies to invoke the deities seeking their benevolence.

Lachenpa

The Bhutia people living in the plateau are called Tibetan and the other falling on the side of peninsular India continues to be called *Bhotia*. The term "*Bhot*" or "*Bhotia*" is very wide in meaning and implication. Bhotia is clearly a generic name given to people of *Bhot* origin. It includes myriads of tribes and clans possessing diverse culture and language and inhabiting over vast geographical boundaries. As evident from above, the Sikkimese Bhotia is one of the many tribes belonging to the corpus Bhotia. They call themselves Sikkimese or *Denzongpa* and speak Sikkimese which is a dialect of Bhotia or Tibetan. Unlike other Bhotia tribes the Sikkimese Bhotias have a distinct political and cultural entity as Sikkimese.

The Lachen valley is inhabited by the Bhutias and they identify them as *Lachenpa.* The word *Lachenpa* means "*Lachen*" is a place of big hill and the inhabitant of foot of the hill is "*pa*". The village is typically traditional and retains its old practice of the "*Dzumsa,*" (political system). The people of Lachen valley are herdsmen and traders. Beside the economic life of the people, depends on agriculture, dairy farming and pastoralist. During the summer season people of Lachenpa go to higher altitudes, to graze their animals. They stay there in the summer months when the land is covered with grass. When winter starts, they come down to the lower altitude with their animals and practice cultivation with cardamom being their principal cash crop. They make butter from the yak and cow milk for their own consumption. Beside, they also collect twice in year, yak hair and sheep wool for sale. The Lachenpa women play a vital role in socio-economic life of the people. The women are mainly engaged in different type of weaving activities like carpet making and woolen garments etc. Besides, the female folk also participate in the dance, music, during the festivals and functions The Bhutias are famous for their weaving, wood carving and '*thanka*' painting.

Buddhism has played a special role in shaping the *Lachenpa* society. The monasteries and monks are pivot around their socio-cultural and religious life. The Lachenpa follows household ritual, marriage and birth or death ceremonies and agricultural rites are conducted by the monks from the Gompas. Their chief deity is the tutelary galaxy of Buddha and Bodhisattvas, followed by the guardian deities, including local deities, family deities, village deities and Khangchendzonga. Most of the deities are related to mountains, lakes and forest. The important festivals of the Lachenpa are the Tibetan New Year, the *Sagadawa*, the *Pang-Lhabsol*, the *Losoong*, and the *Lhabab-Duchen*. The *Tashi -Tagye* is a popular theme of Bhutia art. These eight symbols, considered auspicious in Mahayana Buddhism, are intimately associated with the life and teaching of the Buddha. The important festivals observed by the Lachenpa community include *Losoong*; *Pang-Lhab-Sol*, worship of the guardian deity, Khangchendzonga; *Kagyat* dance or *mask* dance and *Saga Dawa*, the blessing of the spirits. Besides, the people are following different types of ancestral beliefs which may be both malevolent and benevolent in nature. Ramesh Chandra noted that, it is largely true that the geography of a particular area or ecology in the broader sense, helps to a great extent in shaping the society at its value systems level (social aspects) as well as its cultural level (material cultural aspects). But it is also to be considered at the same level how well other institutions help people to respond in a cohesive manner to the needs arising out of ecological settings satisfying demands of institutions simultaneously. A sense of reciprocity between the intuitions and ecology fulfill the requirements of the people deserves attention from anthropologists for its elucidation. It is noted that various social and religious institution in any society are largely shaped in the manner, or present set of prescription, which fit in the frame work of need- direct or indirect at different levels of the people to which terms given for their recognition are "adjustment" and/ or "adaptation" (Ramesh Chandra 1981).

THE NATURE

The nature of K.B.R. centers around the forest, land, hills and rivers. Dzongu is a mountains land, its length and breadth forty miles on each side, bounded on the south-east by river Tissta, on the north-east by the river Talung and on the other side by the mountains Khangchendzonga. The rivers are about 2,000 ft above sea-level and the average height of the hills is about 12,000 ft.The river valley are hot, humid and somewhat malarious. Most of the houses and cultivated land are situated between 3,500 ft and 7,500 ft above sea-level. Above the cultivated land is the forest from which wild produce is gathered and is also use as hunting place and grazing land for cattle. Above the forest level comes first the rhododendron forest and then the snows, rarely visited except by hunter searching for musk-deer and other wild animals. The climate of the Tulung valley is excessively wet, even for the Himalayas; it is only in the autumn month- from the end of September to the end of November – that there is no rain. In the Dzongu there are a great number of mountain streams running down from the snows to the river. The Dzongu consists of six numbers of Gram panchyat and the settlement pattern of the villages have no sort of geographical unity, the houses are either isolated in the fields and forests, or gathered in small groups of three or four families.

Physically the Lachen valley occupies highest human habitation region of the north Sikkim. The habitation area is situated about 5,000 ft in height. There is no place below the height of 6,234 ft in the region. The whole region is enclosed on all sides by the Great Himalaya with different heights between 17,000 ft, to 28,000 ft. This region is the upper catchments basin of the Tista within the Himalayas. Due to the opening in south, monsoon clouds penetrate into the far northern region and cause comparatively high rain fall, which is not common in other parts of the Himalayas. Temperature is also not uniform throughout the region and varies with altitude, rainfall, nearness to the perpetual snowline, etc. The Tista with its tributaries, namely, the Lachung, Zemu, Lhonak and Sebozungetc has divided the region into separate units. The human habitation is restricted to a height of almost 12,000 ft, along the Lachen or Tista valley. The concentration of the population is mainly restricted to the Tista and Lachung valley. The villages are situated on glacial terraces which are now a few hundred feet above the river bed, as in Khedum, Lema, etc. in the Lachun valley. In the higher region of Yathang or Kalem of the Tista, where the valley is still U-shape and the river has not yet down gorges, villages are situated in the flat valley bottom near the stream. The settlement pattern is controlled by physiography. Where there is ample space as in Yathang, the settlement is scattered; where there is a small circular basin, as in Lachen, the settlement is compact and where there is a strip of land formed by a glacier, as in Khedum, the pattern is liner.

The life and culture of Lepcha and Bhutia appear in the lap of natural surrounding by forest, river and hill. The ecological setting of these people makes a deep relation on their socio-economic as well as of their belief system. The nature is so deep –rooted in their life and culture that they cannot isolate themselves from the forest, hill etc. The Lepcha and Bhutia villages are mainly situated in the buffer zone of the K.B.R area. The house type of the both the communities are rectangular in shape, which is made by wooden or bamboo walls, roof is thatched with grass, leaves and cane. Forest, river and hill play a major role of their economic life. The people are exploiting the forest product as per their necessities. They procure different type of edible roots, tubers, fruits, flowers, leaves, herbs, shrubs, medicinal plants, bee-hives and wild animals (edible) from the forest for their sustenance. In the past, hunting was one of the most important sources of food requirement. Due to imposition of forest rules now-days the hunting has became less. The utilize of forest and hill resources like bamboo, cane and wood are very close to their social life. Supply of raw materials from forest and other sources is very immense for making domestic utensils, basket weaving crafts and blanket making, which help them in procuring their bread. They make baskets of different shape and sizes. Basketry is one of the important sources of earning cash money. Besides, the Lepcha and Bhutia are engaged in making various type of household utensils like bamboo and wooden pot, used as *chi* (country liquor) or tea drinking cup, mat for sleeping, wooden container for preservation, make various kinds of vessels. On the other hand, the Lachenpa are very famous for making eight lucky signs, thanka painting and yak products. The Lachenpa women engaged themselves in different type of blanket and carpet making. Now-a-days, the younger generation makes various types of bamboo and cane items, due to demand of the tourist people. The present scenario indicates that after impact of tourism, the products or the artifacts have became a new source of income for the people. The raw materials are procured from the K.B.R. region. In this situation the Lepcha and Bhutia life and culture seem to have originated, develop and flourished in the lap of nature. They are dependent on the forest and hill to such extent that their whole life and their economy revolve round the forest and hill. The above facts reveal that the importance of the forest in the matter of supplying shelter, food, drinking, indigenous medicines and raw materials for their crafts, is very immense. Thus, the economic activities of the Lepcha and Bhutia are closely inter-woven with forest and hill.

SOCIAL ASPECT

Lepcha is a homogeneous interlocking community. They appear to subsist fairly well in the mixed communities, to a great extent adopting the habits, culture and even the language of their neighbours. They also share with them the religion of Lamaism, which is the official religion of the State. Lost in the overwhelming mass of alien people, the Lepchas have no social organization and since Lepcha life is based on the social group they have been left with little except their appearance and their gentleness which can be called Lepcha (Gorer 1987).

The Lepchas are divided into groups by birth and marriage; these groups are the patrilineal clan, or *ptso* and the immediate and extended family. Lepcha have a very small number of kinship terms; they exclude all the category of cousins and except for the mother's brothers, make no distinction between the paternal and maternal lines. The people younger than the speaker too do not make any distinction of sex; the same word is used for a younger brother or a younger sister, for a son or a daughter, for a nephew or a nice. Only in the case of children's spouses different words are used for son-in-law and daughter-in law.

Lepcha belongs to a patrineal clan or *ptso*, which is originated from some supernatural or legendary ancestor beliefs. The function of the *ptso* is the regulation of marriage and the prevention of incest; an exogamic unit. In the same *ptso* are allowed to marry if they are separated by nine generations from a common ancestor. Each *ptso* is under the guardianship of certain supernatural, who are worshipped by all the male members of the *ptso*; every third year all the men of one place arrange together a sacrifice of an ox. The sacrifice is entirely under the direction of the *Mun*. The ceremony performed for the benefit of particular individuals.

The family is not only a social unit, but also has its own religious position with accompanying ceremonies. The family forms an economic unit and their good or evil fortune depends on the property of the head of the family as well as on the initiative and ingenuity displayed by himself, his wife and their grown up children. The old members of the family assist according to their ability in the common work and the children will be drawn into the daily work being given whatever work is suitable to their age. The members of the family also assist their neighbors in their work and join in the general work of the villages.

It may be said that the Lepcha of Dzongu possess neither arts, crafts, though they show considerable dexterity in adapting natural materials to domestic uses. The most important single material for the Lepcha is the bamboo or other the numerous verities of different bamboo that they grow and recognize. In the house bamboo is used for the floor ceiling, wall and balcony; out of it water-carries and an occasion water conducts are made. The drinking vessels- *potyout* is used to drink *chi*, a sort of bear which is prepared by pouring boiling water on fermented grain. This is taken through a straw—*pa-hip* pin and brooches which are made from bamboo. Bow and arrow is the only hunting weapon of the Lepcha. Plates are usually replaced by big leaves, but there are a certain number of rudely carved wooden plates which is used on a ceremonious occasions. The Lepcha weave strong and regular mats and baskets out of the bark of bamboo and various reeds, which they employ for various purposes.

Lepcha houses are rectangular building raised a meter high above the ground on stone piles which go round three sides of the building; the east side is left open, and the space underneath serves as a shelter at night for domestic animals. The building itself is made of wood, plaster, bamboo and thatch. All buildings have the floor which is usually woven bamboo; the walls are always of bamboo covered with plaster, occasionally with wooden supports. After compilation the house the Lama and *Mun* appease *Tashi-chene* and on the day first of all incense leaves are burned to savely the demons who live in the earth below the house and who may have inhabited the trees of which the house is built. Then an ox is sacrifices by the *Mun* and offered to entire gods, and then the head, right foreleg and left hind portion of sacrificed ox are given to the carpenter, who has worked on the house as his fee. After this a *laminas* ceremony with music and reading from the appropriate books is performed. At the end of which the chief lama present will anoint the house pillars with blood, chi, liquored and butters starting with the western pillar and proceeding to the northern, eastern southern and central. Finally all present throw rice mixed with flour at the pillar shouting in a voice as loud as possible. This ceremony is meant to avert illness from the inhabitants of the house.

The Lepcha believed that, natural objects ; all supernatural, good and bad though eternally living out side the world have innumerable manifestations with which this world is filled. These manifestation or replicas of the supernatural choose various natural phenomena for semi-permanent habitation, agreeable phenomena lakes or fruits tress or fruitful land – if the supernatural are generally benevolent; disagreeable place useless tree, water-falls rocks or barren ground is the supernatural are generally malevolent. Each type of supernatural nature has a preference for particular kind of habitation; thus all the dent moong-fever devils – live in big isolated trees sabdok moong –skin disease devil – in out crops of rock. According to Lamaist beliefs everything the world possesses a soul, for the soul is the animating princi all life without whose intermediary nothing could move or gr

The deity *Angu-brung* is related to stone goddess, during the overtake path if the people not obey the goddess, they will suffer from any disease. All the functions are appeased by *Boongthing*. During the puja of *Boongthing* scarifying chicken, egg, banana, rice etc. is common practice. A youth generally join hunting team at the age of fifteen years. He became a new member of the team and he observes the senior hunter and learns tecqunic and requisite rituals. During his first visit to hunting he is not allowed to carry bow and arrow. After getting permission form the senior member he acquires a bow and arrow from an elder brother or uncle or a friend. After hunting one hundred animals, he is allowed to eat his own hunt. Before that all the hunt meat is consumed by the family members.

The Bhotia of Sikkim are divided into two groups, the Tondu Rushi, which has four exogamous units (rue) namely Chechuthapa, Sandarpa, Kachopa and Sengapa; and the Beb Tsen Gye with eight rue, namely Gensapa Namchangopa, Chungiapa, Ithempa, Venchungpa, Veinpunadikpa, Namnakpa and Machangpa. These rues are differentiated from each other on a social and territorial base. In case of Lachen valley Sandarpa, Sengapa, Namnakpa and Chungiapa are the majority groups in the area. The groups are traditionally endogamous. One cannot marry one's own member. The marriage rule was endogamous at community level. It is observed that adult marriage is in vogue and generally the wife is younger than the husband but there are many cases where the wives are older. Now the people follows monogamy is general practice, except in the North district, where fraternal polyandry is noticed. Until recently polyandry was practice on a wide scale in Lachung and Lachen but now the occurrence has declined; although there are some men who have more than one wife. The married Bhutia women were a striped apron called the *pangden* as a symbol of marriage.

As for rules of inheritance, property is inherited only by sons. Sons get equal shares except the youngest; who generally stays in the house and looks after his mother and younger sisters and therefore is entitled to a little extra over the others. Other sons usually go out and seek other professions. The settlement of the Lachenpa people is formed near the foot of the hill. The house type is rectangular in shape. The house is generally made by wooden *ara* in structure. The house is divided into several rooms. The rooms consist of Puja ghar (*Chho-ka*), bed room (*Ne-sa),* kitchen room (*Thap-sa)* and bottom part of the house known as (*Ogong)* is generally used as store purpose. On account of the occasion of the opening day of the house and inauguration of the house the Lama appease the God for the welfare of the house. On these days, all the relative and friends attend the function and foods.

Birth

The term pregnancy is locally known as *Fuchi-mo*. During delivery, if the pregnant women feel uneasy, the traditional witch doctor *Jhakri* appease the benevolent spirit to save women and her new born child with the help of *Gurudongmar lake* water and flower. Her husband is allowed to massage lower abdomen part with the help of *Chowri ghee*. *Chowri* is female Yak. The delivery house is separated from the main house. The delivery house is locally known as *Bho*. After delivery the mother stays separately with her new born child. The system is locally known as *Zim-chung*. The abdominal chord of the new born is cut by an experience lady with the help of knife. To dry chord, a ghee made of yak milk is used generally after boiling to sear of naval point of the new born baby. The old lady *(Dai)* is locally known as *Teu*. The husband berries the placenta (*shamo)* beneath the earth. They believe that by doing so evil spirit will not harm to mother and child. The first breast milk is not given to the child; they believe that it is harmful to the new born child. Which locally known as *Om-cope*. After 10-12 days the mother is allowed to enter the kitchen or the main house. During the pregnancy period the mother observed restriction of some food items. The mother should not drink more water. She is restricted from yak, sheep meat and vegetable also. During the pregnancy period, in evening time the mother is not allowed to go out side of the house. The people believe that, the mother may get effect from evil spirit. This system is locally known as *Phiru-makham*. It is also observed that the pregnant woman is not allowed to go to the forest and not to cross the river. The system is locally known as *Na-che-na-manju*. The child at the age of six or seven years they perform name giving ceremony locally known as *Me-yaksha*, when the child baby's hair is removed for first time. The process is locally known as *Tap-che*. All the function is performed in presence of Lama all relative enjoy feast.

Marriage (*Bree*)

The physical signs of puberty of Lepcha - the beginning of menses and the growing of the breasts- are believed only to occur through the external influence either of a man or supernatural namely by *Kandoo moong*. On the puberty occasion the people appease *Kandoo moog* for save of the girl. Berofe marriage the mun performs ritual in the groom's house before being taken to the girl's family. On the day, they sacrifice pigs and other gifts. This puja offered to the *rum-faat-bu*; by the *Mun*, and Lama also participates in the ceremony. Likewise the family members also appease the deities by offering burned *chi*, buttered cup and rice to *ptso* and so to the *Komsithing* and *Tarbong-bo* (clan deity). The people believe that, after appeasing the gods bless the marriage and make it fruitful.

The Lepcha marriage consists of a number of rituals and customary practices all along the different stages of the wedding process. The important practices are *Nyom-vyat* (quest for the bride). *Ashake* (joining or the linking function). *Bree* (the wedding ceremony). Before marriage the *Boongthing* perform ancestor puja like *Vick-rum, Mukung-rum* and *Hit-rum* and other God and Goddesses of marriage, and seek their blessing for the success of the new couple.

Marriage-(*Nin*)

The Lachenpa generally follow arranged marriage. Now-a-days, some cases of love marriage are also there. Marriage in a Lachenpa family is arranged through negotiations by the paternal or maternal uncle of the boy who goes to the bride's place. The age of marriage is generally eighteen to nineteen years for girls, but now-a-days, age of marriage is followed. The family members of both parties negotiated and fixed marriage date. To finalize the marriage function from groom house is locally known as (*Fumu-ta-juse*). On the other hand from bride house finalize the function locally known as *Fu-ta-juse.* The marriage day finalization is locally known as *Kha-dick-sa.* The invitation is extended orally to invite the relative and friends. The system is locally known as *Phu-she.* The marriage ceremony is performed during day time. The dowry system is till exiting in the society, the bride house generally gives dowry as yak, sheep and cash before marriage day. The dowry system is locally known as *Ree*. On the marriage day, yak and sheep meat is common for the invities. To day some modern food is introduce in the function. The marriage function is performed in the bride house. The marriage symbol of girl is *Paugden* and the boy used *Bakhu*. After three days of marriage function, the bride and groom coming groom house on the day the bride offer his mother-in-law sheep meat, ghee (yak), cloth and sweet also. This system is locally known as *Faluk.* Similarly the bride and groom is coming bride house, on this day the groom house offer cloth, gold and money so that the new couple can build their new family. The Lama performs the marriage ceremony.

Death- (*Afung*) Lepcha

The Lama believed that the soul wanders for forty-nine days in a sort of purgatory, after which it is judged and rewarded and sent on to its next incarnation, whether it be on the earth as another human being or as an animal or to haven for a period of blessedness or to hell for a period of torment, where *Mun* believe that the soul is conduced to the rumlyang, where it is born again as a tiny child, very often of a different sex to its former life; in the rumluang the child grows up to maturity and leads a happy and immoral life among all the other death, a life similar to that hare on earth except that there is no death or disease or want.

The Lepcha perform participating rites by worshiping their ancestor deities like *Lee-rum*, *Ajo-sekeo, Mukung-rum, Vick-rum* and *Hit-rum* after death occurred in the family. It continues for five weeks. The system is locally known as *Duney*. *Chumi* puja is performed after the forty nine days; on the days all the relatives and friends come and join the puja. After one year the family members perform *Lamchat puja*. On this day both the Lama and *Boongthing* are join the puja. It will continue consequently for three years. The Lachenpa follow Buddhism. The supernatural belief system is related to malevolent and benevolent spirits in nature. The life cycle rituals, i.e., birth to death centers round monastery or gumpa.

Death- (*Me-shi-sa*) Lachenpa

In the case of death, the Lachenpa people first call all relatives and the Lama. The house member informed the Lama about the death in the family which is locally known as *Lama-Chunna.* The dead body is kept for three days in the house and Lama performs puja for welfare of the remaining house hold members. During the period yak ghee lamp and resin are generally used by the people. This is locally known as *Kubur-yak-she*. During the period, all the family members and Lama generally use vegetable food and *Chang* as a food items. After three days, the dead body is brought to the Gumpa, where puja is performed for the dead person. The system is locally known as *Kubur bak-she.* Then the dead body is taken for crimination and the first son generally lets the pyre of the dead body. After forty nine days, *Tha-chne* puja is performed by the family members. On the day, the family members hoist one white flag in front of the house as a mark of memory of the dead. After seven days the family members perform one function and all the relative are invited on this occasion. Finally after forty nine days the family member's perform *Tha-chne* functions. On that day, all the relatives and friends join the function. The yak meat is served compulsorily to the invitees. This marks the end of the death purification rites of observation and the family is treated pure to have interaction with other society members on normal pattern.

The Lechanpa have the custom of worshipping ancestors from the paternal side as *Pho-lha* and from maternal side as *Mo-Lha*. The names of the ancestors are invoked and oblations offered in a ceremony. The invocation of *Masang Khyong-dyudh* precedes the other. *Masang Khyong-dyudh* is invoked as the greatest *Pho-Lha*, the greatest saviour of mankind and the King of *Dab-Lha*, in the *Pho-Lha* ceremony. Every clan of Sikkimese Bhotia is required to perform the *Pho-Lha* ceremony every year in accordance with the prescribed rituals of worship. A Sikkimese Bhotia is required to know his *Php-Lha* and *Mo-Lha*, failing which he may suffer the forfeiture of social recognition. This is why the maternal uncles of the both the bride and groom are required in the solemnization of a marriage in Sikkimese Bhutia custom. As a matter of fact, a marriage cannot enjoy any social respectability in the absence of the maternal uncles, who symbolize the purity of *Ryudh* (clan) *Khoong* (Gribe) and *Gyudh* (race).

It is also noticed that, *Ghe Bumsa* managed to appease the spirit by accepting him as his protector deity of clan (Pho-Iha) offering right arm of Yak as sacrifice and thereby averting the wrath of the spirit. *Ghe Bumsa*, thereafter, worshiped masang *Khyong-dyudh* as his chief *Pholha* (Chief Protector Deity of clan or Kula devata) by offering right arm of a Yak as sacrifice every year. The patrimonial clan deity is called *Pho-Lha* and the matrimonial one is called *Mo-Lha*.

Before *Lossong* festival *Gutor* is perform by monks in the monasteries. The people pray for a good harvest and even better prospects for the next crop. During the festival the people perform the *Chaam* dance at the monasteries. The dance symbolized the exorcizing of evil spirits of the year and the welcoming of the benevolent spirits for the New Year. The people also participate in archery competitions as a mark of the festival. The men become gods during the festival and don attires with mystical symbols. The *'Kagyed'* (eight teachings of the Guru) dance forms an important part of the *Gutor* ceremony and is held on the 28th day of the 11th month at the monasteries.

The deity *Angu-brung* is related to stone goddess, during the overtake path if the people do not obey the goddess, the people suffer from any disease. All the functions are appeased by *Boongthing*. During the puja the *Boongthing* is scarifying chicken, egg, banana, rice etc.

THE ROLE OF POLITICAL SYSTEM IN THE SOCIETY

In the early days, *Dzongu* as part of the Maharajah of Sikkim is private estate, which divided into twelve villages, each village had a Mandal. The Mandal finalized all type of disputes. In the year of 1975 Sikkim enlist as 22nd state of India and people follow modern democracy in their day to life. The traditional political system of Lachenpa i.e., *Dzumsa* is constituted of two clusters. One cluster is elected by the local people and other body is from religious cluster i.e., Lama from monastery. The traditional political system is to maintain every sphere of life and culture of the society. The role of development is divided in two dimensions i.e., for welfare of the society and religious performance for wellbeing of the society.

From the above few pages it is observed that, the social life of the Lepcha and Bhutia centre on beliefs and practices. The belief system is centre around the supernatural phenomena and monastery. They have developed series of beliefs within their eco-cultural niche.

THE SPIRIT

It is evident that, the Lepcha follow two religions simultaneously-Buddhism and traditional religion i.e. based on *Mun* and *Boongthing*. The Lachenpa of Lachen valley follows Buddhism (Tibetan type). The spread of each religion corresponds to the ecological setting to a great deal. In general both the religions work to give a smooth running to the Lepcha and Lachenpa people in terms of fulfillment of their needs arising out of the ecological setting. In addition, something beyond human control is recognized as the "supernatural" and with the power of other secondary deities. There are gods and goddesses at different levels in orders to religious life of the Lepcha and Lachenpa starting from individual to regional level. The people living in harsh surrounding in the forms of mountains, jungles and fearful location, their belief in supernatural and in the god becomes more entrenched in day to day life. They believe in number of supernatural powers who wiled a profound influence on their life and culture by controlling and directing their day to day affairs. Most of the misfortunes, ailments, accidents, disease, failure in hunting and crops, are taken to be in the hands of some evil spirits. The super natural power is conceived as benevolent and malevolent in nature.

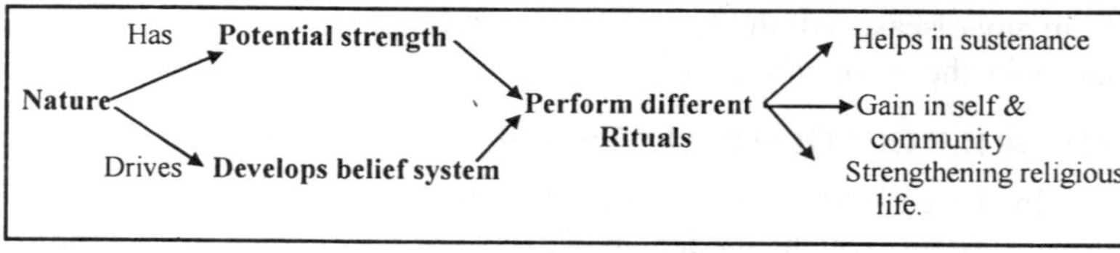

Schematic representation of Man- Nature relationship.
Developed after Ramesh Chandra model (Ramesh Chandra 1981).

The Lepcha and Bhutia are living in the midst of forest and hills. They have been dependent upon the forest for their subsistence and develop a beliefs system keeping in harmony with surrounding. The life and culture of the Lapcha and Bhutia is the reflection of their economy, self- image existence and beliefs in the supernatural world; thus interdependence of "man" and the "nature".

According to nature, structure and function, the supernatural powers are considered either benevolent or malevolent. They are conceived and accommodated by offering numbers of worships and sacrifices. However, the people are afraid of such powers because these are taken to be causes of sickness, death, accident etc. Consequently, such deities will be discussed at family, village level and other deities are exclusively related with their economy life.

The belief system of Lepcha and Bhutia can be categorized in three segmentations i.e. Nature; Social life and Religious life. The schematic diagram tries to represent as how the Lepcha and Bhutia people depend on nature in their social and economic life. To utilize the natural resource the people appease god and goddess to maintain their easy lives. Thus the men are depending on nature; on the other side man also depends on the religious belief for their satisfaction.

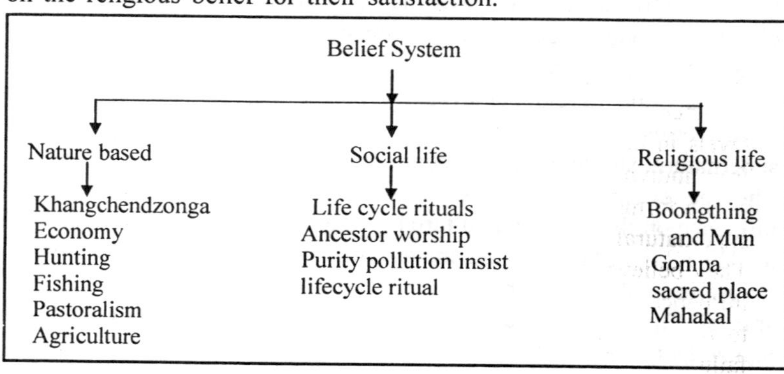

The economic life of the both communities is depending on nature. The daily needs mainly of shelter, food (fruit, root and tubers) fuel and medicine are all part and parcel of human life. To procure such essential items they appease different types of gods and goddess.

The people believe that, Khangchendzonga is the god of wealth, gold, diamond, silver and brass etc. The God Khangchendzonga also saves them from bad evil, the evil is locally known as *Leader*. The evil *Leader* is believed to be inhabitant in the hill area and destroys all wealth. To protect them from evils the people appease Khangchendzonga deities. The Lapcha and Bhutia keep the image of Khangchendzonga deities inside their houses. The color of image is generally brown. The concept of brown is related to the Lama people who use brown colored dress and they are the people who engage themselves for welfare of the people. The use of color for Khangchendzonga deities is developed from Lama people. On the seventh day of September the puja is performed by the people. During the puja the people perform *mask* dance locally know as *Siwa.* The dance is related to both the belief system i.e. malevolent and benevolent in nature. The *Siwa* dance is to appease for welfare of the society. The dance reflects various kinds of activities; related to aware or led to live the individual as well as society. Similarly the Lepcha perform *Tendong-lho-faat* worship. On 8th August, the Lepchas worship *Mount... Tendong*. The people believed that, the *Mount Tendong* saved their race from destruction by great flood. The *Boongthing* worship *Mt, Tendong* at Gangtok. The Lepcha from different part of the Sikkim attend the function.

Chu-faat

It is an age old folk dance of the Lepcha. It is performed on the fifteenth day of the seventh month of the Buddhist calendar, every year. The dance is performing in honour of the Mount Khangchendzonga and its associate peaks, *Mt Pandim, Mt Kabru, Mt Simbrum* and *Mt Narshing.* The Lepcha believe that the five snowy peaks are five hidden treasure such as Salt, Medicine, Minerals, Sacred books and Food grains. The entire dance team carries green Bamboo leaves and butter lamps in their hands perform ritualistic dance with the devotional songs.

Agriculture is the important occupation of these people and these people practice a large number of religious rites related to this occupation. The Lepcha believe that without the assistance of the supernatural deity *Sakue rum* the Lepcha will not survives and the deity *sukum rum* is the protector of agriculture crops. They believe that this deity is to be honored for bountiful and unhampered growth of the plants and production. This is celebrated in a collective way and in the agricultural field itself. Beside, deity *Aanyu rum* is worshiped for good harvest of cardamom. The *Sakue-rum* deity is related to plantation, the head of the family offer ancestor's deity for better crops. After harvesting the family members offer new crops for their ancestor. The function generally performed by the priest i.e. *Boong thing*. On the day, the people offer their ancestor Bird- (*Pha*), Fish- (*Hu*), Chura- (*Tafa)*, Ginger- (*Hing*) and local made liquor *Chung* etc. It is also observed that, five numbers of bamboo pots used in the puja, which is locally known as *Puchhut*. All the bamboo pot filled up with the pieces of above mention items are kept in front of the house. After the function is over the bamboo pots are brought inside the house. They observe some rules and regulation during the festival. On full moon and dark mun nights this festival is not observed by the people. The people believe that, if the function is not conducted by the family members the family members may suffer from any disease.

According to the age old experience the people abstain from taking some forest food items because their ancestors had not identified such items for consumption. The root is locally known as *Taral*. The wild bird locally known as *Tinpitfo* and leave of *tut* tree and not allowed to be taken as food. The people before going for hunting appease *pong-rum* god as they believe that if not hunter may face problems in the jungle. After return from hunting the hunter appeases *mut-fat deity*. On the day, he offers two chicken, two eggs, rice, wheat tarma and *Chung*. The women folk are not allowed to participate in the puja.

Zo-mal–lok

It is a popular dance of the people depicting the sowing, reaping and harvesting of paddy. The dance is performed by the people generally with all the relatives and friends while working on the fields. All participants enjoy feast. *Boongthing* also join in the dance.

Green Tara

Green Tara is a forest God the of Lachenpa. The God is having four types of images. The forest God protects the people from wild animals like tigers, snakes and other ferocious animals inside the forest. The *Garuda* or *khung* puja is related to snake. The every Lachenpa family kept image of the *Garuda* in their house to avoid from snake bite.

Social life of the Lepcha and Bhutia is very close to different beliefs systems which are governed from the nature base. The people are performing various rites and rituals on different occasion like ancestral or clan worship, birth, marriage and death etc. Here some examples have been given for understanding; as how the people are very close to supernatural belief system their social life.

Animistic faith of religion necessitates for blood offering every sacred performance. It is observed that, Lepcha are very god fearing and every moment of their life is guided and controlled by the *Mun* and *Boongthing*. It is seen that different spirits play a major role in dealing with his mode of life and destiny. Ancestor worship is very common among the Lepcha. The worship locally known as *leerun*, the traditional priest *Boongthing* performs the rites to appease the ancestors. They sacrifice chicken in the names of grandfather and grandmother respectively. It is also a practice to keep a sum of rupee ten or twenty-five separately in the names of these ancestors every year. In emergency cases they can use the fund as loan but it must be repaid afterwards. This is an exceptional process of economic management of the Lepcha derived as a manifestation emerged out of nature-man-spirit complex.

A-Thing

It is a puja is related to ancestral deity. The Lepcha faced with any social and medical problem; appease ancestral deity to save them from evil or malevolent spirit. The puja is performed continuously for three years in succession. The puja is conducted by *Boongthing*; who offering a pig for ancestor along with *chi or chang* (local rice bear), bamboo leafs, ginger and ghee, etc. The pig blood smeared on the body individual the family members. After performing the puja the invitee's friends enjoy the feast.

The Lepcha perform different types of festivals on various occasions round the year. Every worship reflects their socio-economic and religious life. In the month of December (mar-*lavo*), they perform "*Nam-Sung*" festival, *Guru Puja* in Oct-Nov-(*eth-lavo*), (*Padin-rum*) and ancestor puja (*Ram-lyot*), in the month of Feb-March, *Rum-Kuk* or *Takpo-bur* and *Kursong-than* puja in the month of April-May respectively. With the blossom of flower grown in the forest, the people come to know about the arrival of the autumn season. In the month of August-September, the people perform *Chu-rum-fat* puja which is related to nature i.e. hill, river, stream etc. The Muk-*zuk-ding-rum-fat* puja is performed after ten days of *Chu-rum-fat* puja. This puja perform for better crops. They think that this puja saves or protects the crops from snowfall or bad weather etc. In the month of September- October, they perform worship *Sekew-rum fat* for nature and ancestor. They offer new crops for their ancestors. *Layang-rum-fat* puja perform in the month of June-July for protection of the village any bad evil or diseases. In the month of August-September the Lepcha worship *Lapcho-rum-fat* for long life. On the way with in the village, any large stone *(Long)* they cross daily, they appease stone and they believe that their life will be of long span like the stone.

Long-rum

It is a female deity having sole authority for all disease. Beside the people also believed in different type of deities related to different disease also. The deity *Ninji-brung* is related to headache, waist pain, stomach pain and body pain etc. The deity *Rangang Ajo* is related to blood vomiting, mental problem fever etc. The deity *Angu-brung* is related to stone goddess. It is said that while overtaking path if the people do not obey the goddess, the people are likely to suffer from any disease. All connected offering and puja etc. are done by the *Boongthing*. During the puja the *Boongthing* scarifies chicken and offer others egg, banana, rice etc. to the deities.

The Lachenpa people have developed or classified some god and goddess, who are related to different types of diseases and ancestral spirits. The god *Sangyar Manla* is considered to be head medicinal god. The people believed that the image of the god having two hands depicts that the right hand keep medicinal trees locally known as *Menslong* while the left hand has a container to keep the ethno-medicinal plants locally known as *tungjeb*. When some one sufferes from any disease the medicinal man *Jhakri* appeases the *Sangyar Manla* god and accordingly the *Jhakri* starts the treatment.

White Tara

It is a local god also known as *Donkar*. If a person of the community commits any sin harmful acts and after realization of his acts work he chants mantra of the *Donkar* god. They believe that by chanting mantras the sin which he earned by committing harm, will completely go out during his life time. It is also believed that after death the person is faced with different types of problems in the other world.

Saga Dawa

It is the holiest Buddhist festival. On this occasion, the people perform the various stages of Lord Buddha's birth to enlightenment and up to the reaching of *Nirvana*. Three important events are celebrated in the festival of *Saga Dawa*. The three-day events falls on the full moon day of the 4th month of Buddhist lunar calendar, which usually falls around the end of May. During the occasion the people participate in singing and dancing.

Lhabad Dhuechen

The festival '*Lhabab Dhuechen*' is performed by the descendant of Lord Buddha. *Dhuechen* means festivals, *Lha* means heaven and *Bab* means descendant. *Pang-Lhab-Sol*. Legend has it that the mother of Lord Buddha *Maha Maya* did not live long after his birth and took rebirth in *Trayastrimsa* or the haven of the thirty gods. After attaining enlightenment, Lord Buddha through spiritual power came to know about the whereabouts of his mother and at the age of forty he ascended to the heavens along with thousands of his followers. Lord Buddha stayed in heaven for three months during which he delivered sermons to his mother and other celestial beings. Lord Buddha had left behind one of his disciples on earth. This disciple and other devotees of the lord could not bear the long separation and longed to hear his preaching, *Maugalyayana,* who possessed miraculous powers, was exhorted to go up to the heaven to request the Lord to return back to the earth. The gods were not willing to let Lord Buddha return back to earth but *Maugalyayana* suggested that as the earthly beings did not have the powers to visit heaven, the celestial beings could come down to the earth to attend his preaching. Lord Buddha finally relented and descended to the earth at a place called *sankasya* along a triple ladder that was prepared especially for the occasion by Viswakarma, the god of machines.

Drukpa Tsheshi

This festival is performed by the Buddhist people on occasion when the Buddha first turned the wheel of dharma. The festival is held on the 4th day *(tsheshi)* of the 6th month (*drukpa*) of the Tibetan calendar around July or August every year. The festival celebrates the Buddha's first preaching of the four noble truths to his first five disciples in a park at Sarnath. The first is the noble truth of suffering. The second noble truth is truth of the origin of suffering Karma and Delusion and their causes. The third noble truth is the cessation of the suffering or the attainment of nirvana. The fourth noble truth is the truth of eight fold path leading to nirvana. The day falls on the fourth day (*teshi*) of the sixth Tibetan month (*drukpa)*. On this day, people also enjoy yak races.

Pang-Lhab-Sol

The '*Pang-Lhab-Sol*' festival is unique for the Sikkim people. The festival is held from the 15th of July and continues till the end of August. The festival also marks the signing of the treaty of blood brotherhood between the Lepchas and Bhutias by *Khye Bumsa* and *Tetong Tek* when the local deities are invoked to witness the occasion. The word '*Phang*' means witness. In this festival the snowy range of Khangchendzonga is worshipped for its unifying powers. Buddhist monks perform rituals and prayers in the name of the Khangchendzonga deities. The monks and devotees go all the way up to *Dzongri 'Dhapla Gang'* to offer prayers and rituals to the deities for good harvest; freedom for the whole country and world free from disease, hunger, famine, war etc.

On the day, the guardian deity is portrayed by *masked Lama Dances* as a fiery red-faced deity with a crown of five skulls, riding a snow lion. To lighten the mood of the spectators, jesters called "*Atchars*" play antics during *Chaams*. The third Chogyal of Sikkim, Chakdor Namgyal is credited for choreographing the *Pang-Lhab-Sol* dance performed by monks on this day.

Losoong

The *Losoong* is performed during the harvesting season at the end of the tenth month of the Tibetan year. As it falls on the 11th month of the Tibetan calendar, it is not the real New Year but it is in fact an agricultural New Year when rice and grains are plentiful and the weather is moderate. Before *Lossong,* a ceremony called *Gutor* is performed by monks in the monasteries. The people pray for a good harvest and even better prospects for the next crop. During the festival the people perform the *Chaam dance* at the monasteries. The dance symbolizes the exorcizing of evil spirits of the year and the welcoming of the benevolent spirits for the New Year. The people also participate in archery competitions as a mark of the festival. The men become Gods during the festival and don attires with mystical symbols. The *'Kagyed'* (eight teachings of the Guru) dance forms an important part of the *Gutor* ceremony and is held on the 28th day of the 11th month at the monasteries. The other religious dances or *chaams* that are performed prior to *Losoong* are - *Rolchaam* (cymbal dance), *Tshamche* (animal headed mask dance), *Shyak* (dance of horned animals), *Namding* (dance of winged animals), *Thakshobalap* (dance of the beasts of prey), *Hdur* (skeleton dance), *Shanag* (black hat dance), *Thoma Tshoglen* (dance of wrathful deities) and *shawa chaam* (stag dance).

Losar

The *'Losar'* (*Lo*-year, *sar*- new) festival is celebrated mainly during the Tibetan New Year. It is celebrated in the month of February. On this day the youth perform *Yak* dances and threw '*Sampa*' as a way of greeting and welcoming the New Year with shouts of "*tashi delek*". The people enjoy with their brocades, jewelry, songs, dance and picnics.

Manichuhung

The functions related to bad and evil spirit are performed every year in the month of May. The Lachenpa worship the deity to protect the bad and evils. The festival is performed for three days continuously and every day bearing different significant. The opening day called *manichuhun, Thukung* means (puja) the day related to appease the witch doctor to protect from any disease or any natural disaster. The second day is called *Mundai* or *Jedu* and it belongs to hills. The third day *Khabu* belonging to plain. Before the festival the junior lamas make different types of icons of the evil spirits. This is made by wheat mixture and dry it finally put on color of the image. In the function they make five big statues and in front of the big figure so many small figure is kept at the time of puja. On the top of each figure the people decorate it with the help of cotton thread. It is altogether six steps. During the step or building making they used five color cotton threads i.e. blue, white and yellow, red and green and top of the five steps or building make one hexagonal with the help of the cotton thread. The making process is locally known as *Dyu*. The five step color cotton thread indicate blue related to sky, red related to fire, green carrying forest and yellow related to land finally white indicate water. The five deities are related to different belief systems of the people. The white color figure locally known as *Pekar Dzeng* the puja related to for peace and avoid of the war. The yellow color figure is locally known as *Men-Lhozong* the puja related to for better agricultural crops. The blue figure is locally known as *Tashi tshring*, the puja related to disease. The red figure is locally known as *Nallah tashi tshring* related to ice raining and avoid thundering. The green figure is locally known as *yeullah which* is related to save the ecological condition and good rain for cultivation. The puja (*thukung*) performed in the Gumpa house. During the puja the Lachenpa offer five animal skulls in front of the figure like white – lion, yellow – tiger, blue – gorur-chung, red-dragon or Dyak, green – taa (horse) accordingly. The people believe that the entire five animals co-related for their survival.

In religious life the people are guided by traditional priests and lamas. In religious life the people obey some sacred place, gumpa, lake etc. Beside they also perform malevolent and benevolent spirit for their survival. The priests are the man who can appeases god and goddess for the welfare of the people.

Manuchokung festival at Lachen

Mun (Lepcha priest)

Manuchokung festival at Lachen

Mun (Lepcha priest)

Role of Boongthing and Mun and Lama in a Society

The life and culture of the Lepcha and Bhutia are based on their nearby surrounding. To maintain their socio-cultural, economic and religious life they develop series of belief system. The belief system related to gumpa or monetary and super natural power. The Lama and *Boongthing* appease god and goddess for welfare of the society.

The religious specialist's *Mun* and *Boongthing* play important role in the magico-religious beliefs and practices of the Lepcha. The priests are an institution between the supernatural power and the common human beings. They use to hold a special position during any festival or rituals. They perform series of ceremonies committed to various rum and *moong* for their conciliation. Beside they also perform puja to other deities related with the Lepcha cultural life. The chief function is related to misfortune caused by the malevolent spirits which they appease it through animal sacrifice and proper propitiation of the supernatural power.

The *Boongthing* is a man who establishes linkage between the family members and their protective *rum*. The attachment of *Boongthing* is restricted to family to clan group. Thus the domination of a *Mun* is wider than a *Boongthing*. The ecological bases of Lepcha religious beliefs are without an uncertainty clear in the different forms of worship where *Boong thing* is more active. The Lepcha believe that their early ancestors had originated from the sacred snow of the Khangchendzonga and with this view they claim to be the children of Khangchendzonga. Khangchendzonga is not only the sacred deity of the Lepcha but also the guardian deity of Sikkim.

The *Mun* is manifestation of supernatural spirits. The role *Mun* is to ward off the misfortunes and illness caused by devils, which is done partly by sacrifices especially animal sacrifice and prophesy at death ceremonies, they summon the soul of the dead man to speak his last wishes through their mouth and then conduct it into the *'rum lyang'*– the place of the gods-where it is reborn as an infant and grows up to an eternal life similar to the life here on earth. It is believed that there are two sorts of *Mun*, a good group called *Tang-li mun* and a bad group called *Mun-mook mun*, the traditional difference between white and black magician. Beside this Lepcha are also practices Buddhism religion in every sphere of their life and culture.

The Buddhism faith has played a special role in shaping the Lachenpa life and culture. The monasteries or gumpa are centered on their rhythm of lives. Every household ritual, marriage, birth or death ceremonies and agricultural rites are conducted by the Lama. Their chief deity is the tutelary galaxy of Buddha and Bodhisattva and other deities are the guardian deities, including family deities, village deities and Khangchendzonga goddess also perform by the Lama.

Mayal, the holy place, occupies an important role in the life and culture of Lepcha. The Lepcha believed that the two old people namely *Adoo Yook* and *Alau Yook*, with their wives namely *Talyeu Nimu* and *Sangove Nimo*, are the spirits of the earth; these two women lie on their backs under the earth and on their bellies are the cultivatable lands; into this *Adoo Yook* and *Alau Yook* send rice and millet and maize, just as if it were human seed from a husband and the women bore and fruit. The *Mayal* worship is related exclusively with the corps of rice, millet and maize. The people perform two puja after, the compilation of sowing and the harvesting of the dry rice. The *Mun* and old Lepcha pray to the holy place *Mayal* for protection from winter; during winter away snow and hail, in the spring to protect next crops and after sowing of each of their grains they offer *sakyou faat* to ensure a good harvest. The place also related to hunting centre and the people appease *Pong rum* deity for god of hunter.

The Gurudongmar Lake is largest and probably the highest in Sikkim. It is one of the sacred lake and many pilgrims visit this place once in a year. It is considered as one of the sacred lakes of the Buddhism and the Hindus. The lake remains milky in color throughout the year and it is believed that Guru Padmasambhava blessed. It is situated at an attitude of over 17000 ft and encircled all around by snow-covered mountains; the sacred lake has a great religious significance as well. This snow-fed milky water of the lake is one of the major sources of Tista. This lake freezes during the winters except at one spot, which the devout believe to have been specially blessed and the blessed water of this lake is believed to posses the miraculous power of granting children to issueless couples.

Bumchu festival is celebrated at the monastery at Tashiding in the month of January or Feburary. The word '*Bum*' means 'pot or vase' and *Chu* means 'water'. During the festival, the pot containing the holy water is opened by the lamas of the monastery. The level of water in the pot foretells the future for the forthcoming year. They believe that if the water is full up to the brim, it foretells a year in which peace and prosperity will prevail. If the water is over the brim and is spilling over, it signifies a year with natural disasters and flood. It prophesies bloodshed and disturbances. If the water level is low or almost dry it signifies famine. A part of the holy water is distributed amongst the gathering of the devotees and the pot is replenished with river water and sealed at the end of the festival to be opened only in the next festival.

The people of Lachenpa perform *Guru Rimpoche's Trungkar Tshechu* puja, on this day; the Buddhists pay homage to the master who first blessed Sikkim as a whole land. The guru is believed to have firmly established Buddhism in Sikkim and introduced his form of tantric Buddhism to the Himalayan kingdom after vanquishing the "*demons*" obstructing the growth of dharma in Tibet. This day commemorates his victory over these demons and the devout believe that the virtues accrued by recitation of mantras on this day are two-fold.

Mahakal- is local god *Mahakal* belongs to Himalaya. The people believe that the god having fives intelligence locally known as *Thor*. The intellect is related to hill, stone and river, stream and tree. The representation of god *Mahakal* picture is having six heads. The main icon is *Mahakal* and other five heads attached with main icon. The five icons are related to hill, stone, river stream and tree. The people believed that, on the basis of the many eyes he protects from bad evil. The people keep the image in their house to save themselves from bad evil. Here people use dark blue color in the icon. Every year the puja performed by the people on seventh September.

Mask Dance is performed by the Lama in the gumpa. Khangchendzonga dance is celebrated in September. The portrayed of Kangchendzonga is fiery red having with crown of five skulls, riding the mythical snow lion. The dancer are all male members. In the dance the war like pomp and panoply, the war deity resplendent the flaming robes, snow lion, comprise the essence of the dance. The festival is known the Bhotia New Year Day. The dance is performed by the male members for success of good over evil is demonstrated. The dance represents eight manifestations of the Guru Rimpoche. The festival is very colorful and spectacular and draws many pilgrim and visitors.

Taboos

As out come of nature-man-spirit complex and interdependent relationship the Lachenpas follow some customary laws to adhere for harmonious life. During the marriage solemnization brides are not allowed to sit on the lap of bridegroom. On the basis of the customary law, during the burial time they arrange nine steps for funeral for females. Similarly, at the time of male's funeral they arrange eight steps for burial.

During marriage the bride sits on an elevated seat than the bridegroom's seat and the bridegroom sits on the floor. After marriage the rule is not strictly followed by the Lachenpa people. The Lachenpa economy depends on agriculture, dairy farming and pastoralist and trading. Beside people of Lachenpa are also very close to forest economy.

Two types of agricultural fields are prepared, namely, (i) *Gosing* in Lachen or *phasing* in Lachung- a permanent field for every year's cultivation; and (ii) *Cheram* in Lachen or *Resing* in Lachung – a temporary field captured from the jungle for only one year or at the most two years and then vacated for generation of forest for 8 to 10 years. Even the season for each crop varies with altitude, soil, temperature, rainfall. For example, potato is harvested in September in the high zone of the Lachen valley, while it is harvested in Lachung in the month of July only.

CONCLUSION

Considering the situation of two areas in different environmental conditions and cultural background, the two communities i.e. the Lepchas and the Bhutias have developed their belief system which have the commonness in conserving nature through the worship of different deities and spirits and maintain the different kind of life cycle rituals. But the manifestation in performing the rites is dissimilar due to differential background. The ecological set-up of the Lepcha and Bhutia have evolved some adjustments with nature through various sets of arrangements at social levels well as religious levels to make their survival.

It is observed that, the Lepcha practice two types of religious path in their day to day life. The traditional priests i.e. *mun* and *boongthing* performs rituals for welfare of the society, which is related to malevolent and benevolent spirit in nature. On the other hand, the Lamaism has got blended in their traditional faith and rituals which are also reflected in their life and culture now-a-days. It is also noticed that the supernatural belief system surrounds their life and culture. The Lepcha people perform different type of festivals during various occasions round the year. The worship is performed in anticipation of betterment. The people also perform "*Nam-Sung*" festival, "*Guru Puja*" (*Padin-rum*), ancestor puja (*Ram-Lyot*) with the help of *Boon thing*. The flowers blossom in the forest in the respective season and on the basis of it they protect future prosperity. In the month of August- September, the people perform *Chu-rum-fat,* festival related to nature i.e. for hill, river, stream etc. The people believe that it would save or protect the crops from snowfall or bad weathér etc. In the month of September- October, they worship *Sekew-rum fat* for nature and in memory of ancestor. They first offer new crops to their ancestors before usually for themselves. In the month of June –July, they worship *Layang- rum- fat* for protection of the village from bad evil or diseases, which is performed by the *boongthing.* In the month of August- September, the Lepcha people worship *Lapcho- rum-fat* for long life. On the way passing through the village, whatever stone (locally known as *Long*) they cross daily, they worship on belief that their life will be long like stone.

The Buddhism faith has played a special role in shaping the Lachenpa life and culture. The monasteries or gumpa are centered on their rhythm of lives. Every household ritual, marriage, birth or death ceremonies and agricultural rites are conducted by the monks from the *gumpas* which are prominent in all the Lachenpa settlements. Their chief deity is the tutelary galaxy of Buddha and Bodhisattva and other deities are the guardian deities, including family deities, village deities and Khangchendzonga goddess. Most of the deities are related to mountains, lakes and forest. The eight symbols considered auspicious in Mahayana Buddhism are intimately associated with the life and teaching of the Buddha. The important festivals observed by the Bhutia community include *Losoong*; *Pang-Lhab-Sol*, worship of the guardian deity-Khangchendzonga. *Kagyat* or *mask* dance and *Saga Dawa* bless the spirits. Beside, the people follow different type of ancestral beliefs and worship malevolent and benevolent spirits in their life. It is also observed that all kinds of painting relating to Buddhism are attached with nature, man and animal figure. Such a series of belief system govern their sustenance.

It is revealed that the two communities i.e. Lepcha and Bhotia inhabitants of KBR of middle and northern part respectively follow nature and ancestor worship. Therefore different kind of deities and spirits are believed to have their abode in streams, mountain slope, forest species, different kinds of stones and various elements of nature. These are worshipped by them in different seasons with the help of traditional priests, though blending of Lamaism is observed in performance of rituals and festivals. This may be due to close touch of the two communities since long. The close touch with Tibet by the Bhotia and adherence of Buddhism by them percolates down also to the life and culture of the Lepcha people. But this kind of performance with the help of traditional priests, Lamas, village members and caste council make them united and help to develop a sense of responsibility in conserving nature in their own way. Above all, nature and spirits are attached as part and parcel of these people in various ways. Here it is the importance of Khangchendzonga Biosphere Reserve which is reflected in terms of man-nature-spirit complex and their inter dependent relationship.

ACKNOWLODGEMENT

First and foremost, I thank to Dr. V.R. Rao, Director –in- charge of Anthropological Survey of India for extending necessary facilities to carryout the study. I also thank to Dr. D.B. Mandal (former, Deputy Director) of the Eastern regional centre, salt lake, Kolkatta, to give me an opportunity to study the K.B.R. Project. I also thank to Dr. Mrs. Kakoli Chakrabarty (H.O.) of the eastern regional centre, Salt Lake, Kolkatta, for her kind co-operation. Author expresses his gratitude to Dr. Ramesh Chandra, Deputy Director, of North-West regional centre, Deharadun for his encouragement and guidance in preparing and finalizing the report. I acknowledge the authority of the Sikkim and the Pipon of Lachen valley for allowing me to in Sikkim. Lastly, I am indebted to the people of Dzongu and Lachen valley for their kind help.

10

Health, Illness and Role of Ethno-Medicine among the Lepchas Living in Khangchendzonga Biosphere Reserve of Sikkim Himalayas: A Study on Traditional Knowledge

Sumitabha Chakraborty

INTRODUCTION

"Health is a state of complete physical, mental and social well-being and is not merely the absence of disease or infirmity" as propounded by World Health Organization (WHO, 1946/1948, p.100). Life of an individual is concerned with 'health'. The idea of ill-health disturbs the rhythm of life and performance capabilities of the individual being. All human groups, no matter how small or technologically primitive, have always been devising ways and means for taking care of the health. Now the discussion begs the question – "What is health?" and the corollary questions – "What is illness?" To view this Wylie cautioned that any attempt to define what health means lays the definer open to attack by critics armed with heavy reference books. Many definitions represent health and illness, which have conceptualized health as 'modes of relationship' – equilibrium and disequilibrium between man and his environment; involving human factors, ecological aspect and social structure (Lehriche, 1973, p. 54). Health and illness have an integral association with the individual as well as society, where the health is a property and illness is a state. In contrary, illness ceases to be something outside the individual, whereas health is an expression of the individual. Sigerist (1943) opined that health simply refers to reveal and assume importance in consequence of the attack of illness. In one of his interpretation, Valabrega mentioned two notions of health and illness – first, the illness, behaviour of the sick and medical practices are considered by endogenous (illness is caused by the magical theft of the individual soul) and exogenous (illness is caused by the real or symbolic intrusion of some objects into the patient's body) concept; secondly, illness may be caused by the action of another man or sorcerer or religious origin, produced by a god or a spirit (1962). While working on the Japanese religious sect, Lebra (1972) observed that sickness or illness in Japanese religious sect is believed to be caused by the neglect of 'religious duties'; and the people of this sect, therefore, be held responsible for their diseases. Saunders (1959) suggested in his writing that every person has cultural guides, which enable him/her to know when he/she may be regarded as sick. It is also mentioned that culture plays a broad role in shaping peoples' ideas about health and illness and their subsequent treatment activities.

Health and illness have close linkages with the therapeutic and preventive practices, which have shown variations throughout the ages. These therapeutic and preventive practices led by the human being are termed as 'ethno-medicine', which is referred to beliefs and practices relating to disease which are the products of indigenous cultural development' (Hughes, 1968, p. 88). All societies have an identical way of health practices, which are not explicitly derived from the conceptual framework of modern medicine. History revealed that since the dawn of civilization, everywhere man searched out both naturalistic and super-naturalistic means to prevail upon the ill-health. In this matter, man only depends on their surrounding 'biome' and developed an attachment with biotic and abiotic creature for coping up various health disorders and illness. Thus, the traditional way of nature cure with herbal medicine got tremendous popularity during the historical period. The first recorded treatise on the collection of 800 plant and plant products was mentioned in *Charak Samhita* (1000 – 800 B.C.) followed by *Sushruta Samhita* (800 – 700 B.C.). These are still identified as the basic guidance for the practice of traditional herbal medicine for ailments and cure.

In the path of development of ethno-medicine, there were two types of healing practices prevalent during the Vedic period – one was relied on magico – religious system while the other combined with naturally grown medicinal herbs and medicines. In the phase of Upanishada, the practice of medicine did not progress much and the belief in demons and goblins remained persistent as before. Most developed phase in this sphere was the period of *Samhitas*, when the treatment by vegetation, animal products and metals had reached on top with magico-religious systems. There were also the effects of nine *grahas* (harmful stars) and eight types of supernatural spirits (*Devas, Asuras, Gandharvas, Yakshas, Pitris, Bhujangas, Raksasas and Pishachas*) considered responsible for the ill health. In this journey of medicinal development, Ayurveda came later but got restricted to a section of learned person only. Lastly the classical modern medicine caught hold the position under the patronage of the ruler and some of the member of higher and more affluent society. The condition of the downtrodden people at that time was unhesitatingly fearful. They started to rely on magico-religious performances with the support of the Ayurvedic herbal medicine, which were prevalent in the vicinity and thus 'ethno-medicine' came into front as a fatal remedies (Roy Chowdhury, 1988; p. 134). Ethno-medicine does not only mean to address the empirical theories of disease causation and its prevention but also effectively addresses the supernatural theories by counter veiling supernatural powers or event. In ethno-medicine, treatment by means of magical and religious virtualization is more effective because the indigenous people much rely on emotional catharsis. Other than this, they have a pharmacopoeia or a rudimentary medical technique, where they have exceptional practical knowledge of exploitation of surrounding nature.

Health behaviour is the another arena, where some of the personal attributes, like, beliefs, expectations, motives, values, perceptions and other cognitive elements are attached with ones own health. Thus Gochman, mentioned that 'personality characteristics, including affective and emotional states and traits, and overt behaviour patterns, action and habits that relate to health maintenance, to health restoration and to health improvement' (Gochman, 1982, p.169). Health behaviour does not mean the clinical improvement or physiological recovery but rather includes an impact or recovery. On the other hand, Kasl and Cobb (1966a) described a different statement of health behaviour as it comprises those actions undertaken by persons. Health behaviour includes responses to bodily signs and symptoms; seeking opinions and advice from persons who are believed to have health expertise. On the contrary to health behaviour, the local people prefer to the traditional way of pharmacopoeia. By indigenous, Pattnaik (2005) perhaps mean to the local people having a vision that is rooted in their culture, lifestyle and livelihood. On one hand they follow the magical and religious rituals by healing, witchcraft, sorcery while on the other hand follow the pharmacopoeia by using herbal medicine and naturopathy. In India, the concept of utilizing the natural and plant products to cure the ailments had appeared in the remote past, dating back to 4500-1600 B.C. during Rig Veda. During the course of time, a number of attempts have been made to improvise the knowledge of ethno-medicine. It was early part of twentieth century, numerous anthropological studies on ethno-medicine had been carried out by the famous scholars like, Evans-Pitchard (on Azande); Kluckhon and Spencer (On Navaho); Redfield, Gillion and Adams (on Maya) and in Indian context ethno-medicine had been studied in the later part of twentieth century by scholars like, P.C. Josh; Balgir Singh; K.H. Bist; S.N.H. Rizvi and so on. Everywhere, it was depicted that the local people coped up the illness, health related issues by administering the traditional medical systems. They tried to interlink cause and affect relationship of health and illness with the supernatural power by observing beliefs, rituals and practices. The local people are regarded as the 'sons of the soil' having a close linkage with the ecological set up of their respective habitation and the economic exploitation of natural resources from generation to generation. But with the advent of numerous life-saving drugs and health related programmes the therapeutics become effective and fast-relieving. How for this type of systematic and advanced mode of therapy is beneficial and accepted by these people is still a matter of debate in front of the researchers as many earlier records have revealed that whenever an alien mode of therapeutics is applied in the fold of an old and already established system; either it is refused in total or accepted a part of it as a supportive remedies.

The present study had been undertaken with a view to understand the health, illness and the role of ethno-medicine among the Lepchas of Sikkim Himalayas in and around Khangchendzonga Biosphere Reserve (KBR). Ethno-medicine has tremendous significance in context of the biosphere; the medicinal herbs are available in abundance in KBR. The entire state of Sikkim is a rich repository of many such endemic medicinal species, which are used by the local people over the centuries. Inhabiting on the lap of KBR the Lepchas utilize these natural resources for illness treatment. The present study is selected under the project 'Man in biosphere: Khangchendzonga Biosphere Reserve' and I got an opportunity to carry out the study. This project was initiated in the form of Cultural Dimension of Tourism but gradually shifted its focus to Biosphere reserve aspect for the emergence of facilitating the resolution of increasing conflict between the people and the protected areas. The KBR is one of such important reserve zone for the treasure and beauty of the third highest peak Mt. Khangchendzonga. It is believed to be the dwelling place of local people's guardian deity – *Kingtsoomzaongbool*. The word *Khang-chen-dzo-nga* means five repositories of god's treasure; like, gold, silver, gems, grains and holy books. The inhabitants of Sikkim, Lepcha and Bhutia always have a notion that the Khangchendzonga and its surrounding natural wealth give lots of things including life saving medicines. So the ecology of it should be saved properly. On keeping this view in mind, the government of Sikkim earmarked an area, which was notified as Khangchendzonga National Park (KNP) in August, 1977. Later on the area was expanded to 1784 sq. kms., in May, 1997. The park occupied about 25 per cent of the total geographical area of Sikkim with an elevation, ranging from 1829 to 8586 meters. The geographical location of KNP extends from 27°19'13" to 27°29'04" north latitude and 88°09'18" to 88°15' east longitude. On 7th February, 2000 the Ministry of Environment and forest, Government of India notified KNP as a biosphere reserve with a total area of 2192 sq. kms. (Map of Sikkim, showing the Biosphere Reserve area). As one of the important biosphere reserves, this KBR embraces many water bodies as sacred lakes, wishing lakes; national parks; Buddhist monasteries etc. This biosphere reserve is one of the richest phytodiversity centers in Sikkim Himalaya. Due to its unique geographical position, the vegetation of this biosphere reserve has invasion of many foreign elements as well as endemic species. KBR includes the largest known population of some endangered species like, Red Panda, Himalayan Black Bear, Musk-deer (*Kastoori*), etc. The KBR is having a rich cultural diversity and abode of tribal groups, who are remarkable for their traditional and harmonious use of natural resources. The KBR is spread over the parts of north and west Sikkim districts. The KBR includes the area of Bakhim, Karjee, Gamgyap, Labdang, Khecheopalri, Chong, Dubdi and Yuksam in the West district; and Sakyong, Pentong, Linzya, Salim Pakhel, Shipgyar of Upper Dzongu; Chungthang, Mensithang, Lachung, Monguthang, and Lachen in the North district of Sikkim as buffer hamlets. There is only one core hamlet, i.e. Tsoka, which lies under the Yuksam-Dubdi Gram panchayat. The KBR is the inhabiting place of some ten communities, viz. the Bhutia, Lepcha, Sherpa, Rai, Chhetri, Mewar, Kami, Gurung, Limbu, Damai. (Booklet of Khangchendzonga Conservation Committee).

The Lepchas of Khangchendzonga Himalayas have their age-old traditional system of therapeutics, which they acquire from their forefathers and practice when they feel to be effective. Due to the advent of various modern treatment facilities available nowadays, are those populations really changing their age-old practice of natural healing and the ethno-medicine? How far their health related beliefs and practices are really changed by the implementation of modern health care system and programmes provided from outside? Is there any stiff resistance prevails against the implementation of such health care programmes? It has also become pertinent, due to the inception of forest protections, regulations and prohibition of forest laws implemented by the Forest Department, illegal extraction and exploitation of forest resources are restricted at large.

Keeping these views in mind, the present account is an outcome of fieldwork, which was conducted in the Lepcha dominated hamlets in the buffer areas of Khangchendzonga Biosphere Reserve with special emphasis on Yuksam of West Sikkim and Dzongu of North Sikkim.

Objectives

The study was conducted with the following objectives:

1. To understand peoples' behaviour towards the disease causation and curative measures of the disease.
2. To explore various symbolic elements (cosmological, spiritual, supernatural) that may have linkages with patient's ill-health.
3. To understand the effectiveness of indigenous preventive measures.
4. To understand as how far the community applies indigenous methods for curing the illness and diseases.
5. To explore the acceptance and effectiveness of the medical specialists.
6. To understand the changing scenario of tourists' influx, and
7. To understand impact of health care programmes on traditional health care systems.

OPERATIONALIZING THE STUDY

The study was conducted in two phases, first phase including two spells (during August – September and November-December, 2006) and second phase (during May – June, 2007). In both the phases, information regarding health, illness and its preventive measures had been collected from the Lepcha community. For the first phase of field work, the area Yuksam, Tsozo and Khecheopalri of West Sikkim district and for the second phase the area Lachen and Dzongu of North Sikkim district was selected.

1. The fieldwork was conducted in six hamlets (locally known as *bustee*) of West Sikkim district namely, Nubgang, Dosthang, Ramgyathang, Lethang, Tsozo and Khecheopalri, which are spread over in 3 Gram-Panchayat Unit (GPU), i.e. (i) Yuksam-Dubdi, (ii) Tsozo and (iii) Khecheopalri. These areas come under the buffer zone – I of Khangchendzonga Biosphere Reserve (KBR). Among the six, the three hamlets (Ramgyathang, Lethang and Khecheopalri) are uniethnic inhabited only by the Lepchas while other hamlets - Nubgang, Dosthang and Tsozo are cohabited with Bhutias; Subbas, Limbus or Gurungs of the Nepalese sub-group, who are in majority there. In North Sikkim, the field work was conducted in Dzongu, an area under the buffer zone – IV of KBR, solely inhabited by the Lepchas only. The Bhutias, Nepalese and any other outsiders are not allowed to reside permanently in the Dzongu.
2. Household information is collected through household census schedule. All Lepcha households of Yuksam-Dubdi, Tsozo and Khecheopalri Gram-Panchayat Unit (G.P.U.) were covered from West district of Sikkim and due to inaccessible terrain; only forty percent Lepcha households were covered from hamlets situated on the hill-slopes of both upper and lower Dzongu area of North Sikkim district. In the household census schedule, major stress was laid on health practices covering both traditional and modern. The kind of remedies, whether it is spiritual or supernatural, natural healing and the practice of ethno-botanical as well as ethno-biotic component as medicines were observed during the course of fieldwork.
3. Information regarding interpretation of the cause of illness, diagnosis, application of therapeutics, administering the healing rituals etc. was collected through observation from both the areas. During the study, the process of collection, preparation and application of medicinal herbs and animal extracts were also observed. Sometimes participant observation was applied for collecting materials, preparing and processing the medicine etc.

A sizeable numbers of medicinal herbs were being collected from both the places and recorded the usefulness of all the samples in regard to their therapeutics.

4. Information was collected through interviews, which was carried out through both structured and open ended questions. For that purpose, the informants are grouped as (i) the educated Lepcha men, (ii) Young Lepcha men, who accompanied the trekking party as cook and porter, (iii) The medicine men (*maondaok*), (iv) The spiritual healer (*boongthing/mun*), (v) The Lepcha people, who have strong faith on traditional health care system and (vi) The Lepcha patients, suffered by different types of ailments.
5. A numbers of case studies were gathered from different stages of the Lepchas, especially from (a) the traditional medicine men, (b) the spiritual healer, (c) the age-old Lepcha men, (d) the person beliefs in traditional medicine, (e) the doctor of primary health centre, for better assessment of ill-health, prevention and therapeutics.
6. Other than the primary data, the secondary information (written by various scholars) was taken into consideration as base line information.

THE STUDY AREA

The area under the study is mainly chosen from the buffer zone of the Khangchendzonga Biosphere Reserve (KBR), which lies in the West and North district of Sikkim. In the west district, the studied hamlets are lying in the revenue villages, viz. (a) Yuksam (under Yuksam–Dubdi Gram Panchayat), (b) Tsozo (under Tsozo Gram Panchayat) and (c) Khecheopalri (under Khecheopalri Gram Panchayat). A total number of 636 households with a total population of 3385 (census of India, 2001) souls are inhabited in west districts, of which about 75 percent are tribal. They are mostly residing in the remote hamlets (bustees), adjacent to the Khangchendzonga Biosphere Reserve. Other than the buffer zone hamlets there is one and the only core zone hamlet, called Tsoka existing in KBR (Khangchendzonga Biosphere Reserve), which is a part of the Yuksam revenue village. During the reign of Namgyal Dynasty this high altitude hamlet was settled for the habitation of few Tibetan migrants. Historical account of Sikkim revealed that in the year 1642, three great Lamas (monks) came from Tibet to Sikkim following the routes of three different directions – north, south and west and ultimately met at a place, called *Nubgang*, which lies in present day Yuksam. It is also revealed from the history that those three Lamas coronate the first Chogyal King, here in Nubgang of Yuksam. Thus Chogyal dynasty, a Bhutia Kingdom had started its rule over the Sikkim. According to the Lepchas, the word 'Yuksam' meant as a meeting place of three monks (Lhabchen Chempo, Gnadak Sempa Chempo and Kathok Rikzin Chempo). To them, Yuksam is considered to be a '*Lakhang*' or altar for offering to the Khangchendzonga guardian deity. It was noticed that everywhere the Lepcha houses are sparsely located in the hill slopes by forming a *bustee*. The distance between the houses are more than the normal set ups.

Table 1: Concentration of the Lepchas in the studied hamlets (West Sikkim)

Revenue Village (West Sikkim)	*Household*		*Population*	
	Total	*Lepcha*	*Total*	*Lepcha*
YUKSAM	364		1951	
(Ramgyathang bustee)	16	16	87	87
TSOZO	89		476	
(Lethang bustee)	33	33	194	194
KHECHEOPALRI	114		556	
(Monastry bustee)	16	15	83	76

Source: Gram Panchayat record compiled with field data.

Table 1 shows the concentration of the Lepcha population in various revenue villages. It was noticed that each revenue village has a number of hamlets popularly known as *bustee*. In Yuksam, there are nine hamlets (*bustees*) like, Topsing, Gerethang, Mangsabong, Yuksam Bazar, Nubgang, Guffa-dera, Dosthang, Tintin, Ramgyathang etc. of which the Lepcha are inhabited in three hamlets (bustee). According to concentration of population, the Nubgang and Dosthang have mixed population – Bhutia, Lepcha and Nepalese. The Ramgyathang bustee is inhabited totally by the Lepchas. The Tsozo revenue village has different hamlets, viz. – Lethang, Tsozo, Seling, Lingay, Putung etc. The Lepchas are the inhabitant in Lethang, Lingay and Tsozo hamlets with hundred percent concentrations, while the other two hamlets – Seling and Putung are inhabited by the Bhutias. It was noticed during the fieldwork that due to shyness and having preferences to live in relatively isolation in the lap of nature, most of the Lepcha bustees were found in remote area amidst in the deep forest. In the monastery bustee under Khecheopalri revenue village the Lepcha houses are built up within an area centering a very old Buddhist monastery. Nowadays, with the advent of tourism industry both Yuksam and Khecheopalri has got tremendous significance. Yuksam attracts both the Indian and foreign tourist for the heritage site of first coronation place of first Namgyal King and it is also famous for the base camp of trekking route to Khangchendzonga; while the Khecheopalri attracts the tourists for its sacred lake.

In north district of Sikkim, the Lepchas are only inhabited in Dzongu, an isolated place separated from the district headquarter Mangan by the river Teesta. Dzongu is a Tibetan word and combination of two syllables, i.e., *Dzon*, meaning hillock and *gu*, meaning nine make to understand that the place Dzongu is the concentration of nine hillocks. Dzongu is somewhat triangular mountainous land having approximately 60 kms. on each side, bounded on the south-east by the river Teesta, on the north-east by the river Talung and on the third side by the mountain peaks of Khangchendzonga. The land is excessively precipitous; the rivers are at about 700 meter above the sea-level and the average height of the hills is about 4200 meter. Except for a few artificially leveled places there is probably not a one square kms., of flat ground in the whole district; and the tracks are very much steep and too uneven for it to be easy for mules to track, let alone horses; all traveling has to be done on foot, and all goods transported by human porterage. The river valleys are hot, steamy and somewhat malicious, and consequently there are no houses right on the river, though the ground is used for raising subtropical plants; there are however occasional houses about 180 meter higher up. Most of the houses and cultivated land are between 1200 meter and 2500 meter above sea level, a relatively narrow band above the two rivers, though occasionally fields are made at even higher altitudes. Above the cultivated land is the forest in which wild produce is gathered, a decreasing amount of hunting done, and to which the cattle are sent up to pasture in the winter months. Above the forest level comes first the rhododendron forest, and then the snow, rarely visited except by hunters searching either for ibex and musk-deer or for the wild aconite which forms the basis of their arrow poison (Gorer, 2005; p. 56).

The Lepchas conceptualize the Mt. Khangchendzonga as sacred in relation to their guardian deity – 'Kingtsoomzaongbool'. They started to believe that this place is their '*Mayel – Lyang*' (hidden city), from where they had originated. In Lepcha folk-tales, a number of mythological stories are present about this land. During the field work in Tolung valley one of such etymological myth portrays – 'One day the demon went down the Talung valley and came to Sakyong (so called because Tag-Kyong-ka was killed there), Pentong, Thong-to, Laven, Tingboong, Lungdem (where he killed the children), A-dong, Ling-them (tem-la tem-la taa he ate each in turn). The village opposite is called Liklyang, the place of crying, because people cried out from there. Rum-nam chased the demon and eventually overtook him at Lasso-tsong-nyong, in the Teesta valley to the west, and there killed him and scattered his flesh over the land. From this scattered flesh the leeches, mosquitoes and the small predatory bird *Kar-hu-fo* took birth. The places where the demon was slain many huge stones were appeared, which was believed as the out-growth of the killed demon's bone'.

The area, Dzongu is divided in two areas – (a) the lower Dzongu and (b) upper Dzongu. (I) In lower Dzongu, there are altogether two GPU (Gram Panchayat Unit) – (i) Gor-Sangtok and (ii) Hee – Gyathang. (II) The upper Dzongu has five gram-panchayat units (GPU) namely (i) Lingthem – Lingdem, (ii) Sakyong – Pentong, (iii) Shipgyard Salim Pakhel, (iv) Tingbong – Linzya and (v) Lingdong - Berfok. It was informed that the total Dzongu is not under the KBR, rather a portion of the upper Dzongu consisting of Sakyong, Pentong, Bay Linzya, Tingbong, Lik, Shipgyar, Salim – Pakhel hamlets are under the KBR. (Map 3 pointing the spot of study). The field work was conducted in Linzya and Bay hamlet of upper Dzongu situated in the buffer area of KBR and one hamlet, i.e., Samdong of lower Dzongu situated outside the buffer zone to assess the significance of the role of ethno-medicine.

Table 2: Concentration of the Lepchas in the studied hamlets (North Sikkim)

Revenue village (North Sikkim)	*Household Lepĉha*	*Population Lepcha*
Hee-Gyathang (Lower Dzongu) (Samdong *bustee*)	268 039	1380 228
Tingbong-Linzya (upper Dzongu) (Lower Linzya *bustee*)	075 017	385 99
Sakyong-Pentong (Upper Dzongu) (Bay *bustee*)	069 011	414 69

Source: Gram-Panchayat record compiled with field collected data.

Table 2, depicts the area wise concentration of the Lepchas in the hamlets of lower and upper Dzongu. In lower Dzongu Hee-Gyathang is the largest revenue village consisting of many hamlets (*bustees*). On the other hand, except Lingthem – Lingdem revenue village, others have small Lepcha population strength. It was found that most of the hamlets in upper Dzongu, revenue villages are situated in very inaccessible terrain. The people have to cross the river Teesta with their traditional bamboo made suspension bridge and have to travel a longer distance on foot through the forest land and inaccessible terrain.

THE PEOPLE

The Lepchas, once the ruling race, are the earliest settlers of Sikkim profoundly proclaimed as '*Rongkup*' (the son of the snowy peak) '*motanchi*' (term for intra-community identity). Their identity can be understood by the following local folk-song:

Rong, rong, rong, Rongkup achule
Mayel Yangcha Rongkup Kaiyu
Ut Kachule
Mayel Yangcha Motanchi
Dungit Kayuache
Motanchina Lencho Thugong
Tamzuk Rumit Sha

The expression of the above legendary song is – '...we are the Lepcha (*motanchi*) keep our identity as the son of '*mayel lyang*' (the land of hidden delightful paradise) up to the last breathe (field data, 2006)'. The history revealed that formerly the ruling dynasty of the Lepchas was extended from the Himalayas down to Titaliya, the plains of Bangladesh. To the east it was extended up to Gipmochi mountain of present days Chinese Tibet and to the west up to Aroon river of Nepal (Tamsang, 1983). About the origin of the Lepchas, there are many views. Some have the opinion that the Lepchas belong to one of the Naga tribes; some have found similarities with the tribes of Arunachal Pradesh and Meghalaya (Ibid). Above all, the Lepchas have always been convinced with the legendary kingdom of '*Mayel*' in the vicinity of mount Khangchendzonga. The Lepcha tradition depicts that in the beginning the first primo-genitors of the Lepchas, *Fodongthing* and *Nazaongnyo* were created by God from the pure, virgin snow of *Kingtsoomzaongboo choo's* (Khangchendzonga), pinnacle and sent them down to live, prosper and spread up all over the fairy land. Therefore, *Kingtsoomzaongboo* is metaphorically expressed as the most superior, supreme god to them. Most of the Lepcha clan thus claims to have mythical connections with this mountain peak, which they worship as their guardian deity.

The appellation 'Lepcha' is derived from the Nepalese term *Lepchey*, which means scurrilous speakers. Originally, the term *Lepchey* was anglicized by the British people and coined the present term 'Lepcha', who proclaimed themselves as *Rongkup* or in short *Rong* that is 'snowy peak'. History of the state reveals that the Lepchas are the oldest inhabitant of Sikkim. They had kings and kingdom. It was believed that at one time the Lepcha dominantly ruled out the whole of north-eastern states including Sikkim. During the reign of Gaeboo Achok, the most authoritative king, the area of his kingdom extended in the highest unit. But the reign of whole Lepcha kingdom was finished within a very short period and the condition of the Lepcha was gradually fallen down. The Lepcha tradition revealed that in the beginning, when Lasomoong Pano, the demon king and his followers gave unbearable trouble to the Lepchas, they had no other way to save themselves but to run away from the country. And as such, many Lepcha had fled towards Tibet crossing the Himalayas; and while fleeing in panic, some went eastward and settled down in China some of them entered into Assam following the Brahmaputra river course and settled down there; still some people moved further southwards up to Burma (present day Mayanmar). However the Lepcha version remains that they have not migrated from the east to Sikkim but it is the Lepchas who had migrated from Sikkim to the northeastern states of India and also to the further upto Southeast Asian countries.

According to the tradition, there were ten divisions of ancient Lepcha families claiming their descent from the ten sons of *Fodongthing* and *Nazaongnyoo*. Those ten divisions of the ancient Lepcha families were called as '*Rong kup kati*', which means ten Lepchas. The Lepcha is also recognized as '*Rong Migyit*'. They have hereditary fixed clan or caste which called *agyit*, means a group of Lepcha people or family under the common ancestor.

The Lepchas are thought to have been living mostly through hunting and gathering from the forests. Since later phase of last century they took to settled cultivation and subsequently adopted the system of cash crop plantation, like cardamom, tea and ginger, in their terrace agricultural field, the Lepchas raise maize, paddy, wheat, barley and millet. The rice is the most important staple food. Millet is commonly used for making local bear '*Chi*'(traditional liquor). Fish is taken occasionally but meat – both fresh and dried are taken regularly. They do not have any inhibition in consuming beef, pork, rabbit, porcupine, monkey, deer etc.

The Lepcha seem to have evolved a strong cultural base. Their folklores, mores, myths and legends, dance, songs have yet cherished and transmitted to the younger generation. The Lepcha have their own ancient religion, named as *Boongthing-ism* and *Mun-ism*. They believe in the existence of God called 'Rum' and to Him they offer their prayers and thanks giving. They also have strong belief in evil spirits, who cause illness and misfortune. *Boongthing* and *Mun* perform all the rituals and religious ceremonies of the Lepchas. Many of the earlier scholars had mentioned that the Lepchas did not have any religion rather they believed in atheism. But in reality, for the God fearing Lepchas; prayers, supplication and worship through the medium of *Boongthing* and *Mun* are no superstition. The worship and prayers by the *Boongthing* and *Mun* are no flight of eloquence, not lip homage of God. They believe prayers and chanting spring out from the core of their hearts. They also believe that prayer is an unfailing means to achieve the purity of heart. The *Boongthing* and the *Mun* plays the role of mediator between God and the people. Lord Tamsangthing, the Lepcha man had first observed the ancient Lepcha religion. It was reflected from their saying and firm conviction that God always listen to the prayers fervently offered by them. That is why; they assemble at a certain place, either at home or in the open place under the bright sun light and pray, salute and bow-down to the Almighty to get the blessings of long life, prosperity and protection from the disease, sickness and misfortune.

Other than the ancient religion; during recent time, the majority of the Lepchas have embraced Buddhism. Gorer informed a very important observation about the nature of Buddhism among the Lepchas, "As a generalization it may be said that the Lepchas have accepted the ritual, the validating mythology, and the organization of Lamaism; what they have completely refused to accept is the ethnic. Like other 'high religious' Lamaism is individualistic; if holds that a person's chief concern should be with his own spiritual welfare. Thus, the key-concept of Lamaism, was and is an alien attitude to disapproved of acts is social, and not individuals it is the society and not the evil-doer, which bears the burnt of wicked acts" (Gorer, 2005; p.135). It was mentioned that in the Lepcha religion both the elements of Buddhism and Bon religion of Tibet mixed with the traditional elements. They manifested the calendar rituals of every 15th day of Tibetan months as a symbolic replica of Khangchendzonga. It was also observed that the exorcism and the atrophic rites performed by the Lamas for the benefit of individuals are numerous and varied other than the calendar festivals. Both of the Buddhist and Christian Lepcha have possessed strong faith on their own ancient religion – '*Munism*' and '*Boongthingism*'.

The Lepcha language as dubbed by many scholars as a 'mystery' language, because it is not related to any other language, prevalent in this region. Some have a belief that the language belongs to the Tibeto – Burman family, while others have found its root in the Austro-Asiatic family. Eminent linguist Suniti Kumar Chatterjee had mentioned in Linguistic Survey of India, Vol. 3 that the Lepcha language belongs to the Himalayan group of the Tibeto-Burman sub-family (cited in Thakur, 1988). In linguistic and cultural point of view all the Lepchas are one, but geographically they are divided into four sections – (a) Renjyongmoo, (b) Illammoo, (c) Damsangmoo, (d) Prommoo. *Renjyongmoo* is the combination of two words; - *Renjyong* means Sikkim and *Moo* means belong to; that means the Lepchas of Sikkim. Likewise, *Illammoo* refers the Lepchas of Illam, a place under present days Nepal. Thus, *Damsangmoo* refers the Lepchas of Kalimpong, *Prommoo* are the Lepchas of Bhutan. In spite of all, they always feel that they are the son of Khangchendzonga inhabited amidst the forest (Tamsang, 1983).

In their perceptions, every aspects of the nature have significant meaning and importance to their life. In one hand, they have traditional religion '*Munism*' by believing the existence of malevolent and benevolent spirit and on the other hand, there is the existence of God - *Rum* and the malignant spirits '*moongs*'. According to them; the cause of illness and misfortune is due to the displeasure of '*rums*' and '*moongs*'. Their religious and healing performances are based on the propitiation of '*moongs*' with ritual sacrifices and incantations. The role of '*boongthing*', perform a linkage between human beings and the '*rums*' (God). On the other hand, '*mun*' can communicate with the soul (*pil*) of the dead person. In Lepcha society, the *mun* is a post of succession and the knowledge of healing transmitted from one generation to other but the post of *boongthing* depends on the knowledge acquired by the person.

SOCIAL STRUCTURE

The Lepchas are kin based community and sub-divided into a number of patrilineal clans, which are locally known as *ptso*. Each *ptso* is considered to have a common supernatural or legendary ancestor. The chief function of *ptso* is the regulation of marriage alliance and the prevention of incest. The Lepchas do not have any centralized authority. In older times, during the reign of kingdom, there existed two division or social classes i.e., (i) *Rongboo* (patricians), (ii) *Mangboo* (plebeians). According to them, the *Rangboo* Lepcha belonged to the mobility classes (Roy Burman, 2003; p. 35), who were appointed by the king as priests; while the *Mangboo* class of Lepcha consists of farmers, potters, carpenters, blacksmiths, weavers etc. At the time of arranged marriage, the Lepcha do enquire about the clan of the bride and the groom, because they strictly follow the rule of *ptso* (clan exogamy). It is observed that the settlement pattern of the Lepchas is also usually clan based. That is why, the clan – *Sandyanmoo, Lutsomoo* and *Hee-moo* is prevalent in Lethang, Ramgyathang and Khecheopalri bustee. It is in their belief that these clans are conferred from the 108 main snowy peaks of Sikkim Himalayas. K.P. Tamang (1983; p. 40) mentioned that in the early period of the Lepchas community life, a kind of social order was embodied to rule by both male and female in terms of patriarch and matriarch. By this order, both the father and the mother are the head of the family at a time and therefore, the male children or sons belongs to the father's clan and the female children or daughters belong to the mother's clan. The girls or daughters inherit her mother's clan from generation to generation till eternity; and as such a daughter or daughters have no right whatsoever over her father's moveable or immoveable properties.

In Lepcha society, the extended family is a psychologically operative group, which renders possible identification with the community as a while. It is their opinion that the extended family imparts positive training to the child and teaches a strong control over behaviour. It is the family level training and education to a grown up child, how to adopt the certain acts taking other people's property, refuses to do work, obey the parents, belief in gods and goddesses (*rum*) etc. It is also note worthy that the Lepcha social organization also renders possible identifications of social approval and disapproval which will support them against the condemnation of another part of the community. As a member of society, they have clear and separate idea about 'shame' and 'sin'. Shame is an unpleasant physical sensation, while sin has some effect on the body when a person performs any wrong doing. While describing the society, the Lepcha men often started that they have no class, creed and ranking among themselves. No one is big, no one is small, and there is no gradation as such. In any decision making purpose only the seniority of age is considered. As a pattern of their social system and set up, they have a sort of traditional communism, where everybody provide service and if necessary manual labour for the need of others. In the phases of life (birth, death and marriage) a multitude has to be fed and in return, who came to attend those, invariably bring millet, rice, maize or whatever they consider necessary as a gift.

The social cohesion and solidarity among the Lepchas is also due to the principle of reciprocity evinced in different facts of life. Low productivity and a delicate balance between man and nature set limits for efficient and intensive economic exploitation of resources. It is their opinion that no condition exists for social status which would inevitably lead to more work and rigorous exploitation of resources. Exchange labour system between kin members, neighbours and barter economy play a significant role in the system of reciprocity. The extensive gift giving practices between the kin members also ensures strong community bonds. The reciprocal ties among the Lepchas are fully legitimized through an institution called 'lobo' (Roy Burman, 2003, p: 46). According to them, this is the networks of individuals involving reciprocal exchange of particular goods and services. Every family is involved in an enduring *lobo* group, which include family members, friends and neighbours and friends usually based on residential propinquity or proximity of working areas. A person can be a member of two or more *lobos*. It depends on nature of activity involved in *bustee* (hamlet). Reciprocity with a wider group – '*Lyhang-cho*' with whom one has obligations of token exchange the village participation in this wider network, as well as the smaller group is essential as a member of the community. In Lepcha society, the household member, especially the male member are also asked to participate in the '*Onlok*' – collective work for community welfare, like bridge making, bridle path construction etc. '*Ochhom*' is the other system institutionalizing friendly ties between people of the same *ptso* or clan or outside – within or without the village. This relationship involves giving help, including material items and services as well as psychological support. A Lepcha person, through this *ochhom* gets labour, cattle, fields on loan basis or any other help. This system is distinguished from any other cooperative networks because; here in this system no reciprocal obligations are involved.

It was evident that among the Lepchas of Dzongu, a system of self-rule is still functioning in the form of an informal council of the elders, which they termed as '*Lyang-ganbu*'. In spite of the existence of the Panchayat, it is very important to settle-up various disputes and difficulties of the member within the community. Disputes regarding marriage alliance, fixing up of bride-price, cultivation of crops, land holding disputes, crimes, disputes within the family members etc. are settled by this self-rule system. It was informed that the moral basis of social formation and social cohesion among the Lepchas is reinforced time to time through various collective village rituals, where everybody has equal role and participation. According to few age-old Lepcha men-folk, the clans or *ptso*, prevalent in their society are conferred from the 108 main snowy peaks of Sikkim Himalayas. Some of them are as like – *Sandyang-moo*, *Luksang-moo*, *Aden-moo*, *Taso-moo*, *Hee-moo*, *Kabo-moo*, *Kacho-moo* and so on. The function of the clans is to regulate the marriage alliance, where clan exogamy is preferred. It was informed that there is a practice prevalent in Lepcha society to bring a wife by agreement with her parents or by serving her parents to their satisfaction. In this case, a marriageable boy prefer to give-up his service in would be in-law's house within the period between betrothal and bringing up wife in his home. Being a human, the Lepcha people have some differences of understanding between the person, social cohesion which sometimes leads to quarrel either among the members of same household or among the members of different households. But whatever it is, according to their belief, any kind of quarrel is the result of the evil action of three spirits or devils, i.e. – *Soo-moong* (enmity of speech), *Ge-moong* (enmity of thought), and *Jhor-moong* (enmity of action). The devil *Soo-ge-Thor* is responsible for the evil trinity. The Lamaic exorcism is performed every year to destroy the evil action of *Soo-Ge-Thor* devils.

HEALTH, ILLNESS AND HEALTH CARE: AN ANALYSIS

Before entering into the main domain of the present report – Health, illness and role of ethno-medicine of the Lepchas of KBR and around of Sikkim Himalayas - it is imperative to reveal some information about the general medical system of earlier days Sikkim. Prior to merging into India as a 22nd Sovereign State, Sikkim had a dynasty and was ruled by the Tibetan king. At that time no medical facilities of western type existed and the local people had only faith on supernatural powers, spirits, manifested in the surrounding nature as a means of cure. The people had never been experienced with any kind of so-called religion teachings rather they followed a rudimentary form of 'animism' by appeasing those supernatural powers and spirits existed in the surrounding nature, whenever they had faced any problem. After the advent of Buddhism, especially the Vajrayana aspect of Mahayana fold of Buddhism the local people began to gain faith on the new dimension of religion because the Mahayana fold also encouraged the belief on supernatural spirits and powers. Thus the two guiding forces – the Tibetan Dynasty and Mahayana Buddhism had developed a kind of holistic medicinal practice in Sikkim at that time, which later got popularized as 'Tibetan Medicine'. Samuel Weiser, being one of the authorities on Tibetan medicine opined that 'there is a very close relationship between Buddhism and medicine'. He also stated that "Lord Buddha was the first, who said Man suffers from the inherent frustration of conditioned existence, and our suffering is caused by the fact of impermanence of all entities and by the endless craving that arises from the delusion, the Dharma" (cited in Tibetan Buddhist Medicine and Psychiatry, Samuel Weiser, 1984). In reality, illness is the reflection of mind to body and of the embodied psycho-organism at large. On a relative plane, illness is said to be caused by a lack of harmony within the microcosm and on an absolute plane, it is understood to be caused by the disharmony originating from the fundamental delusion of duality and ego's self-existence (Weiser, 1984). In the arena of traditional medical practices in Sikkim, Veena Bhasin while making her observation of the opinion that in spite of the prevalence of Tibetan pharmacopoeia, the state has the abundance of flora and fauna which have tremendous value in ethno-medicinal purpose of the local people. She also pointed out that the state has high attitude, difficult terrain, and inaccessible passes (Bhasin, 1997). The local people had to manage all these vagaries of nature and uncontrolled difficulties, out of which a belief in the supernatural powers and spirits had developed in their mind.

According to the belief of the local people the illness or disease may happen due to the pleasure and displeasure of the supernatural powers including deities, spirits, and ghosts or by some magical means. The beliefs pertaining to various diseases and their cure are also based on the past experiences and traditional logic. The various categories of illness are treated with worship and appeasement accompanied by animal sacrifice. On the other hand the diseases caused by magical means are treated by exorcism. In spite of these, there is also prevailing a supernatural basis of folk-healer treatment where most of the folk healers claimed that unless a medical concoction has been empowered by a special benediction, it will have little effect. It is noteworthy that nowadays, the traditional medical practices operate simultaneously along with modern allopathic system.

Lepcha Medical Practices

Lepcha Medical Practices

The concept of health and illness among the Lepchas is fully guided by the belief in supernatural. Accordingly, the cause of illness can be classified into two categories – (i) Disease caused by supernatural beings, their displeasure and actions, which are beyond their control; and (ii) diseases caused by the magical means like witchcraft and sorcery. The system of cause, effect and cure is an enclosed system limited to the traditional knowledge, which provides the manifestation of explanation and control in the face of disorders, chaos and inexplicable circumstances. It is their belief that if the cause of illness is a spirit, the effect is then spirit possession. The ideas of health, illness and disease have individual importance in Lepcha mind. As like others, they also believe that health is related with tension, mental stress and strain. When a man suffers with tension mental stress and strain, illness automatically appeared without any cause of disease. The Lepcha feel that any kind of health disorder may not cause any disease all the time. Simple cough and cold, headache, bodyache is not experienced as an illness or disease by them. According to them, disease is of two categories – (a) Curable and (b) non-curable. The people also have the opinion that due to carelessness some disease can be turned into a non-curable disease. According to their perception 'illness' has two aspects – i.e. (a) Psycho-analytical (based on the existence of spirits, ghosts, evil doers), (b) medicinal (based on the existence of some noncurable fatal diseases like, tuberculosis, cancer, cholera, diarrhea etc.). The Psycho-analytical aspect of illness is cured only by means of propitiation of deities and appeasement of spirits, ghosts etc., while the 'medicinal' aspect is cured by the application of traditional herbal medicine first and if not cured then they apply modern allopathic medicine.

According to tradition, health, illness and diseases have linkage with mythology. One such important mythology about Khangchendzonga and the residing 'guardian deity' – *Kingsoomzaongbool* is this that – '*Kingsoomzaongbool*' is the creator and protector of the Lepcha people. Whenever the people have faced any kind of difficulty, they go to the high altitude away from Dzongri (a high altitude area) and propitiate the deity so that their difficulties can be solved. According to their belief, the displeasure of the 'guardian deity' would bring disease, unhappiness, illness, bad crops, drying up and displacement of lakes and streams. Therefore, every year, in the month of August, '*Pang-Lhab-Sol*', a religious festival is organized throughout the state. In course of the discussion, it is revealed that a sterile woman can give birth to the child or any kind of chronic dreadful disease can be cured with the propitiation of the 'guardian deity'. Thus they feel that the Khangchendzonga should be protected and the people should follow the rules and norms of preservation of its greenness, lest any kind of natural disaster, like, landslides, heavy rainfall and earthquake would destroy the people. It is in their tradition that the illness and diseases follows certain performance of rituals, like – (i) the propitiation of '*kul-deota*' (clan deity); propitiation of earth deity (*Hee-ula jivda)*, propitiation of guardian deity; appeasement of malevolent spirits, ghosts believed to be residing in the nature or on the natural objects (snow clad mountain, lakes, streams, stones, mountains, forests etc.); (iii) goes to consult the traditional medicine men (*Maondaok*) first and (iv) if not cured, rarely goes to the government health centre, during recent time.

During the discussions, it is also pointed out that the faith in supernatural power-gods - *Rum* and demons – *Moong* is an age-old tradition before the advent of Buddhism, introduced in their society by Lama Lhotsung Nankha Gigma. Both *Rum* (God) and *Moong* (demon) can be doing harm in the form of fatal injury, epidemics, mishaps, disease etc. and also can snatch out ones' life, if they really become dissatisfied. At that time, the *Mun* and *Boongthing*, the folk-healer is to be consulted. The *Mums* and *Boongthings* are considered by the Lepcha to be the media for communication to the God (*rum*) and the devils or demons (*moongs*). It is believed by the people that the *Boongthings* are supposed to be able to communicate with all the devils/demons (*Moongs*) except the 'Dom *moong*', who causes *Leprosy.* It is the opinion of the *Mun* and *Boongthing* that different types of illness are caused by other *Muns*' indulging in propition of *moongs* (devil/demon) which can be treated with worship and devotion of respective *moongs* accompanied by animal sacrifice. The Lepcha folk-healers (*Mun and Boongthing*) stated that if those *rum* and *moong* (God and devil/demon) are ignored or any disrespect is shown to them by defiling or polluting by nature's call etc. may invite the wrath of the particular individual – the people may suffer from the serious sickness and sometimes even die. They informed that one of such *moong* is 'Lungzee' normally resides in the big stone present at the entrance of a *bustee* (hamlet). *Mun* and *Boongthing* also agreed that if *Rum* (god) is angered it appears in malicious guise and then referred to as a demon, and may cause sickness and other misfortune. A group of aged Lepcha of Yuksam and Dzongu opined that other than the influence of *Rum* (god) and *Moong* (devil/demon). The sickness, disease may also cause by magical means, which is treated by exorcism. In this sphere the folk healer (*Mun* and *Boongthing*) took initiative steps. By counting of the rosary beads and throwing off the dice, the folk-healer divines what is actually troubling the patient and then suggested that sacrifice is actually necessary or not. In psycho-analytical aspect of illness, disease may caused by the evil spirit and according to them, all evil spirit reside in the upper part and as well as in the lower part of the earth. To get rid of those evil spirit, in almost all Lepcha houses of both in Yuksam and Dzongu, a kind of structure was found, what they termed *Namgo* (for the evil spirit of upper part of the earth) and *Sago* (for the evil spirit of lower part of the earth). It is a common belief that this structure seemed to protect all kind of malevolent spirit. This interpretation of the Lepcha has resemblance with popular Hindu mythological interpretation of *marta* or *patal* (below the earth). According to them, the underworld or beneath the earth is full of darkness and is the abode of all malevolent spirit, which may be the root cause of dreadful diseases and illness; while on the other hand the place above the earth is full of brightness and considered as the abode of both malevolent and benevolent spirits. The people stated that as because of the presence of their 'guardian deity' – *kingsoomzaongbool* in the Khangchendgonga peak and the peak is above the earth, the malevolent spirits could not affect much to the people. From this opinion, it is felt that the conception of dichotomy – 'sacred and profane', 'good and bad', 'bright and dark' etc. are prevalent in Lepcha mind. It was informed that there are number of spirits, demons and deities in the Lepcha society, whose harmful action is responsible for disease and illness. Among all of them, few important, spirits, demons and deities as recognized by the people are mentioned as below:

(i) The demon *mung-nong-chuk* and its evil action.

(ii) The deities *Rum-na-na-cho* become arrogant.

(iii) The spirit *Thing-na-na-cho* and its malevolent action.

(iv) Jungle spirit *muzom-na-chuk-chumboo* and its harmful activities.

(v) Household deities *Sakya-tofion-lee-Rum* and its harmful action.

(vi) Principal household deities *Mukung-Rum* and its evil action.

(vii) The deity *Veek-Run* and its evil action, believed to be present in the surrounding of a house of a person.

(viii) Nature spirit *yougebo* and its evil action.

(ix) Nature spirit – Dzongo and its evil action.

(x) The deity *Lungno* and their evil action.

(xi) The spirit *Makryum, Sor, Dut-chaim* and their malevolent effect.

(xii) The spirit *Muzom, sipundi, Anee* and their malevolent effect.

(xiii) The demon (*mong*) – *Dut,* Tshen, *mamn, Cu, Gey-bo, Cyang-shergnyu, eetgnyn, Thyakdum,* pankar, tong-Thing.

Lepcha medicine man

It is feared that due to the harmful effect of demon, deities and spirits the people become sick by heart disease (*alut-dak*), stomach disorder (*tubok-dak*), rheumatism (*aku-dak athung-dak*), vision problem, nose bleeding (*jukmar-vee*) etc. which can be cured by the magico-religious performances. During the study they also informed that they have strong faith in cosmology in relation to health, illness and disease. Both eclipses (Solar and Lunar), stages of waxing and waning of moon, falling of stars, sudden visibility of any constellation in the sky etc. are believed to have a direct effect on peoples' health, especially on the pregnant lady, new born baby and the children of lactating stage. During pregnancy, both would be father and mother have to follow certain taboos, which are believed to be essential for safe delivery and as well as for the protection of any deformities of the expected child. They also informed that any kind of disrespect of that taboos may cause epilepsy and blindness to the new born child. It is also in their faith that sacredness of the natural objects, like streams, lakes, rivers, trees, stones has direct or indirect relation with the illness and disease.

They informed that whenever the sacred river, lakes and streams got polluted by any means of sinful activity, it either dries up or displaced from its place of origin and this may cause epidemic in that area. They also have the opinion that the high density water in the sacred rivers and lakes would maintain the seasonal change and indirectly would not affect the health of the people, but on the other hand the low density of water would disturb the seasons and people may fall ill or their health may be disturbed.

Health, illness and disease have direct relation with the behaviour of the people's belief. It was observed that the people in general hesitate to accept the modern means of health practices. They informed that it is their belief as well as the cultural make-up to accept the traditional way of spiritual healing by means of magico-religious activities or practices. The age-old Lepcha people stated that the activities or performances of the doctors and nurses are merciless in nature while taking blood or giving any injection or even at the time of any operation. According to their understanding the traditional way of implication of ethno-biotic (using of plants and animal parts) medicine is more effective one, even in the present day. It is their opinion that implication of various ways of modern family planning measures are an impious activity, which sometimes create a cultural shock to the would be mother as well as to the whole family.

BELIEFS AND ILLNESS

Many of the early writers and researchers mentioned that the Lepchas are 'animists' and the references to devils' habitation in the desiderata for a house site might suggest that such a term was justified. Because the Lepchas, on the one hand believe in ghost, demons and on the other hand they have the belief on Gods and goddesses. They also have the religious attitude towards various natural objects. All supernatural being, good and bad, though eternally living outside the world, have innumerable manifestations. These manifestations, or replicas, of the supernatural, chose various natural phenomena for semi permanent habitation, agreeable phenomena - lakes or fruit trees or fruitful land – if the supernatural are generally benevolent, disagreeable places – useless trees, waterfalls, rocks or barren ground – if the supernatural are generally malevolent. Each type of supernatural has a preference for a particular kind of habitation, thus all the *dent moong* – fever devils – live in big isolated trees, *Sabdok moong* – skim disease devils – in outcrops of rock.

According to them everything in the world possess a soul, for the soul is the animating principle of all life, without whose intermediary nothing could move or grow. But the souls of objects and animals below the vertebrates are very weak and transient things; they are easily killed and never reincarnate.

The word with which the Lepchas invariably refer to the habitations of supernatural is *li*. The houses of supernatural particularly malevolent supernatural – are avoided, because the devil might be annoyed at the intrusion on his privacy would show his resentment by inflicting illness on the intruders. Similarly the supernatural would resent any injury done to his house, such as cutting down his tree or chipping off parts of his stone, and would punish the rash man by paining him in that portion of his body which corresponded to that portion of the house which had been destroyed; thus cutting from the top of a tree or a rock would result in head pains, from a branch or an outcrop in arm ache, and so on. Consequently the recognized habitations of devils are paid the respect of avoidance and should a man be forced to go near to one of an evening he would perhaps burn a little incense – either juniper leaves or rice mixed with butter so that the devil shall be gratified and not pursue him. One such spot was in between the area of Tingboong and Linzya just beside the road side gorge, where the two outcrops are believed to be the homes of *Sabdok moong* and his wife *Loo moong*. This female devil causes a specific skin disease, and if a person / or a passerby urinate on that spot should suffer from a non-curable genital disease. Her stone will be anointed with holy water by a lama and with milk by a *Mun*.

It was informed that there is a lake 'Luksom partam', high up in Dzongu, from where life is believed to be created. Sterile couples who wish for children should visit this lake, spend the night on its bank copulating and then in the morning throw into the water a silver rupees and a *chimi* (altar light) to please the gods. If necessary this may be repeated annually for three years. The connection between water and birth runs all through the *Mun* mythology. People viewed that in divine world where the two gods *Tak-bo-thing* and *Narzong-nyou* live there is a stream called *Lungfung* which represents the birth of male children and a well called *Rungzel oong-lap* which represents the birth of female children. This well is guarded by a supernatural boy called *Sathim ong*.

RITUALS FOR CURING ILLNESS

The rituals are performed for the benefit of individuals, households and the geographical area at large. Among many of such rituals few important rituals are mentioned below. The people have the belief that observance of these rituals is essential for curing the illness. In these ceremonies, *Mun, Boongthing* and Lama play an overwhelming role.

A. Cherim Ceremony: In the *cherim* ceremony, which is held twice in a year - once at the beginning of the rains and second at the beginning of winter respectively to ward off epidemic diseases like malaria. Three separate rituals are performed for this; two by *Mun* and the one by the Lamas. In such communal sacrifice at least one individual from each household has to be present and each household contributes a little amount of grain and *Mun*'s participation is necessary.

The first part of the ceremony consists of offering to the devil spirits. This ceremony is called *rum* after the name given to the chief article of sacrifice. In a large basket filled with earth and covered with a banana leaf into which are kept a number of eight pieces of each article manifesting 'demon's walking stick' consisting of decorated bamboos with flowers inserted in holes, water in a container, milk, tea and *chi* (country liquor); pieces of mica; stems of warm wood decorated with threads, fresh eggs, heaps of grain and dried bird, dried fish and ginger. The offering articles also includes two *ta-ming* which consists of long sticks to which are attached and wrapped in leaves samples of every sort of food and drink. When the offerings have to be made, the *Mun*, sitting opposite to the people, intones a long chant to invoke the gods (*rum*) and then takes the eggs and touches them to his forehead while keeping his eyes shut; the line which he envisages inside the eggs foretells the future health of the community.

The second ceremony – '*Tsandong*' is also performed by *Mun*, consists of offerings to the Gods of Khangchendzonga and the plains. The offerings consist of rice, butter, *chimi* (a variety of wild fruit), a rupee and eight eggs. The offering is made in two parts; first grain and strained *chi* (traditional liquor) are thrown out by the *Mun* and her assistant and later a goat is dedicated and then sacrificed. These two ceremonies together take about four hours time. At least one member from each household has to attend this ceremony. Usually the male members attended the ceremony. In this ceremony prayers are also attributed to the God of mountains (*Sungmul*) from the protection from snow, hailstorm and blizzard. The people present in this ceremony are busy in cooking, eating, gossiping and watching the preparation.

The third ceremony is performed by the Lamas with the preparation of a very elaborate ceremonial object. The chief of these are the '*deu*', the 'nine – storied palace', consisting of elaborate regular polyhedral in different colour threads supported on bamboo splinters through a central bamboo. This 'palace', which took over four hours to complete is made to mollify the demons or ghost of an old king of Tibet called *Dayom*. In his lifetime this palace and monasteries were destroyed so that he had nowhere to live. In revenge his spirit roams about harming people. The palace is offered to beg his pardon and to persuade him to return home without hurting the people in the neighbourhood. The foreground of the structure was occupied by an elaborate representation of the female demon *Mamoo Moong*, portrayed as a snake-haired female riding on a tiger and surrounded by hundreds of lesser objects. The demon was principally made out of buckwheat powder and it was impressed on the onlookers. According to the sacred books, when the whole object has been made, the invocation and readings from the Holy Scriptures begin with the accompaniment of musical instrument. An offering of boiled rice and fresh buckwheat bread is cleared and *cherkem* is offered to the demons. The *Mamoo Moong* herself is summoned and gratified with the offerings of copper pots and clothes. When the demon *Mamoo Moong* is presumed to be in a good mood or temper, her image is taken – off the temporarily erected altar and handed over to all present during the observance to wave out the malevolent action. Lastly the image is carried out with a procession and immersed into the junction of three streams. It is a perception that if any animal has not devoured within three days, it is a sign that there will be serious sickness in the coming season. Before taking out the image a *Mun* sang a song alone for thanking the god for coming and blessing them and now to go back. On these occasions, *Mun* always sang more or less a sacred song.

B. Shokbu – Rum Ceremony: This ceremony is followed by the Lepcha people during the month of summer season to propitiate the *Yomgebo* god (rum) and nature spirit. It is a belief of the people that during onset of summer season people are affected by various seasonal diseases like diarrhea, dysentery, cough and cold etc. which may cause by the ill effect of that *yomgebo* deity (*rum*) and the spirit residing in the nature. According to them, the sun god, *Yomgebo* is most powerful among the all and people must appease the sun god. The Lepcha people offer millet, maize, buckwheat flour to the *yomgebo* and the nature spirit. It is worth mentioning that no animal is sacrificed in this ceremony. *Boongthing* plays an important role to propitiate the god and the spirit without taking any food. By seeing the yoke of the egg offered by every individual household, *Boongthing* can feel about the future health status of that particular household. Either the member of the household would really get affected by any diseases or not during the coming season can be foretold by the *Boongthing*. At the time of initiation of this ceremony, *Boongthing* sits facing the east, he also decorates the place by making a platform made of bamboo poles, bamboo vessel for the offerings, wooden bowl for *maung chi* (traditional millet beer) etc. The whole propitiation is preferably done on the bank of a river or a stream. This ceremony is not performed in the household premises rather the place is chosen on the top of the hills, presence of the people from each household is necessary.

C. Parnap festival: This ceremony is performed to appease the demon, known as *Zengo*, who is believed to be residing in Tolung gompha. This ceremony is performed every year turn wise by the every household. It is the perception of the people that the appeasement of the demon *Zengo* may protect their health from any dreadful diseases. It is also told that the Lepcha, whenever completed the construction of their house, organize this ceremony in the newly built house as if to purify the house and ward off any harm caused by demon to the house. *Boongthing* or *Mun* are responsible to propitiate the rituals in their traditional way. On the day of the ceremony one cock and one hen is sacrificed to venerate the demon and on the next day the house-owner organize a feast to which the relatives, kith and kin members and the neighbours are invited. On the other hand, during the span of one year every household within a *bustee* contribute the food grains (millet, maize, and buckwheat), money and *maung-chi* (millet-beer) as per their capacity and assimilate together. At the time of yearly festival, during the month of June, one of the members of that *bustee* carries away those assimilated articles to the Thollung monastery and performs worship by a Lama. This *parnap* ceremony, according to them is performed for overall prosperity, happiness and well-being of the *bustee*. The people believe that any kind of disregard and carelessness may cause harm to them and they may die by the dreadful sickness.

D. Apang Moong / Sor moong: To get rid of genito-urinary disease or violent death, a goat is put in a snare having three knots tied in its length, first of all, all the members of the afflicted household must touch the knots and then the *Mun* would call on all the devils to be contended with the blood of the sacrifice and not to take the patient, after which he throws the rope into the air. If the rope falls end outwards (i.e. the end away from the goat falls towards the door), it means that the devil is satisfied and if it falls towards the house the prognosis is bad. After this the animal is killed and the *gazook* and *sha-fot* offered to the devil/demon with a plate and a pot filled with rice, a rupee and a ceremonial scarf (*Khada*), together with some of the invalid's ornaments and clothing and also a cup of *chi* with different grains in it. Then the *Mun* constructs a phallus out of wood, which is called in its guardian function *moong long tik*. This phallus is set up between two stones leaning slightly forward, somewhere in the forest, and anointed with the blood of the slain animal and *chi*. This will keep the devil/demon away from the area and household.

E. Num-een moong: The young children death caused by infantile diarrhea, which is believed to be caused by a demon named *Num-een moong*. To drive away that demon (*moong*) the Lepcha people sacrifice a goat or a sheep. Even after the sacrifice of an animal if the person continues to be troubled by the *moong*. Then the troubled person stands on the right side of the stream and the *Mun* on the left of it. Then a 'gateway' is made over the stream of two bundles of elephant grass and brambles, while the *Mun* holds in each hand a bundle made out of wild raspberries, nettles and some other thorny and prickly plants. These bundles are dipped in water and peek over the sufferer several times. A bamboo *chi* (beer) holder filled with blood and *chi* and shut up at both ends and a leaf filled with fried rice, meat and blood are peek over the patient and thrown through the gateway for the demon. The branches of thorny plants are thrown through the gateway and finally the gateway is filled up with thorny plants, so that it looks like a tree. The *Mun* does this at two other places; one is some way apart on the streams and the other is either above or below the first one. After completing the *Mun* must return straight to his own house without meeting anybody. If he meets people *Num-een moong* will start haunting him.

It was told that *Num-een moong* is the demon released by the death of young children. Older people who die do not let loose a devil/demon. The *Num-een moong* persists for about three years after the child's death.

F. Sipundi: The Lepcha when attacked by food poison is believed to be caused due to the effect of a malevolent spirit called *sipundi*. It is also believed by the people that when the malevolent spirit *sipundi* made a tremendous effect on the Lepcha, they die instantly. Sometimes its effect gradually harms the people. At this time, the Lepcha experienced with various physical agonies and ailments and their physique becomes feeble. Some of the people also get affected by jaundice and started decreasing their health. The *Boongthing* is called out and he is the person who can trace what kind of supernatural power really affected the person. He also suggested the best way one Lepcha can do. Whenever the malevolent spirit *sipundi* affect the person, he/she will be cured by folk medicine of herbal medicine.

G. Amee: It is another type of malevolent spirit usually believed to be residing in the fruits, vegetables and grains heaped outside the Lepcha houses. This malevolent spirit is said to be the cause of limb pain, whenever a Lepcha person get effected by limb pain it is believed that he or she might have stolen the other Lepchas articles. They also believed that for the cure of the malevolent effect of *Amee* the affected person must have to go to the owner's house and confess his wrong-doings. If the owner of the article simply rub the limb and effected person get relief.

H. Lung-Zee: One of the most special spirits is *Lung-zee*, interpreted as an equivalent sort of guardian spirit for a particular object of nature. These objects are such that they catch the eye straightaway may be a huge tree, a crag, a tarn, a cave, a cluster of trees, a special hillock and other natural objects. They are supposed to have some sort of a limit or boundary around the object in which they have come and taken up the abode. The belief is that if the spirit is ignored, and the object defiled and polluted by answering the call of nature, or men and women indulging sexual intercourse anywhere in its vicinity, there is the possibility of the whole village getting sufferings by any infections disease, or at least the culprit or culprits receiving punishment by a series of diseases and sometimes death may also occur in the family. In order to ward off ill effects of such spirits to the people try to abide by the norms pertaining maintenance of the nature in most harmonious way. For that matter they restrict themselves from wood hewing in the area, where *lung-zee* is apprehended to be present. They believe that a pond or a stream is the abode of a *lung-zee*. They do not irritate it by throwing stones in it. It is believed that the *lung-zee* is present in a crag, they do not dare to collect honey combs, hornet grubs or flowering edible orchids from it. *Boongthing* and *Mun* perform the job to detect where the *lung-zee* originally resides and give the instruction accordingly.

Supernatural power and the illness: According to Lepcha, the illness may occur due to the displeasure or dissatisfaction of the supernatural power on whom they have no control. These supernatural powers are sometimes benefited them and sometimes cursed them as well in the form of illness and diseases. This type of harmful supernatural power have its own jurisdiction which are mentioned below (Table 3, 4 and 5):

Table 3. Malevolent power of the God (*rum*)

Position	*Local Name*	*Causes*
Village God	*Langrum*	Responsible for headache, fever, drowsiness
Household deity	*Tongthing*	Eye infection
Household deity	*Lee-rum*	Cause the disease like diarrhea, dysentery, stomach, disorder etc.
Common deity	*Tsandong rum*	Cause epidemic like malaria, jaundice
Common deity	*Lung-no rum, Ajo Gyantho*	Responsible for severe stomach pain, diarrhea, dysentery.
Seasonal deity	*Shukbu-rum*	Responsible for various seasonal disease like Cough and Cold, Phenomonia, diarrhea, dysentery etc.

Table 4. Malevolent power of the demon/devil/ghost (moong)

Position	*Local Name*	*Causes*
Place of dense forest, rock and cave	*Duet-Tshen moong*	Responsible for rheumatism (*akn-dak/athmg dak*), headache, Bodyache, joint and limb pain, high fever
Places of flowing streams, rivers	*Manoo moong* (female ghost)	Responsible for whole body pain.
places of flowing streams, rivers	*Loo-moong* (female demon)	responsible for specific skin disease, wounds, fatal injury

Position	*Local Name*	*Causes*
Places of a village boundary	*Lyang shergynu* (female ghost)	Responsible for miscarriage, frequent vomiting, lose of appetite of the female folk.
Places of outcrops of a rock	*Sabdok moong*	Skin disease, sore etc. is caused due to the ill effect of the *moong*
Places of roadside area	*Arof moong*	Accident, suicide

Table 5. Malevolent power of the evil spirit

Position	*Local Name*	*Causes*
Reside in the nature as a whole	*Dzengo*	Cause of different dreadful diseases like TB., Pneumonia lung disease.
Reside in the tree trunk	*Apang moong sor moong*	Cause of genitor-urinary disease. Cause for violent death.
Reside in the dead child's soul	*Num-een moong*	Cause of infantile diarrhea
Reside in the open barren field	*Sipundi*	Cause of food poison and jaundice
Reside in the fruits, vegetables and grains	*Amee*	Cause of limb pain, whole body pain
Reside in a huge tree, a crag, a tarn, a cave, a cluster of trees, a hillock	*Lung-zee*	Cause of various infections disease. The whole village got affected.
Reside in the huge stone situated at the entry point of the *bustee*	*Sandong Long-chuk*	Cause of various common diseases like headache, bodyache, limb pain, nose bleeding (*jukmar-vee*), heart disease (*alut-dak*), stomach disorder (*tubok-dak*)
Reside in the open air just outside the house	*Maknyam*	Cause of vomiting, stomach pain, diarrhea
Reside in the dense forest	*Sor*	Cause of loose motion, piles, abnormal delivery etc.

From the list of few supernatural powers mentioned above it can be seen that the Lepcha world of vision is completely guided by beliefs. Even in nowadays, these traditions get due importance. The Lepcha take the measure, to propitiate those supernatural evil power first by the *Boongthing* and *Mun*, if it is not cured they opt, for the better option of Traditional herbal medicine by consulting the medicine men - *Maondaok*. If the health situation becomes aggravated then they go to the Primary health centre and opt for modern medicine.

Some Warding-off Practices

Many of the so called Lepcha superstitions and beliefs stem out from the mythology, legends and folk-lore. The people explained that 'due to the absence of any knowledge of science, we have a kind of experience by trial and error, and have evolved our own method of talking the various problems of our lives' (narrated by the Lepcha age-old person, Chewang Duk Lepcha of Dzongu and Pasankit of Yuksam area). There are some warding off practices and beliefs as what is not supposed to be done in the Lepcha society which have great relevance with the concept of illness are mentioned here –

1. In the Lepcha mind whistling at night is absolutely forbidden. It is believed that if the whistling is done '*Sang-rong moong*', a huge creature, living in the high altitude forest would come down whistling at the dead of might and may cause various harm including killing of the person, who had done whistling.
2. The women-folk of the Lepcha society have a belief that when two women are pregnant, and if the women themselves or their husbands, knowingly or unknowingly exchange articles, the sex of the foetus in the womb also gets changed - the male becoming female and otherwise.
3. It is a popular belief that pointing at a rainbow with the index finger is supposed to result in gnarled fingers like those of the lepers. The reason behind it is they believed that the rainbow is a supernatural being and having a spirit. The Lepcha should respect it and pointing at it with the index finger, which we consider as a sign of disrespect.
4. If someone in the family commits incest, they fall victims under the curse of '*Khum*'. It is believed that this particular curse will directly affect the children in the house; the children may fall sick and often die. They have also a belief that if any family have made any dealings with the curse affected family, the later will be

affected by a special curse called '*Tyup*' by which the contacting family will suffer from dangerous type of diseases.

5. It was told that if anyone gives away a certain article or a thing to someone else, he must not receive it back. The fear is that if this is done, one is sure to develop a sore or gangrene at the elbow joints by '*Kather nyom*', which literally means in Lepcha language 'The elbow curse'. It is believed that the elbow sore will get so bad that the some bone marrow will ooze out from the arm bone.
6. During pregnancy both mother and father strictly follow some restrictions, like (i) would be father generally avoid any type of bamboo work. If he does so he should avoid making any knots, (ii) would be father avoids nailing work. Even if he is bound to do that, he should remove the nails after finishing the work. (iii) Both would be father and mother and other members of that household do not eat any meat of fastened animal. They have a restriction even to see the fastened dead animal. It has a popular belief against these that if the would-be-parents do not follow this, their child will be affected by epilepsy. (iv) They have also popular belief that would-be-parents should never see solar eclipse, lunar eclipse, falling of star and cosmic ray. On the day of eclipse both of them are strictly confined into the room. It has a belief that disregard of such traditional rules would be the cause of giving birth a blind child. (v) During pregnancy, mother and father are restricted to cross the cattle rope. They believe that if they did so the new born baby may die of fastening of rope or strangulation.

Traditional Healer: *Boongthing* and *Mun*

The Lepcha since long believed in psycho-somato traditional healing practice - *Boongthingism* and *Munism.* They believe in existence of God called *Rum* to whom the *Boongthing* and *Mun* offer their prayers and thanks. *Boongthing* and *Mun* perform all the rituals and religious ceremonies of the Lepchas. Many of the earlier writing mentioned that for the God fearing Lepchas, prayers supplication and worship is performed through *Boongthing* and *Mun.* It is not a superstition, not any flight of eloquence and not even lips homage to God. The living quality of *Boongthingism* and *Munism* is demonstrated by the loyalty it has commanded from its followers, the Lepchas. *Boongthing* and *Mun* is the mediator between God (*rums*), devil/demons (*moongs*) and the

Lepchas. The *Boongthing* ward-off the evil spirits by sacrificing the animals and other things. Both of them are invited to officiate during clan/community rituals or even for worshipping the family deities. Their assistance is also invariably sought for curing sickness of individuals. *Boongthing* are supposed to be able to communicate with the malevolent and benevolent demons/devils (*moongs*). The institution *Mun* is hereditary in nature, but the institution *Boongthing* can be learnt from the other *Boongthing*. The Lepcha believed that apart from the service of warding off the malevolent spirits, *Boongthing* are also sought for during the wedding to invoke the gods and goddesses. The *Boongthings* are more popular among the Lepchas in general as their service is frequently sought. *Muns*' performance is restricted to different social functions. *Mun* plays a pivotal role in agriculture related observances. According to them the *Muns* are hierarchically classified in their status. Every classification has definite performance. *Pilden Muns* are the superior one who has the capacity to communicate with the dead person's soul. Some of the *Muns*, known as *Mun Mook-Mun*, are thought to be the evil doers who cause hardship to the people. The *Mun-Jyum-Mun* category *mun* perform the activities as like the *Pilden mun*, except for that they can not communicate with the dead person's soul but can cure the sick person by herbal medicines. The *mun* having the specialized knowledge of using herbs is considered as *Tangli mun*.

Health Care System in West and North Sikkim

From the study it was noticed that the Lepchas of Ramgyathang hamlet follows the dual system (both traditional and modern allopathic medicine) of medical practice, while the Lepchas of another set up, i.e., Lethang and Khecheopalri, preference is different. They prefer traditional way of health care over the modern one. In Khecheopalri monastery bustee the Lepchas are influenced by the monastery and the healing practices of the lama. During the study it was observed that the infant group in general is treated by both traditional and modern medicine. In this context it was learnt that whenever the intensity of illness becomes severe, they prefer to go to the Health Centre. The age-old person always prefers the traditional medical practice by appeasing the supernatural power and by applying the ethno-medicine. To them, a kind of regular health disorder, like, loose motion; cough and cold; snake bite; injuries, etc. are not at all cared seriously. The acute ailment like, eye infection; severe chest pain; continuous fever; tuberculosis; malarial infection etc., carry some importance and for that purpose they initially consult the *boongthing, mun* and after that take the ethno-medicine. If it is not cured, then they have to consult the doctor. It is noticed that education plays a key role in the Lepcha society of west Sikkim district. The Lepcha, who have no education generally, prefers the traditional medicines to cure their illness, while the educated persons prefer to consult the modern medicine men, the doctor. Of course there are some exceptions found in the Lethang hamlet, where few high school students want to give much value to their traditional medical practices by following the ethno-medicine. Amongst them those who are affluent in these three set up prefer to consult the modern medical system. In Khecheopalri the role of lama is much more than the services of *Boongthing* and *Mun* in view of existence of a thought there.

In North Sikkim it was noticed that for the health care in lower Dzongu, people seemed more traditional with some leaning towards the modern system. But in the upper Dzongu maximum number of Lepcha population prefer only to the age-old traditional system keeping faith on the services of *Mun, Boongthing* and also the Lama. Living in the close proximity with nature and forest the people take the ethno-medicine and ethno-biotic components for healing up their illness. People informed that the lower Dzongu area is situated in the close proximity of the district headquarter Mangan and they have easy access to go there and treat their ailments in the district hospital. However, the Lepcha who reside in the farthest places like Linzya and Bay, have to adopt their traditional system as an effective means of health care as there is no hospital facilities available. In all the three studied hamlets it is noticed that the infants are looked after carefully, whenever the infants fall sick the *Maondaok*, traditional medicine man, is consulted along with *Boongthing*. Another important point is the impact of education and awareness which plays an important role in health care system. People of upper Dzongu specially the areas, like, Linzya, Bay, Salim-Pakhel; the Lepchas have less access to take up the modern health facilities. The Lepchas of upper Dzongu depend on traditional system first, then dual mode (traditional as well as modern medicine) and finally, when health care needs the modern medicine is used. The reason behind is the belief on supernatural power and strong religious faith compel them to stick on the age-old tradition.

Ethno-biotic medicine

Ethno-biotic medicines comprise of both botanical and animal body parts to treat the people from ailments. In Sikkim, the Lepchas have the treasure of botanical medicinal resource and as well as the knowledge

Table 6. Medicinal Plant Used by the Lepchas of West and North Sikkim

A. West Sikkim

Vernacular Name	*Botanical Name*	*Parts used*	*Disease/ailments*
Chuli	*Abroma augusta*	Bark, by making bark juice, granules of bark paste	Menstrual disorder
Teil	*Artemisia Nilagirica*	Leaf by making juice, paste and boiled into the water	Nasal bleeding, benemicidal and skin treatment
Chimcharch	*Begonia sp.*	Leaf and petiole by making the juice and boiling into the water	Stomachache
Aniomukh	*Codonopsis Viridis*	Leaf by making juice and boiling into the water	Infant diarrhea
Roo-pa-tong	*Costus speciosus*	Rhizome by boiling and consumed as vegetable	Urinary disorder and food poisoning
Shykhyok-Kung	*Engelhardtia spicata*	Green bract by making paste and consumed as juice	Stomach ailments and throat pain
Ulak-rikh	*Hemiphragma heterophyllum*	Fruit consumed directly	Throat pain and tonsillitis
Kalkung	*Juglaus regia*	Nut consumed by boi8ling and fried	Rheumatism

Vernacular Name	*Botanical Name*	*Parts used*	*Disease/ailments*
Yayena	*Rubia cordifolia*	Root by making paste	Astringents in cuts and wounds
Sambrung-kung	*Schima wallichii*	Fruit consumed directly and dried up sometimes make a paste and applied directly	Dandruff
Mongrip	*Siegesbeckia orientalis*	Leaf by making juice boiling in water and leaf-paste	Sores
Zangoo Much	*Spilanthes acmella*	Inflorescence by boiling in mastered oil	Toothache
Pusore	*Thysanolaena maxima*	Root by boiling of root making a paste.	Boils, sores and gastric problem
Tungkung	*Trichosanthes tricuspidata*	Root, stem and seed by making juice and paste of roof and stem by boiling the seed	Food-poisoning snake biting rheumatism
Dinshing	*Abies wabbiana*	Leaves and gums by making paste of leaves. Gum mixed with oil of roses	Stomachache, Tonic astringent, internal hemorrhage Tuberculosis. Gum used internally for intoxication and externally for headache

Vernacular Name	*Botanical Name*	*Parts used*	*Disease/ailments*
Riklok	*Acorus calamus*	Root and Rhizome by making power of roof. Boiling the Rhizome	Expelling intestinal worm insect repellent diarrhea
Mordo-Kung/ Kohul-Kung	*Actinodaphne Hookeri*	Leaves and seeds by extracting oil from seeds	Urinary disorder diabetes, oil extracting from seeds used in sprain of muscles
Yel, Yel-Pote	*Aesandra butyraceae Diploknema buty raceac Maduca butyraceac*	Fruit by making ointment of the fruit, oil cakes by making juice of the Bark	Asthma, rheumatism.
Harrasiris	*Albizzia Lebbeck*	Root, seed, leaves by extracting oil from the seed; by making powder from the root bark	Roof- disease of blood, leucoderma, itching, piles, skin disease inflammation, cry-sepals, bronchitis. Flower- Asthma seed-oil-leprosy roof bark powder – It strengthen the gums
Iakmar	*Albizia procera*	Leaves	Applied in ulcers, being anti cancerous properties used in cancers.
Singriang	*Albizia stipulate*	Bark by making lotion from the bark	Cuts, scabies and other skin disease.

Vernacular Name	*Botanical Name*	*Parts used*	*Disease/ailments*
Yel, Yel-Pote	*Aesandra butyraceae Diploknema buty raceac Maduca butyraceac*	Fruit by making ointment of the fruit, oil cakes by making juice of the Bark	Asthma, rheumatism.
Harrasiris	*Albizzia Lebbeck*	Root, seed, leaves by extracting oil from the seed; by making powder from the root bark	Roof- disease of blood, leucoderma, itching, piles, skin disease inflammation, cry-sepals, bronchitis. Flower- Asthma seed-oil-leprosy roof bark powder – It strengthen the gums
Iakmar	*Albizia procera*	Leaves	Applied in ulcers, being anti cancerous properties used in cancers.
Singriang	*Albizia stipulate*	Bark by making lotion from the bark	Cuts, scabies and other skin disease.
Langi Tungrap	*Ammomum sabulatun*	Seeds by making seed oil and seed juice	Heart and Liver disorder, hypnotic appetizer Indigestion, vomiting, enlarged spleen, bulge of rectum, gonorrhea

Vernacular Name	*Botanical Name*	*Parts used*	*Disease/ailments*
Langi Tungrap	*Ammomum sabulatun*	Seeds by making seed oil and seed juice	Heart and Liver disorder, hypnotic appetizer Indigestion. vomiting, enlarged spleen, bulge of rectum, gonorrhea
Tangaruk	*Aphanamixis polystachaya*	Bark and seed by making bark juice and seed oil	Spleen and liver disease, tumors abdominal complaints, rheumatism
Tuk-Gnyel	*Artimisia vulgaris*	Whole plant by making the juice and sometimes paste.	Asthma, itching, antibacterial and antifungal properties.
Ramsukung	*Artocarpus heterophyllus*	Fruits, latex, leaves, roots by making tonic from fruits.	Leaves ash healing ulcers, roof useful in skin disease, asthma, diarrhea
Sungyenkung	*Artocarpus lakoocha*	Fruit, plant	Ripe fruit- Improve Taste Eye trouble Appetite Plant- Spleen, bone fracture, tapeworm
Chee-Kung	*Bauhimia purpurea*	Roots, Bark, flowers by making juice.	Control diarrhea, animal bite.

Vernacular Name	*Botanical Name*	*Parts used*	*Disease/ailments*
Makrik/Sungung Rik	*Bauhinia vahlie*	Seeds, leaves by making leaves tonic	Diarrhea, dysentery, stomach disorder
Rhar-Kung	*Bauhinia variegate*	Bark, leaves, flowers, buds and flowers by making astringent tonic	Toothache, ulcers, skin diseases, diarrhea, cough bleeding piles.
Sutung Kung	*Berberis aristata*	Root, Bark, Branch lets fruit by making paste and juice from root bark.	Skin disease, diarrhea, jaundice, eyes infection roof extraction is hypo-glycaemia and anticancer.
Sangli Kung	*Betula utilis*	Bark by making bark tonic bark paste	Convulsion, bronchitis, blood and ear leprosy, bark paste use in fracture of bone.
Sunga	*Callicarpa arborea*	Bark by making tonic, paste	Bark tonic – Cutaneous diseases, rheumatism, gonorrhea Bark paste- insect biting, scorpion sting skin disease
Kapher-Buk	*Canna edulis*	Roots, Seeds, leaves and flowers	Roof:- Fever, leprosy flowers – Eye diseases

Vernacular Name	*Botanical Name*	*Parts used*	*Disease/ailments*
Nambo Kung	*Cannabis sativa*	Leaves, seeds by making leave juice seed oil, leaf powder	Leaves:-hysteria, spasmodic cough, asthma, neuralgia, diarrhea Plant:-diabetic, hypertension
Manyan	*Carica papaya*	Fruits (Latex), seeds	Cure inflammation, enlargement of spleens, piles, ringworm, skin disease. Seeds are used as antibiotic
Ruglim	*Celastrus paniculata*	Seeds and leaves by making seed oil, leaves paste and juice	Seed oil: improves memory power Seeds:- rheumatism, gout, paralysis, leprosy
Songsor Kung	*Cinnamomum tamala*	Leaves, bark by making juice and paste	Leaves: Scabies, reaction of piles, heart troubles, bad taste, Brain tonic Bark:- gonorrhea, antibacterial.
Tamshap Rip	*Cissampelos paraeira*	Leaves, barks roots by making leaves paste	Roof:- dyspepsia, dropsy dysentery, urinary trouble Leaves:- scabies, septic ulcers

Vernacular Name	*Botanical Name*	*Parts used*	*Disease/ailments*
Karhyo	*Citrullus colosynthis*	Fruits, roots	Fruits:- Cures tumors, leucoderma, ulcers, asthma, Jaundice Roof:-inflammation of breasts, pains in joints.
Sangatrani	*Citrus maxima*	Fruits, leaves	Fruit: Leprosy, asthma, cough, mental aberration, epilepsy, chest complaints Leaves:- Tonic for brain, vomiting, abdomen gripping, headache, eye troubles
Chalum	*Citrus reticulate auram tium*	Fruits and flower by making juice from flower	Dried skin of the fruit- useful in dyspepsia Flower juice: antispasmodic and sedative

B. North Sikkim

Vernacular Name	*Botanical Name*	*Parts used*	*Disease / Ailments*
Aetok koong	*Rhododendron arboretum*	Flowers and Petals by making dried powder	Fresh and dried flower petal cures dysentery and diarrhea clear the bones of fish stuck in the throat.
Ausoodaong	*Menthe arvensis*	Leaves and young shoots by making juice and paste	Remedy for headache and cholera, used as stimulant and digestive
Kadaorip	*Rosa clamascena*	Petals, buds and roots, by making paste and juice of buds and roots	*Petal paste* is applied in cuts, stops blood discharge. *Buds and Roof*- Cure Tuberculosis.
Kajyoo khyaamoong	*Datura fistulosa*	Roots, leaves and seeds by making paste, juice and dried powder	*Leaves*- rheumatic swelling, sciatic and inflammations complaints *Seeds powder* – smoke of seeds powder cure asthmatic fits.
Kanyim	*Amaranthus tricolor*	Roots, stalks and Leaves by making juice	Astringent in diarrhea, dysentery and hemorrhage of the bowels. Juice is effective for excessive menstrual discharge
Kazoo	*Urtica parviflora*	Roots, leaves and flowers by making juice, powder	*Roofs*- Fracture and dislocation. *Pounding roofs*- gonorrhea. Juice is taken as tonic for cleaning after child birth.

Vernacular Name	*Botanical Name*	*Parts used*	*Disease / Ailments*
Kahlyaabi	*Hibiscus esculentus*	Fruits- Gums and gelatinous substance of the fruits	Cure gonorrhea, burning sensation while urine and painful urination.
Kashyum koong	*Rubus ellipticus*	Roots, shoots	Cure colic pains and kill the intestinal worms in children.
Kaong ki koong	*Prumus Pudum*	Bark, branches by making paste and soaking liquid	*Bark*:- paste is applied for healing up fracture of bones, *Soaking liquid of small branches* stops abortion.
Kaong hi koong	*Semicarpus amacardium*	Roots, barks and fruits by making paste	Paste is applied to cure all kinds of skin disease.
Kuntim paot	*Piper longum*	Fruits by making juice, powder	Cure Asthma, cough, rheumatism, gonorrhea, piles, and spleen. *Powder fruits*- applied with black pepper powder and milk good for development of breast.
Took koong	*Gynocardia odorata*	Seeds by making oil and paste	*Seed oil*- very useful for leprosy, also used for eczema and other skin disease and chronic rheumatism.
Gey bookhanaok	*Dichroa febrifuge*	Roots and leaves, by making paste and juice	Decoction of roof cures fever. Very useful for malaria and other type of fevers.

Vernacular Name	*Botanical Name*	*Parts used*	*Disease / Ailments*
Gok-Rip	*Michelia champaca*	Bark, flowers and fruits by making juice as tonic	*Bark* – reduce fever and ejects phlegm from throat and lungs by coughing and spitting. *Flowers and Fruits*- cures nausea and fever. Promoting urine in kidney diseases and in gonorrhea.
Tuk chyer koong	*Albizia julibrissin*	Bark and seed by making powder, juice and paste	Cures piles and diarrhea. *Root Bark powder*- strengthens gums for teeth. *Juice of young leaves*- cures might blindness.
Tuk nyil	*Artimisia vulgaris*	*Whole plant including leaves* by making paste young shoot by boiling in the water.	Cures skin diseases and ulcers, nose bleeding, clear the block in nostrils. Cures gout and rheumatism. *Young shoot*- increase and promotes appetite digestion
Tukpitrik	*Paederia foetida*	*Leaves*, roots and fruits, shoots by making powder juice	*Young leaves and shoots*- cure convalescent rheumatism. *Leaves juice*- cures diarrhea of children *pounded fruits*- protects toothache.

Vernacular Name	*Botanical Name*	*Parts used*	*Disease / Ailments*
Tumbaar rik	*Mussaenda frondosa*	Flowers, roots, by making paste juice	*Flowers* – cough, asthma *Root juice*- jaundice *roof paste*- skin eruption ulcers.
Tung loo koong	*Bombax malabaricum*	Gum or juice roots	Cures dysentery. *Young roofs*- cures gonorrhea
Durbi hyur	*Red fungas*	Whole body of the fungus by making powder	Dried red fungus soaked in worm water to cure arching ear.
Naong ryoopaot	*Zanthoxyllum acanthopodium*	Seeds and bark by making tonic, distilled arrack of fruit	*Seed and Bark tonic*- cure fever, dyspepsia and cholera *Distilled arrack of fruit* massaged to cure gout and rheumatism.
Paong mook	*Cynodon dactylon*	Roots, whole plants by making decoction, juice	*Decoction of roofs*- cures dropsy and syphilis *Fusion of roofs*- stops bleeding of piles *Crushed roofs*- cures chronic gonorrhea *Juice of plants*-cures cuts and wounds,
Pudin ayok mook	*Drymaria cordata*	Leaves and plants by making ash and paste	Inhaling of Smolder leaves and plants cures nose blockage and headache cure diphtheria, pneumonia, good chronic sinus infection.

Vernacular Name	*Botanical Name*	*Parts used*	*Disease / Ailments*
Pur vok koong	*Alstonia scholaris*	Bark, root by making paste and juice	*Bark*- cure skin disease, rheumatism. *Root*- juice taken with milk cures leprosy.
Phago koong	Not collected	Bark, seeds by making paste and ashes powder	*Bark paste*- cure fresh cuts and wounds *Bark ashes*- cure chronic wounds. *Powder of seed*- cures throat, lung sores and typhoid.
Braong paot	*Phyllanthus emblica*	Barks, fruits by making juice, paste	*Bark and fruits*- cures diarrhea and dysentery, helps digestion. *Fresh juice*- mixed with milk cure gonorrhea mixed with honey cure white leucorrhoea relieves pain in urine trouble and burning sensation to the vagina.
Booshi kaa	Not collected	Roots, bark leaves and flowers by making paste, juice	Remove phlegm, bile impurities of blood cures cough, asthma, fever, vomiting, leprosy, tuberculosis. Leaves are valuable antiseptic.
Ruklim	*Celastrus paniculata*	Seeds by making juice and paste	Cure rheumatism, paralysis, leprosy and scabies.
Rung kyen	*Swerita chirata Hain*	Whole plant	Cures intermittent fevers, acidity and bilious dyspepsia cures lever function.

Vernacular Name	*Botanical Name*	*Parts used*	*Disease / Ailments*
Sangaa koong	Not collected	Bark by making powder	Bark powder soaked in water cures Pneumonia.
Safok jyu	*Rubus molnecarnus*	Fruits, leaves by making paste, juice	Cure passing of urine by night of the little children useful for promoting the menstrual discharge.
Kasimji	Not collected	Apex and Tender leaves	Put in the cold boiled water and extracting gelatinous substance cures tonsillitis.
Sahaor paot	*Cydonia oblonga*	Fruits by cooking and pounding	*Pounded fruits*- cures extreme headache *Cooked fruits*- stimulate the heart in case of heart failure
Saong koong	*Abies webbiana*	Leaves by making paste and extracted oil	Leaves juice mixed with ginger, cardamom, clove sugar cure asthma, bronchitis extracted oil heat up internal hemorrhages and tuberculosis
Soo gook koong	*Ficus cunia*	Roots, fruits by making juice	Cures leprosy and urinary bladder complaints.
Kaol koong	*Juglans regia*	Bark, fruits by boiling only in water	Destroys and expels intestinal worms cures rheumatism
Payezu koong	Not collected	Bark by boiling in water	Cures diabetes.

Table. 7 Biotic Components Used by the Lepchas of Sikkim:

Name of the disease	*Application of Animal body parts*
Poor vision/eye sight	Apply the lukewarm blood of Leech
Calf pain and turning over the calf muscles	Apply the burnt tail of peacock (*mung young tuk shyin*) by smearing over the calf muscle of human leg.
Inflammation or swelling of groin or armpit	Apply the burnt cocks' quill (*hik tsaong kaop*) by smearing over the inflammatory or swelling portion.
Fresh cut and wounds	Apply the spider's web (*sung gryaong saong*) and bandaged properly
Pneumonia, Bronchitis, other lung sores and Typhoid	Apply the pounded paste of Round worm (*tarekbu*), which is available under banana plant.
High fever	Prescribed to take the soup of cooked flesh of black toad without patch without mixing salt.
Pneumonia	Prescribed to take the soup and flesh of cooked Green toad without patch.
Epilepsy and High fever	Prescribed to take the soup o palm and finger of monkey without mixing salt.
Tuberculosis	Consume the liver and flesh of monkey (*su-hu*)
Snake bite	'Kastoori', navel of Sabar (musk-deer) is applied.
Gall bladder pain	Prescribed to consume the boiled flesh of Bear

Name of the disease	*Application of Animal body parts*
Cut, wounds, skin disease	Black frog's skin (*luk pak taluk*) used as band aid.
Malaria (*dangdulat*) and Food poison (*enng*)	Prescribed to take the gall bladder soup of black Bear (*san-ha*)
Asthma	Prescribed to take the gall bladder soup of monkey (*su-hu*)
Malarial fever	Prescribed to consume the roasted stomach of porcupine (*Sattin*) with the gelatinous juice of *aloe vera* (*ghreta kumari*).
Vomiting of Pregnant Lady	Prescribe to inhale the smell of the burning ash of porcupine's barb.
Liver malfunction	Prescribed to dip the navel of Sabar (musk deer) in the water for over night and then consumed it.
Ill effect of poisonous mushroom	Prescribed to take the roasted skin and meat of Deer (*Su-ku*)

of effective utilization of animal body parts. Here, vegetative and animal body parts together mean 'ethno-biotic medicine'. According to them, the history of medicine of the Lepchas in *Mayel Lyang* can be traced to the remote past. The earliest mention of the medicinal use of plants is found in the traditional tale of Lord Tamsangthing, perhaps the oldest repository of Lepcha knowledge having originated along with Pundim Choo, i.e. the mountain peak of Pundim. Later '*Boongthingism*' and '*Munism*' came into existence; the properties of various medicines have been told in detail.

The Lepcha medicine men called '*Maondaok*' utilize the locally growing plants which are found useful after trial for treatment of diseases. Besides plants they use scores of minerals and animal originated medicines for treatment of diseases. While discussing the traditional medicine, the Lepcha men informed that the traditional medicines are not prescribed to outsiders. The Lepcha medicine man, *Maondaok* uses flowers, roots, tubers, barks, leaves etc. of plants and also the body parts of the animals for traditional medicine. No written records are available as from when this traditional knowledge came into being to serve as life saving means. On their opinion, the Lepcha medicine men (*Maondaok*) have built their experience from generations, often over centuries. Due to the inherent secret nature of the medicine men, the knowledge and use of some of the really efficacious vegetable drugs are disappearing. The people are by nature generally superstitious and cherish in inherent belief that if the secrets which were handed over to them from their elder generation, are once given out to an unauthorized person, the efficacy of the plants will vanish. However the traditional system of the treatment of disease practiced in the olden times by the Lepcha medicine men is fast disappearing. It is obviously stated that those resources have full of potentiality as traditional drugs (Table 6 and 7). Few of them were collected during the fieldwork at west Sikkim (Yuksam) while few of them were collected during the field work at North Sikkim (Dzongu). The list of utilization of medicinal plant and ethno-biotic component are mentioned Table 6.

Table 6 demonstrates use of various biotic medicines in concerned diseases and other ailments. In addition, it was recorded that a kind of *pinkish mica flake dust* which is sour in taste licking to the tongue. This mica flake dust is believed to be an effective medicine for curing the tonsillitis of the children upto the age of ten years.

CASE STUDIES

Case – I

Mr. Norfey Lepcha, an aged Lepcha man of approximately 76 years old, stayed in Linzya bustee of upper Dzongu. He had a small patch of terraced land on which he cultivated the millet (*maung*), buckwheat (*phaphar*) and mustard grams (*rai*). The annual yield never be satisfied the demand. He admitted that before introducing the forest act, they used to go to the forest land on high hills for collecting various natural forest resources (honey, timber, wild animal etc.). But nowadays it is impossible.

He admitted that the Lepcha life is always encompassed with beliefs. Due to the habitation in an inaccessible, rugged terrain of mountain slopes the Lepcha in general have faith on 'nature'. He informed that every action has a cause behind it and that's why every illness is the resultant factor of the deeds of any supernatural beings. He cited emphatically that any illness is not exactly turned into diseases, but whenever a Lepcha become sick, as he believed would be the cause of either of some malevolent spirit, ghosts (*moong*) or the displeasure of the deities (*rum*). He also intimated that every object in the surrounding nature has 'soul' in it and whenever these souls become arrogant cause many harm to them either in the form of disease, properly losses, fatal injuries and even death. According to him, this can only be cured by the sacred activities of *Boongthing* and *Mun* and sometimes the lama would call upon for the sacred readings. He also believed that illness, misery can only be solved in traditional way and there is no medicine required for that. In consequence with, he admitted that during his lifetime neither he took any modern medicine, nor he goes to the hospitals. He admitted that whenever the illness or diseases were not cured by the worship of deities or appeasement of the spirits he would take the herbal and biotic component to make him cure. After the implementation of forest act, the practices of ethno-biotic therapeutic measures become rare.

Case – II

Mr. Chewang Lepcha, a middle aged Lepcha man of Namprikdang *bustee* of upper Dzongu. He is an educated fellow having post graduate degree in Modern History. At present he is working in the education department at Gangtok and stays at Gangtok for few years. Though he stays at Gangtok but he frequently visit his native place whenever the chance come.

While discussing about the importance of health, disease and its remedies, he admitted reluctantly that every community have its own tradition and it should be obeyed by following the rules and regulations, because man is a social being. He awfully admitted that since remote past the Lepchas depend on beliefs, rituals and practices from the core of their heart. He admired it but vis-à-vis he also admitted that the blind support on traditional beliefs and practices towards the deities (*rum*) and *moongs* (spirits/ghosts) is not so effective all the time. He cited that the use of traditional healing and ethno-medicine would not be so active in different dreadful diseases like malaria, tuberculosis. In this case the modern medicine can cure the disease. Due to the Lepchas blind faith on the malevolent activity of *rum* and *moong* and the performance of *Boongthing* and *Mun* regarding illness and disease, many Lepchas lost their lives. According to him, for any kind of dreadful disease and illness, the Lepcha should follow the pharmacopoeia of modern medicine and when the disease or illness is felt to be the cause of the displeasure of supernatural being, it might be cured by traditional healing or with the help of ethno-biotic therapeutics by applying herbal medicine. Both traditional and modern system can run side-by-side.

Case – III

Mrs. Pasankit Lepcha, an aged lady of 26 years is a resident of lower Lingthem *bustee* of upper Dzongu. After completing her graduation she got married and nowadays, she is a housewife having two small kids. She had the opinion in favour of practicing the modern medical system for illness and diseases. Why is it so? In reply to that, she described, during her childhood days she had a tremendous faith on traditional system of natural healing, beliefs on the existence of *rum* and *moong*. But at the time of her first pregnancy, she once ate the meat of a goat which was killed by rope-knotting. The womenfolk made her fear by saying that her would be child either will be a patient of epilepsy or become dead. The lady got puzzled and consulted with *Boongthing* and *Mun*. They demanded a good amount of money and also prescribed sacrifices of goat and cow and many things have to be offered. She actually was unable to spend all these expenditure at that time and decided to consult with a medical practitioner in nearby PHC (Primary Health Centre). After checking her, the nurse of the PHC told that everything is quiet normal and prescribed to take few medicine and pre-natal check up. After one month of this incident an expert medical team from Gangtok had visited to the bustee for periodical check up. She appeared there for the check up. The expert Lady Doctor checks her condition and told after that she was normal. The Doctor also insisted her to take pre-natal courses regularly which will protect her baby from every deformities, she informed with great pleasure that she followed every instructions and attended the regular check ups. Finally, she give birth her first son. Since then, she relied on the modern therapeutics.

Case – IV

Mr. Top Tshering Lepcha, A traditional healer – *Boongthing* an aged man of about 67 years. He is the only *Boongthing* of Lethang *bustee* of West Sikkim, prefers traditional way of healing. He lives alone in the extreme end of the bustee along with 20 numbers of goats and a small patch of vegetable ground as his belongings. He become busy most of the days with his healing performance and whenever he is free used to go with his flock of animals.

Top Tshering admitted that a *Boongthing* can perform the healing activities for both malevolent and benevolent purposes. Even today the healing is part and parcel of the Lepcha society. He informed that even came later the *Boongthingism* and *Munism* has captured an important place in the Lepcha belief system. He narrated that a *Boongthing* have the capacity to predict the future condition of a person by counting the rosary beads and by seeing the yoke of an egg. In Lepcha society, it is believed that a *Boongthing* can only ward off the evil spirits (*moong*) and vis-à-vis also propitiates the deities (*rum*) for well-being and prosperity of the people. According to him, the illness and diseases in the ancient time can only be cured by the appeasement and propitiation of *rum* and *moong*, where *Boongthing* prefer the role of a mediator. Being a *Boongthing*, Top Tshering claimed that he can communicate the message with the spiritual being by means of enchanting parables with a kind of hallucination and offered a prayer to the spiritual being not to create any harmful effect to the person. For the performance of any traditional ritual a *Boongthing* demanded various items like eggs, hen, *maung chi* (millet beer), even ox and buffaloes as sacrificed item, which he brings after the ritual. According to him, this kind of traditional healing is the tradition of the Lepcha. Being the son of the *Mayel Lyang*, the Lepcha always belief in nature. If nature persists, the traditional system of remedies will also survive.

Case – V

Dr. (Mrs.) Anusha Lama, a physician of Govt. Primary Health Centre, Yuksam of 33 years of age is a resident of Yuksam of West Sikkim. By profession she is one and only lady doctor holding the post of chief

Medical Officer (CMO) of the Primary Health Centre, Yuksam. In the course of discussion the doctor told that by habit the Lepchas are shy, innocent and very much careless in regards to their health. She also informed that the Lepchas even today totally oriented by their traditional belief system. They always tried to make linkages of health disorder with the evil deeds of supernatural being. It is in their opinion that everything including many of the nonliving things also has souls. That is why each and every health hazards, any kind of mishaps, sufferings, any type of distress have caused of dissatisfaction and displeasure of various deities (*rums*) and spirits, ghost, demons (*moongs*). This kind of blind faith can not be released and in medical science no such drugs has ever been discovered to cure these. She admitted that for any kind of illness, disease the Lepcha first prefer the service of traditional healer what they called *Boongthing* or *Muns*, if it is not cured then the medicine men (*Maondaok*) is to be called off and ultimately when the health condition become so much aggravated they forcibly come to either PHC or Hospital. The doctors try their level best, sometimes they succeed and sometimes not. She also admitted that after conducting frequent medical check up camp and organizing medical campaign few of the younger generation shows interest in modern medical practices. Some of the younger womenfolk individually come and consult with the doctors about their problem.

CONCLUSION

In the discussion held in earlier pages it has been attempted to delineate the fact that irrespective of consideration of caste, class, and creed; 'health' is an important feature to all human groups. The ill-health disturbs the rhythm of life and the performances of the individual being. On having a separate identity health and illness remain as both sides of the same coin - if health is a property, then illness is a state. The failure of health causes illness and cure becomes essential. Being an original inhabitant of natural abode, the Lepcha of the Khangchendzonga Biosphere (KBR) in West and North district of Sikkim are not an exception to that. But according to their perception, every health disorder or health hazards are not contemplated as 'illnesses'. Like others the Lepcha also have dependency on age-old ethno-medicinal system. The health, illness, behaviour of the sick and medical practices among the Lepchas primarily follows the path of their own traditional and cultural essence. According to their belief, everything in the world possesses a 'soul', and illness is the reflection towards the disorder of that 'soul'.

While describing the illness and therapeutics, it has been found that the idea of the health, illness and diseases has individual significance among the Lepchas. Any kind of illness may not be the cause of disease, as cough and cold, headache, bodyache are not experienced as a disease. The illness of the Lepcha is either caused by the dissatisfaction of various natural being which are considered to be an animate object; the arrogance and dissatisfaction of spirits, demons, and ghosts, believed to be residing in the nature; or by the displeasure of various deities related with the nature. In accordance with the rules of prevention against illness and diseases the Lepcha primarily follows the path of appeasement of various benevolent deities; or propitiating the malevolent spirits, demons, ghost by employing the service of the traditional spirit healers and priests, called *Mun* and *Boongthing*. Also they pray for the services of the Buddhist monk; called Lama for the holy readings of Buddhist scripture. The second option for health cure is use of herbal therapeutics with the consultation of traditional medicine men (*Maondaok*). According to them, the disease and illness will be cured by these in most of the cases. However, if it is not possible, then they are advised to go to the Primary Health Centre or District hospital for their treatment through modern medicines.

At the beginning of this report it has been discussed that the Khangchendzonga and its peaks bear tremendous significance in every sphere of socio-cultural and religious life of the local people. They try to maintain its holiness as far as possible. The 'Panglhab-sol' ceremony, one of the best noted religio-cultural festival is performed everywhere in the Sikkim with pomp and posh during the month of August-September of every year to mark the cultural and religious identity of the local people. After declaring the 22nd sovereign state of independent India, Government of Sikkim had realized to protect the ecosystem of the area and formed KNP (Khangchendzonga National Park). Later on 7th February 2000, the earmarked national park area was extended further and formed KBR for the sustenance of some of the rare variety of flora, fauna and cultural heritage of the local inhabitants. Being an inhabitant in the buffer hamlets of KBR, the west and north districts of Sikkim, the Lepchas try to protect the green forest ecosystem and maintain a symbiotic relationship with natural resources. According to them, '*Kingtsoomzaongboo*', the guardian deity resides in the Khangchendzonga pinnacle from which they are believed to get birth. It is also believed that the surrounding nature is the abode of spirits, ghosts, demons, which may create harm to them if those creatures were dissatisfied by the action of the people. Since time immemorial the Lepchas have developed an intuitive relationship with environment. They have extremely rich knowledge of varieties of plants, beasts, insects and flowers and some have the capacity to identify the particular species which are beneficial for them. All aspects of their life and their performances follow the nature. Their song, dance and music are speaking out the beauties of nature.

During the discussion about the family structure, it was informed that during earlier period people preferred the extended type of family for group hunting vis-a-vis gathering, shifting cultivation and security, but with the advent of time when the people began practicing terrace cultivation as one of the important subsistence, the nuclear type of family become preferred. During the later phase as the terraced field become scarce for unequal sharing among the brothers the formation of nuclear type of families get its value in their society; what was observed in the Lethang hamlet of west district of Sikkim. The fact of family formation has direct or indirect bearing on health practices, as revealed by the Lepchas. According to their opinion in a nuclear family the members of the family prefer to cure their ailments with modern medicines as there is scarcity of number of family members. It is observed that the nuclear family composed by the young couple has the tendency to adopt modern pharmacopeias for curing the physical ailments. Among the Lepchas, those have still retain the accessibility of exploiting natural resources follow the use of botanical and animal parts as ethno-medical treatment.

ACKNOWLEDGEMENT

The author expresses heartfelt indebtedness to the Director-in-Charge, Anthropological Survey of India, for giving the opportunity to work among the Lepchas of Sikkim Himalayas. The author is deeply indebted to Dr. D.B. Mondal, coordinator of this Project for involving in this project. The author also expresses indebtedness to Dr. Ramesh Chandra, Deputy Director (C), NWRC, Anthropological Survey of India, Dehradun for painstaking efforts to rectify the report by giving valuable suggestions. The author is deeply indebted to Dr. A.K. Singh, Ex-Senior Human Ecologist, Anthropological survey of India, Kolkata for giving the valuable suggestions at the time of formation of the Project Proposal. The heartfelt thanks go to the Lepchas of Ramgyathang, Lethang, Khecheopalri hamlets of West Sikkim district and Samdong, Linzya and Bay hamlets of North Sikkim district for extensive cooperation and helpful treatment during the course of the study. The author also expresses thanks to Mrs. Deepa Saha for giving continuous support in typing the manuscripts. Last but not the least, the author expresses thanks to Mr. A. Dinda and Dr. Umesh Kumar and other team members foı giving continuous encouragement.

References

Ackerman, E.A. (1963). Where is a research frontier? *Ann. Ass. Geogr.* 53, 429-440.

Affeld, D. (1975). Social aspects of the development of tourism. In *United Nations, Planning and Development of the Tourist Industry in the ECC Regions*, United Nations, New York, pp. 109-15.

Bansal, B.L. (1994). *Bon its Encounter with Buddhism in Tibet.* Eastern Book Linkers, Delhi.

Banerjee H.N. (1990). *Introducing Social and Cultural Anthropology.* K.K. Publication, Calcutta.

Basnet, L. (1974). *Sikkim : A Short Political History.* New Delhi: S. Chand and Co. Pvt. Ltd.

Bezbaruah, M.P. (2002). *Frontiers of New Tourism.* Gyan Publishing House, New Delhi.

Bhadra, M. (1992). *Sikkim : Democracy and Social Change.* Calcutta: Minerva Associates Pvt. Ltd.

Bhasin, V. (1989). *Ecology, Culture and Change.* Inter India Publications, New Delhi.

(1990). *Habitat Habitation and Health in the Himalayas*, Kamala Raj Enterprises, New Delhi.

(1997). Social dimension of politics: The case of tribal democracy in Sikkim. *Journal of Human Ecology*, 4 (1); pp. 63-78.

Bhasin, M. K and Bhasin, V. (1995). *Sikkim Himalayas- Ecology and Resource Development,* Kamala Raj Enterprises, New Delhi.

Bhattacharya, A. (1950). *Bangla Mangal Kavyer Itihas* (in Bengali). Calcutta Book House. Calcutta.

Bose, S. (1966). The Bhot of Nothern Sikkim. *Man in India*, Vol. 46. No. 2.

Census of India. (1991). *General Population Tables and Primary Census Abstract.* Part- II A and II B, series – 22.

Census of India, (2001). *Sikkim: Series 12, Final Population Tables*. Directorate of Census operations, Government of India, Gangtok.

Census of India (2001). *Population Atla*. Census Report, Sikkim.

Chakraborty, J. (1994). Ethnic consciousness and cultural revivalism, among the Lepchas of the eastern Himalayas. *J. Indian Anthrop. Soc*. 29: 179 – 186.

Chapman, G.P. (1970). Perception and regulation: A case study of farmers in Bihar. *Trans. Inst. Br. Geog*. 62, 71-94.

Charles, C. Hughes. (1968). Ethnomedicine. In *Encyclopaedia of Social Sciences,* Sills, D. L., Vol. 9 and 10, p. 88.

Chattopadhyay, Kamaladevi (1975). *Handicrafts of India*. Indian Council for Cultural Relations, New Delhi.

Chawla, Romila (ed.). (2003). *Global Tourism*. Sonali Publications, New Delhi.

Chorley, R.J. (1971). The role and relation of physical geography. In *Progress in Geography*. Vol. 3 (Eds C. Board et al.). Methun, London.

Chowdhury, M. (2006). *Sikkim. Geographical Perspectives*. Mittal Publication, New Delhi.

Crowley, D.J. (1972). Crafts. In *International Encyclopedia of the Social Science*, Sills, D.L., Vol. 3 and 4, London: Collier. Macmillan Publishers.

Danda, A.K. (1991). *Tribal Economy in India, (Tribal Studies of India Series, T-143)*. Inter-India Publication, New Delhi.

Dark, P.J.C. (1978). What is art for anthropologists? In *Art in Society: Studies in style, culture and aesthetics,* Greenhalgh, M., and Megaw, V., London: Duckworth.

Das, A.K. (1987). The Lepchas of West Bengal: A socio-economic and cultural profile. In *Himalayan Heritage*, Raha, M.K. (ed.), Gyan Publishing House, Delhi.

Department of Forest (2006). *Household and Population Structure of Fringe Villages of Khangchendzonga National Park*. Government of Sikkim. Gangtok (unpublished).

Department of Forest (2006). *Report of Khangchendzonga National Park and Biosphere Reserve* (unpublished).

Desai, Mamata (1988). *Eco-system and Ethnic Constellaction of Sikkim*. Best Books Calcutta.

Dinda, Amitava (2007). Evaluation of eco-tourism activity: A case study of Sundarban Tiger Reserve. In *Man in Biosphere: A Case Study of*

Sundarban Biosphere Reserve Mandal, D. (ed), Gyan Publishing House on behalf of Anthropological Survey of India, New Delhi, pp. 241-264.

Forde, Daryll (1934). *Habitat, Economy and Society.* Methun and Co. Ltd., London.

Forest Department. (2007). *KBR.* Govt. of Sikkim.

Foning, A.R. (1987). *Lepcha: My Vanishing Tribe.* New Delhi: Sterling Publishers Pvt. Ltd.

Fox, W. (1990). *Towards a Transpersonal Ecology: Developing New Foundations for Environmentalism.* Shambhala Publications, Boston.

Gangopadhyay, S. (1983). Human Adaptation in the Sikkim Himalaya: Some Observations, paper presented at the workshop *Human Adaptation in the Extreme Climate* on the 27th June, 1983, at Anthropological Survey of India, Calcutta.

________(1985). Transhumance in the North Sikkim Himalaya: A way of environmental management. In *Impact of Development on Environment* (ed.), Vol. 1, Bireswar Banerjee, Geographical Society of India, Calcutta.

________(1988). *Nature of Human Adaptation in the Tista Valley of Sikkim: A Geographical Analysis.* Ph.D thesis, Calcutta University.

________(1989). Human adaptation in a changing situation: A case study of Lachung: *A* village in the Sikkim Himalayas. In *Acculturation and Social Change in India,* (ed.), S.C. Panchbhai, M.K.A. Siddiqui, Anthropological Survey of India, Calcutta.

Gazetteer of Sikkim (1973). *Gazetteer of Sikhim.* Oriental Publishers, Calcutta. Government of Sikhim.

Geoffrey, Gorer. (1987). *The Lepchas of Sikkim.* Gyan publishing House, Delhi –110007.

Gochman, S. David (1982). Labels, systems and motives: Some perspective for future research. *Health Education Quarterly; Children Health, beliefs and health behaviour*, Gochman, D.S. and Parcel G.S. Spl. Issue, Vol. 9, pp. 167-174.

Gorer, G. (1938). *Himalayan Village: An Account of the Lepchas of Sikkim.* London: Thosmas Nelson and Sons Ltd.

Gorer, Geoffery (2005). *The Lepcha of Sikkim.* New Delhi, Gyan Publishing House.

Gowloog, R.R. (1995). *Lingthem Revisited: Social Change in a Lepcha Village of North Sikkim.* Hari Anand Publication, New Delhi.

Gulia, K.S. (2005). *Human Ecology of Sikkim.* Kalpaz Publications, Delhi.

Haeckel, E. (1866). *Generelle Morphologie der Organismen.* 2 volumes. Georg. Remer, Berlin.

Hannah, L. and Lohse, D. 1993. *Annual Report, Conservation Institutions,* Washington D.C.

Holloway, Christopher (1985). *The Business of Tourism,* Mac Donald and Evans, Ply mouth, p. 22.

Hooker, J. D., and Murray, J. (1855). *Himalayan Journals: Notes of a Naturalist.* Two Volumes, London. Reprinted 1980, Today and Tomorrow's, New Delhi.

Jafari, J. (1974). The social costs of tourism to the developing countries. *Annals of Tourism Research.* 1:227-262.

Joshi, H.G. (2004). *Sikkim: Past and Present.* Mittal Publications, New Delhi.

Khangchendzonga Conservation Committee (2002). *Khangchendzonga: The Sacred Mountain – A Biodiversity Conservation Hand Book.* Published by K.C.C., Yuksam. Committee.

Khangchendzonga Conservation Committee (2002). *Brochure of Khangchendzonga and its People.* (unpublished).

Krishna, Akhouri Promod *et al.* (2002). Human Dimensions of Conservation in the Khangchendzonga Biosphere Reserve: The Need for Conflict Prevention, *Mountain Research and Development.*

Lea, John. (1997). Tourism's economic impacts. In: *The Earthscan Reader in Sustainable Tourism,* Lesley France (ed.), U.K. Earthscan. Publications, pp. 166-169.

Lehriche, C. and Danglas, G. (1973). *Health and illness: A Social Psychological Analysis.* London, Academic Press.

Lepcha, S.W. and Mandam, H. (1981). Who are the Lepchas? *The Eastern Anthropologist,* p. 34.

Mac Naught, and. Timothy, J. (1982). Mass tourism and the dilemmas of modernisation in Pacific Island communities. *Annals of Tourism Research,* 9(3): 359-381.

Mandal, H. et al. (2004). *Development of Tourism in Sikkim.* Anthropological Survey of India, Kolkata.

Mandal, K. and Ray, S. (2007). Economic condition of a delta vllage: A study in biosphere reserve in Sundarban. In *Man in Biosphere: A Case Study of Sundarban Biosphere Reserve,* Mandal, D.B., Gyan

Publishing House, New Delhi on behalf of Anthropological Survey of India, Kolkata.

Maity, D. and Chauhan, A.S. (2001). Kanchanjunga Biosphere Reserve. In *Floristic Diversity and Conservation Strategies in India,* Singh, N.P. and Singh, K.P. Vol. V, Kolkata, Botanical Survey of India.

Mathews, H.G. (1977). *International Tourism: A Political and Social Analysis.* M.A. Schenkman Publishing Company. Cambridge.

Mittermeier, R.A. (1988). Primate diversity and the tropical forest: Case studies from Brazil and Madagascar, and the importance of the mega diversity countries. In *Biodiversity,* Wilson, E.O. (ed.), National Academy Press, Washington, D.C.

Modi, Shalini. (2001). *Tourism and Society : Cross-Cultural Perspectives.* Rawat Publications, Jaipur and New Delhi.

Morris, J. (1938). *Living with the Lepchas: A Book about the Sikkim Himalayas.* William Heinemann Ltd. London.

Nunez, T. (1963). Tourism, tradition and acculturation: Weekendismo in a Mexican village. *South West Journal of Anthropology.* 34: 328-36.

O'Malley, LSS. (1907). *Darjeeling District Gazetteer.* Reprint, Gyan Publihsing House, Delhi.

Pant, K. (2003). The boon called village tourism. In *New Approaches in Tourism Management,* Ranga, Mkesh and Nigam D. (eds.), Abhijit Publications, Delhi.

Park, R.E. and Burgess, E.W. (1921). *Introduction to the Science of Sociology.* University of Chicago Press, Chicago.

Pattnaik, B. (2005). Ecological bases of Indian traditions: Search for an indigenous vision. *The Eastern Anthropologist,* Vol. 58, No. 3 and 4.

Porter, A.E. (1931). *Gazetteer of Bengal and Sikkim,* Vol. V, part I and II, Delhi: Usha Publication.

Porter, A.E. (1987). *Gazetteer of Bengal and Sikkim.* Vol. 5, Part I & II, Usha Publication, Delhi. Reprint 1987.

Raha, M.K. and Chakravarty, S. (1996). Tribal economy in the Himalayas: Persistence and change. In *Dimensions of Human Society and Culture,* Raha, M.K., Gyan Publishing House, New Delhi.

Rai, S.C. and Sundriyal, R.C. (1997). Tourism development and biodiversity conservation: A case study from the Sikkim Himalaya. *Ambio,* 26: 235-242.

Raina, A.K. and Lodha, R.C. (2004). *Fundamentals of Tourism System.* Kanishka Publishers, New Delhi.

Raina, V.K. and Srivastava, B.S. (1981). Tectonic evolution of Sikkim Himalayas. *Contemp. Geosci, Resin Himalaya*, Vol. Dehradun.

Risley, H.H. (ed.) (1894). *The Gazetteer of Sikkim*, Bengal Government Secretariat, Calcutta.

Risley, H. H. (1891). *Tribes and Castes of Bengal: Ethnographic Glossary.* Firma Mukhopadhyay.

Ritchie, J.R.B. (1988). Consensus policy formation in tourism: Measuring resident views via survey research. *Tourism Management* 9:199-212.

Robinson, D.W. (1997). Strategies for alternative tourism: The case of tourism in Sagarmatha (Everest) National Park, Nepal'. In *The Earthscan Reader in Sustainable Tourism,* France, Lesley (eds.), U.K., Earthscan Publications. pp. 176-186.

Roy Chaudhury, A.K. (1988). *Man, Malady and Medicine: History of Indian Medicine.* Calcutta, Das Gupta and Co. (P) Ltd.

Roy Burman, J.J. (2003). *Tribal Medicine: Traditional Practices and Changes in India.* New Delhi, Mittal Publications.

Saeed, Taalat (1995). *Cultural Heritage of Sikkim: A Survey.* Bulletin of Research Institute of Tibetology, Gangtok.

Sharma, Ramesh (1983). *Images of Sikkim: The Land, People and Culture, Sikkim.* Department of Tourism, Gangtok, Ringsum Publication.

Sharma, R.D. (1993). Energy consumption survey in the Aravalli Project Area. *Survey Project Report No. 3, Aravalli Project*, Haryana Forest Development, Gurgaon, Haryana, p. 107.

Sigerist, H.E. (1943). *Civilization and Disease.* Chicago, University of Chicago Press.

Singer, H. (1956). *Ethnological Field Research in Chitral, Sikkim and Assam*, Hidyotidk- Gilologishe Meddeleser, XXXVI.

Singer, H. (1967). *The Lepchas–Culture and Religion of a Himalayan People.* The National Museum of Denmark.

Singer, H. (1967). *The National Museum of Denmark.*

Singh, A.K. and Patil, S. (2007). *Man in Biosphere: A Case Study of Nilgiri Biosphere Reserve.* Gyan Publishing House on behalf of Anthropological Survey of India.New Delhi, pp. 241-264.

Singh, K.S. (ed.) (1993). *People of India: Sikkim.* Vol. XXXIX, Segal Books, Calcutta.

Singh, K.S. and Manoharan, S. (1993). *People of India National Series: Languages and Scripts.* Volume – IX, Appendix – V, p. 311, Anthropological Survey of India, Oxford University Press.

Singh, N.P., Mudgal, V., Khanna, K.K. and Srivastava, S.C. (2001). Medicinal Plant. *Floristic Diversity and Conservation Strategies in India*, Vol. IV, Botanical Survey of India, Kolkata.

Sinha, A.C. (1975). *Politics of Sikkim: A Sociological Study*. New Delhi: Thomson Press (India) Ltd.

Sinha, A.C. (1983). *Studies in the Himalayan Communities*. Books Today. New Delhi.

Smith, Valene (ed.), (1977). *Hosts and Guests- The Anthropology of Tourism.* Philadelphia, University of Pennsylvania Press.

Subba, T.B. (1988). Migration and ethnic relation in Darjeeling and Sikkim. In *Social Science and Social Concern*, Chakraborty, S.B (ed.), Mittal Publications, New Delhi.

Sutton, W. (1967). Travel and understanding notes on the social structure of touring. *International Journal of Comparative Sociology*, 8 (2): 212-223.

Steward, J. (1936). The economic and social basis of primitive bands. In *Essays in Anthropology in Honour of Alfred Louis Kroeber*, Lowie, R.H. (ed.), pp. 31-50. Berkeley: University of California Press.

(1938). *Basin-Plateau Aboriginal Sociopolitical Groups* (Bureau of American Bulletin 120), Smithsonian Institution, Washington, DC.

(1955). *Theory of Cultural Change: The Methodology of Multilinear Evolution.* University of Illinois Press, Urbana.

Stoddart, D.R. (1965). Geography and ecological approach. *Geography*, 50, 242-251.

Sundriyal, R.C., and Sharma, E. (1996). Anthropogenic pressure on tree structure and biomass in the temperate forest on Mamlay Watershed in Sikkim. *Forest Ecology and Management*, 81: 113-134.

Tamsang, K.P. (1983). *The Untold and Unknown Reality about the Lepchas*. 2nd edition Mani Printing Press, Kalimpong.

Thakur, R.N. (1988). *Himalayan Lepchas*. New Delhi, Archives Publisher and Distributors.

UNESCO (1976). The effects of tourism on socio-cultural values. *Annals of Tourism Research,* IV (2):74-105.

Valabrega, J.P. (1962) La relation therapeutique, malade et medecin. Cited in *Social Factors in Relations to Chronic Illness,* by Graham Smith (1963).

Verma, Rajesh (2007). *Sikkim – A Guide and Handbook.* Published by R. Verma, New Delhi.

Weiser Samuel (1984). *Tibetan Buddhist Medicine and Psychiatry.* New Delhi, Samuel Weiser Inc.

World Health Organization (1946). *Health and Illness.* Bulletin, New York.

APPENDICES

APPENDIX-I

Villages in the Fringe Zone of KBR

Revenue Block (West Sikkim)	*Households*	*Population*
Dubdi	69	402
Yuksam	364	1951
Tsozo	89	476
Khacheopalri	114	556
Meli	116	623
Melliaching	109	589
Topung	52	286
Singrangpung	47	227
Nambu	146	859
Kongri	71	442
Labdang	80	456
Dhupidara	76	493
Narkhola	82	510
Mangnam	64	380
	1,479	**8,250**

Revenue Block (North Sikkim)	*Households*	*Population*
Lachen	1609	2923
Shipgyer	166	695
Tung	52	201
Lachen Forest Block	12	32
Salim Pakel	132	615
Lingthem	210	1161
Lingdem	97	542
Tingbong	164	1001
Lingzah-Tolung	80	397
Sakyong-Pentong	41	196
	2,563	**7,763**
Total	**4,042**	**16,013**

APPENDIX-II

Conat Attitude Survey Questionnaire

Class	*Response Context*	*Questions asked for CONAT assessment*	*Yes*	*No*
A	Conservation related concern	1. BR is important for healthy bio-diversity.		
		2. Felling of trees and wildlife killing should not be allowed.		
		3. Felling of trees, wildlife hunting and grazing will adversely affect bio-diversity.		
		4. BR is for benefit of our future generation.		
		5. Although more land is required for agriculture / other livelihood practices, but it is necessary to protect the land inhabited by wildlife.		
		6. BR is for outsiders, we have nothing to do with it.		
		7. BR is also the abode of Guardian Deity and is essential for a healthy environment.		

Class	*Response Context*	*Questions asked for CONAT assessment*	*Yes*	*No*
B	Socio-Economic related concern	1. BR is for outsiders and for those who enjoy nature viewing. We do not enjoy this as we have to face problem from BR.		
		2. It is good if local people are allowed to hunt in the BR.		
		3. It is good if local people are given free access to BR for timber, fuel wood, fodder and other NTFP collection as well as for livestock grazing.		
		4. Since there is dearth of land, it would be good if some land is given with in BR.		
C	WTA/WPA related concern	1. Wildlife of the BR is causing us trouble, we should be allowed for wildlife hunting.		
		2. BR is beneficial and we are willing to pay the price in terms of conservation restrictions.		
		3. BR conservation may cost us culturally also, but we are willing to accept it.		
D	Participatory concern in the BR concept	1. We shall participate in researches related to BR conservation.		
		2. We shall volunteer for training for capacity building on value addition in NTFP, cultivation of medicinal plants, plantation work, social forestry, nature tourism promotion and conservation education.		

Glossary

CIC	Community Information Centre
Dokpa	Herders grazing in high altitude
Dzumsa	Village Council of Lachen village
Goatwalla	Herders grazing in low altitude
GREF	General Reserve Engineering Force
ICDS	Integrated Child Development Scheme
KBR	Khangchendzonga Biosphere Reserve
KCC	Khangchendzonga Conservation Committee
Km	Kilometer
KNP	Khangchendzonga National Park
m	Meter
PWD	Public Woks Department
Sq. km	Square Kilometer
VLW	Village Level Worker

Index

A

Above Poverty Line, 113, 114
Adhiya System, 133
Agricultural
  Activities, 138
  And Non-agricultural Labourers, 321
  Labour, 325
  Operations, 25
  Practices, 19, 31, 271
  Rites, 209, 347
  System, 25
Agriculture, 92
Agro-Forestry System, 25, 210
Agro-Pastoral Economy, 72
Alpine
  And Sub-Alpine Grazing Land, 27
  Economic Region, 54, 56
  Flora and Fauna, 53
  Land, 24
  Meadows, 56
  Pastures, 53
Amee, Malevolent Spirit, 402
Anglo-Saxon Craft, 143
Angu-Brung Deity, 352
Animal Rearing, 119
  And Herding, 122, 123, 125
Animism, 336
Animistic Faith of Religion, 361
Apang Moong/Sor Moong, 400
Architecture, 142, 146
Argentina, 229
Art and Craft, 97, 144
  Artifacts, 190
Artifacts and Performing Arts, 153
Arts, 159
  Crafts and Performing Arts of Lachen, Bhutia and Crafts, and Performing Arts, 159
  Domestic, 159
  Performing Arts, 159
  Religious, 159
Australia, 225, 228, 229, 291
Ayurveda, 375
Ayurvedic Herbal Medicines, 375

B

Bajrant, 38, 40
Baku, Traditional Dress Worn by Women, 101
Bambo Crafts, 156
Banapala Sheep, 47, 53
Bangladesh, 384
Bans—Asari, 38
Barren Forest, 274
Basic Infrastructure, 197
Basket Weaving Craft, 349
Bay of Bengal, 21
Belief System, 336, 358
Beliefs and Illness, 396
Below Poverty Line, 113, 114
Bho Yaks, 48
Bhotia
  Kingdom, 381
  Lama, 71

Of Sikkim, 352
Bhurkan (Matresses), 53
Bhutan, 20, 24
Bhutia, 52, 57, 95, 115, 146, 208, 260
And Lepcha, 65, 66, 96, 97
Art, 147, 347
As Lachenpa, 66
Community, 32, 90, 117, 146, 147
Followers of Buddhism, 71
Girls, 312
Lachenpas, 87, 90, 100, 104
Lepcha and Nepalese Communities, 192
Lepcha and Nepali, 205
Lepcha, Nepali and Tibetan Refugees, 202
Of Lachung, 52
People, 346
Population, 343
Religion, 147
Settlements, 297
Women, 147, 172, 244
Bhutia's Economy, 146
Bhutias, 24, 77, 78, 83, 297
Biodiversity, 15, 16, 18, 19, 31
Conservation of-, 17
Loss of-, 15
Pristine, 17
Biological
Communities, 15
Diversity, 15, 197
Conference, 17
Reserve (BR), 17, 36, 57, 63, 65, 111, 118, 121, 129, 134, 135, 143, 190, 196, 280, 296, 377
Areas, 60
Concepts, 17, 33, 57
Development, 18
In India, 19, 31, 65
Management, 31
People's Perception, 134
Dubdi, 134
Lachen, 135
Principles, 57
Resources, 143
Salient Features, 269
Birth
(Ceremonies), 353
(Rituals), 317, 318
Blanket (Rari), 170
Making, 349
Blankets and Carpets of Yak Hairs, 51
Bodhisattavas, 347
Body Decoration, 141
Bon Religion of Tibet, 386
Boongthing, 352, 355, 361, 399
Local Priest, 146
Traditional Healer, 406
Ward Off Evil Spirits, 407
Boongthing-ism, 386
Border of Assam and Burma, 145
Bride Price, 390
Broad Leaf Forests, 143
Oak, Birth, Maple, Chestnut—Ash Alder, 143
Buddha (Lord), 61, 147, 347, 363
And Bodhisattavas, 146
Buddhism, 24, 62, 71, 72, 77, 95, 96, 146, 180, 182, 208, 214, 274, 321 330, 332, 345, 357, 386, 390
And Hinduism, 368
And Local Culture, 97
And Medicines, 391
Faith, 367, 371
Sikkim State Religion, 214
Buddhist, 202
And Christian Lepchas, 387
And Hindus, 294
Festivals, 147
Lamas, 61

Lunar Calendar, 182
Monarchy, 65, 71, 76, 143
Monarchy, Yuksam Birthplace, 76
Monasteries, 191, 197, 377
Monastery, 382
Monks, 183
Orders, 266
Religion, 262
Buffer
And Transition Zones, 31
Zone, 28, 36, 59, 65, 66, 143
Bumthing (Religious Priest), 319, 327
Burkeson, Traditional Blanket, 170
Byaji System, 133

C

Canada, 229
Capacity Building Training, 41
Cardamom, 27, 148
Cropping, 54
Cultivation, 271
Lepcha Principal Cash Crop, 326
Principal Crop, 146
Carpet
Making, 147
Weaving Traditional Activity, 169
Weaving, 168
Carving, 141, 146
Case Histories, 328-330
Case Studies, 254, 426-432
Azo Kesang, 81 Yrs., 254
Chhangma Lachenpa, 257
Jason Lisinski, 36 yrs 256
Madan Gurung—Azu Dorjeelopen, 257
Mitale Ayyanger Aged 23 Yrs old, 255
Pema Gyalsing Bhutia, 256
Samir Gajjar, 356
Tenzing Gyalso Bhutia, 54 yrs Old, 254
Central Africa, 15
Centre for Environmental Education, 280
Chanp Wood Species, 41
Chan—Tooni, 43
Chaom Dance, 184
Chauri Khiang, 291
Chemical Dyes, 173
Cherim Ceremony, 398
Chiabhangjang La, 21
China, 20, 229
Chinese
Aggression, 1862, 144
Occupation of Tibet, 1959, 144
Chitra, Bamboo Mat, 162
Chogyal
Dynasty, 296
Phuntshog, 266, 267
Chola Range, 21
Cholamu, 52
Chopta Valley, 80, 86, 125, 144
Chortens, 239, 240
Chowri, Female Yak, 353
Christianity, 96
Chubipas People, 146
Chumbi Valley, 21, 146
Chupi, Dried Cheese, 51
Clan Exogamy, 312
Clans, Jamyong—Tsaltelim, 305
Classical Medicine, 375
Clay Mask, 176
Colonialism and Imperialism, 199
Commercial Crops, 25, 26
Common Supernatural or Legendary Ancestors, 387
Community, 156
Bhutia, 32, 117, 146, 147
Chhetri, 156
Endogamy, 312
Gurung, 156, 170, 211
Information Centre (CIC), 79, 104, 244, 279, 280
Lepca, 32, 144, 313, 379

Nepali, 209
Coniferous Forests, 22
Conservation, 15, 17, 57
Functions, 17
Conservation of-, 17
Ecosystem, 17
Landscape, 17
Of Biological Diversity, 111
Species, 17
Craft, 141, 143
Defined, 142
Museum, 190
Crafts of
Dzongu, 156
Lachen, 156
Western Sikkim, 154-155
Craftsmanship, 142, 145
Craftsman, 142, 180, 191
Of Lachenpa, 177
Cross Breed Cattles, 47
Cross Breeding Centres of Darjeeling and Kalimpong, 47
Cultural
And Ecological Damages, 201
Landscape, 70, 84
Life in Yuksam, 95
Treasurers, 197
Cycle Tour in Hilly Roads, 251

D

Dairy Farming, 146
Dalai Lama Foundation Dharmshala (HP), 277
Dance(s), 181, 359
And Music, 158
Chu Faat, Age Old Folk Dance, 359
Losoong, 364
Zo-Mal-Lok, 360
Death
(Afung) Lepcha, 355
(Me-Shi-Sa), Lechenpa, 355
Ceremonies, 321, 347
Purification Rites, 356
Deciduous Sal Forest, 23
Degraded Forest, 34, 274
Demons and Goblins, 375
Denkhya, 21
Dense Forest, 274
Development of Ecotourism, 212
Developmental Programme, 111
Devil Spirit, 398
Dhakar Tashiding Monastery, 216
Dhopthapas, 146
Dhungro, Wooden Mug, 162
Divorce, 324
Dokpas, 90
Community, 77
Dolep and Salep, 52
Dolma (Tara), 179
Domestic Tourists, 238
At Lachen, 234
Flow, 281
From West Bengal–Assam, 201
Dominant Species of Temperate Forest, (DSTF), 22
Cinnamon, 22
Ghoge Champ, 22
Phalat, 22
Shrub Live Oak, 22
Donkun, 52
Downtrodden People, 375
Dress, 211
Drukpa
Festival Performed by Buddhist People, 363
Tsheshi, 362
Drukpas, 146
Dubdi
And Labhing Revenue Village, 71
And Lachen Villages, 138
And Lachen, 112
Economic Life, 117

Monastery, 113, 136
First Buddhist Monastery, 214
Oldest Buddhist Monastery, 214
Revenue Village, 32
Dufuk Cave, 295
Dzo, 80, 81
And Horse, 56
And Yak, 211
Hybrid Male Animal, 121, 123
Hybrid of Cattle Hybrid Yak, 51
Dzongri, 61, 267, 291
Area, 143
Dzongu, 62, 66-68, 144, 149, 190, 340, 341, 347, 348, 382
Area, 38
Division, 383
Reserve Area, 32
Dzumsa System, 60
Local Governance System, 60

E

Eastern Himalayas, 20
Eclipses (Luna and Solar), 395
Ecological
Balances, 11
System, 16
Ecology, 335
Cultural 335
Economic Activities, 121
Peoples Role, 130
In Dubdi, 130
In Lachen, 131
Economic
And Ethical Diversity, 69
And Social Development, 17
And Social Relics, 130
And Social Relics, Dubdi, 132
And Social Relics, Lachen, 133
Development, 15, 17, 19, 195
Exploitation, 376
Economy, 18, 47, 59, 66, 68, 70, 77, 85, 92, 111, 131
Impact of Tourism, 240
Primitive, 111
Ecosystem, 15, 16, 17, 19, 31, 266
Conservation in Biosphere Reserve, 60
Health, 16
Eco-Tourism, 65, 196, 212
In Yuksam, 212
Education
And Exchange, 17
And Hygiene, 100
At Yuksam, 276
Educational Programme, 102
Effects of Tourism in Local Communities, 195
Eight Lucky Signs, 239
Emotional Catharsis, 375
Endangered
Himalayan Bear, 29
Red Panda, 29
Species, (ES), 47, 377
Himalayan Black Bear, 377
Musk Deer, 377
Red Panda, 377
Endemic Flora of Khangchendzonga Biosphere Reserve (KBR), 22
Anenone, 22
Maponia, 22
Sikkim Rhododendron, 22
Uvaria, 22
Endogenous and Exogamous Concept, 374
Environment Impact, 253
Environmental
Conservation, 33, 57
Issues, 60
Erosion in Moral Behaviour to Tourism, 252

Ethnic
- Communities, 276
- Groups, (EG), 25, 86, 209, 266, 275
- Chhatris, 209
- Damais, 209
- Gurungs, 209
- Kamis, 209
- Lepcha, Bhutia, Nepalese, 260, 261
- Limbus, 209
- Magars, 209
- Murmis, 209
- Rais, 209
- Tamangs, 209
- Peoples of Yuksam, 156

Ethno-
- Biotic Medicine, 408, 425
- Medicine, 375, 376, 378, 391
- Medicines Role, 378

Evil Spirits, 327
Exchange Labour System, 389
Exogamous Clans, 330
Exorcism, 387

F

Family Welfare Centre, 279
Fauna, 23
Feeding and Management Practices, 48
Female Demon, 399
Festivals, 68, 176, 183, 347
- Bumchu, 183, 368
- Drukpa Tsheshi, 183
- Lhabab Dhuechen, 182
- Losar, 184
- Losoong, 347
- Namsoong, Lepcha's Indigenous Festival, 146, 184
- Pang-Lhab-Sog, 61, 97, 183, 347, 363
- Parnap, 400
- Phang Lhabsog, 61, 68, 97
- Saga-Dawa Buddhist Festival, 347, 362
- Saga-Dawa, Holiest Buddhist Festival, 182
- Tibetan New Year, 347

Festivals of Buddhist of Sikkim, (FBS), 147
- Lhabah-Duchen, 147
- Losoong, 147
- Pang-Lhabsol, 147
- Sagadava, 147
- Tiben New Year, 147

Firewood, 40, 41
First Chogyal of Sikkim, 266
Five Year Plan (10th), 143, 293
Flora, 22
- And Fauna, 153

Flow of Foreign Tourist, 225, 229
Fodder in Dzongu, 43
- Nibara—Tilipat, 46

Fo-Kho, Traditional Dress, 101
Folk
- Songs, 141
- Traditions, 201

Folklore, 141, 405
Food Classification, 111
- Animal Herding, 111
- Farming and Industrial Economy, 111
- Classification, Food Gathering, 111
- Hunting and Fishing, 111

Food
- Habits, 211
- Security, 19, 31

Foreign
- Tourism, 29
- Tourist from England—Israel, 201
- Tourists, 238, 260

Forest
- Economic System, 112

Management, 112
Resources, 112, 190
Rules, 349
Types, 22
France, 291
Fringe Set-up, 66
Fringe Villages, 65, 66, 68, 79, 111, 205
Cultural Landscape, 65
Economic Life in-, 111
Environmental Background, 72
Population Structure, 206
Fringe Zone of Khangchendzonga Biosphere Reserve (KBR), 114
Fruit Crops, 25
Fuel Wood, 37
Consumption, 253
Pattern, 39

G

Gaechala, 291
Gangtok, 22
Gaon Bure, Head of Village, 326
Genes, 15
Genetic Diversity, 18
Geographic
Division of Lepcha, 387
Information System (GIS), 33
German Federal Agency for National Conservation, 197
Germany, 291
Netherlands and France, 225, 228, 229
Ginger, 27
Gipmochi Mountain (near Chinese Tibet), 384
Glaciers and Glaciated Lakes, (GGL), 343
Chholhamu, 343
Chopta, 343
Green Lake, 343
Guruchongmar, 343
Lhonak, 343
Zemu, 343
Glaciers and Snow Clad Range, 27
Gnong-Samdong Village, 38
Gochala, 63
Gocharan Land, 27
God Khangchendzonga, 359
Goechala, 212
Gram Panchayats, 149, 150, 348
Gram Panchayat (Dzumsa), 124
Gram Panchayat Unit (GPU), 379
Grazing, 91
Grazing Areas, 53
Chungthang, 53
Lima, 53
Yangthang, 53
Grazing Routes of Migratory Livestock, 52
Green Lake, 80
Green Tara, Forest God of Lepcha, 360
Growing Consumption of—, 266
Guardian Deity (ies), 347, 364, 385
Guru Rimpoche's Trungker Tshechu, 182, 369
Gurudongmar Lake, 114, 368
Gurung
And Chettri Ethnic Categories, 275
Community, 170, 211
Semi Nomadic Shepherd, 53
Gurungs and Limbus, 25
Gutor Ceremony, 184
Gyalsheng, 267
Gyalwa Lhatsun Chempo, 143

H

Habitat Degradation, 47
Handicraft
Craft Centre, 85
Items, 77
Works, 121
Handloom Items, 167
Hanju, Men's Upper Garment, 304

Healing, 376
Health Care System, 407
Health
  Illness, 373-432
  Role of Ethno-Medicine among Lepchas, 373
  Restoration, 375
Heart Problems, 278
Henley Centre for Forecasting, 199
Herbal System of Treatment, 277
High Mountain Valley, 123-125
Himal Rakshak Force, 54, 56
Himalayan
  Health Exchange Programme, 277
  Kingdom, 182
  Red Panda, 24
  Snow Cock, 24
Hindu Nepali Population of Sikkim, 210
Hinduism, 96
Holy Caves in Sikkim, (HCS), 62
  Dechen Phu in West, 62
  Khandu Sang Phu in South, 62
  Lhari Nying Phu in North, 62
Holy Lakes in Sikkim (HLS), 62, 143
  Barcho Marpu, 62
  Dafuk Yum Tso, 62
  Kar Bru La Tso, 62
  Kathok Tso, 62
  Khecheoparli, 62
  Phyu Cho Karpu, 62
Holy Lakes,
  Bar Cho, 143
  Dafuk Yam Tso, 143
  Ka Bur Latso, 143
  Karthok, 143
  Khachepetri, 143
  Morpu, 143
  Phuchokarpu, 143
  Surma Ten Tso, 143
  Tso, 143
Horticulture, 26
  System, 25
Hunter Gathering Society, 111

I

Illegal Extraction and Exploitation of Forest Resources, 378
Immigrants, 24
Impact of
  Biosphere Reserve, 190
  Tourism, (IOT), 195-263
    On Local Communities, 195
India, Land of Multi-Ethnic Communities, 141
Indian
  Border, 79
  Fourteen Biosphere Reserves, 339
  Tribal Situation, 336
  Tribes, 336
Indigenous Knowledge, 141, 143, 192, 205
Indira Gandhi National Open University (IGNOU), 279
Industrial Revolution, 112, 265
Industry and Economic Development, 15
Infrastructural Facilities, 98, 101, 191, 192
Infrastructure Development, 201
Inter-Community Marriage, 331
Inter-Cultural Contacts, 195
International Tourists, 291

J

Jalep La, 21
Japanese Religious Sect, 374
Jat Katua, 40
Jhankris, 210
Jimdars, 145
Joint Family, 96
Jungloe of Sapse Settlement Area, 96

K

Kagyal Dance (Mask Dance), 147

Katus—Tarsing, 41
Kauto-Chanp, 41
Kazis, 208
Khams, Tibetan Province, 24
Khangchendzonga, 15, 65, 67, 68, 72, 146, 183, 202, 212, 359, 367, 371, 377, 387
 Deities, 71, 76, 96, 143, 216, 231
 Expedition, 217
  God, 99
  Jurisdiction, 280
  Mountain, 71
 Mountain Range, 24
  Region, 144
  Trekking Trail, 216
  Water Falls, 295
 Highest Mountain in the World, 21
 Highest Mountain Peak, 68
  Hills, 339
Khangchendzonga Biosphere Reserve (KBR), 15, 57, 61, 63, 65, 66, 112, 143, 192
 Buffer Zone Forest of-, 47
 Ecology and Conservation, 31
 Endemic Flora, 22
  Festival Songs, 185
   Bhutia Song, 187
   Love Song, 183, 186
   Marriage Song, 185
   Namsung Festival Song, 185
 Heavy Snowfall, 53
 Highest Peak, 28
  Impact of Tourism in—, 195-263
 Importance, 68
  In Sikkim, 196, 266
 Jurisdiction, 377
 Bakhim, 377
 Chong, 377
 Dubdi, 377
 Gamgyap, 377
 Karjee, 377
Khecheopalri, 377
 Labdang, 377
 Sakyong—Lachen (In North), 377
 Yuksam (in West), 377
 Land Use Cover, 34
 Main Features, 28
 Newest Biosphere Reserve, 27
 Of Sikkim Himalayas, 65
 Spread over Major Areas of Sikkim, 19
 Study Area, 32
  Tourism Industries in-, 193
Khangchendzonga Conservation Committee (KCC), 41, 62, 63, 77, 79, 102, 105, 202, 211, 2112, 236, 237, 240, 243, 280
Khangchendzonga National Park, (KNP), 66, 66, 77, 79, 81, 102, 143, 206, 212, 213, 268, 377
Khang-Chen-Dzonga Water Falls, 214
Khasi
 And Mizo Tribes of Arunachal Pradesh, 208
 Language, 24
 Tribes, 24
Khasis in Meghalaya, 145
Khechedpalri, 65
Khesmehal Land, 27
King of Dab-Lha, 356
Kingdom of Mayal, 145, 345
Kinship, 312, 313
Kinship Terms, 315-317
Konro, 162

L

La, Jalep La, 21
La, Nathu La, 21
La, Tangkar La, 21
Lachempa Society, 346

Lachen, 66, 67, 77, 80, 85, 89, 98, 103, 121-124, 126, 137
and Bhutia, 348, 349
and Lachung Package Tour, 80
and Lachung People, 52
and Lalchung, 60
and The Lachung Valley, 26
and Yuksam Valley, 190
Forest, 342
Traditional Gram Panchayat, 114
Monastery, 99
Tourism Development Council, 212
Valley, 60, 77, 80, 101, 144, 146, 152, 173, 190, 342, 343, 346
Village, 32
Lachenchu (River), 101
Lachenchu-Tributaries-Laserchu—Mainchu, 101
Lachenpa, 72, 77, 78, 344
Village, 32
Lachung Valley, 52, 146
Lahasa Valley, 72
Lake,
Gurudongmar, 114, 144, 212, 217, 353, 368
Kathok, 239
Khechaopalri, 214, 294, 295
Sumer, 267, 291
Green, 80
Lama(s), 176, 266, 267, 302, 320, 321, 322, 381, 387, 398
Lhatsum Chembo, 266
Rinzing Chembo, 266
Sempa Chembo, 266
Lamaic Buddhism, 261, 263
Lamaism, 25, 72, 345, 369, 386
Lamaist, 349
Buddhism, 330
Land
Slide Forest, 274
Use, 34
Use System, 25
Language Behaviour, 253
Language Pattern, 96
Laser Valley, 114
Latung and Denga Settlements, 124
Lechenpa Community, 347
Lepcha, 24, 96, 145, 148, 208, 274
Aa Deng Puchutu-Lookblumu, 305
And Bhutia, 360, 364, 367, 370
And Bhutia Study, 335-371
And Nepalese, 147
Are Hunters and Gatherers, 324
Are Mongoloid People, 345
Are Non-Vegetarian, 304
Clan, 306, 345, 385
Community, 32, 144, 313, 379
Dwellings, 302
Economic Life, 324
Land and Forests, 345
Economy, 331
Exogamous Patriarchal Clans, 305
Folk Dances, 208
Folklore, 346
Hat, 159
History, 296, 297
Homogeneous Interlocking Community, 349
Houses, 351
Language, 24, 206
Marriage, 311
Marriage Pattern, 331
Marriage Rituals, 354
Medical Practices, 391
Medicine Men (Moondaok), 425
Mythical Connections, 345
Of Dzongu, 350
Of Khangchendzonga Himalayas, 378
Population, 381, 384
Settlement (Lenang), 302
Social Organisation, 388

Social System, 388
Society, 305, 307, 310, 311, 345, 388, 394, 405
Patrilineal, Patrilocal and Patriarchal, 310
Socio-Religious Life, 327
Superstitions, 405
Territory, 68
Tribe, 321
Women, 324
Lepcha, (Dzongu), 146
Lepchas, 117, 293-333, 376
And Bhutia, 183, 377
Are Animist, 396
Deities, 146
Etbumoo, 146
Itbu Debu Rum, 146
Khongchen Konglo, 146
Rum, 146
Tamsang Thing, 146
Lethang and Tsozo, 294
Lichen Tourism Development Committee, 237
Life Cycle Rituals, 345
Limbu, 95, 103
Lingdim Revenue Village, 384
Lingdom Gram Panchayat, 152
Literacy Rate, 100, 273
Livestock, 272, 273
Local
Deities, 347
Economy, 195
Market Rate of Carpets, 169
At Dubdi, 169
At Lachen, 169
At Yuksam, 169
Lodge Operation, 41
Lodges in Lachen, 86
Logistics Functions, 18
Long-rum, Female Deity, 362
Lord Buddha, 98, 182 see under Buddha (Lord) also
Lord Padamasambhava, 214
Low Mountain Valley, 124
Lukuni, Traditional Dress Making Material, 170
Lungnak La, 268
Lung-Zee Spirit, 402

M

Magical and Religious Rituals, 376
Magico-Religious
Beliefs, 367
Performance, 375
System, 375
Mahakal, 369
Maharaja of Sikkim, 144
Mahayana Buddhism, 147, 179, 345, 345, 347, 391
Festivals of Hindu Nepalese (MFHN), 147
Baisakhi, 147
Dasain, 147
Makar Sakranti 147
Teohar, 147
Man and Biosphere (MAB), 17, 196, 293
Programme, 17
Man, Nature and Spirit, 335-371
Management
Of Biosphere Reserve Resources, 60
Plans, 16
Strategy, 19
Mandarin Orange, 26
Mandro, Bamboo Mat, 162
Mangan,—Gnathang, 22
Marital Alliance with Bhutias, 312
Market Economy, 80
Marriage (Ceremonies), 353
Marriage Procedure, 318
Bree (Marriage), 318
Khachong (betrothal), 318
Mask (Mahakal), 177

Mask
    Dance, 192
    Making, 176
        Ancient Craft of Sikkim, 176
Material Culture, 142, 252
Maudgalyana, 182
Mayal, The Holy Place, 368
Meadows, 53
Mech, 145
Medical Development, 375
Medicinal
    Aconite, 22
    Centres, Sub Centres, 277
    Ginseng, 22
    Herbs and Medicines, 374
    Herbs, 22, 36, 376
    Jatamanshi, 56
    Kurki, 56
    Kutki Root, 22
    Plants, (List and Details), 409
    Plants, 56, 154
    Plants, Bikh, 56
    Spikenard, 22
    Treatment, 277
Mega-Diversity Zones, 15
Migration, 146
    From Nepal, 145
Ministry of Environment and Forest, (MEF), 18, 213
Minor Forest Products (MFP), 37
Mizae and Gnyapo, Variety of Blanket, 174
Modern Health Care System, 378
Modernisation, 252
Moguthang and Donkung-Chulemu, Attraction for Trekking, 73
Monasteries in Sikkim and Their Kinds, 237
    Gomp, 237
    Gompas, 237
    Tak-Phu, 237
Monastery (ies), 76, 237, 345
    Buddhist, 191, 197
    Dubdi, 113, 239
    Dubdi-Oldest Monarchy, 71, 76,136
    Khecheopalri, 407
    Or Gompa, 147
    Pemayanetse, 214
    Sanga-Choling, 214
    Tashidong, 183, 214, 368
    Yuksam Dubdi, 214
Monastic Life, 72
Moguthang and Donkung-Cholamu— and Tourist, 73
Monsoon Storms, 21
Most Below Poverty Line, 115
Mother Language, 276
    Bhutia, 276
    Lepcha, 276
    Limbu, 276
Mount
    Kabru, 212, 359
    Khongchendzonga, 61, 62, 345, 145, 202, 212, 294, 321, 377, 384
    Narsingh, 212, 359
    Pandim, 212, 359
    Simbrum, 359
Mountain Institutions, 280
Multiparty System, 65
Mun, 305, 321, 351, 367, 397, 400, 407
    And Boongthing, 367, 370
    Or Lama, 317
    Religion, 345
Mun-ism, 386
Muns and Boongthing, 327, 393, 398, 406, 408
Mural, 146
Music, 141, 142, 147
Music and Dance, 141, 143
Musk Deer, 24, 348, 369

Mutanchi Lhom Aal Shenzum (MILAS), 62
Mythological Land, 68
Mythology, 392

N

Nambu, Traditional Dress, 158
Namgyal
  Dynasty, 296, 297, 380, 381
  Chakdor, Third Chogyal of Sikkim, 183
  Chogyal Phuntsog, First King, 73, 143, 208, 296
  Maharaja Sir Thutob, 146
  Pinchoo, 24
  Tensung, 267
Namkha Jigme, 214
Namkha Jigme, Follower of Padmasambhava, 214
Nathu La, 21
Nathula Rangi, 52
National Information Centre, (NIC), 279
Natural
  Dyes, 173
  Economic System, 202
  Resources (NR), 17, 18, 19, 31, 32, 60, 63, 143, 376
  Vegetable Dyes, 175
Nepal, 20, 21
Nepalese Broad Divisions, (NBD), 147
  Bahunds, 147
  Chhetries, 147
  Damis, 147
  Gurungs, 147
  Kamis, 147
  Limbus, 147
  Magars, 147
  Murmis, 147
  Rais, 147
  Tamangs, 147
Nepalese Communities, (NC), 95, 115
  Brahman, 115
  Chhetris, 115
  Gurung, 115
  Kami, 115
  Limbu, 115
  Pradhan, 115
  Rai, 115
Nepalese, 147
  Women, 148
Nepali, 57, 209, 260
  Immigrants, 297
  Population, 209, 210, 275
  Society, 210
New Zealand, 229
NGOs, 57, 212
  Role of-, 62
Nigeria, 229
Nine Grahas (Harmful Stars), 375
Ninji-Bruns, Deity, 362
Nirvana, 182, 362
Nomadic Sheep Herders, 54
Non-Participation Observation Techniques, 293
Non-Timber Forest Product (NTFP), 19, 36
Norbugang Chorten, 214
Nyingmapa, 266
Nyngmapa (Nyingmapa) Sect, 214

O

Oak Forests, at Hayapatal Merger of Sikkim into India, 56
Oil and Natural Gas, 265
Orange Cultivation, 26
Other Communities, (OC), 95
  Chetri, 95
  Gurung, 95
  Lepcha, 95
  Mongar, 95
  Newar, 95
  Rai, 95
  Tamang, 95

P

Paintings, 141-143, 146
  And Sculptures, 199

Panchayati System, 239
Panchayatiraj System, 60
Pangden, Traditional Dress, 101
Panglhabsol Festival, 61
Park at Sarnath, 183, 363
Participatory Rural Appraisal (PRA), 33
Pastoral System, 53
Pastoralism, 46, 70, 89, 90, 146
Patriarchal Clans, 350
Pelling and Yuksam Tourist Spot, 294
Pemayanetse Monastery, 214
Pentong Gram Panchayat, 152
Performing Arts, 141, 146, 152, 153, 181, 190
Period of Upanishads, 375
Phichue, Tista Tributary, 144
Pho-Lha Ceremony, 356
Pigs, 50
Pipon, Zumsha Head, 60
Places of Tourist Interest at Lachen, (PTIL), 218
- Chopta Valley, 218
- Chungthang, 219
- Gran Lake, 219
- Gurudongmer Lake, 218
- Thangu, 218

Plantation, 35
- Crops, 25

Planting Methods, 26
Po-Chut, Drinking Country Liquor, 162
Poetry, 141
Po-Kho, 211
Political System, 326, 357
Polyandry, 98
Po-Potak, Long Musical Instruments, 166
Population of Lachen, 206
Population of Villages Studied, (PVS), 148
- Dubdi, 148
- Khechipalri, 148
- Tsozo, 148
- Yuksam, 148

Population of Yuksam, 206
Porter, Cook and Guide, 84
Potato
- Cultivation, 27
- Major Crop, 92

Poultry, 50
Prayer
- Flags, 62, 239
- Wheel, 98

Preservation of Monuments, 197
Primary Health Centres (PHCs), 277, 278
Pristine Ecosystem, 196
Programme of UNESCO, 17
Promotion of Arts, Crafts —, 197
Prostitution and Drugs (PADS), 205, 252
Protected Areas, 17
Psycho-Somato Traditional Healing, 406
Ptso Supernaturals, 305
Puntang, Musical Instruments, 166

R

Rabdentse Ruins, 214
Rangang Ajo, Deity, 362
Rari Making, 170
- Processing Weaving, 170

Rathong Chu, 272
- Main Drainage Line, 71

Rathong Hydro-Electric Power Project, 280
Recognised Spirits, Demons and Deities, 394, 395
Red Hat Sect, 143
Religion of-, 95
- Bhutia (Buddhism), 95
- Lepcha, (Buddhism), 95

Religion, 99
Religious
- Arts, 159

Ceremonies, 176
Mask Making, 159
Protected Lakes, 62
Thangka Paintings, 159
Wood Carving, 159
Remarriage of Divorce/Widow, 324
Remote Sensing, (RS), 33
Reserved Forest, 279
Resource
Management, 66, 68, 88
Materials, 153
Rhododendron
And Juniper Firewood, 56
Forest, 347
Rig Veda, 376
Rituals, 376
And Festivals, 369
For Curing Illness, 397
Rituals—Death Ceremonies, 209
River
Lachen, 21, 114
Lachenchu, 342
Lachenchu Tributaries, 342
Lasachu—Rabom Chu, 342
Lachung, 21
Rangit (Rangeet), 21, 213
Rathang Kola, 295
Rathangchu, 97, 98
Talung, 144, 347
Teesta at Chungthang, 114
Tista, 21, 144, 268, 347
And Rangit, Tributaries, 29
Roadi (Blankets), 53
Role of
Art, Craft and Performing Arts, 145, 152, 189
Boongthing, 366
Dzumsa, 104
Educational Institutions, 103
Ethnic Medicine of Lepchas, 390
Non-Governmental Organisations, 62
Rongkup, 145
Route of Gezong—Yuksam, 83
Russia, 229

S

Sacred Species, 19, 32
Groves, 19, 32
Landscape, 19, 32
Mountain System, 19, 32
Water Bodies, 19, 32
Saga Dawa, 147
Sakyong-Penfong—Shipgyer, 68
Salvation, 147
Sanga-Choling Monastery, 214
Satellite Imagery, 34
Scheduled Tribe, 115
Sculptures, 141, 142
Second Phase Area of Study, 379
Secondary Occupations, 119, 120, 127, 128
Sedentary Paddy Cultivators, 54
Seed Potato Production, 25
Settled Cultivation, 203
Settlement Pattern, 113, 114, 295
Settlements, 39
Settlements, Geychen, 39
Settlements, Khongtay, 39
Settlements, Norbugang, 39
Settlements, of Bakhim—Yuksam, 213
Settlements, Tshoka, 39
Settlements, Yuksam, 39
Shamanism, 210
Sheep, 50
Sherpas, 95
Shifting Cultivation, 203
Shokbu-Rum Ceremony, 399
Sikkam, 19-22, 23, 24, 25
Biodiversity and Ecotourism Project, 40, 41
Ethnic Groups, (SEG), 24
Bhutia, 24
Kingdom, 25
Lepcha, 24

Highly Prone to Erosion, 27
Himalayas, 31, 114, 121
Land Locked Indian State, 191
Livestock Wealth of-, 47
Multi-Ethnic, 202
Nepalese, 24
Pastoral System, 25
Population, 46
Rich Heritage in Handloom Women Artifacts, 167
Sikkim's Administration, 60
Sikkimese
Culture, 192
People, 346
Singalila
And Chola Mountain Ranges, 21
Range, 21, 56, 66, 268
Snow Leopard, 24
Social
And Cultural Impacts, 197
Control, 141
Forms, 142
Organisation, 98
Structure, 336
Welfare Department, 85
Socio-
Cultural Life, Impact of Tourism on-, 251
Economic and Cultural Issues, 19, 31
Economic and Ecological Indicators of Settlers, 59
Soil Degradation, Problem of-, 27
South
America, 15
China, 15
Southern Tibet, 145
Special Sacrifices, 306
Species, 15, 17, 18
Diversity, 16
Of Birds, 29
Of Butterflies, 29
Of Timber Woods, 41
Spirits,
Benevolent, 208
Malevolent, 208
Spiritual World, 336
Status of Women, 323
Freedom of Movement, 324
Stone Goddess, 352
Study Area, 380
Khecheopalri, 380
Tsozo, 380
Yuksam, 380
Subsidiary Economy, 118
Subsistence Economy, 195
Sumer Lake, 267, 291
Supernatural
Power, 357, 375, 376
Spirits (Eight Types), (SS), 375
Asuras, 375
Bhujangas, 375
Devas, 375
Gandharvas, 375
Pishachas, 375
Pitras, 375
Rakshas, 375
Yakshas, 375
Surrogate Marriage, 331
Sustainable Development, 15, 17, 196, 197
Sutchang, Long Musical Instruments, 166

T

Talung Valley, 383
Tamang, 95
Tangkar La, 21
Tankas, 239
Tashi Tagya, 347
Tashi-Chene, 351
Ceremony to Pacify the Demons, 302

Tashidong Monastery, 183, 214, 368
Technique of Thanka Paintings, 180
Technologies, 111
Terrace Cultivation, 325, 331
Tey-Gyap-La Valley, 213
  Thangu, 52
Thangu
  And Chopta Valley, 114
  Valley, 125
Thanka Painting, 97, 147, 158, 179
  Buddhist Belief, 179
  Life of Buddha, 179
  Tools for Meditation, 179
The Spirit, 357
Three Monks, 381 see under Lama(s) also
  G Sempo, 381
  Kathok Rikzin, 381
  L Chemo, 381
Thub Athuk, Lepcha Chief, 296
Thumse, Bamboo Basket, 162
Tibet, 21, 24, 51, 72, 79, 85, 105, 144, 266, 297, 399
  And Bhutan, 208
  Autonomous Region (TAR), 268
  Burman Family, 208
Tibetan, 85, 115, 266
  And Bhutan Borders, 21
  And Bhutias, 211
  Border, 52
  Buddhism, 25, 267
  Calendar, 183
  Community, 90
  Culture, 98
  Dress, 304
  Dynasty, 391
  Horned Eagle, 24
  Medicine, 391
  New Year, 365
  Plateau, 52
  Region, 20
  Settlers at Thangu, 52
  System of Medicine, 277
Tibetans, 57, 77
  And Bhutias, 273
  Or Khampas, 296
Timber, 33, 41
Timber Wood in Dzongu, 43
Tista
  And Lachung Valley, 348
  Valley, 21
Topography of State (Sikkim), 25
Tourism, 65, 67, 71, 77, 84, 92, 98, 136, 137, 190, 195-197, 252, 261, 291, 326, 377
  At Lachen, 230
  At Yuksam, 219, 238
  Development Programme, 191
  Development, 197, 203
  Impact of-, 189
  In Khangchendzonga Biosphere Reserve (KBR), 212
  In Yuksam, Dzongri, Goechhala Trekking, 201
  Industry, 143, 145, 152, 153, 189, 190, 191, 192, 195, 197, 201
  Main Resource, 280
  Social and Cultural Impact of-, 198
Tourist
  Flow at Lachen, 231-233
  Flow in Sikkim, 260
  Impact of Local Culture, 239
  Related Economic Activities, 120, 129
  Season, 326
  Trekking Corridor, 216
Trade
  Route, 144
  With Gangtok and Kalimpong, 85
  With Tibet, 79
Traditional
  Agriculture, 46, 202
  And Modern Medicines, 407
  Art, 141, 143
  Art and Craft Items, 103

Blankets in Lachen, 170
Communism, 388
Council, 104
Economy, 80, 85
Knowledge, 60, 373, 392
Medicine System, 376
Medicine, 425
Occupations, 203
Shifting Cultivation, 19, 31
Societies, 19, 31
System of Rural and Folk Medicines, 277
System of Therapeutics, 378
Village Council (TVC), 98
Traditions and Beliefs, 141
Training and Education, 388
Trans-Border Trade, 79, 87
Transport System, 83
Travel Agencies, 241, 245
Travel Agents Association of Sikkim, 41
Trekking, 201, 291
And Tourism, 130
Corridor, 40, 253
Corridor of Yuksam-Gochala, 40
Operators, 250
To Dzongri, 294
Tour to Lake in Lachen Valley, 80
Tourism, 54, 56, 121, 253
Tourists, 225
Tribal
Groups, 377
Religions in India, 336
Tribes in Arunachal Pradesh, 145
Tributaries of Tista, 21
Tsandong Ceremony, 398
Tsoka, 267
Core Hamlet, 377
In Yuksam Revenue Block, 269
Tsong
And Mangtabong, Land Cover Map, 36
Area, 35
Tsozo, 65
Tulung Valley, 348
Tung Bam, Bamoo Pot, 166
Tung Kyung Bamboo Pot, 166

U

UK, 225, 228, 229, 291
UN, 265
UN Development Programme, 237
UNESCO (United Nations Educational, Scientific, and Cultural Organisation), 17, 18, 31, 196, 198
Upanishads, 375
Upper Dzongu, 150, 151
Upper Dzongu Gram Panchayat, 341
Urban Tourists, 196
Urbanisation, 265, 266, 280
US, 225, 228, 229, 291

V

Valley,
Chopta, 80, 86, 125, 144
Chumbi, 21
Lachen and Yuksam, 190
Lachen, 26, 77, 80, 101, 144, 146, 152, 173, 190
Lachung, 26, 52, 146
Lahasa, 72
Talung, 348, 383
Thangu, 125
Tista, 21
Tista and Lachung, 348
Value System, 19, 32
Vegetables at Beam Zee, 92
Village
Dzongu, 339

Dubdi Village, 113, 115
Lachen, 69, 72, 72, 73, 114
Studied, 113
Yuksam, 95, 79
Villages
And Khangchendzonga Biosphere Reserve, 69
Dhoopi—Sardung, 54
Studies, 294
Khechupodi in Western Sikkim, 294
Lethang, 294
Tsozo, 294
Under Wards, 273

W

Wage Labour, 195
Warding Off Practices, 405
Water Resources, 69
Weaving, 141
West Bengal, 20
West Sikkim, 54, 57
Wheel of Life, 239
White Tara, (Donkar), 362
Wildlife Poaching, 56
Witchcraft, 376
Wood
Carving, 175, 192
At Lachen, (Rate), 178
At Yuksam, (Rate), 178
Consumption, 33
Wooden Mask, 158
Making, 177
World Health Organisation, (WHO), 373
World Tourism Organisation (WTO), 197

Y

Yak, 27, 51, 90, 274
And Sheep, 52
Herders, 56
Herding, 56
Meat, 356
Yak/Dzo, 202
Yeshey Dolma, Maharani, 146
Yorkshire Breed, 47
Yuksam, 32, 62, 63, 65-67, 69, 71, 73, 76, 77, 79-81, 86, 88, 96, 97, 102, 105, 136, 190, 192, 202, 214-216, 243, 245, 252, 262
And Dubdi
Area, 43
Blocks, 37, 39, 41, 48
Villages, 41, 37
And Lachen of KBR, 197, 212, 260-262
Bazar, 71, 82, 83, 89, 102, 103, 274, 275, 326
Communities, 73
Communities, Bhutia—Damai, 7
Connected with Telecommunication Network, 279
Dubdi Gram Panchayat, 113, 204-206, 210, 214, 237, 273, 275, 377
Education at-, 276
Entry Point—, 267
First Capital of Sikkim, 216
Growth of Urbanisation, 265-292
Health Practices, 277
Land use In-, 88

Main Entry Point to KBR, 63

Multi-Ethnic Village, 73

No Bank, Financial Institutions, Insurance Comps, 278

Reserve Forest, 71

Resource Base for Tourism, 292

Village, 120, 143

Yuksam-Gochala Trek Route, 51

Yuksam-Goechhala Trekking Corridor, 35

Z

Zemu Glaciers, 99

Zoning System, 17

Zumsha System, 60